D0904982

THE
FOURTH REICH

THE
FOURTH REICH

Klaus Barbie and the
neo-Fascist connection

Magnus Linklater,
Isabel Hilton
and Neal Ascherson

with
Mark Hosenball in Washington,
Jon Swain in Paris
and Tana de Zulueta in Rome

HODDER AND STOUGHTON
LONDON SYDNEY AUCKLAND TORONTO

British Library Cataloguing in Publication Data
Linklater, Magnus
  The Fourth Reich
   1. Barbie, Klaus   2. Fascism – Bolivia
  I. Title   II. Hilton, Isabel
  III. Ascherson, Neal
  320.5′33′0984   F3326

ISBN 0-340-34443-1

Copyright © 1984 by Magnus Linklater, Isabel Hilton and Neal Ascherson. First printed 1984. All rights reserved. No part of this publication may be reproduced or transmitted in any form or by any means, electronic or mechanical, including photocopy, recording, or any information storage and retrieval system, without permission in writing from the publisher. Printed in Great Britain for Hodder and Stoughton Limited, Mill Road, Dunton Green, Sevenoaks, Kent by St Edmundsbury Press, Bury St Edmunds, Suffolk. Photoset by Rowland Phototypesetting Limited, Bury St Edmunds, Suffolk. Hodder and Stoughton Editorial Office: 47 Bedford Square, London WC1B 3DP

Acknowledgments

This book began its life in La Paz, Bolivia. It moved rapidly to Rome, Washington and Paris, and only then set out on the long journey back to Trier in West Germany where its origins truly lie. This is the *geographical* explanation for the multiplicity of names on the title page. But there is a more important one. In no country where we worked did the information to be mined come easily from the seam. The process required skilled journalism, and the intimate local knowledge that only a foreign correspondent in place can acquire. We were lucky to have the best of both.

The authors and contributors are divided almost equally between the two leading British Sunday newspapers, the *Observer* and the *Sunday Times*. The book has, however, been researched and written independently of both publications. We are grateful for the tolerance and support of friends, colleagues and editors on both papers who may have found our enquiries intruding on the day-to-day business of journalism, but did not (to our knowledge) complain. We owe much to our book editors on both sides of the Atlantic – Ion Trewin of Hodder and Stoughton in London, and Marian Wood of Holt, Rinehart and Winston in New York, who lived with this unpredictable monster for eighteen months, and gently nudged it on to the right trail whenever it showed signs of plunging off into the jungle.

The sources, documentation and printed works which underpin the book are listed at the back, but it could not have been put together without the special help we received at every level in the different countries where our research was conducted.

In Bolivia, the investigation presented its own, special difficulties. The public record is virtually non-existent, partly because of Bolivia's general condition as a third world state, but more as a legacy of its singular political conditions: past regimes have treated Bolivia as a feudal fiefdom, and ministers leaving office have tended to insure their future security by removing all documents pertaining to their deeds, even on occasion taking the furniture with them. Under these circumstances, we were heavily dependent on individual knowledge. Our subjects – politics, paramilitary activities and drug dealing – were sensitive ones, and we are especially grateful, therefore, to those who were so generous with their information. Amongst the officials, we would like to thank Mario Rueda Pena, Minister of Information; Mario Roncal, Minister of the Interior; Gustavo Sanchez, Subsecretary of the Interior; Dr Carlos Salinas, Ministry of Defence; the staff of the Comptroller General's office, of San Pedro prison in La Paz, of the *alcaldia* in Cochabamba and of the Clinica Petrolera and Trumpillo airport in Santa Cruz. Many professional colleagues helped, both with first hand knowledge and with advice on how best to tackle the many obstacles we encountered. Among them we would like to mention in particular Peter McFarren, Lupe Cajias, Rene Bascope Aspiaza, Mabel Azcui, Ligia Novillo Torrico, Juan Leon, Mery Flores and Andres Solis. Other colleagues, who helped us with sensitive contacts, have asked not to be thanked by name: we owe them a debt of gratitude. We are also grateful to the many diplomats in La Paz, some of them actors as well as observers in our drama, who talked to us with welcome frankness. Members of the Jewish and the German communities in La Paz, Santa Cruz and Cochabamba were generous with their recollections as were many individual members of the Bolivian armed forces who demonstrated by their example that not every Bolivian military man is a drug dealer or a coup maker. Amongst others who were generous with time and expertise were Gonzalo Montes, Mirna Murrillo, Gregorio Iriarte, Marcus Domic, Dr Hanibal Aguilar Penarieta, Noel Vasquez of COB and Hans Hiller. Of Barbie's friends, we are particularly indebted to Alvaro de Castro; we would also like to thank Consuela Carrion and Adolfo Ustárez. We were glad of the first hand accounts of Jean Napoleon LeClerc, Col Gary Prado, and the many others who helped us but who, in the precarious conditions of Bolivia, prefer not to be thanked by name.

In Peru, we owed much to Enrique Zileri and the staff of *Caretas* magazine, to Albert Brun and to Dr Santos Chichizola. But we are specially grateful to Volkmar Johannes Schneider Merck who opened the lid on many of the most startling activities of Klaus Barbie in South America and later submitted patiently to long interviews as well as furnishing us with his collection of the papers of Friedrich Schwend. In Argentina, the indefatigable Maria Laura Avignolo was an invaluable source of suggestions and advice. We are also heavily indebted to Juan Joffre for his help and to Carlos Tortola and the "Comandante" for their invaluable eye witness testimony.

In America we relied heavily on documents supplied to us by the US Army, the US Justice Department, whose report on Barbie's connections with the US Counter Intelligence Corps after the war was a seminal source, and, eventually, the CIA. A full account of these documents appears at the end of this book, but we would like to record our gratitude for the astonishing wealth of material we received under the Freedom of Information Act – it fills two drawers of a filing cabinet. We cannot, alas, say the same for Britain, where the Foreign Office, who hold just thirty-two pages of official documentation on Barbie, deliberated for six months, then announced that no papers would be released, on the grounds that events which took place in 1946 might yet endanger national security . . .

In Washington, we worked closely with the television network ABC who were enormously helpful in pursuing Freedom of Information actions with us; special acknowledgments are due to John Martin, the ABC news correspondent who jumped on the Barbie story at the outset and stuck with it to its conclusion; to ABC News Vice-President Bob Murphy, who authorised the partnership with us; to Lionel Kestenbaum and Barry Goldsmith, the Washington lawyers whose brilliant work brought the litigation to a rewarding conclusion. On the government side, we owe special thanks to former Justice Department investigators Alan Ryan and Richard Sullivan; US Army lawyer Tim Hatch; US Army Intelligence FOI officials Tom Conley and Jim Sletchta; Justice Department lawyer Lee Strickland; and officials of another agency who went out of their way to help but would rather not be named. Thanks are also due to Bill Lewis and George Chalou of the US Federal Records Center at Suitland, Maryland; John Taylor of the National Archives; Darnell Stuart of the State Department's FOI office; the Institute for Policy Studies, Washington; former US intelligence agents Erhard Dabringhaus, Eugene Kolb, Robert Taylor, Jim Milano, Bob Schow and Earl Browning, with special mention of Herbert Bechtold who gave us much time and valuable material. Cynthia Jabs baby-sat the Washington end of the book while one of the authors was on holiday; finally, Carole Donoghue gave over several draughty Saturdays in the National Archives thumbing through worm-eaten documents, and then spent months tolerating the obsessions and clutter which attend an enterprise of this scale.

It goes almost without saying that this book would never have been contemplated had it not been for the tireless dedication of Serge and Beate Klarsfeld in Paris, whose work in locating and then identifying Klaus Barbie in Bolivia led to his return to face trial in France. We owe them a special debt of thanks for allowing us to make such generous use of their files, records, expertise and time. Frederique Laurent gave us some valuable advice on the French connection with black terrorism. On the central period of Barbie's career, we would wish to record our gratitude to Claude Bourdet, Raymond and Lucie Aubrac, Lise Lesèvre, Dr Frederic Dugoujon, Henri Monjaret, Charles Adam, Jacques Delarue, Yves Leridon, and Simone Lagrange, whose experience of the terrible events in Lyon in 1943 and 1944 provides the world with first-hand testimony of searing eloquence.

In Italy, we were obliged to the journalist and writer Gianni Flamini whose knowledge of right-wing terrorism is impressive and whose help and generous advice was greatly appreciated. In the labyrinth of black terror, with its myriad groups and cast of characters, the most helpful guides were Italian magistrates whose persistence in pursuing enquiries over the years has often been conducted at great personal risk to themselves; they have their martyrs, including Vittorio Occorsio and Emilio Alessandrini, murdered in the course of their duty. We would thank Giovanni Tamburino, now a member of the Italian Magistrates' Supreme Council; Luciano Violante, ex-investigating magistrate, now parliamentary deputy and professor of law; Luigi Fiasconaro; and Gerardo D'Ambrosio. Finally, warm thanks to the Florence magistrates Pierluigi Vigna and Rosaro Minna whose investigations into a colleague's murder may have turned the tide in bringing right-wing terrorists to trial. The Italian Ministry of Interior put helpful information at our disposal. Particularly useful was the direct knowledge of the officers of DIGOS, the Italian anti-terrorist squad.

In Spain, where the judiciary has not yet acquired the independence of their Italian colleagues, the situation was more delicate. It is barely ten years since the death of General Franco, and some of his own police officers were implicated with foreign terrorists, notably the Italian, Stefano delle Chiaie who, with Barbie, occupies centre stage in this book. We cannot therefore cite our Spanish sources except to say that they were well-placed police officers and that their help was invaluable. We can only hope that they will find this book, as they promised they would, of interest.

In London, Bradley Smith, professor of history at Cabrillo College, Santa Cruz, helped us at the outset of this project through his constant encouragement and criticism, and his generosity with his own time and research in the Public Records Office in London. Stuart Christie, who has collated a wealth of fascinating material on black terror and delle Chiaie in particular, was constantly helpful to us. Xavier Vinader, temporarily in exile from Spain, provided an encyclopaedic knowledge of black terror. We would also like to thank Sir Fitzroy Maclean for helping us to trace the sinister Dr Krunoslav Draganovic; Mrs Stephen Clissold who generously handed us her late husband's invaluable manuscript on the subject; and Stella Alexander who took an enormous interest and provided crucial new information on the Draganovic saga. Amongst others who helped were: James Dunkerley of the Latin American Bureau;

Lance Pope and E. B. ("Crash") Abbots, vigilant sentries of democracy in the post-war British zone of Germany; the staff of *Searchlight* magazine; the Wiener Library; the London Library; the Islington public library; the Board of Deputies of British Jews.

On Barbie's early life, special thanks for help given in Trier, West Germany, to Peter Reinwald and Lt-Col Eberhard Klopp; to Dr Krapp, director of the Friedrich-Wilhelm-Gymnasium; the local historians Dr Emil Zenz and Edgar Christoffel; and Willy Torgau. In Munich, to Frau von Kotze of the Institut für Zeitgeschichte. In Dortmund, to Dr J. Högl of the Stadtarchiv. On Barbie's post-war career, we were grateful for the help of Oberstaatsanwalt von zur Mühlen and Staatsanwalt Schmidt in Munich; Frank Thönicke of the Hessische Nachrichten in Kassel and two officers of the political police in Kassel better left anonymous; Staatsanwalt Rainer Schilling and Dr Bernd Kroner in Frankfurt; Rolf Timmermann in Hamburg; Werner Dietrich, Peter Höbel, Juliana and Hans-Christian Ströbele, Dieter Zach, Alexander Ginsburg, and, for her tireless interest in the Fiebelkorn connection, Brigitte Heinrich. Deep gratitude too for the hospitality, sympathy, assistance and ideas of Gitta Sereny and Don Honeyman, without which our research both in Germany and in Austria would have been far harder.

In Holland, we thank Ben Braber of Amsterdam; Dr David Barnouw of the Rijksoorlogsdokumentasie; J. W. Reitlinger; Henk Glimmerveen.

Finally, a tribute to Andrée Rivez, the Frenchwoman who, through a combination of misfortune, treachery by others, and love, was drawn into the role of a collaborator with the Abwehr during the German occupation of Dijon and Lyon. When we finally found her in West Germany, she was already a sick woman, suffering great pain. In spite of this, she received us with kindness and dignity, and provided her own unique evidence about wartime France and about her association with Barbie in Germany after the war. Recollecting her tragic life was plainly an agony for her, but perhaps also a cleansing confession. Andrée Rivez never dared return to the land which, in spite of everything, she loved so much. She died on November 13 1983, on the day which Germans call Volkstrauertag, the day when all those who perished in the bombings and the battles and the concentration camps of the Second World War are mourned.

Magnus Linklater,
Isabel Hilton,
Neal Ascherson,
London, 1984

Contents

PROLOGUE   15

PART ONE: The Old Order   21

Chapter 1: "An Impeccable Comrade"   23
Chapter 2: Apprenticeship in the Ghetto   45
Chapter 3: The Gestapo Mission   63
Chapter 4: The Killing of Jean Moulin   81
Chapter 5: Bloodbath   97
Chapter 6: Selection of a Henchman   132
Chapter 7: The Petersen Bureau   151
Chapter 8: The Good Father   182

INTERLUDE   197

PART TWO: The New Order   199

Chapter 9: Black Terror   203
Chapter 10: In the Service of the State   215
Chapter 11: Klaus and Fritz   235
Chapter 12: The Nazi-Hunters   249
Chapter 13: Fiancés of Death   266
Chapter 14: Coup d'État   285
Chapter 15: The Past is Present   303
Chapter 16: The Last Defence   321

Principal Characters in South America   333
Glossary   335
Bibliography   338
Index   343

Illustrations

Between pages 160 and 161
Barbie in uniform[1]
The children of Izieu[1]
The Barbie family[2]
Barbie's SS portrait[3]
Jean Moulin[4]
Kurt Merk[2]
Herbert Bechtold[5]
Eugene Kolb[5]
Colonel Jim Milano[5]
Visa form[6]
Transit document[6]
Bolivian identity card[7]
Stefano delle Chiaie (and inset)[8]
Pierluigi Pagliai[8]
Barbie celebrating[9]
The Fiancés of Death[7]
General García Meza[10]
Colonel Arce Gómez[10]
Alvaro de Castro[9]
Barbie and Schwend[11]
Barbie handcuffed[7]

Acknowledgments
1. Klarsfeld
2. Bechtold
3. Berlin Document Centre
4. Keystone
5. Bower
6. US Justice Department
7. *Stern*
8. Ansa
9. Serre
10. McFarren
11. *Caretas*

Prologue

Flying in a military C-130 Hercules is like being trapped in a barn during a hurricane. There is a cavernous darkness relieved only by a few feeble lights, a tumult of noise, swaying and vibration, the din of webbing straps flailing against the sides of the aircraft. There are no windows and no proper seats. The passenger clings to whatever he may for support, more like a captive animal than a man.

The prisoner sat on the metal floor, huddled in his parka, his hands clasped in front of his knees. When the television crew switched on their lights, the face that blinked up at them was old, drained, expressionless.

The Bolivian journalist crouched down nervously beside him.

"May I ask you some questions? What is your name?"

The prisoner answered: "On the way to the airport, a man said to me: 'Are you Klaus Altmann?' I told him, 'In Europe, I was called Klaus Barbie.'"

The journalist persisted.

"Nevertheless, there is some doubt about your nationality, because you changed your name to come to Bolivia."

"I didn't change my name. I didn't change anything. I took another name, like lots of other people who change their names, because one has a right to defend oneself . . ."

The prisoner began to ramble; he was weary and defensive. The questions went on, the answers got nowhere. Finally the journalist signalled that the interview was nearing its end.

"Do you think your life has reached its last phase?" he asked.

"I understand so. Just as my wife's life reached its final stage."

"Are you afraid of death?"

"No, I've never feared death and I do not fear it now . . ."

"Do you regret anything in your life?"

"No, personally, no. If there were mistakes, there were mistakes . . . but a man has to have a line. No?"

The journalist ordered the lights to be switched off, and the prisoner's face vanished into the darkness.

It was the night of February 4 1983. After nearly forty years of liberty, Hauptsturmführer Klaus Barbie of the SS had begun at last to pay for his crimes. The new civilian government of Bolivia had expelled him, and the Bolivian transport plane was taking him back to Europe.

He thought he was on the way to West Germany. He had not been told that the Hercules was bound for the French territory of Guyana, and that he was to be handed over to the French authorities to stand trial for crimes against humanity, committed during the war when he was chief of the Gestapo in occupied Lyon.

The charges would be detailed, specific, geared to a terrible period of twenty-one months in 1943 and 1944, when the tortures and massacres carried out in Vichy France earned Barbie the title, Butcher of Lyon.

But the significance of Klaus Barbie goes far beyond Lyon. The background of his life is a huge canvas, covering Germany, Holland and Latin America, in which France forms one section only. Italians, Bolivians, Croats, and above all Americans, are present in this enormous group portrait, together with the rulers and rebels, the policemen and secret agents, the criminals and terrorists of a dozen nations.

"One has to have a line. No?" Barbie told his interviewer. This book is about what Barbie was, and what he did.

It is important first to make clear what he was not. Barbie does not, for a start, belong in the first rank of Nazi criminals. He was not one of the authors of the policy of genocide like – after Hitler himself – Bormann, Himmler, Heydrich, Kaltenbrunner. He was not a "desk murderer" like Adolf Eichmann, who organised the Jewish deportations to the gas chambers throughout Europe. He was not even one of the local SS commanders in charge of supervising the killing, like Stroop in Warsaw, Globocnik in Lublin, or Höss and Stangl, the commandants of Auschwitz and Treblinka.

Barbie was a field officer, one of those who used the guns, who hunted, murdered and tortured for their masters. And, as such, he was only one among thousands. For every French town where Barbie took his Einsatzkommando to kill and burn, for every St Genis-Laval or St Claude, there were a dozen Polish or Russian villages where more appalling massacres took place. The trial of Klaus Barbie will not rank with the great Auschwitz hearings of 1963, or with the Eichmann case.

But it is not Barbie's service to Hitler alone which makes him important. The whole sweep of his career, on two continents and under many masters, offers a lesson which no single court of justice can encompass.

Barbie himself is the last man to understand his own significance. Astute rather than intelligent, energetic rather than creative, callous rather than imaginatively violent, he is an average specimen of Fascism, the creed which the British writer Esmond Romilly called "that mixture of profit-seeking, self-interest, cheap emotion and organised brutality".

Hunched on the floor of the empty cargo plane taking him from Bolivia to French captivity, his comments on his own fate still struck exactly the note of amoral, tinpot fatalism which he had absorbed from the years of Nazi propaganda so long before.

"Death is cruel, and that is how it has been in the history of the world, beginning with Cain who murdered Abel . . .

"The first part of my life was my youth, the second the war, the third Bolivia. The balance is that I have suffered a lot . . .

"Whoever wins the war was right. If you know history, you know the words, *vae victis*, woe to the conquered, from the Romans. Who wins the war, wins everything; who loses, loses everything . . ."

The Barbie lesson has three parts that stretch far beyond these banalities. The first is that it has proved possible, after all, to build a living connection between the two Fascist generations; between the survivors of the European dictatorships of the 1930s and the international right-wing terrorism which only began to emerge as a dangerous force in the late 1960s, and which reached its destructive peak with the bombing at Bologna station in August 1980, when eighty-four people died – the worst terrorist outrage in Europe since the war.

Around Barbie, the unrepentant Nazi veteran, there gathered in Bolivia some of the most savage and professional killers of the Italian ultra-right, accompanied by romantic worshippers of the swastika from Germany, France and even Switzerland. In the Bolivia of President García Meza, they found a welcome, and, for a time, power. They brought, too, the technologies of repression, from the old world to the new: Barbie introduced the fully-developed concentration camp to Bolivia, and lectured on the use of electrodes applied to the human body to extract confessions, a technique first developed by Gestapo interrogators in France. Together with the Italian terrorist, Stefano delle Chiaie, he organised the squads of mercenary thugs which held down Bolivia by murder and intimidation, and which are seen performing the same task in El Salvador today.

Not only the Bolivian dictatorship but General Pinochet in Chile, the officers who directed the "dirty war" in Argentina in the 1970s, and today's exponents of counter-terror in Central America have drawn deeply on the skills and services of this very special immigration from Europe.

The second lesson of Barbie's career is that justice is often one-eyed in a polarised world. Klaus Barbie owes fifty years of practice in his profession to the cold war. His credentials as an anti-Communist remained as stainless in South America as they were in the Germany of his distant youth. In the post-war years, when many SS veterans cynically transferred their loyalty to Soviet Communism as the "victor in the world struggle for survival", he resisted firmly all invitations to work for the East. It was this that made him so appealing to the Americans who recruited him in 1947, and which later induced South American dictators to trust him. Compared to his reliability in the global war between ideologies, Barbie's excesses during Hitler's "anti-Bolshevist" crusade counted for little.

Finally, this is a study not only of a man but of a caste. Throughout history, societies have maintained a staff of untouchables, those who do the dirty work without which civilisation could not function, and who are despised, sometimes even persecuted, for undertaking it. There have always been night-soil carters, pawnbrokers, abortionists, unlicensed pedlars, smugglers of brandy in times of prohibition. The caste gets no thanks from the society that employs them. In response, they have developed a sour solidarity among themselves.

Barbie's caste is one that has been a growth area in our own time: those who act secretly and beyond the law in government service – spies, security police, "special forces" and counter-insurgency teams. They are hidden from democratic supervision and public inspection. They enjoy a broad licence to violate privacy, deceive, burgle or blackmail, and on occasion to torture and to kill. Although they are paid for it out of public funds, nobody likes what they do. Inevitably they feel a certain paranoid kinship with others who operate in these fields. Much as the licensed pawnbroker finds himself drinking a gloomy pint of beer in the understanding company of the pickpocket, so did American agents of the Counter Intelligence Corps feel less lonely when comparing interrogation techniques with an old hand from the Sicherheitsdienst, the secret service of the SS. Those whose profession is secret violence – a trade much in demand – constantly cross moral frontiers.

Klaus Barbie did what he considered to be a good job for his country, and is now identified as a war criminal. The men and women he hunted in France, the Résistants who were seen during the war by many a sober French citizen as irresponsible gangsters, were soon marching down the Champs-Elysées in Paris, sanctified as heroes. For Italy, Barbie's comrade Stefano delle Chiaie was the most feared right-wing terrorist in the land; for Bolivian governments, he was a valued and respected expert in counter-terrorism.

All through Barbie's life, state security and political terror and organised crime revealed their fundamental affinity. At the end and climax of his career, all three finally merged into the carnival of misrule that was Bolivia under military dictatorship.

This, then, is the story which connects the Third Reich in Germany to the military regimes of South and Central America, which leads from one age of Fascism to another, which tells how the defeated old man in the belly of a military plane evolved from a lonely little boy who once dreamed of becoming a Catholic priest.

PART ONE

The Old Order

CHAPTER ONE

"An Impeccable Comrade"

In the German city of Trier, in the years between the wars there lived a man famous for his wisdom, his erudition, and his gentle sense of humour. He had remarkably bright comprehending eyes. He was a historian, a writer and a scholar, as well as one of the town's religious leaders. Among his friends he numbered most of Trier's prominent citizens: the Roman Catholic bishop, the chairman of the regional council, the mayor of the city. Old men still alive in Trier remember sitting at his feet in those days, listening to him talk about history and philosophy or about the politics of those violent years in Germany.

In 1938 it became impossible for him to live any longer in this city on the western borders of Germany, which for eighteen years had been his home. Taking his family, he left for Holland, hoping to return in better times. Two years later the Nazi armies poured into his refuge. In 1942 the snatch squads of the SS rounded him up, and he was sent with thousands of others to the concentration camp at Theresienstadt, north of Prague. From there in May 1944 he was deported to Auschwitz. He was not an old man. But he was too old for the SS doctors making the selection on the railway platform. They decided he was not worth working to death. They sent him to the gas chambers.

The name of this man was Adolf Altmann, and he was the chief rabbi of Trier. And though he died at Auschwitz there was one more indignity to come. Seven years after his murder, an SS man from Trier stole his name. Klaus Barbie, who had taken part in the terrorising and deportation of the Amsterdam Jews, was looking for a new identity. French demands for the extradition of the man journalists called the Butcher of Lyon were becoming too insistent, and Barbie was preparing for an escape to South America, to a new life in a securely distant continent. He needed a new identity to inscribe in his false papers for this new life, and Altmann was the name he chose for himself, his wife, his son and his daughter. It is not possible, and nobody in Trier today believes it possible, that he selected the name accidentally. The choice was deliberate: a savage parting jest against history. Altmann is not a particularly common name. In Trier there had been only one Altmann family; their last home had been in the Zuckerbergstrasse next to the synagogue, before it was burned out and plundered by stormtroopers in the anti-Jewish pogrom of "Crystal Night", November 9 1938. For the Nazis of Trier, Adolf Altmann had been the supreme target of their hate, slandered persistently in the half-pompous, half-hysterical articles of the *Trierer Nationalblatt*, the Nazi daily paper.

In 1951 Klaus Barbie looked around and saw a conquered, timid, repentant Germany. Not only was every city rebuilding its synagogue out of public funds, but the new Bonn government was anxiously seeking reconciliation with an imperious, unforgiving state of Israel. He, at least, had not changed his views. He would not ask pardon for deeds he in no way regretted. And there was this private, satisfying little way in which he could show his contempt. On March 23 1951 the steamer *Corrientes* sailed from Genoa for Argentina. On board, bound for Bolivia, there travelled a family of four under the name of Altmann.

Klaus Barbie was born in 1913, the last year that the huge, confident and prosperous German Empire spent in peace. But he grew up in another Germany that seemed to be dying: its frontier provinces torn away, alien troops on its soil, the Empire overthrown by a workers' revolution, the economy shattered, and the population demoralised by poverty, unemployment and inflation. And in Trier, the city where he grew up, these miseries evoked a special quality of outraged patriotism, the passions of a Grenzstadt, a town that had always stood on a disputed frontier.

Though there are some challengers, Trier is probably the oldest city in Germany. It stands on the middle reaches of the Mosel river, with the French and Luxemburg frontiers only a few miles down the highway to the west, and ever since Roman times it has been a fortress astride one of Europe's main invasion routes. To the Frankish barbarians and the troops of Louis XIV, for Napoleon and the American and French armies advancing down the Mosel valley towards the Rhine, Trier has been both prize and victim. In the nineteenth century, instead of the factories of the Industrial Revolution, there came Prussian barracks and military roads; with the fresh militarisation of Trier, the traditional markets in France were cut off and the economy languished.

Even in the early years of the nineteenth century Trier was a decaying little town within its enormous Roman walls. And it was there, in an old house on the Brückenstrasse where Napoleon's military governor had lived, that Karl Marx was born in 1818. Ninety-five years later – on October 25 1913 – thirty miles away on the Rhine, Klaus Barbie entered the world. Though Trier was to be his home city, there was a good reason why he was born not there but in Godesberg. His parents, Nikolaus Barbie and Anna Hees, were both village school teachers in the Eifel, the high volcanic hinterland which lies to the north of Trier, and when Anna became pregnant they were not married. For the sake of both their careers, it was better that Anna should travel away to have the baby where she was not known. She returned after the birth, and on January 30 1914 she and Nikolaus were married in the little town of Merzig in the Saar, where most of the Barbie family came from.

Six months later, the First World War began. Nikolaus was twenty-six and he volunteered at once. He was to serve the full ordeal of four years at the front. He returned a shattered man, suffering from a severe bullet wound in the neck. He was never again to feel at peace with himself or with the world around him.

That world had altered almost out of recognition. Alsace and Lorraine, bordering on Trier, had been returned to France, while the Saar, Nikolaus's own country, had been torn away from the Reich and placed, to all intents and purposes, under French influence. Trier, like most of the rest of the Rhenish province west of the river, was under French military occupation and, to the horror of the population, was patrolled by ferocious-looking North African colonial troops. Worst of all, the French were encouraging a movement to separate the Rhineland from Germany altogether and to set up puppet "autonomous republics" under French control. At first, this idea held some attraction as a way of breaking free of Prussian domination; the young Konrad Adenauer, at the start of an extraordinary career which was to make him the first chancellor of West Germany some thirty years later, was among the Catholic politicians who played with the notion of Rhenish separatism. But as the real French design became clear, most of the genuine support dropped away.

The peak of the crisis, for Trier and for all Germany, came in 1923. Although Klaus Barbie was only nine years old, the violence and upheaval of that year were to mark indelibly his future life and his attitudes. Early in 1923, in order to force overdue reparation payments, French and Belgian troops occupied the Ruhr. The German government called for "passive resistance" by all state employees. Many, less patient, resorted to sabotage. Among them was a sinister right-wing freebooter named Albert Leo Schlageter, who was betrayed to the French and shot by a firing squad at

Düsseldorf in May of that year. Schlageter was instantly canonised as a national hero by the young Nazi movement; many years later, he was to become a crucial figure in Barbie's personal mythology.

In Trier the French reacted savagely to the strike by state employees. Several hundred families, mostly railwaymen's but also including those of many local government officials and school teachers who refused to work, were turned out of their homes and driven from the Rhineland. At the Friedrich-Wilhelm-Gymnasium, Barbie's future school, the boys demonstrated in the streets and were charged in the Hauptmarkt by Moroccan cavalry laying about them with the flat of their scimitars.

By then the Barbies were living in the village of Udler, in the Eifel hills above Trier. There was chaos and often shooting all over the Eifel as the separatists declared shortlived "autonomous republics" under French military protection. All this the young Klaus Barbie saw with a child's intensity: his country exploited and dismembered by its neighbours, Trier and the Eifel around his home awash in legends of patriotic resistance to the foreigner. He said many years later that both his parents had been involved in the struggle against the separatists, which may well be true – less likely is his boast that his father fought in the battle of the Ägidienberg, in which armed farmers defeated a large separatist column. At ten, politics were already all around him, and he would also have heard how, in November 1923, a little-known nationalist fanatic named Adolf Hitler had marched his followers against the government in Munich and seen them scattered at the first volley.

Udler is a tiny hamlet – pigs and chickens still stray in the road and large dung heaps scent the air beside most houses. As a child, Barbie could walk in the forests and, in summer, go swimming in the Pulver Maar, a volcanic crater filled with water. But he never felt quite right in Udler. During the war years 1914–18, with his father away, he had been brought up in his mother's home village of Mehren, a few miles away. As a teenager he was to write: "This Eifel village of Mehren, lying among the beautiful lakes of the volcanic Eifel, became my home and it still is." (For "home" he used the intense, untranslatable German word *Heimat*.) "Like my mother, I too am a true child of the Eifel, which leaves the mark of its grave, austere character on every person who has grown up there . . ."

This reference to his mother, to his special love and loyalty to her and to her village, carries also an implicit rejection of his childhood at Udler and, in some sense, of his father. Klaus Barbie's feelings about his father are a complex, ominous mixture of admiration, respect for his war record, fear and, perhaps, underlying hatred. He was, and remained, very much a mother's boy.

Nikolaus Barbie was the village schoolmaster at Udler. The family lived over the tall, bare schoolhouse that still stands at the end of the village next to a mound covered with flowering broom. He was not badly off by local standards; he had a small holding of five *Morgen* (just over a hectare), which the pupils had to dig for him, some goats, and he could afford to slaughter two pigs a year – one for the family, another for the market. A photograph still exists of the school class: Nikolaus, in a high, hard white celluloid collar, stands at the side, one arm round the small figure of Klaus in a sailor suit. In the front, cross-legged, sits Klaus's younger brother Kurt, a handicapped child who was to die some years later.

But Nikolaus Barbie had a dark side. He drank with increasing persistence and desperation. Sometimes his wife Anna, remembered in the village as "an angel, a Madonna", had to take his classes when he was incapable, and she used to beg her brother to obtain her husband's pay packet at the beginning of the month: "Get it off him, before he boozes it all away." Nikolaus also beat the children with a savagery that made the villagers uneasy, hard-living small farmers though they were.

It was a difficult childhood. There is no reason to suppose that Nikolaus spared the rod with his own boy. Moreover Klaus was the teacher's son. As he wrote at the age of nineteen, in the biographical essay required for permission to matriculate, "my education was very severe, for as the son of the teacher I had to give the best example to the other pupils". But the villagers remember him as a quiet, sweet-natured little boy, often invited to meals at their homes. "He was so harmless," one old man recalls. "We all thought he would make a priest." He was certainly a devout child, and seems at one time to have played with the idea of studying theology. With both parents in the teaching profession, there could be no question of not going to grammar school and then to higher education. At Easter 1925 Klaus, aged eleven, was sent to Trier where he entered the Friedrich-Wilhelm-Gymnasium.

It was, and is, the most important secondary school in the city. When Karl Marx studied there, it was the only grammar school in Trier. In the time of both Marx and Barbie it was housed in a magnificent baroque building that had once been the Jesuit headquarters; it was right in the heart of town, and the boys had only to pour out of the door and down the Jesuitengasse to find themselves in the middle of whatever parade, riot, or ceremony was going on. Its tradition is one of a vigorous but liberal Catholicism, intimate with the Catholic hierarchy of Trier but certainly not dominated by it. It was an atmosphere very much to the young Klaus Barbie's taste.

For the first time he was on his own. At the outset he was lodged in the Aloysius-Heim, a somewhat chaotic Church-run hostel in which the boys were left to sink or swim (the rector had just died). "The self-reliance that . . . I developed in these conditions was the foundation for my further development," he wrote in 1933. A year later, however, an older school friend persuaded him to move into the Konvikt, a much stricter hostel intended for future seminarists. "Punctuality, order, and the spirit of comradeship were developed in me over the three years that I spent in that strict house," he wrote.

Then, suddenly, things changed. Nikolaus Barbie's behaviour in Udler had grown intolerable, it seems, and he was persuaded to take early retirement. About 1929 the family left Udler and moved down to Trier, into a flat on the Viehmarktplatz, and Klaus left the Konvikt to live at home. The move turned out to be a disaster for Klaus. All that is known about what took place is contained in some reticent sentences in his matriculation essay.

From now on, I was to live with my mother and father again. My joy was great – but how disappointed I was! The truly bitter suffering I had to experience in my years between Third and Sixth Forms must for ever remain my secret, and a warning for my future life. All I can say is that those years made of me a mature person. That period taught me how bitter life can be, and how terrible fate can be.

Nikolaus Barbie was to die of cancer four years later, but it sounds as if his violence and his alcoholism, rather than his illness, turned the family life of the Barbies in Trier into a domestic hell.

One consolation for the move was that, released from the Konvikt, Klaus could enjoy a much freer leisure life. His interests, however, were still idealistic, still strongly coloured and formed by the Church. He joined a Catholic young men's group, and for sport, which he increasingly enjoyed, entered the Deutsche Jugendkraft, a powerful and highly organised federation of Catholic sports associations which existed throughout Germany. He also joined the Männerfürsorgeverein (something not unlike the YMCA), which undertook relief work among the destitute and unfortunate. "I paid many visits to prisoners, who made a deep impression on me. In conversation with these people, I heard many tales of bitter human suffering and misfortune . . . It was an excellent addition to what school could offer me."

So far the picture is of a rather shy, lonely boy seeking comfort and company in social work, emotionally crippled by his awful family situation, far from being a non-conformist or a rebel. But in Trier the Nazis were beginning to become an ugly feature of the street scene. At the outset they had been insignificant, and Trier, where the most powerful political force was the Catholic Zentrum party, gave them little encouragement. In 1930, however, the Nazi party won over sixteen per cent of the city's vote in the general elections. Although this was still a poor performance compared to many other parts of Germany, they felt confident enough to carry the battle into the streets. Lacking any significant Communist enemy in Trier, the Nazis concentrated on the Social Democrats and the Jews. There were battles at public meetings, beatings, marches that ended in pummelling and bloodshed. In 1931 the SA (stormtroopers) ambushed and beat up a Jewish children's group returning from a hill walk. The same year they attacked a parade of the Catholic young men's association – one of the very groups to which Klaus Barbie belonged. Violence grew to a climax in 1932: there were shootings, political murders, knifings, incessant fighting in the street as the stormtroopers' hit squad, kept on permanent alert in their headquarters, the "Brown House" on Jakobspitälchen, swarmed out to attack its enemies. Trier was an example of how the effect of energetic terrorism can be out of proportion to numbers: even as late as 1932 the NSDAP (Nazis) in Trier had only 880 members, despite a visit by Hitler himself. Although they were winning neither mass membership nor elections, they were winning the battle where it mattered: in a town where a jeer at a procession could bring an SA man springing out of the march to slash the heckler's face open with a knife, the will to resist the Nazis was disintegrating.

When Hindenburg appointed Adolf Hitler Chancellor of Germany on January 30 1933 the city of Trier surrendered almost without protest to the onslaught of the victorious Nazi minority. Armed SA squads pushed their way into police headquarters and announced that they were now an auxiliary police force. All over the district Communists were rounded up. A rally of the Zentrum party, held in the Catholic Citizens' Union Hall (next door to the house where the Barbies lived), fell apart in tumult as screaming Nazis smashed chairs over the heads of their rivals. "Lay a finger on me and you're fired tomorrow," shouted an SA thug as a police officer moved to restrain him. The crowd fled, and the Nazis were left triumphantly singing the Horst Wessel song among the wreckage.

On April 1 1933 Klaus Barbie joined the Hitler Youth. He was nineteen years old. The earnest, awkward boy had been transformed; the committed Catholic youth with a sense of mission towards the unfortunate had suddenly turned into a young militant in a party that was revolutionary, neo-pagan, and attached to the doctrine that the weakest should be driven to the wall. At the end of that year Barbie wrote: "The mighty national uprising drew me, like every true German youth, along in its wake, so that today I stand as a serving member in the great retinue of the Führer." In this clumsy miming of Nazi jargon there can be sensed the sweatiness, the eager servility of a real convert. Exactly how the conversion came about is not known. Klaus Barbie fell prostrate before Hitler's triumph in the month of March 1933, in the company of millions of others – the Märzgefallenen (March casualties) as their opponents afterwards called them. His decision for Hitler meant, on the face of it, a total rupture with the conservative traditions of the Barbie and Hees clans – small-farming stock on both sides in the Saar and the Eifel – a breach with the Catholic piety of his family and especially of his mother, a rejection of the enlightened liberalism of the Gymnasium. The clean, self-disciplined, neatly dressed boy already on course towards a respectable middle-class career had defected to the violent, foul-mouthed buccaneers of the streets.

And yet it may not have seemed to him quite like that. National Socialism was a bundle of assorted and often contradictory causes and beliefs, held together only by the binding-cord of Führer and party. For the young Klaus Barbie it seems to have been above all the blazing nationalism of the movement that attracted him, the promise to right the wrongs of the Versailles Treaty which had robbed the Reich of its frontier provinces, the chance of giving at last to this "young nation" the proud place in Europe and the world to which it was entitled. Other elements in the party's creed, its physical violence along the road to power and especially its anti-clerical scorn for the Catholic Church, may well initially have been less attractive to him. But here Barbie, like many other young people hesitating on the brink of commitment, found much to reassure him. In March 1933 the new regime had almost abandoned its onslaught against the Churches; a phase of temporary conciliation had begun. In February Hitler had taken care to invoke the blessing of Almighty God on his endeavours, and in March he claimed that "the national government sees in both Christian confessions important factors for preserving our folk-identity. Their rights will not be infringed." The German Churches, terrified at the apparent victory of the Antichrist, snatched gratefully at this offer of compromise.

Nowhere was this gratitude more dramatically illustrated than in Trier. Bishop Bornewasser, convinced that Hitler was a responsible statesman who regretted the anti-Christian "excesses" of his supporters, decided to offer the regime his most precious token of approval: a public showing of the Holy Robe in Trier cathedral, supposedly the robe Christ wore on his last journey to Golgotha. One of the most famous relics in Catholic Europe, the robe was only exhibited at supreme moments in history, and its showing involved the organisation of an international pilgrimage. The bishop could not have invented a more perfect stroke of international propaganda for the new Nazi authorities. On July 20 the German government signed a Concordat with the Vatican. Three days later the showing of the robe began: stormtroopers and party members in uniform acted as official stewards and lined the approach to the cathedral; Nazi dignitaries stood side by side with the bishop at the cathedral door to welcome important foreign guests. In the next few months millions of pilgrims, many from France, Italy and Belgium, made their way to Trier and came away impressed with the cordial, respectful relationship between state and Church in the new Germany.

"And what did the people find who came from abroad?" asked Barbie rhetorically in a school essay.

> Instead of chaos and civil war, they found the greatest order and calm. The brown-shirted "murder gangsters" turned out to be delightful people, obliging in every way . . . It was all due to the firm, decisive government of Hitler that the pilgrimage passed off so brilliantly and without incident . . . Some 422,000 foreigners visited Trier in this period and learned to respect the new Germany.

There is a curious tone of suppressed contempt about this essay (a poorly-done, wooden piece of work that earned only a "satisfactory" mark). If the Church-state truce of 1933 had made it easier for Barbie to join the movement, he had lost his respect for religion by the time the essay was written nearly a year later. In the same examination paper he evades a question about "the religious effects of the pilgrimage" by observing lamely that "it is hard to talk of a success of the pilgrimage in the religious field, as this affects the

31

inner human being". He prefers to write about the political triumph of the occasion. And in his words about foreign pilgrims finding the Nazis to be "delightful people, obliging in every way" there is even a hint of cynicism, a quality until then absent from Barbie's character.

Though he joined it, Barbie took no direct part in the Hitler Youth. The movement was intended for boys between fourteen and eighteen, and he was already nineteen when he joined. Instead he became a Führer with the junior branch, the Deutsche Jungvolk, which took boys between the ages of ten and fourteen. The work involved organising meetings and expeditions and physical and para-military training, as well as offering some elementary teaching of Nazi doctrine. But at the same time, Barbie lent a hand as an unpaid volunteer with the Nazi party office in the quarter of Trier-Central, the local *Ortsgruppe*. Its leader, then and for some years to come, was Karl Horrmann, an enthusiastic gentlemen's tailor and outfitter who gave over part of his own house in the Brückenstrasse to the party and to the German Labour Front. The Karl Marx House, which now accommodated the offices of the Nazi newspaper, was a few yards down the same street. Barbie's home was five minutes' walk away, and the Nazi offices for the whole Trier district, occupying the Brown House, were no further. It is a small, cosy city.

The year 1933 was not only one of political choice for Klaus Barbie. It was also a year of private tragedy and disaster. In June, Kurt, Klaus's younger brother, died: "my only, dear brother". Then in October Nikolaus at the age of only forty-five succumbed to cancer of the neck, which Klaus appears to have attributed to his old war wound. "This was an immense blow for me and for my mother," he wrote. With the death of Nikolaus the family finances, and with them the plans for Klaus's future, collapsed. "Fate, through the death of my father, frustrated my cherished desires," he wrote in the matriculation essay a few months later. "I had wished to study philology, but the financial situation in which I now found myself made that impossible for me. I have resigned myself to seeking a career in the middle ranks of the civil service, although this type of officialdom does not particularly appeal to me."

There was to be no chance of going to a university after all. Small as Nikolaus's schoolmaster's pension must have been, it would evidently have made the difference. Now there was nothing left in Klaus Barbie's life but his work in the National Socialist movement, a future for Germany but no private prospects for himself. It was an embittered, self-pitying young man who sat out his last terms at the Friedrich-Wilhelm-Gymnasium and took *Abitur*, the state matriculation examination that would have entitled him to university entrance at Easter 1934. Did he really see only the prospect of sitting at a clerk's desk, of a life of mediocre bureaucracy? He was twenty years old and impatient to be gone. Immediately after taking *Abitur* he volunteered to do six months' work in the new Labour Service (Reichsarbeitsdienst), and disappeared for a long energetic summer with pick and shovel at Niebüll, in the northern province of Schleswig-Holstein. From this experience of hard physical work and comradeship in "constructing the new Germany" he returned, by all accounts, a more convinced and dedicated National Socialist than ever.

He came back to Trier in late October 1934. Hitler was already reducing unemployment throughout Germany, but Barbie was unable to find a job. He took up his old voluntary work, leading a *Fähnlein* (a unit of about 120 boys) in the Deutsche Jungvolk and working unpaid at the party offices in Brückenstrasse. And now, unpredictably and mysteriously, the course of his life took its decisive turn. On February 1 1935 Barbie was appointed adjutant to Karl Horrmann, the party leader in the vital quarter of Trier-Central. It was an unexpected, brilliant appointment for a young man of twenty-one who was not yet even a party member (he only joined two years later, when it was a mere formality). And, good as this appointment was, there was something even more important that could not be spoken of. In a curriculum vitae written in 1940 for internal SS use, he wrote laconically: "Through my work for the NSDAP branch in Trier-Central, I came in contact with the Security Service of the SS Reichsführer, for which I at first worked on a voluntary basis." Klaus Barbie had been recruited by the Sicherheitsdienst of the SS, the party's own secret service. His unpaid work for the SD began on the day he was appointed Horrmann's adjutant; seven months later, on September 26 and "on the basis of my own application", he became a full time, paid member of the SD. Barbie's real career had begun not as a mere Nazi militant, not even as an ordinary member of the élite "Corps under the Death's Head", the black-uniformed SS, but as a novice in the inmost gang of all.

These two posts, the public and the secret one, together form a career leap that is not easy to explain. Old people in Trier today puzzle over it. Klaus Barbie was for most of his schoolmates a remarkably unremarkable boy, without particular talent, unobtrusive: it is not merely reluctance to recall the Nazi period that has left behind such a dim memory of him. Yet this "leap" clearly indicates that there were some Nazis in Trier who regarded Barbie as a very useful and talented young man indeed, a new comrade who showed promise and was worth trusting. How did Klaus Barbie earn this trust?

On the face of it, he had not done anything of special value to the movement. He had been a junior youth leader and he had given his unpaid services to the party's office in the Brückenstrasse for some eighteen months, interrupted by his absence in the Labour Service. None of this was remarkable, and he must have been winning his spurs in some other way about which his contemporaries knew nothing.

There is one probable explanation. Up to 1933 Barbie had been a member of the Catholic youth movements, and until 1934 was a pupil at the Friedrich-Wilhelm-Gymnasium. The Gymnasium is described in Nazi documents of the time as "a hotbed of clerical opposition", while the party in Trier identified the grasp of the Catholic Church on young hearts and minds as its most formidable ideological challenge for the future. These groups had to be watched, penetrated and eventually broken up. The party knew that the solemn promises in the Concordat and in Hitler's speeches of early 1933 were no more than a tactical deception, and Albert Müller, regional party leader and a pitiless enemy of the Church, worked steadily in public and in secret to undermine these Catholic youth groups. In 1934, more than a year after Hitler had taken power, a member of one of these groups was charged with treason for possessing a leaflet with the song "Hurrah Viktoria":

> . . . We sing our songs
> Through the night of Hitler's struggle,
> They won't catch us,
> We don't fancy that Hitler,
> We are Christ's Kingdom, and we will triumph:
> Hurrah, Viktoria!

The campaign to have the crucifix removed from classroom walls and replaced by Hitler's portrait (the cross was transferred to hang over the door, while Hitler acquired the place of honour over the blackboard) met dogged resistance in the old schools. As late as 1937 one of Barbie's old teachers at the Gymnasium turned all the class desks around to face the cross above the door, so that the pupils had their backs to the Führer. He was denounced, but it is worth remarking that nothing worse happened to this bold schoolmaster than a transfer to another school.

It seems entirely plausible that Klaus Barbie was informing on his teachers, on his fellow-pupils, and on the Catholic youth movements for at least his last two years at the Friedrich-Wilhelm-Gymnasium. It is clear from the archives that an informer network existed at the school from as early as 1933 and probably well before. By joining the Hitler Youth in April 1933 Barbie would have partly blown his cover, so this hypothesis would suggest that his connection with the Nazis may go back further still. If this is correct, Barbie would have been one of the most important Nazi informers in the city, placed as he was in the heart of what the *Nationalblatt* called "the blackest bastion of the Zentrum".

His reports presumably went to the party branch in the Brücken-strasse. There is no reason to disbelieve Barbie's statement, given in a later document for internal SS purposes, that he did not come into direct contact with the Sicherheitsdienst (SD) in this period when he seems to have been a schoolboy informer. Yet another of his SS statements places this initial contact at "the beginning of 1935", when he became Horrmann's adjutant, or at the earliest a month before he was engaged as a "voluntary" SD helper. In one later version of his life story, Barbie claimed that it was Karl Horrmann who originally asked him if he would like to work for the Gestapo or the SD, adding that one of the fringe benefits would be an almost free education in law. Horrmann certainly knew about the family's desperate financial plight (his own son later lodged in the same house as Barbie's widowed mother) and about Klaus's frustrated ambition to enter university.

About the nature of the voluntary "help" he now offered the SD in 1935 there can be little doubt. "Voluntary helper" was a common euphemism for a Vertrauensmann or V-Mann, an informer and spy, on whose reports the Sicherheitsdienst based its intelligence appreciations and its surveillance of the party itself.

The SD had been set up in 1931. Its founder and leader was Reinhard Heydrich, the cold embittered young man who had been sacked from the German navy at the outset of a promising career. He was directly responsible to Heinrich Himmler, the Reichsführer SS. At this time, the SS had three branches: the Allgemeine-SS (general SS, later to provide much of the senior staff for the concentration camps), the Sicherheitsdienst (SD), and the Politische Bereitschaften (Political Alarm Squads), which eventually evolved into the Waffen-SS. Initially Heydrich intended that, after the conquest of power by the Nazis, the SD would become the main security police force of a National Socialist Germany, but this dream was never fully realised. The rise of the Gestapo, which combined the existing criminal and political police with the SS, frustrated Heydrich's plan, and the SD developed instead into the party's own special intelligence service, leaving the arresting and intimidating to the Gestapo and concentrating on the wider study of opposition inside and outside the party. In the late 1930s Himmler described the SD's "primary fields of activity" as Communism, political activity by religious persuasions, and reaction (i.e. conservative opposition). "The SD is only concerned with major ideological problems." Under "religious persuasions" could be included the "Jewish question".

The SD-Hauptamt (headquarters) in Berlin soon collected an extraordinary mixture of fanatical Nazi intellectuals, professors versed in Nazi ideology, and freebooting misfits with giant ideas about the "world fate-struggle against Judaeo-Bolshevism". For the Jew-baiting violence of the SA and of Julius Streicher, editor of the crudely anti-Semitic *Der Stürmer*, in particular, they had nothing but contempt; such excesses only alienated world opinion and showed a vulgar misunderstanding of the problem. At this stage the SD wanted to solve the "Jewish question" by forced emigration; its experts on Jewish affairs, who came to include Adolf Eichmann, diligently studied Jewish history and cultivated sympathetic contacts with the Zionist movement.

When Barbie first encountered the SD, the service was also compiling files on the party itself. In the endless struggle between competing institutions which reflected Nazi ideology (the survival of the fittest), the SD was eventually forced to abandon this activity, but in return it was established as the only legitimate political surveillance and counter-espionage service of the party. The Gestapo, though under Himmler's control, was a state organ, while the Abwehr was essentially a military intelligence service concerned with foreign espionage and counter-espionage.

In joining the SD Barbie was also joining the SS. Because of the horrors for which the SS were responsible, above all in wartime, the "Order of the Death's Head" now appears as the ultimate expression of all the murderous savagery that the Nazi system was to release against Germany and Europe. But this was not at all how the SS looked when Barbie first encountered it. In 1933–4 it was the SA in their brown shirts (a far larger organisation) who were responsible for the violence in the streets, for the beating-up of Communists and Jews, for the placarding or smashing of Jewish shops. It was the SA under Ernst Röhm which made no secret of

its ambition to become a Nazi people's army to supplement and
perhaps supplant the Reichswehr, the regular army, still regarded
with deep respect and awe by the population. In contrast the SS,
in their sleek black uniforms complete with collar and tie, seemed
to personify an orderly, disciplined side to National Socialism. It
was no accident that after March 1933 a large number of aristocrats and upper middle class intellectuals from the universities
joined the SS (in 1938 18.7 per cent of the Obergruppenführer
[generals] of the SS had titles). For such men the SA stood for the
dangerously revolutionary and turbulent side of the Nazi movement. The SS, on the other hand, seemed to preserve the notion of
an élite that was not merely racial but to a considerable extent
social as well.

In June 1934, while Barbie was away swinging a shovel in
Schleswig-Holstein, Hitler had launched the "Blood Putsch" that
broke the power and ambitions of the SA. Hundreds of SA leaders,
including Röhm himself, were massacred, and the instrument of
murder was the SS. It was the Order's first taste of blood, and the
first mass killing carried out by the Third Reich.

It was to be an instructive year for Barbie. In July 1934 the
new Nazi mayor of Trier had banned Jews from all municipal
swimming-pools, and "No Jews" notices went up all over the city.
In the autumn, the regime brought in the "Nuremberg Laws" for
"the protection of German blood and German honour" banning
Jews from public service, forbidding marriage or sexual intercourse
with "non-Aryans", stripping Jews of Reich citizenship. A Trier
historian, Dr Edgar Christoffel, has collected some of the *Nationalblatt* headlines of this period:

"Bestial Jewish Cattle Dealer Attacks Girls"
"Jew Persecutes Mentally Handicapped"
"Jews Poison Sport"
"Jewish Insurance Swindler"
"Jewish Fiend: Thirteen German Women Dishonoured"
"Jew Exploits War Widows"

and so on. To protect his community, Dr Adolf Altmann was
to endure four more years of this abuse before he finally left for
Holland.

Meanwhile the pressure on the Church and especially against
its youth groups intensified. Here and there resistance sprang up;
a priest in the village of Rascheid hoisted a flag with the Christian
cross in his garden, and when party officials arrived with the Trier

police to remove it a riot broke out in which a crowd of several hundred attacked the police, forcing them to summon reinforcements. But these were isolated incidents.

Klaus Barbie was not content to remain a mere informer for his new friends. In the course of 1935 he applied for full membership in the Sicherheitsdienst. He was still not a party member, and on September 1, now nearly twenty-two, he left the Hitler Youth. Some time that month he was summoned to Berlin and interviewed personally by Reinhard Heydrich at the SD headquarters at Wilhelmstrasse 102. He was evidently thought to have performed well, and made a good impression on the SD chief. On September 29 1935 he was granted full paid membership in the Sicherheitsdienst, which brought with it membership in the SS. He received an SS number (272284) and a few days later moved from Trier to Berlin.

In Berlin he was attached to Amt II (Department II) in the SD-Hauptamt, where he remained just over a year. Amt II, whose general duty was "combating opposition", was the most lively department in the SD. Its second section, styled in the office jargon as Amt II/2 and later to be reorganised as an independent Amt III, was led in 1936 by Professor Reinhard Höhn. At first concerned with "anti-opposition action", it was transformed later that year by the arrival of the dynamic Otto Ohlendorf as Höhn's deputy. It became the section dealing with "areas of German life", and in this guise organised a "mass observation" service from informants all over the country. They produced reports of such disconcerting frankness and objectivity about the state of public opinion that Ohlendorf was eventually to fall foul of the party itself and to embarrass Himmler. The first section of the department, styled Amt II/1 (later renamed Amt II/112) studied the "Jewish question": here again, the SD went its own independent way as Edler von Mildenstein, Adolf Eichmann and others in the section cultivated their secret contacts with Zionist centres and underground Jewish groups in Palestine. The young recruit Barbie, fresh from the provinces, must have looked with awe on these eccentric and voluble stars of the Hauptamt. On one memorable occasion, he found himself playing volleyball with Heinrich Himmler, the supreme Reichsführer of the SS, in the Hauptamt courtyard: "he seemed very stiff, shy but polite", Barbie recalled long afterwards.

As a trainee Barbie was at first given a taste of normal police work. He was sent over to Berlin Police Headquarters on the Alexanderplatz, where he did a spell with the murder squad and then, much more entertainingly, with the vice squad, raiding lurid night bars and brothels under the guidance of "Uncle Karl", the squad's commander. Later he graduated to the SD training school at Bernau, outside the city, and to the Security Police (Sipo) Leadership College in Berlin's Charlottenburg district.

Barbie, with his passion for sport, was lucky enough to be in Berlin in the year of the 1936 Olympics. While the prostitutes he had rounded up with the vice squad sat crossly peeling potatoes to feed the competitors (a punishment thought up by Artur Nebe, the Berlin police chief), Barbie invited some of his childhood friends from the Eifel to stay with him and see something of the Games – and no doubt of young Klaus in his new black uniform. Among these friends was a girl from Mehren who had been close to Barbie when they were both in their teens; she had been a regular visitor to his mother's village in the school holidays from Trier. Later they had quarrelled: Barbie, after returning from his Labour Service, had written her a letter in which he paraded his new beliefs and poked fun at religion. She broke off the friendship, but the chance of seeing the Olympics seems to have overcome her reservations. In Berlin all she could extract from Klaus about his work was that "he worked for the Reich Chancellery", the office of Hitler himself. (This was an impressive substitute for the truth; as an intelligence trainee he could not reveal that he was with the Sicherheitsdienst.) But his beliefs had not changed, and neither had hers; they parted, and met again only some years later when Barbie visited her family in the Ruhr. "My mother, a Christian woman, raged at the Nazi regime in Klaus Barbie's presence. And when I realised that he belonged to the Gestapo [*sic*], I went even further. But neither I nor my mother ever suffered any reprisals for our views from Klaus Barbie," recalled Barbie's friend, who returned to live in the Eifel, but prefers to remain anonymous.

By now, in any case, Barbie was increasingly involved with another young woman. Regine Willms, suitably Aryan with blue eyes and fair hair, was two years younger than Barbie and the daughter of a postal official in Trier. Although Regine was born in Osburg, just south of the river Mosel, her family came from a village only a few miles from Mehren and Udler in the Eifel, and it seems likely enough that Klaus and Regine also met while spending summer holidays with their grandparents in the country. Coming from a solidly Catholic family of four children, she was a firm, quiet young person with little of Barbie's nervous ambition. She attended the Auguste-Viktoria school for girls in Trier, leaving early to do a one-year "women's course" in domestic science. From there she went to the beautiful little hill resort of Manderscheid, in her own countryside, and spent six months working in the kitchens of the Eifler Hof hotel to improve her cooking skill. And in 1936 she was to be found at the other end of Germany, in the Berlin that Rhinelanders traditionally disliked so much, living with a family and looking after their children. This would have been a difficult move to explain were it not for the fact that 1936 was also the year that Barbie spent in Berlin.

By October of that year, his training completed, Barbie was sent into the field, transferred to the staff of the SD Oberabschnitt (major region) West, located at Düsseldorf in the Rhineland. In this wealthy, confident city, where a few years before, Germany's biggest industrialists and bankers had listened to Hitler's personal appeal and agreed to give him the financial support the NSDAP desperately needed, traditional politics still flowed on beneath the surface of the Nazi power monopoly. Barbie was given charge of a "desk" in the Düsseldorf branch of Amt II, sections 122 and 123. His work was to study and report on two areas of politics, the so-called "centre" movements and rightism. The first group included "democratic organisations and pacifists"; the second was made up of "reactionaries, right-wing populism" (völkische Opposition) and "National Bolshevism" – this last a curious variant of Fascism that looked towards the Soviet Union as a model of patriotism, discipline and revolutionary order.

It took him some time to find a home, and in the course of his search two women were on his mind: Regine Willms, and his mother Anna. Barbie eventually rented a flat at Feldstrasse 19, a comfortable, middle-class street in the north of the city, and in June 1937 he and his mother, fetched from Trier, moved in. The same day Regine arrived from Berlin. To satisfy the proprieties she was found a room with another family in the same house. She took a job with the local National Socialist Welfare Office looking after children in a day nursery.

They were to remain together in the Feldstrasse for over two years. Barbie was steadily making a solid reputation for himself in the SD as a keen, rapid, and tireless intelligence man in pursuit of what remained of political opposition. His commanding officer in Düsseldorf was Brigadeführer Freiherr von Schade, one of those aristocrats attracted to the SD. Von Schade, who had at one time been on Himmler's personal staff in Munich, was an ineffectual figure owing much of his career to the influence with Frau Himmler of his well-born wife. He was none the less capable of recognising Barbie's potential. He wrote in Barbie's personal file that he was "an upright character, qualified for his job. From the SS point of view, there are no reservations about him. Professionally, he is one of the best desk officers in the Oberabschnitt." Another senior SS officer in Düsseldorf, in a written reference to support Barbie's promotion, described him as "an extremely hard-working and responsible colleague", and later, in another reference, added that he was "an impeccable comrade. His service achievements are excellent. His bearing and conduct as an SS man on and off duty are immaculate."

In the autumn of 1938 Barbie was obliged to do a three-month spell of compulsory military service, which he spent with the 39th Infantry, Düsseldorf's own territorial regiment, at Wesel on the lower Rhine. So he missed the spectacle of blazing synagogues, the flames reflected in the shattered glass windows of Jewish shops, which was offered by Düsseldorf and almost all other German cities that November on "Crystal Night". Neither was he available to be drafted into the Einsatzkommando (operational commando) formed of SS, SD and Gestapo men to follow the German troops into Czechoslovakia and terrorise the Sudetenland in those autumn months. Earlier that year, Hitler had annexed Austria. And even before this, in 1936, German troops had marched into Trier as the Nazi regime defied Britain and France by reoccupying the demilitarised Rhineland. A few more conquests and triumphs were to come: the rump of Czechoslovakia was occupied in March 1939, and that summer brought the Nazi-Soviet pact with its secret protocol for a new partition of Poland. But here Hitler reached the limit of expansion that could be achieved without a European war. As the crisis over Danzig built up in 1939 and it became obvious that Germany was seeking a pretext to invade Poland, the Western democracies prepared to fight.

As the European crisis thickened, Klaus Barbie and Regine Willms set about the business of getting married. For an SS man this was no simple matter. In 1931 Himmler's "SS Marriage Decree" had laid down the procedure for a lengthy physical, political and genetic examination of groom and bride. "The aim is a heredit-arily valuable clan of the German nordic species. Marriage permission will be granted or withheld exclusively on grounds of racial and genetic health." By 1939, in practice, this tedious procedure was beginning to break down: so many SS men were ignoring it that the penalty, originally expulsion, was rapidly being scaled down. But Barbie was not senior enough, and perhaps not bold enough, to defy the decree. The bulky file of their marriage request has been preserved intact, beginning with the application to apply

41

for an application form, which was sent to the SS Race and Settlement Head Office in January 1939. Each had to submit to a minute physical examination to determine their suitability as breeding stock, backed by full accounts of the illnesses and causes of death of their parents and grandparents (here Barbie lied about his father, leaving a question about alcoholism blank). Each had to produce, on the basis of painstaking research through parish registers, a full "ancestor table" going back to the eighteenth century to confirm that no non-Aryan blood tainted their nordic descent. Two SS referees were obliged to fill out a long questionnaire about Regine's political attitudes and social behaviour. Among other character questions, the referees had to state whether she was "child-loving or not child-loving", "comradely or dominating", "thrifty or extravagant", "domesticated or fickle, fond of finery", and at the end, "did the future bride and her family actively support the National Socialist uprising, or are they now reliable defenders of the National Socialist World-view?" In March Barbie tried to hurry the procedure along, arguing that he wished to get engaged at Easter. Permission came through on March 30 1939 but only on condition that Regine first completed a course of "motherhood training". It then turned out that all the approved courses were booked up for months ahead. Weeks of further delay followed. When Regine finally found a place in a motherhood course and enrolled, it was postponed and then cancelled because of the outbreak of war in September 1939. More letters from Barbie explaining this situation were required before the final permit was granted on April 10 1940. It was not until May 1 that Barbie was able to report triumphantly to the Race and Settlement Office in Berlin: "I hereby announce that on April 25 1940 I was married to Miss Regine Willms in the Düsseldorf register office. Heil Hitler!" In fact, Klaus and Regine probably considered that their marriage had begun some time before. Many years later they would talk about their earlier, "real" wedding, conducted in a forest under an oak tree according to some SS fantasy of "traditional nordic rites".

As often happens in wartime, marriage for the Barbies marked the beginning of a long separation. Both Barbie's private and his official lives were disrupted. Early in 1939, the whole structure of the security services had been remodelled and shaken up, as the SD-Hauptamt, the Gestapo, and the Sicherheitspolizei (Sipo) were, after much wrangling, amalgamated under the Reichssicherheitshauptamt (RSHA) in Berlin. This process was more or less complete by the outbreak of war. The existing departments were now renumbered, so that the SD Amt II now became Amt III of the RSHA ("areas of German life"). The big SD Oberabschnitt regions were broken down into smaller districts. Many SD men displaced by these changes were recruited into the Einsatzkommandos, which moved across Poland behind the fighting troops that September, slaughtering Jews, Polish intellectuals, priests, hospital patients, and any other Poles who seemed a possible source of inconvenience or trouble. Barbie did not serve in Poland, but he was reassigned from Düsseldorf on October 1 1939 to the SD-Abschnitt at Dortmund. The household at Feldstrasse broke up: his mother went home to Trier and found a temporary flat in the Fleischstrasse, later moving into an apartment in a magnificent old house in Liebfrauenstrasse, which had been part of a nunnery and stood only a few yards from the cathedral. Regine, a month after Klaus left for Dortmund, found another flat in Düsseldorf and kept her job at the day nursery.

Dortmund was not far away – less than an hour on the train from Düsseldorf – but it was an utterly different city. This was a coal-mining centre with powerful Social Democrat and Communist traditions, where a small but devoted left-wing resistance was still holding secret meetings and smuggling in leaflets and instructions from German political refugees in nearby Holland. Their groups had already been penetrated by informers in 1939; those arrested were tortured in the cells of the local prison, where some died or committed suicide before they could be sent to concentration camps. Soon after Barbie arrived in Dortmund, there was trouble with the coal miners when the owners cut the traditional Christmas bonus to families by forty per cent. The protests reveal the sullen, confused mood of the German working class, its underlying loyalty to the old trade unionism tainted by new elements of official racialism. After older miners had talked young colleagues out of refusing to go on shift, the men relieved their feelings by chalking rude slogans and caricatures on the coal-wagons coming up to the surface. "Christmas bonuses sink, the white Jews stink!" was one. "The black Jews have gone, the white ones have moved in", was another.

It may have been in Dortmund that Barbie got his first taste of foreign intelligence work. It was an important part of the SD's assignment in Dortmund to intercept and infiltrate the flow of clandestine support to left-wing resistance groups in the coal-mining basin, and this support was coming largely from Holland. The Dortmund SD probably also put agents across the frontier in an effort to penetrate the anti-Nazi exile centres in the Netherlands.

Many years later, apparently to divert attention from his true war record, Barbie was to claim that he had worked for Amt VI (foreign intelligence) of the RSHA, which would have carried out such operations in Holland. But there is nothing whatever either in his SD personal file or in surviving RSHA papers to confirm this. These documents suggest only that during his seven-month spell at Dortmund, Barbie initially carried on with his old job of monitoring centre and right-wing political groups. After the 1939 departmental reshuffle, however, he was assigned to the Dortmund desk of section III/C, which was concerned with "cultural matters" (i.e. religious organisations); Dortmund, like Düsseldorf, was a mainly Catholic community.

Another great change in his life was now approaching. On April 20 1940 Barbie was promoted to Untersturmführer (second lieutenant). With glowing references, he had become a commissioned officer: no doubt he wore his new black uniform, with the diamond-shaped SD badge on the right sleeve, to his wedding five days later. On May 10 the "phony war" in the West ended as German armoured divisions drove into Belgium and Holland. Just over two weeks later, on May 29, Untersturmführer Barbie followed them into the land where Adolf Altmann, the chief rabbi of Trier, had made a home in exile. Barbie was transferred to Holland to join the Sipo and SD commandos already scouring through the Dutch population for political opponents. The career that was eventually to make Klaus Barbie notorious throughout the world, the profession of an expert counter-guerrilla leader, had begun.

CHAPTER TWO

Apprenticeship in the Ghetto

The German invasion of Holland began on May 10 1940. Three days later, with resistance collapsing and the city of Rotterdam in flames, Queen Wilhelmina fled to Britain. On May 14 the Dutch army surrendered. On May 29 the newly commissioned Untersturmführer Klaus Barbie arrived in Holland and was assigned to the Aussenstelle (outstation) of the Sicherheitspolizei and SD in Amsterdam.

In the archives of the Federal Republic of Germany at Koblenz, there has survived an expensively produced little book with a long title, *Annual Report for 1942 on the Operations of the Amsterdam Aussenstelle of the Commander of the Sicherheitspolizei and SD for the Occupied Netherlands*. It is written in a jaunty, chatty style, like the annual report of a company working under trying conditions in a foreign country. Its glossy cover bears a photograph of the Sipo/SD headquarters in Amsterdam, huge banners with the SS rune draping its façade. At the end, there are tables and graphs, the flow charts of repression. The curve recording arrests soars to an immense peak in the month of July 1942; the next table, breaking down this production achievement by departments, shows that the peak was entirely attributable to the work of Amt IV/B and its sub-section IV/B-4.

This was the department dealing with the Jews, and July 1942 was the month in which the mass deportation of Jews to the extermination camps in Poland began. The first train left on July 15 1942. The last, carrying the leaders of the German-sponsored "Jewish Council" left on September 13 1944. There were ninety-three trains in all, carrying 112,000 men, women and children to the east. Most of the Jews from Holland went either to Sobibor, where 43,000 perished, or to Auschwitz, where 60,000 died. After the war some 3,000 returned. Of the dead, something over 14,000 were Jews of German nationality who had fled from the persecutions of the Third Reich to Holland. Among them was the chief rabbi of Trier, Dr Adolf Altmann.

The annual report, in its introduction, apologises for not "honouring" the work of all the Sipo/SD departments in Amsterdam by describing their successes in detail. "Discussion of the achievements of the other areas of the executive branch, especially the substantial participation of the Aussenstelle in the accelerated solution of the Jewish question in the occupied Netherlands, could not be undertaken on the grounds of the especial need for secrecy and for lack of space."

Klaus Barbie was not himself in Holland when the great deportations began – he had left in March 1942, after almost two years in Amsterdam. But he shares the responsibility of those SS and SD officers who herded the Jews, with whips and dogs, into the sealed trains four months later. From the beginning of his service in Holland, Barbie worked in the department assigned to hounding Jews and freemasons, becoming an assistant in Adolf Eichmann's Amt IV/B-4 when it was extended to Amsterdam in March 1941. In all the preparations for the crime, the segregation of the Amsterdam Jews, the progressive removal of all their civil rights and above all the systematic terrorising of the Jews into submission – an essential preliminary – he played a central part. By those few left alive to remember, Klaus Barbie is well remembered in Holland.

He arrived in Amsterdam at a time of intense political confusion, not least among the German occupation authorities. The Queen had left the Dutch civil service in place, to preserve what it could of national independence after the catastrophe, and the Germans did not attempt to remove it. Instead, Hitler appointed Arthur Seyss-Inquart as Reichskommissar with four Generalkommissaren under him to deal with the main areas of administration. Much the most important of these was Hans Rauter, a tough and fanatical Austrian Nazi who had known Hitler personally for almost twenty years, who now became Supreme SS and Police Chief for the Netherlands and Generalkommissar for security. His SS file described him as "redoubtable, battle-hardened, obstinate, energetic and with experience of the world". The rivalry between Seyss-Inquart and Rauter, who regarded himself as responsible primarily to Heinrich Himmler and constantly went over Seyss-Inquart's head for authorisation, was to last throughout the German occupation.

These conflicts over occupation policy were not mere personal quarrels but directly affected what happened on the streets of Amsterdam and other Dutch cities, and dictated how the security police, with Klaus Barbie, would operate. In May 1940 Seyss-Inquart stood for a moderate line towards the Dutch; the Reichskommissar hoped that the trauma of defeat would now make the Dutch disposed to abandon their old loyalty to the House of Orange and accept a "new order" regime friendly to Germany. The SS view, in contrast, was that the "Germanic" nature of the Dutch could be at once exploited.

And there was a third element in occupation calculations: the Dutch Nazi movement (NSB) led by Anton Mussert. For Mussert, the German conquest should have meant his own triumphal appointment as the Dutch "Führer", ruling a Fascist Holland through an exclusively NSB regime and treated by Germany with the deference due to a small-scale Mussolini. To ambitions like this, Seyss-Inquart's policy was a slap in the face. Mussert and his lieutenants attached themselves to the departments of the Reichs-kommissariat and offered servile advice. But Mussert felt cheated of power, chained to the status of a mere collaborator.

The Dutch people soon let Seyss-Inquart down. On July 29 1940 the nation boldly celebrated the birthday of Prince Bernhard, wearing carnations and laying wreaths on monuments to the House of Orange. Hitler called Seyss-Inquart to Berlin and screamed abuse at him: the "soft hand" policy was obviously not working. New and harsher regulations were imposed on the Netherlands. In September Mussert was finally introduced to Hitler. The stock of the NSB in Germany rose, and the self-confidence of the move-ment – bitterly loathed by most of the Dutch population – was inflated. Still Mussert was not, then or ever, granted real political power.

It was becoming clear to Rauter and to Dr Wilhelm Harster, commander of the security police and SD in the Netherlands, that Dutch resistance was going to be a major problem, already developing from the spontaneous emotions of the July "Anjerdag" (carnation day) into structured underground networks. The fight against all kinds of political opposition went into a higher gear, and it is now, in late 1940, that the first detailed account of Barbie enters the record.

He was a small man, with a healthy look and a smooth face. His face was square, but rounded at the corners. The most striking thing about that face was the bitter, tight lips, like a thin slash across his face from which now and then a cutting, sarcastic remark emerged. And his laugh was mocking.

Charlotte van Tongeren, now in her eighties, is remembering the man who sent her father to his death. General Hermannus van Tongeren, a veteran of the Dutch army in the East Indies, was a leading freemason, and the task of Barbie's department was not only the repression of the Amsterdam Jews but the breaking up of all "international organisations", especially the secret brotherhood of the Freemasons with its liberal tradition, which had already been a target for the SD in Germany itself. Worse still, from Barbie's point of view, the Amsterdam Freemasons had some Jewish members. The general came under surveillance at the very beginning of the occupation, and was ordered to report daily to the German police authorities.

But van Tongeren was also involved in the first moves towards establishing a resistance movement. His other daughter, Jacoba, acted as a courier in the underground, and was to become a leading figure in the resistance network known as "Group 2000".

The Dutch Freemasons were finally banned in the autumn of 1940. But they continued to organise private gatherings, and on October 10 the general was warned by a frantic telephone caller that the first of a group of Freemasons who had arrived for a coffee meeting at a hotel in the busy Leidseplein, in the centre of Amsterdam, had been arrested. General van Tongeren set out on foot and walked about the Leidseplein, grabbing other masons on their way to the hotel and sending them home.

On the following day three SD officers appeared at the family's flat. The general was out so they bundled his daughter Charlotte into a waiting car and ordered her to tell them where he had gone. "The barber," she suggested untruthfully. A brief tour of central Amsterdam ensued, until the Germans grew tired of her lies and brought her home. And they were in luck: as the car drew up, General van Tongeren arrived at his own front door and was seized. Another mason, however, had seen Charlotte's abduction and had followed at a safe distance in his own car. He telephoned to say that he recognised the three men who had arrested her father. They were Hauptscharführer Otto Kempin, Johan Peter (Josef) Kalb, a half-Dutch art dealer, and Klaus Barbie.

Charlotte's family was allowed to visit the general in prison once a fortnight, but before each visit she or her relatives had to go to the Sipo/SD headquarters to collect a permit.

Kempin and Kalb always had to sit at the enquiry counter [she remembers]. Barbie sat a bit behind them at his own little table, with a radio which he would sometimes turn up very loud. And he would make jokes. The others had to laugh at them dutifully. My father warned us all against him. He said: "Be careful of Barbie! He is the nastiest and the cleverest of the lot!"

In March 1941 van Tongeren broke the news to his daughters that he was being deported to Germany. Already emaciated and shaking with fever – he had kidney disease – he was loaded into an unheated freight wagon and taken to the concentration camp at Sachsenhausen, just north of Berlin. Before the train crossed the frontier he managed to throw out a note to his family: "Last greeting from native soil. Life is hope and hope is life. Your old boy." He did not last long in the camp. After an outdoor roll-call lasting three days and nights in the cruel Prussian winter he was taken to the hospital block, and died a week after his arrival in Sachsenhausen.

On April 1 Barbie rang Charlotte van Tongeren and summoned her to his headquarters. "Your father has died of an infection in both ears," he told her. "He has already been cremated." A month later a policeman came round to the house and delivered a small dented metal urn of ashes. And yet this was not quite the end of General van Tongeren, for as Grand Master he had arranged for the Freemasons' funds to be withdrawn from the bank and hidden for the future use of the new-born resistance. They were well used: the underground newspaper *Vrij Nederland* was financed by the fund, and in 1942 the general's daughter Jacoba drew 600,000 guilders from her father's "legacy" and used it to purchase arms.

Meanwhile the noose was being drawn steadily tighter round the Amsterdam Jews. Back in the summer of 1940 German regulations, hardly noticed by the population at large, had forbidden Jews to act as air raid wardens and had banned ritual slaughter by Jewish butchers. There was much more fuss about the October 1940 decrees obliging all state servants – who included academic staff – to produce signed declarations of Aryan descent; the universities were outraged, and there were several student demonstrations. But this pace was too slow for the anti-Semitic thugs of Mussert's NSB. In December 1940 gangs of Dutch Fascists began to raid the Jewish quarter of Amsterdam, breaking windows and beating up the inhabitants.

Amsterdam's Jews fought back. This was one of the oldest and most sophisticated Jewish centres in western Europe, its self-confidence rooted in the tolerant and democratic society of the Netherlands. Another source of militancy, principally among the large refugee population which had moved to Holland from Germany and Austria, was Zionism: the refugees had reconstructed in the Netherlands a highly organised Zionist network of camps, farms and youth groups preparing "pioneers" for emigration to Palestine. The first NSB raids were soon answered by the appearance of

Jewish self-defence squads, and early in February one of Mussert's men died of injuries received in a street battle.

The Germans had not instigated this confrontation – they had little direct control over the Mussert movement – but they could not tolerate the emergence of a successful anti-Fascist Jewish militia in an occupied city. A few days later there was a fresh crisis. Two German Jews named Cahn and Kohn ran a popular ice-cream parlour, the Koco, on Van Woustraat in south Amsterdam, and their younger Jewish customers decided to organise protection for them against NSB marauders. They equipped the two not only with a guard armed with metal coshes but with a large ammonia spray flask. There had already been some NSB threats to Koco. On the evening of February 19 the ice-cream parlour was already closed when there was a sudden battering on the door and the sound of voices and boots outside. The two owners jumped to the conclusion that it was an attack by Mussert thugs – apt to bolt if they met real resistance – and prepared to defend themselves.

They were tragically wrong. Outside was a German police patrol, led by Willy Lauhus, one of the senior officers of the Amsterdam Aussenstelle, which had come to investigate a rumour that a secret meeting of supporters of the House of Orange was taking place at Koco that night. And with this patrol, according to his own account given many years later, was Klaus Barbie.

The owners tore open the door and, as the first intruders charged in, let off the ammonia flask. Pandemonium followed; the saloon filled up with gas, and coughing German policemen blazed away with their pistols at figures seen in the haze. In 1982, in an interview with *Stern* magazine, Barbie described with relish how he had smashed a heavy glass ashtray over Cahn's head and split his skull open. This must be one of Barbie's boastful fantasies, for Ernst Cahn was able to escape to his own home, where he was later arrested and taken off for interrogation. All the refined sadism of SD torture would not make him give away the names of the Jews who had given him the ammonia flask, and he was shot on March 3.

The Koco affair was to pitch all Holland into crisis. The next day, Hans Rauter, Generalkommissar for security in the Netherlands, told Himmler that his Jews were out of control and asked permission for a crushing counter-blow.

And on February 22 and 23, the whole German police force in Amsterdam poured out on to the streets to raid the Jewish quarter. They were led by Colonel Knolle, the deputy security police commander in the Hague, who brought his dog with him to Amsterdam to take part in the fun. Over four hundred young Jewish men were rounded up. They were deported first to Buchenwald and then to the quarries of the concentration camp at Mauthausen, where thousands of prisoners had already perished. None of them returned home alive, and 160 of them were sent from Mauthausen to die in the experimental gas chambers of the Nazi euthanasia scheme at Schloss Hartheim.

And then something happened which took the Germans totally by surprise. The Dutch rebelled on behalf of their Jewish fellow-citizens. Leaflets appeared calling for "Solidarity between the vic-timised Jews and working people . . . strike! strike! strike!", and on February 25 and 26 1941 a general strike took place not only in Amsterdam but in Utrecht, Hilversum and other big towns. The famous "February strike" was not merely the first mass strike against Nazi occupation in Europe, but – almost more remarkable – it was launched by the Communist party of Holland at a time, four months before Hitler's attack on the Soviet Union, when Communists in the rest of Europe were following the party line of Stalin's Nazi-Soviet Pact and staying out of active resistance.

The Germans put the strike down with ferocity – and with some refinement. A week before the Koco riot, they had persuaded the leaders of the Amsterdam Jews to set up a Jewish Council, an essential instrument in the Nazi technique of gradually neutralising and manipulating Jewish communities throughout Europe. Now Rauter pulled in Professor David Cohen, one of the two chairmen, and threatened to have another three hundred Jews arrested and deported if the strike did not end within twenty-four hours.

The Germans then turned on their own men, those who had bungled by completely failing to predict the "February strike". All around Barbie, desk drawers were being hurriedly cleared and quick farewell office parties organised as Rauter and Harster, the Sicherheitspolizei commanders in the Hague, fired the officers they judged responsible and replaced them. Sturmbannführer Wilkens and Hauptsturmführer Ditges, who had run the Amsterdam Aus-senstelle between them, were thrown out and replaced by the formidable Willy Lages. Karl Ditges had been an old friend of Barbie's from their days together in the pre-war Düsseldorf SD, and a useful supporter in office disputes in Amsterdam. But Barbie, recently promoted to the rank of Obersturmführer, seems rapidly to have won the confidence of Lages, his new commanding officer, and learned to work closely with another of the March incomers, the evasive, neurotic Rhinelander Ferdinand aus der Fünten.

In Berlin Himmler and Heydrich had made changes which now

filtered through to the Sipo/SD in Amsterdam. A "Central Office for Jewish Emigration" was set up, on the model of those in Berlin and Prague: both Heydrich and Adolf Eichmann, now the leading SD "intellectual" on the Jewish question, still thought of a "final solution" based on forced emigration rather than genocide. At the same time, the new RSHA section IV/B-4 was established in Berlin, the "Jewish section" under Eichmann, which spawned its own new branches and sub-branches in the Hague and Amsterdam.

In practice, Barbie was busy in both these offices. He assisted aus der Fünten to run the Emigration Office, which dealt directly with the Jewish Council, and he also worked for sub-section IV/B-4 which, in Amsterdam at least, dealt with Jewish resistance rather than the Jewish question in general. It was probably in his "emigration" capacity that Barbie took part in late March 1941 in the clearing of a Jewish work-village, or pioneer training farm, at Wieringermeer in northern Holland. He found that most of the teenage boys and girls were from Germany, young exiles who had been shovelling the Dutch mud in the firm belief that they would soon be departing to dig good kibbutz earth under the Palestine sun. They watched the arrival of their Nazi fellow-countrymen, with their green fatigues and skull-and-crossbones badges, with disgust. But for the moment nothing worse was to happen than a forced return to Amsterdam where they were farmed out with foster-parents.

May 14 1941 marked the first anniversary of the Dutch surrender to Nazi Germany. But the melancholy of Amsterdam's citizens was lightened by a huge explosion, as a time bomb went off in a German officers' club on the Bernard Zweerskade; later the same day the switchboard of the Luftwaffe base at Schiphol airport was burned out by an incendiary device. The Germans shuffled through various reprisal plans, and resolved to take it out on the Jews. A few days later, Willy Lages sent Barbie round to the Jewish Council offices. He had instructions to avoid creating suspicion. Professor Cohen was surprised when Barbie shook him warmly by the hand and told him he had decided that the young Jews ought to be allowed back to the camp at Wieringermeer. It was a matter of persuading Lages, he implied. A few days later, the board of the council paid him a return visit to discuss the idea further. On June 9 they were again suddenly summoned back to see Barbie once more; it was a matter of fixing transport, he said, and he would like to have the list of addresses at which the young pioneers had been lodged in Amsterdam. "We'll take them back by bus, the same way we brought them."

Cohen and his colleagues withdrew for a moment to discuss this. It seemed an odd request: after all, the Jewish Council itself could perfectly well notify the young Jews about when and where to meet the buses. But they decided not to make difficulties, with Barbie and Lages apparently in such a sunny mood, and agreed to hand over the list. Two days later, on the morning of Wednesday, June 11, Cohen and the second chairman of the council, Asscher, were ordered to report instantly to SD headquarters on the Euterpestraat, where they were locked in a room by themselves and held incommunicado until evening. Then the door opened and Lages appeared, followed by his full staff, to inform them that three hundred Jews had been arrested as a reprisal for the bombing of the officers' club nearly a month before.

The list of addresses had been distributed to the German security police and their Dutch auxiliaries on Tuesday, and on this Wednesday it was not only the male Jews from Wieringermeer who were arrested but dozens of others, dragged out of cafés, clubs and houses and brought to the Euterpestraat. Cohen and Asscher did not understand how Barbie and Lages had tricked them until they were released. Then, downstairs, they found themselves facing the boys whose addresses they had so trustingly handed over to the Germans.

The young men were transported to the quarries at Mauthausen. A surviving German document dated December 1941 tells more eloquently than any description what awaited them there. Out of the 425 Dutch Jews sent to that concentration camp in February and the new wave of victims from Wieringermeer in June, only eight remained alive.

After the June raids, the name of Klaus Barbie begins to fade out of the Dutch record. There is a letter addressed to the RSHA in Berlin, dated from Amsterdam on July 4 1941, in which he reports the birth of a daughter, Ute Regine, in Trier on June 30. There is also a surviving letter to Barbie from one of his Dutch informers, dated December 24 1941. These are the only firm traces of his presence, although the SS records show that his posting to Holland continued until March 1942. This sudden lack of evidence is curious. In 1979, talking to the West German journalist Gerd Heidemann, Barbie claimed that he had been attached to a special unit in the Russian campaign during those months, "suppressing partisan resistance". No evidence of any kind survives to confirm this; as an old man, Barbie often lied about the past to make himself interesting. If he remained in Amsterdam, working with section IV/B-4 to prepare the final disposal of the Dutch Jews, the absence of traces may be explained by the fact that most of those who had contact with him died in the gas chambers. But the "Russian interlude" cannot be entirely excluded. If it happened, Barbie would have served with the Einsatzgruppen, the mixed police and SS battalions who slaughtered hundreds of thousands of Jews, partisans, Communist party members and innocent civilians as the German armies advanced into Russia.

In Holland that summer the remorseless pressure against the Jews continued. In August all Jewish children were removed from Dutch schools. In September, after telephone cables had been cut near Enschede, there was another wave of mass arrests and deportations; the same month Hans Rauter forbade Jews to change their addresses without police permission. In December, a month after the Reich had stripped all German Jews living abroad of their nationality, all non-Dutch Jews resident in Holland were ordered to report to the Central Office of Jewish Emigration as a preliminary to deportation.

By now the decision had been taken by Hitler that the entire Jewish population of Europe was to be exterminated, a decision merely ratified by the "Wannsee Conference" of Nazi and SS leaders in January 1942. Step by step, the Jewish Council was forced by the Germans to move the Amsterdam Jews into camps, the first station on their way to the gas chambers. In the month that Barbie left Holland, March 1942, all Jews in the Netherlands were ordered to wear the star of David. Four months later, the planning for the "final solution of the Jewish question" in Holland was completed, and the first sealed trains moved eastwards towards Sobibor and Auschwitz.

To a horrified witness of the June raids in 1941, Klaus Barbie said: "This is just the beginning!" For once he was telling the truth.

After the Jews of Holland, the Jews of France were to receive Barbie's attention. Did he know where the trains were really taking them? With so many of his old SD comrades from Berlin and Düsseldorf now working the machinery of the death camps, he must have known. And once – but only once – he told an outsider after the war how he had killed Jews with his own hands. They were French Jews, and the person he told, who carried Barbie's story like a secret scar to the end of her life, was a Frenchwoman. The strange journey which took her into Barbie's life began in France, at the outset of the war.

For most of France, the "real" war began as the German offensive launched itself westwards through the Ardennes on May 10 1940. For an unlucky few, those who lived on the frontier with Germany, there had been no "phony war", no interval of apparent peace in the eight months between September 1939 and the "Blitzkrieg". Among those who learned early the experiences of disruption, flight, loss and chaos was a young woman named Andrée Rivez.

She was twenty-four when it began. She was an Alsatian by birth, from a family which had a tradition of fanatical patriotism to France, developed in the half-century 1871–1918 when Alsace and Lorraine were annexed to Germany. In 1939 Andrée and her mother were running the Hotel de la Gare at St Louis, the little town which stands right in the corner of Europe where the Swiss, German and French frontiers run together; it was a good hotel with a famous wine cellar, thriving on the custom of railway travellers crossing the border. And there was another attraction about the Hotel de la Gare: Andrée – tall, slender and dark-haired – was outstandingly pretty.

Among themselves, the regular drinkers and diners wondered why such a beauty had married a useless boor like Böhm, a travelling tea salesman who seldom appeared except to demand money. It was a question Andrée bitterly asked herself. Essentially, she supposed she had married in order to escape the attentions of her stepfather, M. Pecquignot. But many people had warned her not to throw herself away at the age of eighteen, and among them was an Englishman named Richardson who also worked in the tea business. Very gravely, he had said to her: "I beg you for the love of God not to marry Böhm." Something about his intensity puzzled her: was there something about her fiancé he knew but dared not quite say? She shrugged; the wedding was only a few days away, and she could not face the uproar of calling it off. So she married Böhm, who contrived to spend the ample dowry she brought him in two weeks.

Now, six years later, she saw little of her husband. War was plainly imminent, and the hotel was prospering; into the frontier station at St Louis came a torrent of travellers on legitimate or shady errands, and with them a stream of refugees from Nazi Germany, Jews and non-Jews. Many of those who broke their journey at the hotel were smugglers; some were spies. The Hotel de la Gare was a perfect listening-post, and the French Deuxième Bureau (military intelligence) had been using it for years as a source and contact point. Andrée and her mother Jeanne knew about it, and were happy to tip off French counter-intelligence about interesting visitors or snatches of suggestive gossip. And Böhm knew too.

Then, in August 1939, the French government ordered the immediate evacuation of St Louis as a potential war zone. Nothing had been prepared; bewildered crowds swamped the railway station without provisions or shelter, and Andrée went across to distribute free food and drink from the hotel and tie name-and-address labels round the necks of the most pathetic refugees of all, the German-Jewish children. Next day the police came to the hotel and accused Andrée and her mother of profiteering. They were given three hours to clear out. A few hours later the hotel was looted by French troops of all its cutlery, linen and wine.

Andrée drove with her mother to Dijon. They rented a flat and enjoyed some months of peace, made more pleasant by the absence of Böhm who had vanished just before the outbreak of war, saying that he had been conscripted to defend the Maginot Line. Their respite ended in May 1940 as the German armoured divisions burst into France and crossed the river Meuse, threatening to cut Dijon off from Paris. The city panicked. In her little car, hardly big enough to hold herself, her mother, their luggage and their large dog, Andrée joined the thousands of vehicles, many with mattresses and carpets on the roof as protection against German bombs, struggling to escape to the west. After a day inching forward in the colossal traffic jam – she wore out a pair of shoes changing gear – Andrée gave up and turned off down a side lane, eventually reaching the town of Autun just as a series of deafening explosions announced the arrival of a German panzer column from the other direction.

For her, the occupation had begun. And in those first days, Andrée Rivez was to experience all the contradictory, unmanageable feelings that later divided France so tragically between those who resisted from the first hour, those who decided to keep their heads down and live as "normally" as they could, and those who collaborated. There was, of course, the sense of horror and shame as the alien tanks, loaded with healthy, fair-haired young soldiers, rolled through the streets. There was the sick recognition that the Third Republic had utterly failed in its most basic duty: to defend France and make it a state worth defending; when France capitulated on June 22 1940 and the semi-Fascist Vichy regime led by the ancient Marshal Pétain took power, much of France accepted the change with resignation, or even with a glimmer of hope. And there was the moment of almost hysterical relief when the German front-line troops turned out not to be slaughterers but young men who – on the whole – behaved in the first weeks with restraint, even some courtesy.

Andrée herself experienced some of that early courtesy. A German general at Autun not only gave her a fifty-litre drum of petrol – an

unimaginable windfall in those days – but added a basket of straw-
berries for the drive home. Back in Dijon, she buried the drum in
the garden (it was eventually used to help the escape of a Frenchman
who had been hiding German refugees from the Gestapo), and
waited for history's next surprise. It was a disagreeable one. A few
weeks later, Böhm appeared at the door. He was evasive about his
war experiences, stayed a few days, then disappeared again with
his belongings. Some days later, the family upstairs broke the news
to Andrée that he had been seen at the Dijon Kommandantur,
where he was working as an informer and interpreter with the
Germans.

The upstairs neighbours smelt trouble and left Dijon in a hurry,
and Andrée was not entirely surprised when a German in civilian
clothes came round and ordered her to accompany him. She refused,
and a few hours later was taken off forcibly by a uniformed corporal
and a private. Her mother assumed she was bound for the torture
chambers. But the two soldiers took her in silence through the
streets to a well-known café, the Rotonde. At a table in the corner,
there waited for her a square-built young man with blue eyes and
a small blond moustache. His name was Kurt Merk.

This moment of encounter in a Dijon café had many consequences. It was, in the first place, the beginning of an improbable
passion between two human beings who were supposed to be
enemies, a passion which was to withstand a world of treachery,
cruelty and killing, which survived the collapse of a continent and
the vengeance of those who held power after the collapse, and which
ended only in death. It was also the start of a long and decisive
interlinking of the fates of Merk and Andrée Rivez with that of
Klaus Barbie, a relationship which later almost certainly saved
Barbie's life and preserved him for thirty-five years from facing
judgment for his crimes.

Kurt Merk was a lieutenant in the Abwehr, Germany's main
military intelligence service. But he was, in his calm, self-mocking
way, a most unmilitary person. He was three months younger than
Andrée, born in the village of Fleinhausen near Augsburg to a
peasant family who spoke the Bavarian-Swabian dialect, and he
had hardly grown old enough to look about him before he was
sucked into the endless regimentations of the Third Reich. Later he
said to Andrée: "It was the Hitler Youth, then the Reich Labour
Service, then military service, then the war . . . eight years in
uniform, and not one single day voluntarily!" He was twenty-two
when he was drafted into the army; war broke out when he was
due to be released, and he served in an artillery regiment in Poland

until his transfer to France in June 1940. There he was noticed by an old army acquaintance, Major Ehinger, an Abwehr officer and a close friend of the Abwehr chief, Admiral Canaris, who was in charge of establishing a counter-intelligence unit based in Dijon. Ehinger extracted Merk from the artillery and brought him to Dijon where, after some months of training, he was put in charge on one of the desks in Abwehr Department III-f, dealing with counter-intelligence and security.

Kurt Merk was not an enthusiastic Nazi. He believed that it was possible to do a good job in counter-intelligence without getting blood on one's uniform, and he detested the SS and SD with their cult of theatrical violence. In this he was in tune not only with Major Ehinger, a tolerant Swabian, but with the whole ethos of the Abwehr. As the war went on, professional rivalry between the old-established Abwehr and the SS intensified into a fundamental political conflict that eventually – in 1944 – was to lead Admiral Canaris and several of his senior staff officers into support for the plot to murder Hitler, and cost them their lives.

When Merk began his work in Dijon and made the acquaintance of the SD – including Klaus Barbie, at first stationed not far from Dijon at Gex – the two services could still preserve the frontier between them. Merk knew Barbie slightly, and while sharing general intelligence information with him, did not get involved in SD operations. But as time passed, and especially after the arrest of Canaris, the Abwehr in France, as elsewhere, rapidly lost most of its independence to the SS and SD. This affected Merk directly, especially after Barbie moved to a much more important post in Lyon. Although he went on trying to keep his own counter-espionage operations to himself and his Abwehr colleagues, it became much more difficult to keep Barbie and his gang of trained killers out of Merk's patch.

But for most of the war Merk was senior in rank to Barbie, a fact which Barbie – who in Lyon wielded much more power – sharply resented. In 1944 Kurt Merk began to receive direct threats from the SS and Gestapo. As they said to him in Dijon, "When we've won this war, then we'll really clean this mess out" – and they meant the Abwehr itself.

Angry and frightened, Andrée knew nothing about these hidden rivalries as she stood before Merk at the café table. This was just another German. And yet he seemed benign. He asked her to sit down, and as he began to talk, she became reluctantly aware of a quality of honesty about him, a gift which Kurt Merk not only possessed but was able to project all through his life. At another table, to her horror, she glimpsed her husband. Merk told her to take no notice. It was time she heard a few truths. Böhm, he explained, had been working for German intelligence for years before the war (now she remembered and understood the warnings of that English tea salesman, who perhaps was not just a salesman). His journeys on business had been espionage missions; his absence during the fighting had been spent not at the front but at Abwehr headquarters in Stuttgart. His latest feat had been to denounce his own wife and her mother as agents of the Deuxième Bureau in St Louis. Kurt Merk was supposed to arrest them, and have them deported to a concentration camp near Regensburg.

It was somehow already clear to both of them that he would do no such thing. But Merk could not simply forget the accusation. There was a way out, however, which only he could offer. He could tell his superiors that he had "turned" her, that she had agreed to work for the Abwehr. And Andrée, seeing no escape, terrified of her husband and worried about what might happen to her mother, eventually consented. Merk seems to have promised that it would be almost a formality, that in reality he would not ask her to become a traitor to her own country in any serious way; it was not the only occasion on which he "hired" people in order to protect them.

Andrée had found safety, and something more. "I fell in love with him, and he fell in love with me," she says laconically today. In a very frightening world, Kurt Merk was both lover and protector. He took charge, he made her feel safe – perhaps safer than she really was, as a Frenchwoman now officially working as a "collaborator". And as she understood more about his work, she saw that he and Ehinger did indeed make efforts to "spare the conquered". They did their job of penetrating and breaking Allied and Resistance espionage nets with great efficiency – Merk was soon reputed to be one of the most skilled counter-intelligence men in France – but they tried to ensure that those whom they caught did not end up in concentration camps or before firing-squads, and kept them as far as possible out of the hands of the Gestapo.

From the surrender of 1940 until November 1942, France was divided into zones: a northern zone including Paris and Dijon which was under direct German occupation and military control, and the "zone libre" – south-eastern France, including Lyon and Marseille – which was free of German troops and governed from Vichy by Marshal Pétain. Soon after the armistice, a third zone was established for the Italians, which ran up the eastern side of France from Nice to Grenoble, while the north-eastern corner of the country, the department of the Nord with Lille at its centre, was annexed by the German military government in Belgium. France had become a country seamed with new and irrational frontiers, and everywhere human beings – ordinary French citizens seeking their families, Resistance couriers, Jewish refugees – were trying to slip across them illegally.

Kurt Merk obtained transit papers for many of these helpless people, though whether he was entirely altruistic in his motives or also interested in studying the border-crossers cannot be known. Andrée recalls today:

> I think perhaps he helped some Allied airmen get into the zone libre. And he helped many Jews cross over, because he could get hold of travel passes for them. I did this too because I could get the forms. It was better than letting those poor people use the professional "passeurs" to take them across, who would often kill or rob them – many of the refugees would have all their money and jewels with them.

Not far from Dijon was a very much more authentic frontier, the heavily-barricaded border with neutral Switzerland. A special Gestapo outstation covered this stretch of the frontier, based in the charming little town of Gex, its steep, terraced streets only ten miles from Switzerland. In May 1942 Klaus Barbie, fresh from a brief three-week sojourn in Brussels, arrived to take over its command. This was his first command and it was a responsible one. The unit had the double task of collecting intelligence from Switzerland and blocking the continuous flow of Allied or Resistance agents crossing the frontier near Geneva on their way to the British and American diplomatic missions at Berne, the Swiss federal capital.

In Gex, Barbie was a busy and fulfilled policeman. Based on a hotel in the town and keeping close liaison with the local Kommandantur in the Château de Prévessin, he often found it necessary to visit the city of Dijon. And it was in Dijon that he first met Kurt Merk. The two men never became friends – the personal and political differences between them were too great. But they recognised each other's talents. And as long as the demarcation of work between them remained clear – the Abwehr dealing with hostile espionage and the Sicherheitspolizei and SD combating the Resistance – open strife could be avoided.

Meanwhile Barbie was remarkably cheerful in his new job. Gottlieb Fuchs, a Swiss citizen attached to the Gestapo as an interpreter, remembers driving back with him one day to Gex from Dijon, the Obersturmführer steering his black *traction-avant* Citroen through the dark green pine forests of the Jura hills and humming aloud the Horst Wessel song. He began to talk adoringly of Hitler. "He was utterly convinced that Hitler would win the war," says Fuchs.

All this changed in November 1942. The British and Americans landed in French North Africa and faced the undefended south coast of Vichy France across the Mediterranean; the large French fleet that had remained immobilised at Toulon since the armistice might now, the Germans suspected, defect and make a run for it across to liberated Algiers. That month the German forces drove across the demarcation line and occupied the entire zone libre from Lyon south to the Riviera. For Klaus Barbie, the operation brought an abrupt end to his assignment in Gex, and he was transferred to Lyon. Merk stayed in Dijon, but the abolition of the zone extended the operational area of Abwehr Department III-f southwards over a huge tract of new territory that included the main centre of resistance in France, the city of Lyon itself. From now on, Merk and Barbie, the Abwehr and the Einsatzkommando of the Sipo/SD, were hunting in the same thicket – and often treading on one another's toes.

And for the French, "Operation Attila" – the extension of German military control over almost the whole of pre-war France – meant the end of the first phase of the occupation. The illusion of normality, the argument that France remained a proud and independent nation under Marshal Pétain, became harder to sustain. The French fleet at Toulon scuttled itself rather than fall into the hands of the advancing Germans, while the angry voice of Gaullism could now be heard not just from London but from Algeria also. The Resistance steadily extended its networks and activity; since Germany's attack on the Soviet Union in June 1941 the French Communist party had added its huge resources of manpower, organisation and experience of clandestine work to the services of the Resistance, although in 1942 there was as yet no unified command over the various groups operating underground. British and Free French agents, couriers and radio operators were being parachuted into France in growing numbers, while the people of northern France could watch the American bomber fleets, newly based in England, draw their comb of white contrails across the sky.

And yet the previous two years had allowed Vichy and the Germans to build a solid institutional base for collaboration. The French police, above all in Paris, worked closely with the Gestapo, whose work in the northern zone would have been impossible without them. The authoritarian regime of Pétain, with its religiosity, its anti-Semitism, and its infantile appeal to antique rural values ("Tilling and pasturing are the twin nipples of France", or "Work, Family, Fatherland!") found support not only from much of conservative Catholic France but from the Fascist and ultra-rightist political formations which had arisen in France between the wars. A "French Voluntary Legion" was raised to combat Bolshevism on the eastern front and, later, Joseph Darnand raised an ill-disciplined and murderous para-military force in the "Milice", which was used to fight the armed guerrilla units of the Resistance and to terrorise the civilian population supporting them. Between the extremes lay most of the French people, instinctively hostile to the occupying Germans and yet offering the minimum of collaboration necessary to stay out of trouble and carry on business as usual.

It was a time of moral snares, and Andrée Rivez was deep in one of them. She was a patriotic Frenchwoman and no traitor by nature or conviction, but she was not inclined towards self-sacrifice either. Faced with the choice of arrest and deportation with her mother, or a "formal" connection with the Abwehr, she had chosen the Abwehr. But Kurt Merk, for all his good intentions, was not able to keep it entirely a formality. Andrée, who received the Abwehr informant number 7284, was too conspicuous, and the war lasted too long. Many years later, Andrée admitted wryly: "There had to be results. After all, it lasted a long time. If it had been a matter of a week or a month . . . but it was years. Yes, there had to be results." Although she could not believe that she had technically become a collaborator – "working with the Abwehr seemed to me about as probable as a virgin giving birth", she says now – Merk was eventually obliged to exploit her contacts and make use of what she knew for German intelligence.

CHAPTER THREE

The Gestapo Mission

On the morning of November 11 1942 a small group of veterans of the Great War and of the 1940 defeat of France, their chests glittering with medals, stood to attention in front of the war memorial in the city of Lyon. They saluted the stone monument engraved with the names of the war dead; then, heads bared, they observed a minute's silence.

It was a simple ceremony but for those who took part an intensely moving one. All of them remembered the great parades that had traditionally marked Armistice day before the war in the secluded Parc de la Tête d'Or, with the military bands, the dipping colours, and the final dying notes of homage from a lone bugler. This time there was no pomp. The Vichy government had banned the customary ceremony for fear of offending German sensibilities, and the Lyon city administration had added its prohibition. So it took courage even to be there, and the group that now stood at the Monument aux Morts was poignantly small. The only sound was a church bell tolling eleven.

Then, from the north, came a new and disturbing noise. It started as a dull rumble and swelled into a full-throated roar. Through the suburbs and down the main boulevards of the city poured an endless procession of German vehicles and uniformed columns of soldiers. "It was a nightmare," recalled Charles Adam, the caretaker at the Hotel Dieu Hospital in the centre of the city. "The whole city was vibrating with the rattle of caterpillar tracks." Shops began to close as word spread: "The Boches are back." People watched, hostile and silent from behind closed windows, as the Wehrmacht marched through the streets.

With tears in their eyes the veterans turned their backs on the motorised columns roaring past. There could hardly have been a more brutal reminder of the reality of France's defeat.

It was the second occupation of Lyon, but the two bore no comparison. The first had taken place immediately after the Nazi Blitzkrieg in 1940 when France was in a state of shock at the suddenness of its defeat. The German troops had taken over with the minimum of bloodshed and had set about wooing the traumatised population with special propaganda in the form of leaflets and posters, which told the people the Germans had come not as conquerors but as protectors. "We were staggered at the freshness and youth of the German soldiers," said Charles Adam. Furthermore they did not stay for long, pulling out after only eighteen days, to leave the affairs of Lyon in the hands of the Vichy government.

The Armistice day occupation of Lyon in 1942, by contrast, had nothing to do with winning the hearts and minds of the people. The troops of the Wehrmacht and the SS who thundered into the city had been hardened by two year's fighting on the eastern front, and knew enough about the ruthlessness of the Russian partisans to expect the worst of the French Resistance. They were in Lyon as part of Hitler's Attila Plan, and their task was the total suppression of opposition within the southern zone of France.

By the morning of November 12 the occupation was complete. Troops guarded the key intersections within the city; the bridges over the rivers Saône and Rhône which run parallel to each other through the centre were secured, with batteries of 37mm cannon and machine guns mounted at each end; tanks, gun-carriers, and tracked vehicles were drawn up in the Place Bellecour beneath the equestrian statue of Louis XIV; armoured cars lined the main boulevards; from the masts of official buildings huge swastika flags drooped in the cold morning light.

The Germans had requisitioned the main hotels – the Terminus, Bristol and Royal – and commandeered Lyon's military buildings for the use of their troops. Outwardly, at least, Lyon was a conquered city. But almost before the German troops had settled in behind their gun emplacements, the first signs of revolt had emerged. At 11 p.m. on November 13, two days after the arrival of the Wehrmacht, a military vehicle parked in the rue Stella was torn apart by a bomb. Crude slogans – Mort à Hitler! A bas les Boches! – went up overnight on the Sun King's statue in the Place Bellecour, and on November 27 a German soldier was wounded in the rue Victor Hugo, a few hundred yards from the heavily protected headquarters of the SS.

Obersturmführer Klaus Barbie drove into Lyon in a large black staff car a few days after the take-over. He had every reason to relish his new appointment. Just twenty-nine years of age, and with the junior rank of lieutenant, he had been given a job of awesome responsibility: Gestapo chief for Lyon, third largest city in France.

Officially, Barbie was unfamiliar with Lyon. As part of the zone libre, the city had been off-limits to German troops. But as a keen and ambitious young officer in Gex, Barbie had made it his business to undertake a number of clandestine missions to the city in the weeks leading up to the occupation. He had visited it in plain clothes, each time equipped with false identity papers and food ration cards. He spoke excellent if over-precise French, with hardly a trace of a German accent, an asset that had enabled him to mix easily and to make casual contact with the Lyonnais citizens, eavesdropping on their café conversations. By the time he drove openly into the city he had built up a fair picture of it and its inhabitants.

The headquarters of the Sicherheitspolizei, which housed Barbie's office, was the Hotel Terminus, a solid colossus of nineteenth-century architecture with dull views across the Cours de Verdun, one of Lyon's busiest squares, and out over Perrache, the main railway station. Its rooms were still lavishly decorated in the baroque style, with panelling, mirrors, columns and frescoes; but Suite 68 on the third floor was different. By the end of 1942 it had about as much charm as a dentist's waiting room.

This was the office of the Gestapo, and Barbie himself directed the transformation. The silk curtains, brocade-covered sofa, and ornate double bed all disappeared, to be replaced by office furniture. Net curtains obscured the three windows.

Downstairs in the faded elegance of the hotel foyer jackboots pounded across the marble floor, a swastika floated from the high vaulted roof, and Hitler's portrait stared down from a dozen vantage points; outside, sentries behind sandbag emplacements guarded every entrance.

From the start, Barbie exerted his considerable power as Gestapo chief with an easy confidence bordering on arrogance. He exercised authority over a broad swathe of French countryside, stretching from the Swiss frontier in the east to the town of St Etienne, thirty-seven miles south-west of Lyon; and from Chalon-sur-Saône in the north to Valence in the south – a distance of 130 miles. Beneath him were several regional offices, but most immediately he was in charge of policing and counter-intelligence in Lyon itself, with its population of half a million people.

It was part of the Gestapo's policy to give junior officers like Barbie responsibilities that seemed to exceed the normal expectations of their rank. The theory was that they would bring to their job a degree of drive and dedication superior officers might lack. They would ask fewer questions – they would be out to prove themselves. Barbie was a perfect example of the theory in practice.

He fulfilled his task from beginning to end with unflagging and ruthless determination.

Although the Wehrmacht was in nominal control of Lyon, the real power lay with the SS: "The SS was a law unto itself," said Jacques de la Rue, a leading French authority on the German occupation. "Although there were Wehrmacht generals stationed in Lyon, everyone knew that the real authority resided in the SS. The Gestapo worked independently . . . Barbie had the authority to commandeer even regular Wehrmacht units for his police operations."

Within the SS, Barbie himself had an unusual degree of independence. Rivalry, intrigue and sometimes confusion at the top of the hierarchy in Lyon allowed him to organise Gestapo operations without the close supervision he might otherwise have expected. Barbie's first commander, Sturmbannführer Rolf Müller, had been transferred early in 1943 to Marseille, and replaced by Obersturmbannführer Dr Werner Knab, a dry, reserved and irritable man.

Knab was a career functionary in the SS who had been posted to Lyon at the age of thirty-four after serving in Norway – where his reputation had been somewhat marred by accusations of cowardice – and on the eastern front where he had redeemed himself as a Gestapo chief in the harsh wartime conditions of Kiev, where German operations against partisans and the Jews had been notorious for their ferocity.

Knab's adjutant was Hauptsturmführer Heinz Fritz Hollert, a thirty-year-old Austrian, with whom he quarrelled almost immediately. Knab requested that his adjutant be transferred, but was turned down. Hollert, who had some influence in the Nazi party in Berlin, used his connections to hang on to his job in Lyon; and Knab, foiled in the attempt, withdrew into himself. His subordinates remember him as ill-tempered and edgy. He chose not to interfere with the day-to-day running of the SS headquarters, and left Barbie and his Gestapo very much to themselves.

Barbie, in fact, was more frequently answerable to the head office in Paris than to his immediate superiors in Lyon. The Gestapo formed section IV (Amt IV) of the Nazi security organisation, the Reichssicherheitshauptamt (RSHA) whose supreme head was Himmler. It covered the kind of work that went to the heart of the SS's repressive mechanism, with specific responsibility for the suppression of Communists, freemasons and Jews; the control of frontiers and passports; and the breaking of all Resistance activities, including underground networks, clandestine radio links, secret codes and anti-Nazi propaganda. Amt IV reported directly to the Sipo/SD headquarters in Paris at 72 Avenue Foch.

In overall charge of the SS in France was General Karl Oberg, a thick-set, short-sighted officer of forty-five, who had been personally introduced to Paris in May 1942 by Reinhard Heydrich, head of the SD, and was to prove an increasingly harsh and inflexible commander. Immediately below Oberg, and directly in control of Amt IV was Obersturmbannführer Helmut Knochen to whom Barbie's reports went as a matter of routine. From Knochen they would frequently go directly to Berlin, and so, on some occasions, this junior SS lieutenant would find himself in receipt of a personal telegram from Himmler.

Knochen's brief to Barbie was simple – to penetrate and break the Resistance in Lyon. As Barbie himself boasted to Gottlieb Fuchs, the SS interpreter: "The capital of the Resistance is also the capital of the fight against the Resistance. If the Lyonnais are not aware of that yet, I am going to ram it into their skulls."

To help him do so, he was instructed from Paris to set up an Einsatzkommando. This was a squad of forty men chosen for qualities of dedication, even fanaticism, in the service of the SS. Just as in Austria and Poland, where Einsatzgruppen had carried out the most vicious purges, so Barbie's squad was to become especially hated and feared in Lyon. Among those who joined was a former ice-skating champion called Litzrodt, an effeminate-looking young man who liked to wear rings on his fingers, many of which he had stolen from his own victims. Litzrodt was to acquire special notoriety later, when the Einsatzkommando started in earnest its campaign against the Jews.

Barbie also worked with two other sections of the Sipo/SD, Amt V and Amt VI. The former, the Kriminalpolizei (Kripo), dealt with street crime, black marketeers and the misdemeanours of German troops. Amt VI was engaged in intelligence-gathering and ran its own network of agents. Since Barbie's work was counter-intelligence – penetrating the Resistance, recruiting double agents, silencing radio stations and eliminating political opposition – he cooperated closely with Amt VI's chief, Obersturmführer August Moritz, a man he found congenial and cooperative.

The Resistance network confronting them stretched far beyond the city of Lyon. Its centres of activity were in Dijon, Clermont Ferrand, Paris, Nice, Marseille, Grenoble, Toulouse, and Toulon. Abroad the key links in the chain were Lisbon, Geneva, Algiers, and finally London.

But it was in Lyon, free for two years from the occupation, that the Resistance had taken root. Although essentially a bourgeois city that had prospered with the growth of its most famous industry, silk, and had expanded into heavy industry, Lyon had always had a strong left-wing core of Socialists and Communists, and it was among these that the first serious signs of organised resistance began.

The underground campaign in Lyon was aided by a certain secretive side to the city, which had a history of harbouring sects, freemasons, and supposedly witches, dating back to the Middle Ages. Its *ancien quartier* was famous for the *traboules*, dark and narrow passageways running from one house to another, turning them into virtual molehills. Claude Bourdet, one of the early Résistants, said: "The minds of the Lyonnais are a bit tortuous, like those homes. There was an extraordinary and conspiratorial atmosphere at that time which the Germans did not notice at first because they were not attuned to it."

There were three key Resistance groups centred on Lyon: Combat, headed by Captain Henri Frenay, which was on the right-wing of the organisation; the left-wing Libération, led by Emmanuel d'Astier de la Vigerie; and France-Liberté under Jean-Pierre Lévy. All three produced underground newspapers, and though publishing them was a highly dangerous operation with the constant threat of discovery and arrest, all three papers thrived.

Frenay's Combat group was the largest and best organised of the three. Frenay himself, a man of enormous drive and energy, might well have become the Resistance's first national leader. He had conceived and helped create the armée secrète, the para-military wing of the Resistance, which carried out sabotage against German military installations, and by the end of 1942 he could claim armed units in some twenty towns, all capable of inflicting considerable damage. But he was not someone who took easily to working in concert with rival groups and he found it even harder to accept outside authority. As General Charles de Gaulle, leader of the Free French in London, began to exert more authority over the Resistance in France and to ask for unity of command, so Frenay found himself at odds with his comrades in arms and out of favour with the general.

In November 1942, when de Gaulle proposed the idea of a national committee to unite the Resistance, Frenay was instantly against it: "We are resisters, free to think and do as we choose," he told de Gaulle in the course of a heated argument in London. "Our freedom of choice is an inalienable right. It is up to us to decide

whether in the political domain we shall carry out orders or not."
De Gaulle's response was firm: "It seems that France must choose
between you and me," he said.

In the general's mind that choice had already been made. He
had appointed as his delegate in France a man who was to become
the great unifying force within the Resistance, Jean Moulin, the
former prefect of Chartres. Moulin did not share Frenay's reservations about de Gaulle. In his view the Resistance movement needed
a supreme commander in whom it could place entire confidence,
and everything he had learned about de Gaulle convinced him that
he was the right man. Moulin had held long talks with him and
his aides in London and had persuaded them not only of the importance of arming and backing the various Resistance groups, but
of accepting such politically delicate matters as the key role to
be played by the Communists, already the most militant of the
Résistants.

On November 27 1942 the leaders of the various groups met in
conditions of great secrecy in Lyon to propose the creation of the
Conseil National de la Résistance. Moulin, code-named "Max",
was to be its leader. That did not mean that the heated arguments
between him and Frenay would come to an end. Their differences
would continue to be a cause of friction. Nevertheless by the time
Barbie arrived in Lyon the Resistance organisation confronting him
was beginning to look formidable. Its chiefs – Moulin, Frenay,
d'Astier, Lévy, and the man appointed by de Gaulle to head the
armée secrète, General Charles Delestraint – were all, in different
ways, skilled and courageous operators.

There was, it is true, a casual amateurism about the Lyon
Resistance which frequently led it to underestimate its German
opponents; but its members could rely more often on help from
ordinary citizens than in some other French cities where the movement was regarded with suspicion or even hostility. "These were
exceedingly brave people," said Bourdet. "They were the people
who got caught. But in Lyon the majority of the population was
ready to help in some kind of way."

As if to demonstrate their confidence, Frenay's group, Combat,
staged a daring coup on Christmas Eve 1942 by freeing Bertie
Albrecht, a woman prisoner who was both a close friend and
Resistance comrade of Frenay. She had been held in a top-security
psychiatric hospital at Lyon-Bron to which she had been sent after
feigning insanity. Frenay himself cased the grounds of the hospital
and set up the rescue; keys made from wax duplicates were slipped
to the rescue group by a friendly nurse; and scaling ladders took

them over the high walls and out to freedom. It was a clear signal to the Gestapo of the defiance of the Résistants.

Much of the intelligence that Barbie was given on these and other activities came originally from an advance element of the Gestapo that had been secretly active in the city well before the occupation. Known as the Donar Mission, it had arrived near the end of September 1942, installing itself in the Casino building at Charbonnières-les-Bains in the western suburbs of Lyon. The mission, headed by Werner Knab's predecessor, Rolf Müller, was equipped with electronic homing devices to seek out the rash of secret radios transmitting intelligence to London, and it accomplished its task with some thoroughness. Dozens of agents were arrested after houses used as transmission points had been tracked down and raided. By the time Barbie arrived a network of some 280 agents, controlled by both the Gestapo and the Abwehr, was in place; the information it had assembled on suspects, informers, and "safe" houses, was impressive.

Nevertheless the first real coup against the Resistance, following Barbie's arrival, was not achieved by the Gestapo at all. Instead it was a raid organised by Barbie's rival in the Abwehr, Lieutenant Kurt Merk, reaching out from his base in Dijon into the very heart of Barbie's patch in Lyon. And it was the beautiful Andrée Rivez, called on at last to produce the "results" that she knew she owed in return for her safety, who made it possible.

To all outward appearances 36 Quai St Vincent, in the heart of the city, was a modest commercial firm called Technica, dealing in construction materials. Behind the façade, however, it was an intelligence factory, almost certainly the biggest single source of military information from France available to the British and Americans. It had been set up in secret in September 1940 by Colonel Richard Serre of French intelligence after the Germans had issued instructions that the two departments of the Deuxième Bureau dealing with Germany and Italy should cease operations.

Instead of obeying these instructions, Colonel Serre, under orders from the French High Command, took the departments underground. Within a few weeks of being officially closed down, both were once again operating from behind the doors of the Technica company on the Quai St Vincent, supplying the High Command with a daily information bulletin on German and Italian forces in France.

But Colonel Serre went further: he made contact with the American military attaché at Vichy, Colonel Robert Schow, and saw to it that he received a copy of every report produced by Technica.

This information, as Serre intended, was passed directly to Washington and on to British and Free French intelligence in London.

The sheer volume of its output, and its professionalism, made Technica, while it lasted, an astonishing source. The German occupation of the zone libre brought a pause while Technica moved its archives out of the Quai St Vincent to the clock-tower of the Hotel Dieu. But soon it was functioning again at full flow.

Among those who knew the secret of Technica was a retired police commissioner called Charles Merlen, who was Andrée Rivez's uncle. One day, when Merlen was visiting Dijon, Andrée introduced him to her lover Kurt Merk. "It was," she says, "the biggest mistake I ever made."

Lyon was in Kurt Merk's area of operations and, loyal to Andrée as he was, his duty came first. It is still not entirely clear what happened as a result of Andrée's introduction, but after the war, when Charles Merlen was put on trial in Lyon, documents were produced from the Stuttgart files of the Abwehr showing that he had been hired as a "V-Mann" (informant) for the sum of 1,500 francs a month, with far bigger premiums after important arrests.

Today, Andrée still insists that Merlen was innocent:

My uncle did not work for Kurt [she says]; he pretended to, but he did not. It may have looked as if he betrayed Technica, but he was in reality so afraid of the Germans that he always carried a pair of socks in one pocket and a toothbrush in the other in case they arrested him. Kurt said to him, "If you have any problems with the Germans, ask Klaus Barbie to do something." My uncle exclaimed, "Oh no, no – I don't want to have anything to do with that one."

Whatever the truth, wherever the guilt lay, Andrée had introduced a German spy-hunter to a man who was privy to a key French espionage ring.

Merk did his work with great thoroughness: on the night of February 16 1943 the Feldgendarmerie, the Abwehr's police branch, aided by the Gestapo, raided the Quai St Vincent offices and arrested everybody. They then went straight to the Hotel Dieu and seized the Deuxième Bureau archives. It was said after the war that the prisoners were "maltreated" during interrogation at the Hotel Terminus, but Merk had promised Andrée that they would come to no real harm, and that they would spend the rest of the war in "a castle" rather than a concentration camp. Long after Merk was dead Andrée discovered that he had kept his word. The Technica detainees were sent to a remote castle at Bruex in the hills of north Bohemia, where they were liberated safe and sound by American troops in 1945.

Barbie himself seems to have stood back from the Technica operation. Admittedly it had been, from the start, an Abwehr responsibility, and presumably Merk had laid down the ground rules. Nevertheless it was Barbie's Gestapo agents who had carried out the raid, and the interrogations had taken place in Barbie's own offices at the Hotel Terminus. He might well have tried to insist that the questioning and subsequent treatment of these enemies of the Reich was done the SS way – hard. Instead, they seem to have been handled with scrupulous fairness.

It was the last time that would happen. From this point on, the tactics would conform to Barbie's own standards of harshness. The symbol of his regime was the École de Santé Militaire, an interrogation centre just across the Rhône from the Hotel Terminus and the Gare de Perrache, on the Avenue Berthelot to which the expanding Gestapo moved in June 1943. Formerly an army medical school, it was a cavernous old building whose thick stone-walled exterior was blackened with soot from the nearby railway sidings. The windows were blanked out with steel shutters, there was a courtyard inside where lorries could unload the prisoners, and beneath it were deep cellars where they were held.

Upstairs was a series of rooms which were equipped for torture: there were bathtubs, to be filled with freezing water for the torment known as *la baignoire*, and there was a range of implements including whips, clubs, syringes, hot irons to burn the soles of the feet, needles to be inserted beneath the finger-nails. Finally there were electrodes to be attached to the most sensitive parts of the human body. The use of electricity, dealing surges of terrible pain to the body, had been previously almost unknown as a weapon of torture. But under the Gestapo in France it became a speciality.

Barbie's offices at the École de Santé were on the second floor. He regarded it as important to demonstrate to his men not only that he was in direct control of operations, but was capable of setting the most ruthless example himself. It was part of his tactics to disparage the opposition. He told his men that he hated the French for what they had done to his father. "I shall never forget that I saw him return from Verdun in 1917 with a French bullet in his neck," he would say, adding dramatically: "It eventually killed him." Those who worked for the French Resistance, he proclaimed, were "terrorists" and, what was more, cowards, with "nothing in their underpants".

The proof, he used to boast, was that every day he would walk back to his office at the Hotel Terminus at 1.30 sharp after lunch – a perfect target for an assassin's bullet. Yet nobody tried to shoot him. In the evenings he would deliberately go for a stroll along the quais with Wolf, his big black Alsatian, even dropping into the occasional café for a casual drink or to meet a contact. On these occasions he passed himself off as a Frenchman if he was in plain clothes, using the nom-de-plume of Barbier (or perhaps Barbié).

It does appear that Barbie won loyalty, even admiration, from his men. "Barbie was a first-class comrade," said Alfred Lutjens, one of his Einsatzkommando officers. "He was intelligent, highly dynamic, the soul of the Gestapo."

Barbie found different ways of instilling respect and discipline in his troops. He himself remembered with pride how he dealt with an SS officer named Sensenbrenner who had stolen property and raped several local girls.

I assembled my Command with much pomp, and, having read out a list of Sensenbrenner's crimes, I condemned him to death to set an example, and ordered his immediate execution. I gave the order for a hanging rope to be thrown over a beam, and a chair to be put underneath. Then I ordered Sensenbrenner to stand on the chair, handed him the rope and told him to put the noose round his neck. At first he wept for mercy. But then he proved his courage. Having understood there was no reprieve, he remained impassive to the end. One of my Command then kicked the chair away.

There is a hint here of two qualities that were to characterise Barbie's increasingly ferocious attitude to those members of the Resistance he interrogated. First, there is no compunction about the act of execution itself, indeed there is every sign that he took some pride in the grim little ritual he was supervising. Then, there is a morbid interest in the behaviour of his victim.

It was often noted that Barbie combined extremes of brutality with an apparently detached interest in the way his victims reacted. Sometimes, if their behaviour struck him as courageous, he would comment on it with something approaching admiration, though it would not restrain him from further assaults if he was in search of information. At other times, intransigence seemed merely to irritate him.

"He was excessively brutal," recalled Hedwig Ondra, one of the secretaries at Gestapo headquarters in Lyon. "He often reproached one of his assistants, Ernst Floreck, for not being hard enough. It was a matter of pride with him to go to extremes."

This reputation for cruelty was deliberately cultivated. It was a policy of the Gestapo to intimidate, and Reinhard Heydrich, its founder, had once boasted that his organisation was regarded with a mixture of "fear and horror".

But to begin with, despite the savagery of his assaults, Barbie appears to have heeded the SS principles laid down by Himmler:

> The SS Commander must be hard, but he must not become hardened. If, during your work, you come across cases in which some Commander exceeds his duty, or shows signs that his sense of restraint is becoming blurred, intervene at once. Anyone who finds it necessary to dull his senses, or forgets himself in the face of the enemy, shows that he is no true SS Commander.

The distinction was lost on Barbie's victims. And with time it seems to have meant less and less to Barbie himself. There is clear evidence that he came to relish the punishment he handed out. Raymond Aubrac, a member of the Libération group, who was arrested and beaten every day for a week by Barbie in June 1943, said bluntly: "Barbie was insensible to the suffering of others. He derived a sadistic pleasure from torturing people. It gave him a sense of power."

Maurice Boudet, a member of a British intelligence network, arrested a month after Aubrac, said: "Barbie was a monster. He always had a whip in his hand. He lashed out without hesitation and encouraged others to do the same. He personally conducted the interrogations . . . He really enjoyed other people's sufferings." Boudet, who survived and was sent to Mauthausen concentration camp, suffered permanent damage at Barbie's hands. There were to be many others.

The success of the Technica operation had owed little to Barbie's own skills. And the next stunning blow to the Resistance in Lyon was also delivered thanks to assistance from outside sources – the first of which was once again Kurt Merk's office in the Dijon Abwehr.

Robert Moog, code-named "Boby", was a tall, fair-haired foreman at an armaments factory in Toulouse, who early in 1942 had joined a Franco-British spy ring known as "Gilbert". Some time in the summer of that year, Moog was visiting Dijon when he was introduced to Merk's office by an intermediary. Recruited for the Abwehr

Moog became a diligent informant known as agent K-30. He passed on everything he knew about Gilbert to the Germans, and when he reported from Toulouse that André Devigny, a twenty-seven-year-old school teacher who was the brains of the Gilbert ring, was planning to sabotage the arms factory where he worked, the Abwehr moved in. Many of the group were arrested, though Devigny himself escaped and went to ground at Annemasse near the Swiss border.

Barbie, who had learned about the penetration of the Gilbert group, felt that Moog might be invaluable to him in Lyon. Flexing organisational muscle, as the SS now could against the weakening Abwehr, he induced Merk to lend him Moog for his own use. Early in 1943 agent K-30 arrived in Lyon to begin work.

A month later Moog was joined by another traitor, Jean Multon, a former member of the Combat group in Marseilles, where he had been known under the code name Lunel. Multon had been arrested and turned, without torture, by the chief of the Marseille Gestapo, and had proceeded to hand over inside information about Combat's operations in the area. The resulting arrests – some two hundred Resistance members were rounded up – was a crippling blow to Frenay's organisation, and it was not long before Multon was identified as the traitor. He was now a marked man in Marseilles, and was handed on to Barbie in Lyon, who thus found under his control two entirely unscrupulous agents with a wealth of knowledge about the movement they had once served.

April 1943 had begun badly for another Resistance group – Franc-Tireur, Jean-Pierre Lévy's section in Lyon. On April 4 Joseph Monjaret, radio operator for Jean Moulin and Moulin's personal delegate to Franc-Tireur, was arrested. He and a number of his fellow members were picked up at a flower shop in the rue Lafayette which was used by the Resistance as a letter-drop. The Gestapo had been tipped off after what Monjaret described as an "indiscretion" by a member of the group.

Monjaret was taken to the École de Santé. There he was confronted by Barbie who interrogated him brutally for several hours. When Monjaret refused to talk, Barbie beat him ferociously with a bull-whip. Later he was tortured for hours by Gestapo agents who held his head down in a lavatory filled with water. They waited until he had almost drowned, then pulled his head up. This was repeated over and over again. Finally, they fastened electrodes to his nipples and testicles and turned on the current in bursts.

Monjaret, however, refused to talk. He was thrown into prison, then deported to Mauthausen, where, remarkably, he survived the war, to be liberated by Allied troops in April 1945. Today he lives in Brittany; he still suffers from the effects of his torture at the hands of Klaus Barbie.

Twelve days after Monjaret's arrest, Robert Moog played his first card for the Gestapo. On April 16 he knocked on the door of a Lyon laundry shop which he knew was used as a letter-drop by agents of the Gilbert group. Inside was Madame Edmée Deletraz, who acted as liaison agent for the group. She was arrested and taken to the Hotel Terminus where Barbie threatened reprisals against her family unless she talked. Finally Madame Deletraz gave in and began to give Barbie what he wanted.

In the course of her confession she betrayed André Devigny, the school teacher, who had escaped to Annemasse. Devigny was picked up on the platform of Annemasse station that night and driven to Montluc prison in Lyon. He later wrote a grim account of his prolonged torture at the hands of Barbie and his Gestapo agents which included the full range of torments – savage beatings, the cold-water treatment of the baignoire, injections, and red-hot irons placed on the soles of his feet. But the worst attack of all came when Barbie unleashed his Alsatian dog Wolf to tear at Devigny's flesh:

I longed desperately for death at that moment [he wrote]. It would certainly have been better to die than to feel the jaws of a dog tearing your clothes and then your flesh without being able to defend yourself . . . Always the same question: "Will you talk?" Always the same reply: "I have nothing to say . . ." The blood formed a network of streaks on my chest and poured down into my trousers. I breathed in gulps. But in spite of everything, I did not feel my courage fail me. On the contrary, I gazed straight into the eyes of the Gestapo agent, straight into his eyes with a look full of hate and disdain . . ."

Devigny never broke. Later he would become one of the legends of the Resistance by being the only prisoner ever to escape from the Gestapo fortress prison of Montluc.

Edmée Deletraz, who had betrayed Devigny, was released by Barbie to act as an agent for the Gestapo. Immediately she reported her arrest and interrogation to the head of the Gilbert network, who instructed her to maintain contact with the Gestapo and report back, acting as a double agent. This she did, though as subsequent events were to show, it was never entirely clear where her ultimate loyalties lay.

Barbie's other double agent, Jean Multon, now performed his first service for the Gestapo chief. Using his credentials as a former member of the Combat group in Marseille, he infiltrated its sister organisation in Lyon with the aim of exposing the Combat chief Henri Frenay himself. Through the lax security that was so often to damage the Resistance, Multon learned that Bertie Albrecht, Frenay's close friend and now his personal assistant, was due to meet her boss and some other associates in Macon, forty miles north of the city.

The rendezvous had been set for 11.30 a.m. at the Hotel de Bourgogne in the Place de la Paix. Multon alerted the Gestapo who staked out the little square; when Albrecht arrived early, they seized her. Realising that she was betrayed, she screamed: "Attention, tous, à la Gestapo! Alerte à la Gestapo!" Her bravery cost her her life. She was last seen being pushed into a Gestapo car, her face swollen from a savage beating, blood streaming down her legs, her hands bound together. She died later in the prison of Fresnes outside Paris, whether through torture by the Gestapo or by suicide is not known. At 11.30 precisely, Gestapo agents raided the Hotel de Bourgogne, but Frenay and the others, alerted by Albrecht's screams, never showed up.

All of these Gestapo coups were gradually leading up to Barbie's most telling blow against the Resistance, though he was unaware of where the trail was leading. The pace of events began to quicken: on May 30, two days after Albrecht's arrest, Multon and Moog, now acting in partnership, learned of another letter-drop, this time at 14 rue Bouteille. It was used by a department of Combat known as Résistance-Fer, whose task was to sabotage the railway links on which the Nazi occupying force depended. In charge of it was a tall, intense young railway engineer called René Hardy. He had developed for Frenay a project known later as the Plan Vert which was intended to disrupt the entire rail system – with devastating results for German communications; a debate had already begun within the Resistance over whether it should be put into action at once or held until just before the planned Allied landings in France.

The discovery of the Résistance-Fer's letter-drop was, therefore, a considerable coup for Barbie. As soon as Multon and Moog reported back to Gestapo headquarters, the house was raided, its owner arrested, and the premises placed under surveillance in case the Resistance continued to use it.

Word that the letter-drop had been "burned" was leaked almost immediately to the Resistance by Edmée Deletraz who had heard about it at the Hotel Terminus and was now fulfilling her role as double agent. All Resistance members in the Lyon area were warned not to use it. The address, as they were told, was now thoroughly compromised.

Nevertheless, running through the affairs of the Resistance was a marked tendency to overlook basic matters of security. Despite the warning, Henri Aubry, chief of staff of the armée secrète under its commander, General Delestraint, now committed an error which played straight into Barbie's hands.

Aubry had been asked by Delestraint to fix a meeting with René Hardy in Paris, and had sent his secretary with a letter setting out the details. The message was in "clear" (uncoded) French; it not only spelt out the time and place for the rendezvous, but it revealed Hardy's secret code name, "Didot". These errors were then compounded when Aubry's secretary delivered the letter to the "burnt" address in the rue Bouteille.

The matter has been debated endlessly since – Aubry himself admits that he made "a grave error". But the damage was done. As soon as it was delivered, the letter was picked up by Moog who passed it on to Barbie. The Gestapo now knew the time and place of Delestraint's rendezvous in Paris, and plans were laid to seize him: Moog and Multon booked sleepers on the 21.50 train for Paris on the night of June 7.

René Hardy claims he knew nothing of all this. It was therefore by purest coincidence that he too was booked on to the 21.50 train on the same night. He was due in Paris for a different rendezvous and he was travelling under his own name.

What follows is dependent on Hardy's word – though it is supported, in its essentials, by Klaus Barbie. On the night of June 7 Hardy pushed his way through the crowds thronging the platform of the Paris train at the Gare Lyon-Perrache. Suddenly he stopped dead in his tracks. There, coming towards him, was Jean Multon, a man Hardy knew from his days in Marseille. Hardy knew, too, that Multon had been recruited by the Gestapo.

There was no time to run. Looking round, he recognised a woman in the crowd who, by a stroke of fortune, was a fellow member of the Resistance. Sidling up to her, he whispered: "If anything happens to me, it's Lunel's fault" (he used Multon's Marseille code name). Then he stepped on to the train and found his sleeper.

By another extraordinary coincidence, Moog and Multon had booked the sleeper next to Hardy's. They too had recognised him on the platform and they knew how important a Resistance figure he was. After discussing the situation, they decided to act. At 1.00

a.m., when the train pulled into the station at Chalon-sur-Saône, Moog raised the alarm with the German police, who boarded the train and arrested Hardy.

Next day a triumphant Klaus Barbie walked into Hardy's prison cell in Chalon to escort him back to Lyon, while Moog and Multon continued their journey to Paris where they picked up General Delestraint.

Thus, at a stroke, Barbie had captured Delestraint, the head of the armée secrète, and Hardy, the mastermind of Résistance-Fer.

But Barbie now believed he might be on the trail of an even greater prize, the leader of the Resistance itself – Jean Moulin, code-named "Max". By Barbie's account, the key to it was Hardy whom he was about to "turn". By Hardy's account that is a grotesque libel. But either way, the net was tightening around Moulin, and Barbie was in no doubt about his importance.

"Every German security unit knew that 'Max' was the chief of the Resistance," said Barbie later. "We had instructions to follow any thread that might lead us to Max . . ."

Barbie was not an imaginative man, but the figure of Jean Moulin appealed to him strangely. As a boy in the Rhineland, Barbie had been raised on the legend of Albert Leo Schlageter, the early Nazi hero and martyr who had been shot by the French in 1923 for leading sabotage squads against their occupation of the Ruhr. Although Moulin was the enemy, Barbie could not escape a sense of recognition – as if Moulin were the Schlageter of France.

And, by an astonishing coincidence, Barbie had in his office the man who had actually led the hunt for Schlageter in the Ruhr twenty years earlier. Superintendent Barthelet of the French Sureté had captured Schlageter after the German had been betrayed by an unknown comrade. Now, under Barbie, Barthelet was a trusted Gestapo collaborator, violently right-wing and anti-Communist, described after the war as "a maniac of repression".

When Barbie had first learned of Barthelet's part in the capture of Schlageter, he had summoned him to his office. Barthelet had at once confessed, but had gone on to point to the parallel that was so fascinating to Barbie: the job that he had once done in France in the Ruhr was precisely the job that Barbie was now doing for Germany in Lyon. Barbie seems to have recognised that. He never arrested Barthelet, despite requests from Berlin that the Frenchman should be forced to reveal the name of the man who had betrayed Schlageter.

To Barbie, as he himself recalled later, there was a powerful sense that history was somehow repeating itself in a looking-glass – that Moulin was Schlageter, and that he, the pursuer, was Barthelet. It continued to haunt him as the hunt came closer to its quarry.

CHAPTER FOUR

The Killing of Jean Moulin

Everyone agreed he was a remarkable man, though not everyone saw him as a natural leader. It was partly a physical matter. Jean Moulin was small and grey-haired, his sunburnt face open but unremarkable, his voice low-pitched. He cleared his throat repeatedly while speaking – only his gestures were flamboyant. Most people, however, remembered a certain calmness in his character, and its warmth. He had a rich sense of humour and was noted for his wit. His sister Laure called him "Jean qui rit".

There could scarcely have been a greater contrast between the two men who might one day have disputed the future of France – Jean Moulin and Charles de Gaulle. Yet the respect they conceived for each other was crucial to the liberation of their country. What they shared was passionate faith in their cause and enormous energy.

A British intelligence officer, Major Eric Piquet-Wicks, who met Jean Moulin in London during the war, wrote later: "I saw in front of me a little man, tranquil and composed, who did not look anything like I had imagined him to be. He was so anonymous, so calm. However, there was something about him that made me think of a coiled spring." Moulin's secretary, Daniel Cordier, remembered him for his total lack of snobbery: "He paid as much attention to those of modest standing as to those who were important." And even Henri Frenay of Combat, who quarrelled with him repeatedly, was won over by his unassuming manner.

That is not to say that he lacked conviction. "He knew exactly what he wanted and how to set about it," said Piquet-Wicks. "There was no doubting the power of his intellect and the rigour of his judgment," said Cordier. And another British officer, a Major Mortimore, who met him in Lisbon, said: "Not one of the Resistance leaders I met made as deep an impression on me as Jean Moulin. His patriotism was overwhelming. His personality forced attention and admiration."

Among those who shared this admiration was Klaus Barbie. In a long (and deeply unreliable) account of his interrogation of Moulin

81

in June 1943, Barbie says he was struck in particular by his self-composure which, he claimed, was remarkably like his own:

> Never, in the course of the interrogation, did Moulin show any fear. He impressed me throughout, not least because of his disturbing physical resemblance to me. Like me, he was calm and decisive. He was head and shoulders above the other professional spies – violent or terrified – that I dealt with. A cultivated man, Moulin was a sensitive and self-possessed politician. Never, in the course of our conversations, did he raise his voice in the slightest. We spoke, the two of us, in an even tone, firm and calm . . ."

Moulin's calmness in crisis, so vital to his task of unifying the Resistance movement, derived perhaps from the knowledge that he had faced the ultimate test of his personal courage and had not failed it. As France's youngest prefect in Chartres during the invasion of June 1940, he had struck a notable gesture of defiance against the Nazis. He had refused to sign a German document falsely implicating a troop of Senegalese soldiers of the French army in atrocities against civilians. Moulin knew they had not been responsible, and would not put his name to a document that dishonoured them.

Enraged German soldiers had beaten him brutally, tortured him, and then locked him up for the night, first in a room containing the mutilated corpse of a woman, then in a cell with a Senegalese soldier who had been beaten to a pulp. Realising finally that he had reached a point beyond which he might be incapable of holding out, Moulin decided to kill himself.

"I knew," he wrote later, "that that day I had been tested to the very limits of my resistance. The next day if the torture were renewed, I would finish by signing. This was my dilemma: sign or die." He noticed some pieces of broken glass on the floor of his cell. "I knew at once what those fragments of glass could do. They could cut a throat as easily as a knife could." Seizing one of them, he dragged it across his throat.

Four hours later Moulin was found in a pool of blood that covered the floor of his cell. He was rushed to hospital where his life was saved by a German doctor; the terrible wound in his throat was stitched up.

Word of his courage spread rapidly. "The Germans have tortured the prefect of Chartres" was a message that not only shocked a defeated nation, but also gave it a hero overnight at a time when one was badly needed. The legend of Jean Moulin had begun.

Within four days Moulin was back at his desk in Chartres. The scars healed gradually, but thereafter he always wore a high scarf around his neck to conceal them. The Germans did not attempt to attack him again, but in November 1940, they ousted him from his post. Soon afterwards Moulin went underground and began travelling through France, gathering information about the various Resistance movements, meeting the men and women who led them, and learning about their differing aims. His cover during this period was an art gallery in Marseille which he ran and for which he collected pictures as he went from town to town. He himself was a skilled artist who was able to dash off brilliant portraits of his friends. His caricatures in the newspapers had been famous.

As he got to know the Resistance better, he began to realise that two things were essential if it was to have any impact on the occupying forces. The first was to unite the movement, and the second was to persuade General de Gaulle and the British to give them the support they needed in the form of money and arms.

Moulin's first meeting with de Gaulle in London came at the end of November 1941. It was crucial for both men. Politically they were far apart – Moulin, unlike the general, was a man of the left – but they conceived a mutual respect: "Full of judgment, and seeing things and people as they were," wrote de Gaulle of Moulin, "he would be watching each step as he walked along a road that was undermined by adversaries' traps and encumbered by obstacles raised by friends." He promised Moulin the support, both political and material, that was needed if Moulin's authority was to be imposed on the difficult and divided Resistance movement.

Moulin returned to France on New Year's day 1942, parachuting at night into a freezing swamp near Marseille and bearing with him a letter that designated him de Gaulle's personal envoy to the Resistance, "to bring about the concerted action of all elements that resist the enemy and the collaboration".

It was to be no easy assignment. Henri Frenay in particular disagreed with him about both the political and military aims of the Resistance, and there were running disagreements between the northern groups and those in the zone libre. But gradually Moulin's diplomacy succeeded in breaking down the barriers – and not least in softening de Gaulle's still haughty and unbending attitude.

In February 1943, when Moulin visited London again, de Gaulle pinned on his chest the highest honour he could give – the Croix de la Libération. "We recognise you as our companion in the liberation of France, with honour and through victory," he announced solemnly. At the same time he gave Moulin the go-ahead to extend his authority from the southern zone to include the northern as well. On May 27 1943 the Conseil National de la Résistance, the ultimate authority representing the entire movement in France, held its first summit conference in Paris – under the leadership of Jean Moulin.

It was a personal triumph. "He had brought about a kind of miracle," wrote the historian David Schoenbrun, "uniting men of very different political views, of highly competitive ambitions and egos, working and fighting under constant stress, with their lives on the line in every meeting and every decision. He had done so against opposition that at times seemed insurmountable."

It is a bitter irony that the CNR's great conference in Paris should have coincided almost exactly with the first blows struck against the Resistance in Lyon by the two traitors Moog and Multon, whose work for Klaus Barbie in the last days of May would lead inexorably to Jean Moulin's destruction. Their infiltration had delivered René Hardy to Barbie, and though there will always be dispute about Hardy's value to the Nazis, there is no doubt that it was the first step on the trail that would yield an even greater prize – the Resistance leader himself, known so far only as "Max".

It is Barbie's contention that the seizing of Hardy on the night express to Paris on June 7 owed nothing to coincidence. He claims that Multon had learned from Resistance sources that "Didot", code name for the head of Résistance-Fer, would be on the train and that he would provide the essential link to "Max". Furthermore Multon gave Barbie a little clue that would help unmask Didot if he attempted to conceal his true identity: he would be wearing spectacles as a disguise, but the lenses would be ordinary glass – Didot's sight was perfect.

As Barbie tells it, when he confronted Hardy in his cell in Chalon-sur-Saône the day after he had been taken off the train, he stepped forward and plucked the spectacles off Hardy's nose. Holding them up to the light, he said in immaculate French:

"False spectacles, no?"

Hardy was speechless. Finally, he managed to stammer: "Who are you?"

"Who am I?" said Barbie. "You will learn soon enough. But first of all, I am going to tell you who you are. These papers of yours were made up in London. They're false. Your name is René Hardy."

He proceeded, he says, to give Hardy a complete rundown on his career, including his work for the Resistance. Finally, Hardy said weakly:

"Monsieur, I give in. What are you going to do with me?"

From then on, says Barbie, it was only a matter of time before Hardy began to deliver up the information he needed.

"Logically," Barbie told him equably as they drove back to Lyon in his Citroen, "you are face to face with death." He then added, almost inconsequentially, that the Gestapo had picked up Hardy's girl friend, Lydie Bastien, in Lyon, and that her future health might well depend on Hardy's cooperation. The result: Hardy told him everything, including details of the famous Plan Vert and as much as he knew about Max. The chief of the Résistance-Fer had been turned.

When Barbie's SS bosses in Paris heard the news, they told Himmler himself, who sent a telegram of congratulations to the young Lieutenant Barbie, instructing him to take personal charge of the operation to capture Max.

It makes a good story. The trouble is, as a military tribunal in Paris determined when it placed Hardy on trial for treason after the war, it is so full of holes that it makes Barbie's testimony virtually worthless. Hardy, for instance, was travelling openly under his own name that night, so the question of his true identity would not have arisen. Multon would not have known him as "Didot", but as "Carbon" – Hardy's code name from Marseille days. Another prisoner, interrogated later in Lyon, says that the Gestapo were still trying to find out who Didot was several weeks after Hardy had been questioned by Barbie. And the Plan Vert to which Barbie refers was not known by that name until later. Finally, as Barbie himself conceded, the telegram from Himmler, which might have been conclusive, no longer exists; it was burned, he says, by his wife after the war.

But if Barbie's account is flawed, Hardy's begins with a lie he admits himself: he failed to inform fellow members of the Resistance that he had been arrested, for fear they would assume he had talked; instead, he claimed to have leapt off the train at Chalon to escape the Gestapo. This deception alone, which he withheld from the tribunal after the war, was enough to have his trial reopened. It left a hung jury unable to decide whether he was guilty or not.

Hardy maintains that he kept Barbie at bay during his interrogation at the École de Santé, that he fooled him by expressing pro-German sympathies, and that Barbie eventually gave him the benefit of the doubt and released him, while maintaining the threat against his girl friend Lydie if he found he had lied. Hardy knew that if he told his Resistance colleagues about his arrest, they would immediately suspect that it was he who had been responsible for betraying General Delestraint. He therefore kept quiet.

Hardy's fears were understandable. The unwritten law of the Resistance held that suspects should be swiftly eliminated if there were grounds for believing they had been turned. And the news of Delestraint's arrest had indeed been devastating. It convinced Moulin that the Gestapo was tightening its ring around him. In a prescient report to London, he said:

> I'm sought now by the Vichy and the Gestapo, who, thanks to methods used by certain elements within the movement, know everything there is to know about my identity and my activities. My task is becoming more and more delicate, and the difficulties increase unceasingly. I have decided to hold on as long as possible, but, if I disappear, I will not have time to brief my successors.

He decided to convene an urgent meeting of the Resistance leaders in Lyon to nominate a successor to Delestraint and to explore new security arrangements to guard against penetration. The date chosen was Monday, June 21.

Henri Aubry, chief of the armée secrète, and the man who had made the initial blunder over the burned letter-drop, now made another ghastly error: after being told in advance about the meeting, he passed on word about it to René Hardy and invited him to come too. This was entirely against Resistance rules. Only those asked by the leader himself were meant to know that a meeting had even been planned.

Aubry arranged to meet Hardy next day, Sunday, June 20, at the Pont Morand, one of the bridges over the Rhône, and give him details of the time and place for the rendezvous. What happened on that day is cited by Hardy's Resistance colleagues as conclusive evidence that he was a traitor – but again Hardy disputes the facts.

Aubry maintains that, as he approached Hardy in a park near the Pont Morand, Hardy was sitting on a bench with a man whose face was hidden behind a newspaper. He could not make out who it was, but would learn later that it was the SS Gestapo chief, Klaus Barbie, on one of his spying missions, dressed in plain clothes. That sensational claim would be backed up by Barbie himself, and by his bodyguard Harry Stenngritt who said that he too had been in the park that day, keeping an eye on his boss.

Hardy vehemently denies it. The fact is, however, that somehow the Gestapo learned about the Resistance meeting. It was to take place next day at the house of Dr Frederic Dugoujon who had a general practice in Caluire, a suburb in the hills above Lyon. There were originally to have been eight people there, including Moulin and Aubry, other representatives of the armée secrète, and two members of the Libération group. Then Aubry invited Hardy, and Moulin asked along Claude Serreulles, a former parachute officer who had just arrived from London. There were thus ten men that Monday afternoon, making their separate ways towards Caluire.

Moulin was clearly worried about security, and confided his fears to a fellow Resistance member. He was right to be concerned: no provision had been made for armed guards or lookouts on the approaches to the house; several of those attending – including Moulin himself – were late, despite a standing rule that punctuality was essential; finally, two of the participants did not turn up at all. "It was," as one of those attending admitted later, "a disaster waiting to happen."

That disaster might still have been averted. Word reached a Resistance office in Lyon at lunch time that the Gestapo knew about the rendezvous. The messenger was Edmée Deletraz, the Resistance double agent, who claimed to have seen Hardy at Gestapo head-quarters. But no one now knew how to make contact with any of those attending the meeting.

Just before 2 p.m. the Resistance men began arriving inconspicuously at Dr Dugoujon's house, a three-storey, ivy-covered villa overlooking a pretty square in the centre of Caluire. Aubry turned up with Hardy – to the consternation of the others who had not been expecting him. The two who failed to appear included Claude Serreulles who had only just arrived in Lyon and took the wrong cable car. Moulin turned up last, and very late, with another of those invited to attend, Raymond Aubrac of Libération. By the time he arrived, it was 2.45.

Moulin, who carried identity papers bearing the alias Jean Martel, and a faked doctor's note referring him to Dr Dugoujon for a rheumatic complaint, was shown into the downstairs waiting room, along with Raymond Aubrac. The others were upstairs, waiting nervously. Moulin and Aubrac had barely sat down when the garden gate outside was pushed open.

"I was sitting by the window upstairs," said Henri Aubry. "Suddenly, the garden gate squeaked on its hinges and I saw a lot of leather-jacketed men swarm through it. I just had time to stand up and say: 'We're cooked . . . the bastards . . . it's the Gestapo!' "

Dugoujon went to the front door, to be met by two of the Einsatzkommando holding revolvers. "Do you have a meeting in your house?" demanded one. The doctor denied it, but the two men pushed past him and walked quickly upstairs. Others poured in at the French doors of another room and followed them. In the upstairs room, Hardy whipped out a pistol, but the others hissed at him to put it away – there was no chance of winning a shooting match. Then the door was flung open. A small, sturdy Gestapo officer walked abruptly into the room and snapped in French:

"Hands up! German police!"

It was Barbie.

"He leapt at me," said Aubry. "In a few seconds I had been slapped, my head banged against the wall, and my wrists handcuffed behind my back."

But it was what Barbie said that really stunned Aubry:

"Well, Thomas, you don't look so good. You seemed much happier yesterday at Pont Morand. I was reading my paper, but the weather was so nice, I thought I would let you enjoy it for one more day since we would meet again today."

This told Aubry two things: it was Barbie who had been the man behind the newspaper in the park, and somehow he had learned that Aubry's code name was Thomas – one he had acquired only a few weeks before. Who was the traitor?

There was hardly time to speculate. Downstairs, Dr Dugoujon had been handcuffed, struck in the stomach, and manhandled into the waiting room where Moulin was already being held. As Dugoujon passed him, Moulin hissed in his ear: "My name is Jean Martel." He protested to the German soldiers who questioned him that he was only an ordinary patient, and produced the doctor's note he had brought with him. But no one was allowed to leave except for some women patients.

Then Barbie came down and ordered all the prisoners upstairs. As they stumbled into the room where the others were now also handcuffed, Raymond Aubrac was amazed to see Hardy.

"We did not suspect him for a moment," he said, "but he had no business to be there, and the coincidence of his presence with the arrival of the SS was troubling. Our anxiety grew when the SS snapped handcuffs on everyone, including Dr Dugoujon's patients, except René Hardy."

Hardy now experienced a series of apparently lucky breaks. In retrospect, they were so extraordinary that his comrades decided they were more than simply coincidence and that he was being deliberately protected by the Germans. He was, for instance, not put into handcuffs because, by the time they got round to him, the Germans had run out of them; instead they wound a thin chain loosely round his wrists. He was also lucky when the prisoners came to be searched – the soldiers failed, mysteriously, to discover the pistol Hardy had concealed in a secret pocket in his jacket sleeve.

His run of luck continued as Barbie, who had been questioning the prisoners without success, impatiently ordered them outside to the waiting Gestapo cars. The German soldier escorting Hardy opened the car door and waited for him to get in. Hardy jerked the chain attached to his wrist, tripped up the guard, and slammed the door in his face. The guard sank to the ground, letting go of the chain, and Hardy set off across the square, zig-zagging through the trees as bullets whined around him. One hit him in the arm and he almost fell, but he managed to take out his pistol and fire back over his shoulder at the pursuing Germans. Then, reaching the edge of the square, he hurled himself down a steep slope, rolled into a ditch where he was concealed from view, and nursed his wounded arm. The Germans called off the search almost immediately and went back to guard the other prisoners.

Those inside the building heard the shots. Aubry, listening from upstairs, was tempted to jump out of the window. But Barbie told him: "Don't be a fool. One person has already tried to make a break for it and, see, he was unlucky. We fired."

Raymond Aubrac, who was outside the building and saw Hardy escape, was immediately suspicious. He wondered why he had not been gunned down by the Nazi guards outside who were armed with machine-pistols. The events that followed were equally strange. Hardy, bleeding heavily from his arm wound, asked for help from two cyclists at the bottom of the hill. He was reported by one of them to the French police who arrested him, took him in for medical treatment, and then transferred him to the prison section of Antiquaille hospital.

While he was there, the Resistance, convinced of his guilt, tried to kill him. Lucie Aubrac, Raymond's wife and a Libération leader, was given orders to execute Hardy as a traitor. She sent him a food parcel containing a small pot of jam laced with cyanide. But Hardy was suspicious and did not eat it.

From Antiquaille, Hardy was handed over to German custody and interrogated once more by Barbie at the École de Santé. Again he claims he gave nothing away. Again, Barbie himself insists he was a willing accomplice. Finally, Hardy was sent to the prison section of the German military hospital in the Croix-Rousse area of Lyon and from there, miraculously, he escaped.

On the night of August 3 Hardy jumped out of the window into a courtyard and climbed over a side gate to freedom. He was reunited with his girl friend Lydie Bastien and the two of them took off for Paris, where Hardy once again immersed himself in Resistance work. He claims, in his defence, that had he really been a traitor he would hardly have sought out Resistance colleagues again. But that is an argument which can work both ways – he could just as easily have been guarding his reputation.

Meanwhile the ordeal of Jean Moulin and the other victims of Caluire was about to begin. The interrogations were conducted by Barbie personally at the École de Santé. He knew, virtually from the beginning, that "Max" was one of the prisoners. Halfway through the first session, a Gestapo agent arrived, threw a fistful of documents on the table, and announced in French: "Max est parmi eux," [Max is among them.]

Barbie rounded on Aubry and a colleague: "You know who he is. You know he's de Gaulle's right hand man. It's not so long since the BBC announced it in London."

That night each prisoner was brought up from the cellars. Barbie compared them with an inexact Gestapo description of Max, shouted at them, and pummelled them with his bare fists. He got nowhere.

This first ordeal lasted several hours; then, none the wiser, Barbie ordered the prisoners to be loaded on to a lorry and brought to Montluc prison, where they signed the register. Moulin signed Jean Martel, born April 22 1897 at Pecuigny on the Somme; French; bachelor; decorator; domiciled at 17 rue Ernest-Renan, Lyon.

Early next day the torture sessions started in earnest under Barbie's personal supervision. The known Resistance members, including Aubry, came in for specially rough treatment. Aubry suffered a dislocated shoulder; three times he was forced to stand in front of a mock firing squad in the prison courtyard. Another prisoner received a terrible beating because, for twenty-four hours, Barbie was convinced he was Max. But, throughout Monday night, and for the whole of Tuesday, nobody talked.

By the afternoon of Wednesday, June 23, however, Barbie had found out. No one has ever disclosed who cracked or how the truth came out – though Barbie has his own version. Whichever way it was, Dr Dugoujon witnessed the consequences that night as he peered through the judas window of his cell, number 129. Jean Moulin was returning from his first major interrogation session, staggering, barely able to walk, with bandages covering his head.

The next day was worse.

Early Thursday morning they took him back to be interrogated at the École de Santé, and they brought him back that night in a pitiful state [said Dugoujon]. He could no longer walk and he was almost carried out by the two guards, his legs dragging, his face all disfigured. They laid him out on the mattress of his cell and left him there all night, the door open, the light burning, with two guards watching. Friday morning they came to get him again.

There were to be several witnesses to Moulin's terrible condition. In view of what they saw of his beaten face, his head injuries, the eyes that looked as if they had been somehow punched back into his skull, Barbie's jovial account of his "conversations" with Moulin is hard to take. Moulin was by then a dying man, yet Barbie insists that they met as equals, fencing with each other, probing for weaknesses, but motivated by a strong mutual respect.

Our conversations revolved essentially around politics [Barbie recounted years later], around his opinion of the struggle that Germany was waging against American imperialism and Bolshevism. I endeavoured at the same time to grapple, apart from his personal life, with his activities in the heart of the Resistance as well as his role as plenipotentiary of de Gaulle. I placed great emphasis on one point: the Plan Vert for the sabotage of the railways.

Moulin told Barbie that he had nothing to say. He had chewed up the paper containing the agenda for the meeting at Caluire as soon as the doctor's surgery was raided. There was no other evidence against him.

Barbie's account of how Moulin first conceded he was "Max" strains credulity. He says that during the first interrogation, Moulin continued to insist that he was called Martel. "I am an artist, painter and illustrator," he told Barbie. "You know – you have all my documents." Barbie sent for a pencil and paper, pushed them in front of Moulin and told him to draw his portrait: "You're an artist, aren't you?" he said.

Moulin took the drawing materials and started to sketch. Suddenly he stopped and, says Barbie, began to laugh: "It was obvious from the first pencil lines that Moulin was incapable of drawing anything . . . in fact, he was particularly incompetent at sketching – I started to laugh too."

91

Barbie then took the "portrait" and addressed Moulin: "You were a top-rate prefect at Chartres. Don't change your profession." Immediately, his face became serious. "I am indeed Jean Moulin," he said. Barbie wrote "Done by Max" on the sketch and kept it. Once again, however, the evidence in Barbie's support is missing. This was another document that his wife inconveniently burnt after the war.

This story of Barbie's is clearly nonsense. Moulin was in reality an artist of considerable ability, a book illustrator of note, and a skilled caricaturist. What Barbie seems to have done is pervert another incident witnessed by the interpreter, Gottlieb Fuchs. In the course of one session, says Fuchs, Barbie passed Moulin a pencil and paper and told him to draw a diagram of the various branches of the Resistance organisation. After sketching for a few minutes, Moulin handed back the paper without uttering a word. It was not a diagram at all, but a grotesque caricature of Barbie. It provoked, according to Fuchs, a fit of uncontrollable rage from Barbie, which he took out on his prisoner.

Fuchs went on to describe Barbie's growing fury at Moulin's intransigence. At one point, after a savage interrogation, Barbie dragged Moulin down a flight of stairs by means of a rope attached to his feet and then dumped him in his cell. Fuchs could hear the body bouncing on the stone steps as Barbie came down at a run. "If that guy doesn't break tonight," said Barbie, "I'll finish him off tomorrow in Paris." What he meant was that his SS bosses at headquarters in Paris expected him to deliver his prisoner to them next day: Barbie did not have much time.

But Moulin did not break. Barbie vented his frustration on the small frame of his victim. He beat him with a whip, with his truncheon, and, most of all, with his bare fists. There was nothing subtle about the treatment, but to Barbie's mind there was no time for anything more sophisticated. Success, he knew, could make his career. The knowledge lent new frenzy to his attacks.

Barbie had miscalculated. He was now no longer seeking information, he was simply unleashing his rage on a man who would not talk. And in the process he was killing him. By the time Jean Moulin left his cell at Montluc prison, he would no longer be in a state to talk at all, let alone deliver the inside information the SS was so desperate to hear.

Far from marking the pinnacle of his career, Barbie's handling of the interrogation would effectively blight it. By Thursday evening he seems to have realised what he had done. At six o'clock that night a German non-commissioned officer was ordered to fetch

Christian Pineau, a Resistance prisoner (later a trade unionist and government minister), from his cell and to see that he brought his razor. For some reason Pineau was the only inmate of Montluc who had been allowed to keep his razor, and he had therefore been designated the prison's unofficial barber. He followed the soldier down the stairs of the prison. All was quiet and still. The German led Pineau outside to a bench in the northern exercise yard. On it a man was stretched. A soldier stood guard, his rifle slung over his shoulder.

"You shave Monsieur," said the soldier, indicating the motionless figure on the bench.

Pineau moved closer and to his horror realised that the man was Moulin. He knew him well. He had been with him in London in March and had flown back to France in his company. Now he scarcely recognised him. Pineau wrote later: "He was unconscious, his eyes dug in as though they had been punched through his head. An ugly blue wound scarred his temple. A mute rattle came out of his swollen lips."

While the soldier fetched water from a stand-pipe, Pineau held Moulin's hand. It was icy cold. He took a mug and a piece of soap and, with a trembling hand, shaved Moulin's face, making sure the blunt razor avoided the bruises.

Suddenly Moulin's eyes opened wide. "Water," he gasped. Pineau asked the soldier to fetch some, and, after hesitating, he did, rinsing out the soapy mug and filling it with fresh water from the tap.

While he was away, Pineau leaned down and whispered some words of encouragement in Moulin's ear. Moulin said five or six words in English, but his voice was so weak and cracked, so distorted by the blood running from the corner of his mouth, that Pineau could not understand. Moulin gulped down some water and drifted back into a coma. The soldier left them together.

At ten that night, the German reappeared and was surprised to see Pineau still there, sitting beside Moulin on the bench, holding his hand. He ordered him back to his cell. With the guard rattling his bunch of keys behind him, Pineau climbed the stairs to his cell. He took one look back at Moulin who was still stretched on the bench. Pineau thinks the Germans left him there all night. He never saw Moulin again. His haggard, battered face haunts him still.

Pineau could not understand why he had been asked to shave a dying man – he thought it might be some macabre Nazi ritual. But in fact it was a mark of Klaus Barbie's panic. He knew that he was answerable for Moulin's condition to his headquarters in Paris, and he was desperately attempting to make him look as presentable as possible.

Next day Barbie personally drove Moulin to Paris and delivered him to SS headquarters in the Avenue Foch. Barbie was seen there by Henri Aubry, who had been brought to Paris for further interrogation. Aubry saw Moulin too, lying on a chaise-longue. He appeared to be in a coma. Aubry then saw Barbie report to an SS general who did not appear to be pleased.

"Barbie clicked his jackboots in front of the general, who remained standing, smoking cigarette after cigarette. 'I hope he makes it,' the general said drily, dismissing Barbie from his presence. 'It's luck that I wish you.'"

Moulin was transferred to an SS villa in the western Paris suburb of Neuilly where other Resistance leaders were being held. Here, General Delestraint and another of the Caluire prisoners both saw him. Moulin was stretched out on a divan, his head bandaged, his face deathly pale, his breathing irregular and feeble. Only his eyes had any life.

Delestraint was asked if he recognised the prisoner as Moulin, but the general, who was later deported to Dachau and shot dead by the SS just a few hours before the Americans liberated the camp in April 1945, replied frostily:

"Military honour forbids me to recognise Max in this injured man you have presented to me."

A German policeman, Heinrich Meiners, was one of the last men to see Moulin alive at Neuilly. He told his French interrogators after the war that he saw a prisoner at the villa who

made a very bizarre impression on me. The prisoner was lying down, then he sat up and I saw him walk a few steps in his room supporting himself on the furniture and on the walls. He had difficulty in breathing and was holding his stomach and kidneys. He gave me the impression of being a sick man who did not have long to live. There was a glazed, haggard expression in his eyes.

Moulin, stubborn to the end, survived for fourteeen days after his transfer to Paris. Some time early in July the Paris Gestapo received orders to transfer him to Germany. He was put on a train to Berlin, but shortly before it reached Frankfurt he died.

A local policeman, who was able to examine the corpse, concluded it was that of a man who had suffered terribly, and arranged for an autopsy to be performed. But the Gestapo countermanded the order and took charge of the body. "It is a secret police matter," they said.

Moulin's body was brought back to Paris and cremated on July 9 1943 at Père Lachaise cemetery. Today his presumed ashes are interred in the Panthéon, final resting place of France's heroes.

On October 19, four months after his death, a Gestapo officer called at the home in Montpellier of Laure Moulin and informed her that her brother was dead. It was not until May of the following year that she was able to obtain a death certificate, which stated that Moulin had died at Metz in eastern France at 2 a.m. on July 8 1943. He was just forty-four years old.

We know nothing of the dressing-down that Klaus Barbie must have received in Paris. Much later, he was to concoct an explanation of Moulin's death. It should be placed on the record, if only to demonstrate Barbie's capacity for deception, or perhaps, for self-deception:

> We kept him [Moulin] permanently in the loft, bound with handcuffs, of course, and always with two guards in his cell. One day, when there was a lot of activity at the barracks, I had to be absent. I left strict instructions for him to be watched, but the two guards who were ordinary soldiers were negligent. They left him alone in his cell – still with his legs and wrists bound – for a brief moment. It was enough for Moulin.
>
> On my return I asked for him to be brought to me. The soldiers returned in total confusion. Fearing the worst, I dashed into his cell. Moulin was stretched on the ground. Bound as he was, he had taken advantage of that one little moment when he had been left on his own to hurl himself with incredible violence, head first, against the wall . . .

It is unlikely that Barbie troubled SS headquarters in Paris with this version of events. The evidence of Moulin's real injuries was there for all to see. But the Gestapo appears to have covered up for him. A report by Ernst Kaltenbrunner, head of the RSHA in Berlin, written eight days after Moulin's arrest, states that various Resistance leaders had been seized but that Max was not among them, having been delayed by a "French police round-up".

A further report from Gestapo headquarters in Berlin, dated September 18 1943, states that SS Reichsführer Heinrich Himmler had sent a personal letter expressing his gratitude to Barbie and four other Lyon SS officers for their "special efficiency in the pursuit of crime and their dogged commitment to the fight against resistance organisations in France". There was no mention of Jean Moulin.

On November 9 Barbie was decorated with the Iron Cross, First Class, with Sword, and a recommendation for promotion went through, stating that "his most meritorious accomplishment has been the cleaning out of numerous enemy organisations".

But it was not until the following year that he was promoted to Hauptsturmführer, and he ended the war still with that lowly rank – captain. As he himself said, many years later: "The capture of Jean Moulin was a triumph for me, but also the worst disaster of my career."

The innocence or guilt of René Hardy has never been satisfactorily established. The question whether he was a traitor or not still divides Frenchmen. Two separate trials failed to resolve the matter, but that has not prevented those who were involved holding strong and certain views about it.

On December 13 1944, after the liberation of France, Hardy was arrested and charged with treason. He was tried by the Cour de la Justice de la Seine in January 1947. The appearance of this handsome young Resistance colonel in uniform with a chestful of medals, and the talent of his flamboyant lawyer, Maître Maurice Garçon, led to his acquittal.

Shortly afterwards, however, a French railway conductor came forward with the evidence that Hardy had been arrested by the German police at Chalon and taken off the train rather than escaping, as he had pretended. Hardy was re-arrested and, at his second trial before a military tribunal in April 1950 he admitted the lie, pleading that if he had revealed his arrest at the time, the Resistance would probably have executed him.

Evidence taken from Klaus Barbie in Germany was read out in the teeth of protest by Hardy's lawyer, Garçon, and the prosecution also produced Ernst Kaltenbrunner's report, which named Hardy as the source of the Caluire tip-off. But again, the German evidence was found to be so full of inconsistencies that it became virtually worthless in court. Even the testimony of the Resistance witnesses was confused, and there were so many examples of security blunders in the preparations leading up to the Caluire meeting, that Hardy was accorded the benefit of the doubt.

Even so, of the seven members of the tribunal four decided that he was guilty – just one short of the number needed for conviction.

CHAPTER FIVE

Bloodbath

Until the death of Jean Moulin, the image that Klaus Barbie had most liked to cultivate off-duty in Lyon was that of the bluff, devil-may-care German officer, tasting the delights of French life in a city where he could throw his weight about with impunity. He prided himself on a certain "style", particularly towards women, with whom he would affect an old-world courtesy. Among his colleagues he assumed a hearty back-slapping manner which he also reserved, on occasion, for the torture chamber.

Barbie considered himself a civilised German: he played the piano, though badly, and enjoyed long if heavy-handed philosophical discussions about German history and the consequences of the war. He prided himself on his knowledge of France and the French language, and he felt at home in the city of Lyon. He particularly enjoyed his daily walks along the quais with his Alsatian, Wolf – the same dog that had so viciously attacked Devigny in the course of his "interrogation"; the danger he exposed himself to gave the little ritual an added piquancy. He liked to move about incognito, rather as he had done in the weeks before his official arrival, listening in to café conversations, and picking up the gossip.

There was nothing noticeably civilised about the way he spent his evenings. Without Regine, who was for most of the war in Trier, he behaved much like any other unattached officer, eating out in expensive restaurants, getting drunk, and frequenting the night clubs which wartime Lyon kept going with undiminished enthusiasm.

His favourite eating places were the Carillon, the Balbo and Le Moulin à Vent, the best restaurants in town; and he would frequently wind up in Le Lapin Blanc, Lyon's most risqué night club, where the girls were pretty, available, and often useful sources of intelligence. His favourite was Antoinette "Mimiche" Morlot, a hostess at the Lapin Blanc. But he also had a lengthy affair with a girl called Thédy who was a secretary at Gestapo headquarters, and who would often be present at interrogation sessions, sometimes actually sitting on Barbie's lap as his victims were tortured.

After the war Barbie would occasionally boast, to some of the American intelligence officers with whom he worked, of his amorous conquests in France; he would give them detailed accounts of his sexual experiences both in Lyon and on his trips to Paris. There was one severe consequence of these adventures. Early on in his Gestapo career, possibly even while he was still in Gex, he contracted a venereal disease. As soon as he consulted a doctor, the matter was entered on his medical record and became known to his superiors. Barbie claimed that it had cost him promotion and accounted for his still lowly rank of captain at the end of the war. The episode, which is also mentioned in classified US intelligence documents held by the CIA, was a cause of great bitterness to him, particularly later when Kurt Merk of the Abwehr ended up with a higher rank, despite what Barbie considered to be his own unswerving devotion to the Führer.

There was, however, another consequence. Barbie confided to Andrée Rivez after the war that, as a result of one of his affairs with a Frenchwoman, he had fathered a child – a baby boy. The mother kept the baby, but has never to this day admitted who the father was. She is still alive, as is the boy, and both live in France. Barbie's natural son is now in his early forties, and quite unaware of the identity of the man who is his father.

In the months following June 1943 and the Moulin affair, accounts of Barbie's behaviour are increasingly grim; several witnesses speak of the unpredictability of his moods, and the way in which they could change rapidly from calmness to fury. "He could be charming for a time, then, suddenly, ferocious, like a bull," said his interpreter Fuchs. And a Resistance victim, Pol Chavet, recalled that "he was able to change immediately from the greatest brutality to a strange gentleness. In the cells I was surprised by some of my comrades who had been interrogated by him and who said he had been quite kind to them."

One of the victims of Barbie's brutality at this time was Raymond Aubrac, who had been arrested with Jean Moulin at Caluire and was being held at Montluc prison. Aubrac was beaten savagely by Barbie, who used whips and clubs indiscriminately during two long interrogation sessions at the École de Santé, but failed to extract anything of value. There was no subtlety about the questioning. Barbie screamed questions at Aubrac in between beatings, and, when his victim fainted, he waited until he revived, then started again.

After each session at the École de Santé, Aubrac was returned to the fortress prison of Montluc, where conditions were by now appalling. The nineteenth-century building, which stood near railway sidings in the third arrondissement of the city, had been closed on health grounds before the war broke out. The Gestapo found that its primitive facilities suited their needs admirably, and so reopened it. It consisted of a main three-storey building with some 130 cells, a one-storey block called "the refectory" containing sixty beds, into which at least eighty prisoners were crammed, and a yellow-painted wooden building which housed two hundred Jewish prisoners of every nationality, crowded even more tightly.

The food was vile, and hygienic conditions revolting. The prisoners washed in groups of twenty in a shed and had to clean their bodies and their clothes as well as use the toilets, all in five minutes. Twenty minutes of exercise followed. The prison diet consisted of hard German bread and a thin soup.

But what the inmates could never forget was the infestation of lice, fleas, and bed-bugs. One prisoner called Schoetker wrote in the diary he kept during his captivity:

The vermin. The bed-bugs make the nights unbearable and all rest impossible. As soon as night fell, this ravenous horde dropped in bunches from the ceilings, the crevices in the walls, and did not stream back again until daybreak . . . I cannot sleep. I am smothering for lack of air . . . The toilet buckets, the blankets that have been used by so many people without ever being cleaned, the stench of men never given the time nor the means to wash themselves, makes the air unbreathable.

Discipline was harsh. Inmates were forbidden to approach the windows, forbidden to lie down in the daytime, forbidden to remain standing or to sing after eight in the evening. They had to stand to attention in the presence of German soldiers.

Barbie himself was rarely seen at Montluc. But the reasons for his visits were almost invariably sinister. On July 31 1943, for instance, he arrived suddenly, and ordered all the prisoners to parade in the courtyard. A routine search had revealed letters hidden among the dirty laundry sent out of the prison to be washed. As a punishment, three prisoners were picked out and Barbie appointed a member of his Einsatzkommando to be the executioner. The prisoners were shot one by one with a bullet in the nape of the neck.

The greatest terror of the day at Montluc was the early morning roll-call. There were two kinds of *appels* – "Sans bagages" and

"Avec bagages". The *appels* with luggage meant deportation and were always accompanied by moving scenes among the prisoners, with those left behind giving scraps of food to sustain the deportees on their long and terrible journeys.

The *appels* without luggage was shorthand for execution by firing squad. These always came at about four in the morning. The harsh electric light suddenly snapping on, the noise of the doors clanging open, the pounding of heavy German boots, and the barked commands, filled the prison night with dread.

> They dressed in silence, always very calm, with an admirable courage [said one former inmate]. We tried to cheer them up by talking of deportation, but they were not fooled. After the embraces of their closest comrades whom they asked to break the news of their deaths to their loved ones, they went to the door where the cell-leader shook each man by the hand in the name of us all.

A few minutes later a salvo would ring out and it was all over.

After the liberation a commemorative plaque was erected on the outer wall of Montluc. It reads: "Here suffered 10,000 internees, victims of the Nazis and their accomplices during the Occupation. 7,000 succumbed."

Although the death of Jean Moulin had been a setback for the Resistance and a severe blow to the morale of its members, it had by no means destroyed the organisation. Claude Serreulles, the "new boy" from London who had lost his way to the rendezvous at Caluire, stepped in to take over as de Gaulle's delegate and sent a telegram to London informing them of the arrests. He moved north to Paris to help hold the movement together after making rapid contact with the leaders in the south.

In Lyon there was a wave of Gestapo arrests followed by frantic reorganisation among the various Resistance groups. They found they could rely to a greater extent than before on help and protection from the citizens of Lyon, who were increasingly mutinous in their attitude towards their Nazi masters. Conditions in the city had deteriorated – food restrictions were now severe and prices high. But the greatest cause of resentment was the forced labour laws.

Early in the year 1943 the Vichy government had passed a law known as the Service de Travail Obligatoire (STO) which meant that every French male of working age was liable to be called up for compulsory labour in Germany. The demand was for a million

French workers, and more than 700,000 would eventually be transported, making the French the largest male foreign-worker group in Germany.

Throughout the summer Gestapo squads, with French police support, had carried out raids to round up anyone suspected of evading the call-up, and to inflict reprisals. Those who lacked correct identity papers, or who held false work documents, could be arrested. Some became Gestapo informers in return for their freedom, but for the vast majority the law was simply a cause of bitter resentment against the Vichy government and the German occupying force.

Barbie himself remarked later that the STO was the best propaganda weapon the Resistance ever had. And a Vichy minister announced scathingly to Gauleiter Sauckel who ran the recruitment programme in France: "If ever the Maquis puts up monuments in France, you will have the biggest. And the inscription will be: 'To our principal recruiting agent, Gauleiter Sauckel, from the grateful Maquis'."

The Gestapo on its own could never have rounded up 700,000 Frenchmen. They relied for help, not just on the French police, but on the newly-formed Milice whose work alongside the Nazis was to bring a new dimension to the "principle of collaboration" that Marshal Pétain had announced to his people after the fall of France.

The Milice was the French Gestapo. It had been set up early in 1943 after a strong hint from Hitler to the Vichy President of the Council Pierre Laval that there must be an efficient counter-terrorist force in France. Like the Black and Tans who brought disgrace to the British name in Ireland in the early 1920s, the Milice was to become loathed and despised by most French citizens for the viciousness with which it pursued Nazi policy.

The man who founded it was Émile-Joseph Darnand, a First World War hero who had become an Obersturmführer (first lieutenant) in the French Waffen-SS. In 1941 he had answered Pétain's call for "a new spirit" in France by founding the Service d'Ordre Légionnaire, a heavily Fascist body sworn to "fight against democracy, against Gaullist dissidence, and against the Jewish plague". Darnand was the perfect Nazi tool. He and his men toured the gaols of France with their firing squads, setting up summary courts and passing sentences of death in secret. In Lyon, where the Milice chief was Joseph Lecussan, the tactics were particularly ferocious, and included secret executions, carried out alongside the Gestapo. Paul Touvier, Lecussan's number two, who ran a gang of some thirty Milice members, was so vicious that he was once actually arrested by the Vichy police for assault, and was only released after the Gestapo had intervened.

Faced with growing French hostility, the German forces in Lyon began taking extra precautions to protect their troops. Key sections of the city were declared off-limits to civilians, and in the city centre barbed wire entanglements blocked the entrances of the hotels and restaurants frequented by German soldiers. Movements within the city became an ever more hazardous business for the Resistance.

But within four months of Moulin's death the Resistance had pulled off two spectacular coups, right under the nose of the Gestapo. The first was the escape from Montluc jail of André Devigny, the only prisoner out of some ten thousand held there in the course of the war to have succeeded in doing so. The second was the dramatic rescue of Raymond Aubrac.

Devigny had discovered a way of dismantling the wooden panels of his cell door and reassembling them like a jigsaw puzzle. In August 1943, on the weekend before the date set for his execution, he managed to slip out of his cell, cross the prison roof and, using a rope and grappling-hook made up of rags and bits of wire, he scaled the outer wall to freedom. Captured by the Germans near the Swiss frontier, Devigny escaped again and finally reached safety after spending five hours immersed in the waters of the Rhine to avoid a German search party with dogs.

Raymond Aubrac owed his rescue to his resourceful wife Lucie who began by simply presenting herself at Gestapo headquarters and demanding to see Barbie himself. "He received me very cynically," she says. "He said Aubrac and his comrades had been sentenced to death, and their execution would take place in the near future."

So on October 21, four months to the day after the Caluire arrests, Lucie staged a dramatic attack on two lorries taking Aubrac and others from the École de Santé to Montluc after an interrogation. A team of Resistance commandos in two Citroen vans ambushed the convoy with guns blazing. The Gestapo guards were gunned down, and though Aubrac himself was wounded in the neck, he and his fellow prisoners got away. Lucie later escaped with him to England where, within a few weeks of arriving, she gave birth to a son.

The Aubrac escape enraged Barbie. A six o'clock curfew was imposed at Montluc prison, and fierce interrogations carried out to find out who had helped organise the ambush. But no one was discovered.

Barbie's operations now began to extend far beyond his original area of responsibility: south-west towards Toulouse, and south-east to Grenoble and the Swiss frontier, a sector which had been the responsibility of the Italian occupying force. With the fall of Mussolini on July 25 1943, the Italian campaign against the Resistance army – the Maquis – in the countryside began to crumble.

> The Resistance in that sector was strong [recalled Barbie later]. The Italians were simply not organised for the struggle against it. It was a rugged area, with mountains and woods. The whole place came under our control, that is to say, under the command post in Lyon. But the struggle was now strictly military, and we acted in liaison with our army.

In August 1943 Barbie received orders from Paris to carry out a "special operation" in the Italian area. He was to go to Grenoble and kidnap two prominent Frenchmen, André François-Poncet, who had been France's ambassador to Berlin before the war, and Albert Lebrun, the last president of the Third Republic, who had resigned in order to let Marshal Pétain take over. Barbie's orders were to bring them back to Lyon, then dispatch them under armed guard to Germany.

"It was a particularly delicate mission, since the region was still occupied by the Italians and we were not supposed officially to intervene," Barbie recounted. He described the exercise in gripping detail in the "memoirs" which he dictated in 1979, portraying it as a daring kidnap under the noses of the Italians, with the team speeding back to Lyon sprayed by bullets from suspicious French policemen.

Unfortunately for Barbie, both Lebrun and François-Poncet also wrote detailed accounts of their arrest and neither of them recalls any shooting. Lebrun says that Barbie lost his way in Grenoble and had to get out to ask a passer-by for instructions; François-Poncet remembers Barbie's nervousness and then his excitement when he realised he had got away with the kidnap: "His face betrayed the most lively satisfaction; his expedition had succeeded; he had plucked us from under the noses of the Italians; there had been no difficulty, no incident; it had been a perfectly executed piece of larceny . . ."

Barbie's sortie to Grenoble had taken him through areas where the Maquis was growing increasingly strong. By October the supply of arms and equipment from London had begun to flow in earnest, dropped into the hills by RAF aircraft to supply Resistance groups, who were attacking German patrols, blowing up factories, and disrupting rail links with increasing confidence.

The British Special Operations Executive (SOE), whose French section was headed by Colonel Maurice Buckmaster in London, had dispatched an experienced agent to review the state of the Maquis in the area, and he had found the Ain region, north-east of Lyon, the best organised, with a network of safe houses, radio transmission points and landing strips.

On November 11, Armistice day, the local Maquis leader, Major Henri Romans-Petit, demonstrated his defiance of the Wehrmacht by parading through the little town of Oyonnax in the Ain at the head of a troop of two hundred armed Maquisards in uniform. They laid a wreath at the Monument aux Morts to the acclaim of an ecstatic crowd which lined the route.

The Gestapo could not allow this defiance to go unpunished. Five days later a group of Gestapo agents descended on Oyonnax accompanied by a detachment of the Feldgendarmerie, and arrested the mayor and the deputy mayor, whom they bundled into their cars. The two bodies were found later, swinging from a tree in the woods nearby. Giving evidence after the war, Oyonnax's police inspector, Maurice Thévenon, said that the Gestapo officers had told him they were "carrying out the orders of Barbie, the chief of the Lyon SD".

That accords with Barbie's own account of his operations against the Maquis at this time. In his "memoirs", he says that strict measures including instant executions were absolutely justified in dealing with the "guerrillas".

"The Maquis were irregular troops," he said, "and our methods of repression could not be other than extraordinary, outside the limits of normal war, just as the Geneva Accords and the Red Cross had anticipated." It was an argument he was to use again when he admitted ordering the execution of two nuns from the convent of Notre Dame des Dombes after discovering 20,000 litres of petrol hidden there by the Maquis. "The punishment had to be meted out without pity," he recalled.

Harsh measures were encouraged by Barbie's commanding officer, Werner Knab. With the defeat of the German army in North Africa, and suspicions of an imminent Allied landing in the south of France, he had been instructed that it was more important than ever to make the area between Lyon and the Swiss border a secure one for the Wehrmacht. But the Maquis seemed to grow daily in strength, particularly in the region of the Ain.

The Resistance was now bold enough to make an attempt on the life of the Gestapo chief himself. Or at least Barbie believed that, though the attack appears to have been more generally directed against his Einsatzkommando. As Barbie recounted it later, a woman appeared one day at Gestapo headquarters, and told him she could lead the Germans to an important member of the Resistance. She gave him an address in Lyon.

Barbie drew up a plan of attack, and at seven in the morning his men encircled the house. As an added precaution they brought the woman with them. Barbie and his men were wearing civilian clothes similar to those worn by the Maquis – fur-collared jackets with large pockets to hold grenades, and enormous inside pockets big enough to take the broken-down Sten guns which the Allies regularly parachuted to the Maquis forces.

As they moved in on the house Barbie sensed there was something wrong. But before he could do anything, there was a burst of rapid fire from inside the building: the Resistance team inside had opened up with pistols, hand-grenades and sub-machine guns. The Gestapo retreated, losing two or three men, then regrouped and turned to storm the building. After two hours of brisk fighting they finally succeeded in capturing it. Among the dead inside was a Gestapo agent who had been sent in to reconnoitre the premises.

Barbie interrogated the woman who had brought him the tip-off. She confessed finally to being a Resistance agent who had been instructed to lead the Gestapo into a trap. "I ordered the woman to be executed and had her body thrown into the Rhône to cover our tracks," said Barbie later.

There were worse reprisals to come. On January 9 1944 two German soldiers were shot dead at the Perrache station in Lyon. Next day the Gestapo surrounded the nearby Quai St Claire, rounded up a number of people, and took them to the École de Santé.

Commissaire Adrian Richard, deputy chief of the Lyon Sureté, told a war crimes investigation team what happened next:

About one in the morning, I was telephoned at home and ordered to accompany Commissaire Divisionnaire Colomb [his chief] to the École de Santé Militaire for an unspecified mission. At the École de Santé we were received by an officer who attempted to explain to us that the Germans had executed a number of people who had staged a rebellion.

To be clear, I should say that we were received by a German officer who was not Barbie himself, the chief of the service. This officer asked us to follow two NCOs to the cellars to identify the corpses. Flanked by the two NCOs armed with sub-machine guns, we went down to the cellars. Penetrating the corridor, we noticed the overpowering scent of warm blood. As we penetrated deeper, we noticed a pool of congealed blood in front of the door of one cell. One of the officers opened the door to reveal a horrifying sight.

Bodies were piled up in one corner of the cell covered in gore. They were young people who had been machine-gunned from the door. They were stuck together, half lying down, and I remember a postman, in uniform, who looked as if he had been cut down by the sub-machine gunfire as he raised himself from a chair. His face was set in a horrifying grimace.

Richard said the position of the corpses made it immediately obvious that the prisoners had not rebelled as the Germans claimed, but had been massacred in cold blood. He counted 180 spent shells on a table. Twenty-two men and women had died that night.

Barbie does not deny the École de Santé reprisals. In his 1979 "memoirs" he claimed that the Gestapo had deliberately left some of the cell doors open so that an escape bid would be made, and had then machine-gunned the prisoners as they came up the stairs.

"We were in the right because they shouldn't have shot our soldiers in the back. It was against all the laws. We never thought that we should have to put up with such atrocities . . ." he said.

That excuse is unlikely to survive the charge of "crimes against humanity" which includes this incident and which is set down for hearing at Barbie's trial in France.

There is another charge, central not only to Barbie's activities in Lyon, but to an understanding of French attitudes towards the worst of the war crimes committed in the course of the occupation. Klaus Barbie has boasted of his ruthlessness towards the Resistance and its agents. He is less forthcoming, however, on the question of the Jews.

In conversations with American officers of the Counter Intelligence Corps after the war he affected an attitude of indifference towards the subject: "He was contemptuous towards the Jews, but he wasn't outspoken to the point of pursuing it," said one of the officers who got to know him well. "He discussed the policy of the Final Solution – Himmler's policy. He said that the best concept was that of culling them out of the Aryan society and re-locating them to an area of their own. He showed no particular enthusiasm for the idea of killing Jews."

That was not how Andrée Rivez, the girl friend of Kurt Merk, remembered it. One evening, in Germany after the war, Klaus Barbie told her of an incident which occurred in the final days – perhaps the final day – of his time in Lyon:

"At the very end," she said, "Barbie rounded up a squad of ordinary soldiers and told them to shoot a group of Jews. They refused and marched off, saying it was not their job and he had no right to give them orders. So he killed all the Jews himself. That is what he told us." To illustrate the point to her, Barbie pulled the trigger of an imaginary gun – and smiled.

Forty years later Andrée Rivez still found difficulty in talking about the incident, one that is quite undocumented. It is the only known first-hand testimony in which Barbie admits that he took a personal hand in killing Jews. Mademoiselle Rivez found the story, and the coolness with which Barbie recounted it, horrifying.

Long before that incident took place, Barbie and his Einsatzkommando had played a central part in the rounding up and deporting of Jews from Lyon to the concentration camps in which the vast majority of them died. In this he was aided by the Vichy government, the Milice, the French police, and by the cooperation, often willingly given, of a small but active minority of ordinary French citizens.

"We managed to steer the French government's own impulses and those of the French police in the same direction as ours," said a Nazi official in 1942. "That way they not only saved effort, they also preserved French self-respect . . . they reduced the odium of the use of force, since it was French force . . ."

The man chosen by the Vichy government in February 1942 to exert that force was a Jew-baiter of long standing, Darquier de Pellepoix, who worked closely with a twenty-seven-year-old Nazi sadist, Hauptmann Theodore Dannecker, brought from Berlin to head the anti-Jewish section of the Gestapo in Paris.

That May Reinhard Heydrich, Himmler's second in command, visited Paris to introduce General Karl Oberg, the new SS commander, to French and German officials, and to urge the immediate pursuit of Nazi policy on the Jews; and on June 30 Adolf Eichmann, head of the Judenamt of the RSHA, arrived in the French capital bearing a brutal directive from Himmler: all the Jews of France were to be deported, irrespective of nationality.

French official cooperation, however, never came up to Dannecker's demanding standards, and when René Bousquet, chief of the French police, turned down a request from Dannecker to arrest twenty thousand Jews in June 1942, Dannecker was so enraged that he threw the telephone in his office on to the floor and smashed it.

The Vichy leader Pierre Laval spent part of the summer of 1942 bargaining with the Nazis over the final total of Jews to be deported; but General Karl Oberg had already starkly spelled out the alternatives: "The trains are ready," he said, "and at any cost and by any means we must fill them. The Jewish problem is not a question of nationality as far as we are concerned. The French police must cooperate with us; otherwise it is we who will arrest the Jews whether they are French or not."

On July 16 and 17 in a round-up in Paris, which is still remembered as the most shocking of the war, 12,844 foreign Jews, including 4,000 children, deprived of their French nationality, were arrested with the active cooperation of the French police and taken to Drancy camp near Paris. They were then deported to Auschwitz.

In Lyon the pre-war Jewish population of some seven thousand had swollen to about ten times that as Jews fled south from the occupied zone and west from the rest of Europe. The first round-ups began, before Barbie's arrival, in August 1942, but the numbers produced were far smaller than the authorities in Paris had anticipated.

Barbie relied for his anti-Jewish operations on a Gestapo lieutenant, Erich Bartelmus, whose reputation was to grow over the next year into that of a brutal torturer and a cold-blooded executioner. Bartelmus had barely half a dozen officers to help him, but he was able to rely increasingly on the services of the Milice, and on the para-military wing of the right-wing Parti Populaire Français headed by Francis André, a Communist turned Fascist, who was given a wide-ranging licence to carry out executions, often without Gestapo supervision.

The first raids led by Bartelmus in January 1943 produced only 150 Jews. He found little sympathy or cooperation from the Lyonnais. Then, on February 9 the Gestapo raided the headquarters in the rue St Catherine of the Union Générale des Israelites de France, the UGIF, which maintained links between the Jewish community and the Vichy government, and, naively, kept the Germans informed about the homes they provided for orphaned Jewish children.

The early morning raid was headed by Barbie who ordered his men to arrest everyone they found inside, then to wait inside the building and pick up anyone who arrived in the course of the day. By the end of the operation at 6 p.m., eighty-seven Jews had been arrested, searched, stripped of their belongings, then loaded on to lorries. All of them were sent to Auschwitz or Sobibor. There were no survivors.

The reports on that day's raid, forwarded to Paris on February 14, were signed by Barbie himself in his capacity as chief of the Einsatzkommando.

The events of 1943 – the forced labour exodus, the rounding up of Jews – would gradually turn the people of Lyon, and French men and women everywhere, against the Vichy regime. But the number of those who were prepared to take the active risk of protecting Jews from arrest was pitifully small.

One exception was Cardinal Pierre Gerlier, head of the French Catholic Church in France, and a man who had begun by being one of Vichy's most ardent supporters. When, towards the end of 1942, Gerlier learned what was happening to the Jews, he took the step – avoided by so many Catholic bishops – of sending out a pastoral letter to all the churches of the region explaining the reality of events, and urging them to extend help and protection to Jews. Later he sheltered the Grand Rabbi of France from the Gestapo, and managed to prevent the arrest and deportation of at least fifty Jewish children wanted by the French authorities.

Gerlier's actions clearly took great courage. They caused an open breach with the prefect of Lyon, Alexandre Angeli, a bureaucrat who followed Nazi orders meticulously, and who threatened Gerlier with arrest unless he handed back the Jewish children. One Vichy newspaper went so far as to demand "the head of Gerlier, cardinal, mad Talmudist, traitor to his faith, his country and his race".

But this kind of intervention remained a sad exception to the general reaction of apathy, failure to grasp the enormity of what was happening – or, worse, active assistance offered to the Gestapo.

There were, in the whole of France, only some 2,200 Gestapo agents. But they were backed up by more than four thousand French agents, known derogatorily as *gestapistes*, as well as ten thousand active members of the Milice. Heinz Röthke, who succeeded Dannecker in July 1942, commented: "The entire operation in the southern French territory was much more dependent on the French police than in the formerly occupied territory. The German strike force there could only exercise a weak supervision over the operation."

The French police were assisted by the willingness of a small but active minority of ordinary people to collaborate, a willingness which stemmed originally from blind faith in Pétain, but which became a kind of mania in which perfectly normal citizens outdid each other in informing on friends, neighbours and relations.

In Lyon, to begin with, informers presented themselves to section VI of the SS in the Boulevard des Belges, headed by Lieutenant August Moritz, Barbie's intelligence partner. Later, when the SS placed notices in the newspaper offering rewards for information, a special bureau had to be set up in the École de Santé to cope with the flow. To head it Barbie appointed a former French police inspector called André Jaquin. To emphasise Jaquin's importance, Barbie had a Lyon tailor design a special uniform for him which was so dazzling that even German officers used to salute him in the street.

Soon Jaquin's office was swamped with informants. One of his assistants described dealing with up to 150 people a day. Jaquin – known as "Milneuf" because of his SS serial number – enrolled thousands of informants, but it was Barbie who paid them.

Lise Lesèvre, a Resistance agent who was interrogated by Barbie, remembers seeing an elegant Frenchman enter Barbie's office and shake him warmly by the hand. After a brief conversation, Barbie signed a chit which he handed over to his visitor, saying loudly: "Pay office, that way!"

The Frenchman walked out, examining the pay slip, then suddenly stopped.

"Is something the matter?" asked Barbie.

"Excusez-moi, Monsieur," said the Frenchman, "but there were two of them . . ."

Probably the most infamous of Barbie's auxiliaries was Francis André of the Fascist PPF. Known as "Gueule Tordue" because his mouth had been twisted grotesquely in a road accident, André was described even by Gestapo officers as vicious. Ernst Floreck, one of Barbie's men, said that he was "very brutal with prisoners".

Testifying after the war – and shortly before his execution – André returned the compliment. He said that Barbie, with whom he worked closely in "anti-terrorist" expeditions, was "very cruel and bloodthirsty". He added that "Barbie supported to the utmost the Jewish sections of the Gestapo in their reprisals against Jews. He covered up for the murderers of numerous Jews." The records show that André's para-military group of vigilantes, called the Mouvement National anti-Terroriste, murdered, tortured and abused scores of suspects in Lyon, both Jews and Résistants.

The MNAT worked in close liaison with Lieutenant August Moritz, chief of section VI, who gave André permission for his men to carry arms and run their own fleet of cars. At first he insisted that he should be present at all "executions" carried out by André's team, but after a while even this stipulation was dropped. Moritz put a house at their disposal at 14 bis Avenue Leclerc, and they also maintained offices at the École de Santé where they joined in the Gestapo's torture sessions.

It is hard to convey the horror which accompanied the maraudings of this bloodthirsty gang, and there are relatively few survivors to recall it. One who did was Lise Lesèvre, who says that after Barbie had beaten her during one interrogation session he summoned André to take over. Swigging down a mixture of cognac and beer, André beat her naked body tied to a chair, with a cosh. When another French auxiliary offered to take over, André pushed him aside. "You ask the questions, I'll hit," he said.

The PPF enriched themselves at the expense of their Jewish victims, and were allowed to keep much of the gold and jewels they seized in the course of their raids. It was a lucrative and bloody business in which Jewish victims suffered worst. But the PPF was frequently outstripped in brutality by the Milice.

Jean Reynaudon, a Lyon Milicien, wrote to his chief, Joseph Darnand, in Paris in 1943:

> In Lozanne, some Jews gave us 600,000 francs. This money was given to our chief as well as some cigarettes and other merchandise. He gave us 200,000 francs for our team's expenses. In Sainte-Fo-les-Yon, we seized three million francs' worth of merchandise from a Jew. We executed him in retaliation for the murder of Philippe Henriot [Vichy's minister of propaganda]. In retaliation for the assassination of our comrade Milicienne Madame Coquand, we mounted a punitive expedition in which we gunned down four Communists, local shopkeepers who had been signalled to us as dangerous.
>
> Voilà, chef, a glimpse of some of our activities since the creation of our team. I think we have done our duty. So why do people treat us like the lowliest of cowards?

Arrest and executions were justified in the name of combating "terrorism". When André's gang murdered Dr Jean Long, a respected figure in Lyon, who was suspected of being in touch with French exiles in London, a note was left pinned to his chest. It read: "Terror against Terror. This man paid with his life for the murder of a Nationalist."

There are few survivors today to recall Barbie's own direct action against Jews. But those who do survive have chilling memories. Simone Kaddouche was taken in for questioning with her parents in June 1944 and interrogated by Barbie in his new office in the Place Bellecour, where he had moved after the destruction of the École de Santé by Allied bombing the previous month. Barbie knew that Simone, who was thirteen, had two younger brothers and began to question her in front of her parents about their whereabouts. Simone recalls that as he talked – at first gently – he was stroking a cat he was carrying in his arms. Simone's mother protested that they did not know where the boys were. They had been sent to a safe home somewhere outside Lyon and she genuinely did not know the address.

Barbie concentrated on Simone. Setting the cat down on his desk he walked over to her and repeated the question. When she did not answer, he struck her on the face. Shocked, her parents rushed forward to stop him, but Barbie drew his revolver and threatened to shoot them if they moved again. That night they were taken to Montluc, where Simone's father was locked up in the yellow-painted Jewish building while she and her mother were taken down to the basement of the main prison.

Next day Barbie told Simone's mother that unless she revealed where her sons were, he would "take care of" her daughter. Unable to give him the information he wanted, Simone was taken from her cell to the Place Bellecour where Barbie began to beat her repeatedly on the face until it was torn and bleeding. She was then returned to Montluc where, according to Simone, Barbie told her distraught mother: "Look at your daughter. You're the one who's responsible."

The beatings continued for almost a week, after which Simone and her mother were taken separately to the Drancy camp, while her father was kept behind to be deported later. Both parents died at the hands of the Germans, the mother in Auschwitz, the father shot in front of his daughter when they met briefly on a forced march shortly before the end of the war.

Simone's account of her confrontation forms part of the prosecution case at Barbie's trial, as does a small but crucial piece of evidence suggesting that he was under no illusions about the real fate of the Jews he rounded up and deported. It has always been Barbie's defence that he was quite unaware of what happened to them after they left Lyon, but Raymond Geissman, a senior official at UGIF, remembers differently: towards the end of 1943 he went to Barbie to plead with him for the lives of a group of Jews who had just been arrested by the Gestapo and were about to be shot. He begged Barbie to deport them rather than send them in front of a firing squad, to which Barbie replied, damningly: "Deported or shot, there's no difference."

But undoubtedly the most emotive, and ultimately devastating piece of evidence about Barbie's anti-Jewish activities concerns the fate of the children of Izieu.

There were about forty of them, Jewish boys and girls aged from three to fourteen, who had been rescued by a nurse called Sabrina Zlatin and her husband Miron. Most of them had already suffered under the Nazis, orphaned by deportations or murder, and they were desperately vulnerable. In early 1943 an empty farmhouse was found available in a little farming village forty-five miles east of Lyon, which seemed to offer a sanctuary for them. Izieu was in the Ain region, about two kilometres up a steep road above the village of La Bruyère. The nearest town was Belley, fifteen kilometres away.

The advantage of Izieu, to begin with, was that it was in the Italian sector which was considered safe. The Zlatins moved into the twelve-room house and took the children with them. There were classes every day, taken by a young teacher from Belley who remembers them as having

a maturity that others don't have at their age. They were children who had already lived . . . they never talked about themselves, their families or their lives. They never said anything; they were very secretive. They were used to being distrustful. They explained nothing, they said nothing.

They were there for nearly a year, but by spring 1944 the Zlatins were growing concerned about the children's safety. The Germans had moved into the area to take over from Italian troops, and had established a garrison just twenty minutes from the village. In April Madame Zlatin left for the south of France to see if she could find a safer haven. The Nazis came while she was away – on Thursday, April 6 at eight in the morning.

There were about a dozen soldiers, as well as Gestapo officers and local Miliciens in two trucks. Julien Favet, a farm labourer aged twenty-four witnessed the events that followed. He was walking up towards the farmhouse when he saw the lorries, which he thought were delivering firewood. As he turned into the driveway a machine gun was jammed into his ribs and he was prodded into the courtyard by a German soldier.

There he saw Germans stuffing the children into the backs of the two lorries "like sacks of potatoes". The children shouted, "Julien,

Julien!" to him, but, "I couldn't do anything," he recalls. "Most of the children were crying. A few were singing bravely. I knew it was finished for them . . .

"The little ones, who didn't know what was going to happen, were frightened by all the violence," he said. "But the older ones knew well where they were going."

One of the children tried to jump off the truck and was beaten with rifle butts. Miron Zlatin, trying not to provoke the soldiers, warned a neighbour to stay away and was kicked brutally for interfering. Eventually all the children, as well as members of the school staff, were packed into the trucks.

Favet, who was covered the whole time by a German soldier, could only watch helplessly. He was released on the orders of a Gestapo officer whom he is certain was Klaus Barbie, dressed in civilian clothes. "I am convinced of it," he says. "It's simply a face one does not forget."

As the lorries pulled away from the village, Favet says he heard the children begin singing a popular patriotic French song which they had learnt from Sabrina Zlatin, "You won't have Alsace and Lorraine".

The raid shattered the little village.

We had ended up by adopting those kids [Favet said]. Nobody expected such a raid. We had reassured ourselves by thinking that the Maquisards could be warned early enough to intervene. It was a month before I dared enter the house. On the table I found baskets of bread and forty-three bowls with the coffee and milk that nobody had time to drink that morning.

The children seized in the raid were taken to Drancy transit camp. Miron Zlatin was shot by firing squad at the French fortress of Revel with two of the older boys. The names of forty-one other children have been found in the lists of the convoys from Drancy to Auschwitz. All were gassed.

Apart from Favet's evidence, there is no proof that Barbie was present at Izieu during the raid. But that evening a telex was sent from Sipo/SD headquarters in Lyon to the offices of the Gestapo in Paris. It read:

Concerning: Jewish Children's Home in Izieu-Ain.
In the early hours of this morning the Jewish children's home "Colonie Enfant" in Izieu-Ain was closed down. Altogether forty-one children aged from three to thirteen were arrested. In

addition all of the Jewish personnel, consisting of ten people, of whom five were women, were arrested. It was not possible to secure any money or other valuables.

The transport to Drancy follows on 7.4.44.

At the bottom, the message was signed: "Barbie SS Ostuf [Obersturmführer]".

That document is the single most damaging piece of evidence against Barbie – the only piece of paper concerning his anti-Jewish activities not to have been destroyed by the Germans; it will form a major part of the prosecution case at his trial. Its stark message is a reminder of an episode which still stands out as one of the most pitiless in the story of Nazi anti-Semitism in France.

But the raid at Izieu was, for Barbie, only a minor interruption to a campaign in the mountains and forests of the Ain, Haut-Jura and Haute-Savoie that was now taking on the appearance of a full-scale military operation. The successes of the Maquis in the countryside had prompted Barbie's commander, Werner Knab, to join the Wehrmacht in flushing out the Maquis bands who were hitting German columns time and again. Barbie's job, as always, was to capture, interrogate and, if possible, turn any of the Maquis leaders he could round up. He used Francis André, the Milice, and, of course, his Einsatzkommando.

In February 1944 they began a series of sudden strikes against the villages of the Ain. One of the first to suffer was Evosges, where Barbie arrived with about a hundred Wehrmacht soldiers as well as Robert Moog the collaborator and Erich Bartelmus. They were convinced that the Maquis were hiding out in the village, but when they got there, there was no sign of them. Then one of the soldiers, searching out-buildings, discovered a barn stacked with bags of flour stolen from the Germans. Barbie took immediate reprisals by shooting one villager, then, when another refused to tell him where the nearest Maquis camp was, he shot him as well.

Two days later he was back in Evosges. He set fire to the mayor's house, then ordered the execution of the mayor himself. Two other villagers suspected of helping the Maquis were shot and their houses set on fire. Then the soldiers drove on, leaving Evosges stunned at the savagery of the attack. "We had not expected them to be so cruel," said one survivor. "We had not imagined they could do anything like this."

Other villages suffered similar raids, but Barbie's crude methods achieved little beyond establishing his Einsatzkommando as a by-word for brutality. If anything it strengthened the support the Maquis already enjoyed in the countryside. In March they succeeded in cutting six train lines, destroying two locomotives, and killing twenty enemy troops.

That month, however, a Resistance leader picked up in Lyon betrayed a whole underground network of more than a hundred agents, including the regional Maquis chief, Albert Chambonnet; and in the Haute-Savoie the Wehrmacht trapped a band of four hundred Maquis on the Plateau des Glières and cut them down.

The capture of Chambonnet – code name "Didier" – owed nothing to Barbie's skill. But he claimed it as a triumph, for he had been attempting, through a series of particularly brutal interrogations, to identify Chambonnet, and thus break one of the most important and effective Maquis groups in the Ain.

Barbie built his reputation as a counter-intelligence agent on the skill with which, he claimed, he infiltrated the Resistance and turned their key agents. But despite his boasts he appears to have developed little subtlety in his methods of interrogation.

Lise Lesèvre, who had worked for the movement virtually from the beginning, was picked up at the end of March 1944 at the Gare de Perrache and found to have compromising documents on her. By an appalling coincidence Lise knew another "Didier", a minor figure in the Resistance, and nothing to do with Chambonnet. Barbie discovered the name in her documents, which she had tried unsuccessfully to destroy, and set out to break her.

She was questioned by Gestapo officers until four in the morning on her first night, but without violence. Then, at seven the next morning she met Barbie for the first time, in his office at the École de Santé. He sat her in a high-backed chair and stood in front of her, tapping his riding crop against his jackboots.

"He was a terrifying spectacle," said Lise. "His eyes darted constantly from one side to the other. I really had the impression of a wild animal about to spring on me.

" 'Who is Didier?' he demanded. 'Where is Didier?' "

Lise refused to answer so he struck her across the face with his fists. When Barbie saw that she was determined to remain silent, he sent her back to her cell. But that afternoon she was brought back, stripped, and hung from a beam by the manacles on her wrists as Barbie lashed her with his riding crop. Over the next nine days she was tortured in various ways, the most terrible being at the hands of Francis André who struck her naked body with a heavy spiked weight hung from the end of a stick and broke one of her vertebrae.

Barbie applied crude psychological torture too by producing the belongings of her sixteen-year-old son who had also been arrested and had written despairing notes to her on his blotter. The messages wrung her heart, but she would not break down.

At one point she fainted after a particularly vicious torture session. She came to in a well furnished room where a woman was playing Chopin on the piano and a soothing Barbie sat cross-legged on a chair smiling at her. "Well done, my dear," he said. "No one has ever held out as long as you. It's nearly over now . . ."

She was then subjected to the terrors of the baignoire, nearly drowning in the bath of icy water until she felt that she would rather commit suicide than endure another session. Finally she was told she was to be executed and was sent to the condemned cell. A Wehrmacht officer told her: "You are very courageous, Madame, I hope there are many German women who will be as courageous as you."

Lise was saved because she was put into the wrong cell. Instead of being taken out to be shot she joined a train-load of deportees and was sent to Ravensbruck where she survived the war. Her husband Georges died of typhus in Dachau. Her son Jean-Pierre was drowned along with hundreds of other prisoners on the *Cap Arcona*, which was sunk by the British outside Hamburg in 1945, the day before the capture of the city.

Today Lise, now in her eighties, still suffers great pain and discomfort as a result of Barbie's tortures. That she has survived at all is a miracle.

On the afternoon of April 6, following the Izieu raid, the Gestapo, with Klaus Barbie at its head, moved on to the town of St Claude, some thirty miles away. Barbie established his headquarters on the fourth floor of the Hotel de France in the Avenue de Belfort, room 50, where the familiar paraphernalia of interrogation and torture were established.

In St Claude, Barbie was on military detail. He wore SS field uniform and a coal-scuttle helmet. A white scarf of parachute silk was wound round his neck. He had leather gloves, carried a 9mm pistol and was often armed with an American machine pistol as well. As the senior SD officer in the town he had overall command of the Wehrmacht troops, including officers more senior to him, a fact they resented. One of them remembers Barbie's swaggering attitude, and his deliberate failure to salute Wehrmacht officers.

On Easter Sunday, April 9, the Germans ordered all the men in St Claude between the ages of eighteen and forty-five to assemble on the Place du Pré, the main square, before 10 a.m. "Any man found inside a house after 10 a.m. will be shot without trial, including sick men," said the order. The village was sealed by German troops. Every exit was blocked by machine gun emplacements; there was no escape.

The men assembled on the square were confronted by Barbie, members of the Lyon SD, and its French auxiliaries. Accompanied by an NCO, Barbie walked down the lines and arbitrarily selected 307 men for deportation. They were herded into vans and lorries and driven to a nearby girls' school where they remained for the night. One of them who hit out at a German soldier was cut down by a burst of fire from a machine pistol.

The following morning the St Claude hostages were taken by train to Bellegard on the first stage of their terrible journey to the Nazi concentration camps. The Jews were weeded out and taken to Montluc prison, but the bulk of the hostages was sent to Compiègne transit camp north of Paris, from where they were shipped in sealed cattle wagons to Buchenwald.

Pierre Vincent, a twenty-one-year-old pharmacy student, was among them:

> We were packed 100 to 150 men where there was room for only forty. The trip was made under such conditions that several of my comrades died during the journey. They died probably from asphyxia, the only outlets being two small windows latticed with iron bars. The journey lasted four days and three nights and the wagons were not opened once. For food we had a loaf of bread distributed to us when we left, nothing else to eat or drink. Several of our comrades became insane during the journey. Neither the dead nor the insane were removed from the wagons. One man went insane on arriving at Buchenwald and was shot down by the Germans on the platform.

Of the 307 men who were taken that day, just over a hundred returned.

Eugène Delorme, the acting mayor of St Claude and the local Red Cross representative, travelled to Lyon a few days afterwards, seeking information about those who had been arrested. He reported to Barbie himself at the École de Santé and found the Gestapo chief cold and intransigent. Barbie reminded him of the vulnerability of his position by telling him that he had killed another local mayor with his own hand for harbouring members of the Maquis. He refused to respond to Delorme's request to send food and clothes to those imprisoned in Montluc, and added sharply: "I hope it's a good lesson for St Claude."

Barbie was back in the Haut-Jura region on April 11. He presented himself at the headquarters of the local gendarmerie in the village of Bouchoux, and arrested a local man, Jean Vincent, who had been denounced as a Maquis supporter. He told Vincent's wife Marguerite that he was taking her husband to St Claude for questioning. Her last sight of him was as he sat dejected in a Gestapo car in the village square. The Germans had just set fire to a house in Bouchoux and martial law had been imposed on the whole district; Marguerite was not allowed to follow her husband and find out what had happened to him.

As soon as she was permitted to travel, however, she hurried to St Claude where she was directed to Barbie's office in the Hotel de France. "He received me just as he was going to leave, and said mockingly: 'Madame, I lost your husband coming down from Bouchoux.' He then left without another word."

Marguerite's worst fears were confirmed five days later when she was told that some articles of clothing which belonged to her husband had been deposited with the Red Cross. A month later a young shepherd found six crushed skulls and the remains of burnt human bones in the crevice of a rock at Les Fournets. In the ashes was Vincent's steel wedding ring which had survived the flames.

At five o'clock on the afternoon of Vincent's death, April 11, a machine-gun carrier rumbled to a halt outside the Joly restaurant in Martinet, a few kilometres from St Claude. Barbie, with a French collaborator wearing a German uniform, sprang out, barged into the restaurant and held up the proprietor, Madame Cécile Joly, at gun point.

"You have two men in your house," he said sharply. "Where are they?"

Madame Joly's husband showed Barbie and the collaborator upstairs: "A few minutes later I heard a storm of gunfire," Madame Joly said. Rushing upstairs, she found her husband slumped on a chair riddled with bullets. "He had been killed from the front. His forearm which he had raised to his face for protection was pierced by a bullet."

A traitor had been at work – there were indeed two Maquisards in the house; one of them was the area Maquis chief, Commandant Vallin, the other a local man called Colliard-Masson. Barbie arrested them both. Then, as Madame Joly bent over the body of her husband, she caught a glimpse of Colliard-Masson whispering into Barbie's ear. At once Barbie's attitude towards him changed. He smiled and nodded. Madame Joly realised at once that this was the traitor.

"I could not help crying out my contempt for him," she said, "yelling at him: 'Traitor!' and accusing him of selling out his own comrades. 'Why, yes, Madame,' he answered as calm as anything."

Barbie twisted Commandant Vallin's arms behind his back with a blanket and battered his head against a wall, demanding information. He got none. Finally, he ordered the captured Maquis on to a lorry and drove them with his Gestapo escort back to St Claude.

The round-up that day had been one of Barbie's successes. As well as Vallin he had captured Joseph Kemmler, head of the Maquis in Alsace. Kemmler's ordeal was graphically recorded by a German corporal, Alfons Glas, who was in the dining room of the Hotel de France when the prisoners were brought in.

Barbie briefly interrogated the other prisoners, then he turned quickly to Kemmler [said Glas]. He interrogated him in French. Kemmler answered, "Never," whereupon Barbie struck him in the face with his gloved fist. He repeated the questions and struck him again. Kemmler started to bleed from the nose and mouth.

Barbie strolled over to a piano a few steps away and, with his gloved and bloody fingers, played a few bars of the song, "Parlez-moi d'amour".

Then he came back to Kemmler and questioned him anew. When he received no response, other than "Never", Barbie hit Kemmler again. The scene continued for about a quarter of an hour. Meanwhile night had fallen. Kemmler was kept at the hotel while the other prisoners were taken elsewhere.

Kemmler was taken upstairs to a bathroom in the hotel where he was plunged into freezing then scalding water. Still refusing to talk, he was tied up and thrown on to the landing where he lay until morning, when he was brought down once again to the dining room.

The interrogation took place at the rear, in a space which was separated from the rest of the room by a glass partition. Glas now watched through the partition as Kemmler was systematically beaten to death:

In the back of the dining-room was Barbie, two Frenchmen in SS uniforms, and Kemmler who was standing up. Kemmler was struck alternately by each of the Frenchmen with the aid of a rope at the end of which was a weight. He was beaten only on the body, between the shoulders and the thighs, not once on the head.

You could see Barbie asking the questions, but because of the glass partition you could not hear them, nor the replies.

Kemmler received about five blows, then Barbie posed some questions which were followed by more blows. This situation continued for about a quarter of an hour. Then Kemmler collapsed for the first time. The French put him back on his feet and the interrogation continued for more than an hour.

When Kemmler was incapable of standing on his feet, the two Frenchmen dragged him to a chair whose arms kept him from falling off. About ten minutes later Barbie and his French aides left the room.

Kemmler could see everything. His head was still raised, hardly leaning forward. His eyes followed our movements. After about half an hour, his eyelids fluttered, he closed his eyes and his head sunk forward a bit. About five minutes later, a pool of urine formed beneath his chair. It was the indication for me that Kemmler was dead.

Three or four SS men returned to collect Kemmler's body.

"The fact that the SS came back only after his death leads me to conclude that they assumed Kemmler would die as a result of the treatment and had even precisely calculated the moment when death would come," said Glas.

Barbie's operations in the Jura hills lasted for five days. It was a brutal, and ultimately failed expedition, since it achieved no obvious strategic goal. There were 56 executions, 456 arrests, and 126 houses and farms burned.

"Fluidity, rapidity and mobility were my three basic principles", had always been Henri Frenay's view of the best way in which the Maquis should operate. During spring 1944 their hit and run tactics continued to harry the Germans; railway lines were sabotaged, trucks ambushed, and German soldiers assassinated. But as the confidence of the Maquis increased they began, fatally, to abandon the Frenay rule.

On June 6 came word of the Allied landings at Normandy and in the next few days the break-out from the beachheads. It was heady news for the Maquis. Convinced that they were about to receive massive Allied support in the form of airborne troops and mortars for a final battle, they gathered in the kind of large concentrations that Frenay had always argued they should avoid. This meant abandoning their strict guerrilla function and fighting as an army. The place they chose to defend was the Vercors plateau, south-east of Lyon.

To begin with they had some success, inflicting heavy casualties on German troops. Their confidence improved as more arms were dropped and volunteers poured into the area; a "République du Vercors" was set up; the approach roads were mined and direct wireless links set up with Algiers and London. But there was still no sign of the expected Allied troops.

On July 14, Bastille day, the Tricolor flew from masts in every village of the Vercors, and at noon, to crown the celebrations, American planes appeared overhead to drop parachutes of red, white and blue with containers of arms. Victory seemed just around the corner.

In fact it was the beginning of the end for the Vercors. The day after Bastille day German bombers attacked the "République" with incendiary bombs; two German divisions surrounded the plateau, and on July 21 they moved in. The massacre that followed will never be forgotten. The SS men killed indiscriminately, inflicting terrible reprisals on the villagers who had supported the Maquis. Then the Wehrmacht took over with ruthless efficiency, crushing the Maquis forces and driving the survivors far up into the fir-clad summits. By the end of the action about five hundred Maquis fighters had been killed along with two hundred civilians.

In Lyon the Allied landings had prompted reprisals of a different nature. On June 12 Klaus Barbie ordered the first of a series of executions at Montluc. That afternoon Roger Bossé, a Resistance colleague of René Hardy, who had already been tortured in the baignoire on Barbie's orders, was ordered out of his cell, along with twenty-three other prisoners. To shouts of "Schnell, schnell!" and "Sans bagages!" they were herded out into the courtyard, handcuffed together and ordered into two waiting army lorries which then drove out of the prison gates followed by two cars full of Barbie's Gestapo men.

The convoy sped through Lyon; Bossé remembers seeing the crowded café terraces in the Place Bellecour, and the rays of late afternoon sunshine dancing on the placid waters of the Saône. But in the backs of the lorries there was despair. "We've had it," murmured one of Bossé's neighbours.

Finally the lorries shuddered to a halt. Bossé saw a country path running between a field of stubble and a large meadow. Then he was kicked and shoved out of the lorry with eight companions. Outside, the two *traction-avants* cars had drawn up next to the lorries, and the Gestapo, machine pistols in hand, were shouting and waving. The small group of prisoners stumbled up the path, driven on by blows from rifle butts. One man, who bent to pick a buttercup, was clubbed to the ground by an enraged Gestapo guard.

Bossé remembers that the air was deathly still. No one uttered a word. Then a Gestapo officer bringing up the rear, ran at the double to the front of the column and shouted in French: "Lie down! On your stomachs! On the ground!" Wearily, almost apathetically, the prisoners found themselves obeying, without a murmur of complaint.

Bossé's head rested on his left arm. He looked for the last time at the grass and the sky. Death, he knew, was only moments away, but he says he was filled with "un élan formidable, positif". It gave him an overpowering desire to live. The Gestapo stood in a line behind. Bossé heard boots crunch on the gravel, and then gunfire erupted all around him. He felt a heavy blow on the back, and then another in the shoulder.

There was a silence, broken only by the groans of his companions and some short bursts of gunfire. He heard jackboots approaching as a man advanced to deliver the coup de grâce. Bossé smelt the sickly scent of blood, his own and that of his comrades. The faces of his close friends from Montluc swam before his eyes.

A bullet hit him, but it was only a small shock. Only later did he realise that it had passed first through the head of his best friend, Jacques, who had been lying alongside him. Then Bossé's own head exploded with a noise like thunder and his mouth filled with his own blood. But through the pain, almost immediately, he realised he could still see. His eyes made out the grass and the woods; the German who had administered the coup de grâce was no longer visible. Bossé heard the tramp of boots fading into the distance, more shooting as the remaining prisoners were massacred, then the sound of engines starting up, and the shouts and chanting of the German troops as they drove away. He had survived.

Barbie was now reaching the last and most terrible phase of his tour of duty in Lyon. The strange contradictions in his character – his abrupt changes of mood and their unpredictability – were still there, but now he showed no pity; at least, no witnesses have yet come forward to suggest otherwise. Some remember him being gentle, or silkily polite, flirting or teasing, indulging in bouts of heartiness and jocularity. But these moods could easily be the prelude to something sinister – a particularly vicious bout of torture, or a black rage in the course of which a man could be killed instantly. Appeals for mercy aroused in him little but irritation. If he saved a life he did it for some unfathomably quirky reason, dispatching a man back to his cell because he liked the way he stood up to torture, or because he was bored by his failure to talk. But these could just as easily be reasons for killing him.

Barbie appears to fit without difficulty into the standard profile of the SS henchman – those described by the historian Martin Broszat as "men obsessed with a sense of duty, faithful servants of the powers that be . . . brought up in a spirit of soulless conformity . . . incapable of criticism and devoid of imagination".

Rudolf Höss, the commandant of Auschwitz, explaining how he was able to supervise mass killings without compunction, said: "I had no second thoughts at the time . . . a long-standing National Socialist could have no second thoughts, still less an SS officer. 'Führer befiehl, wir folgen' [Führer, command – we follow] was for us no empty phrase, no mere slogan. We took it with deadly seriousness."

But Höss was a Nazi puritan. Barbie was a sadist. He enjoyed inflicting pain, and he liked to inspire fear and to watch its effect on his victims. Mario Blandon, who worked for the Maquis leader Albert Chambonnet, and was tortured by Barbie in June 1944, remembers him showing off by deliberately shooting a prisoner in cold blood as he pushed him in front of him down the stairs at the École de Santé, watched by the other prisoners. "The head split apart while the man somersaulted to the bottom of the stairs like a rabbit," said Blandon, himself a trained Resistance killer. "To get that effect, you need to be exactly three steps behind. Barbie just laughed . . ."

On operations in the Jura, Barbie shot prisoners without remorse and in an apparently arbitrary manner. One such execution was witnessed by Georges Delaye, an electricity board employee. "The whole scene lasted a few seconds," he recalled. "Then the German officer ordered a snack to be brought to him which he munched away heartily while continuing to come and go."

But it was not these isolated acts which earned Barbie the title, Butcher of Lyon. The worst was yet to come.

Werner Knab, Barbie's commanding officer, was determined that the war of attrition being waged by the Wehrmacht in the countryside would be matched by SS reprisals in Lyon itself, to demonstrate that, despite Allied advances in the north, the German hold in the south was still secure.

On the night of July 26, a bomb planted by the Resistance blew up in the Moulin-à-Vent restaurant in the Place Bellecour. Three packages of high explosives had been placed on a shelf of telephone directories on the first floor of the premises, and they were clearly intended to kill as many as possible of the senior Wehrmacht and Gestapo officers who regularly dined there. The restaurant was one of Barbie's own favourite eating places, across the Place Bellecour from his new headquarters. Just conceivably, the bombs had been intended for him. As it was, they did not go off until 11.45 in the evening, after the Moulin had closed. There was considerable damage, but no German casualties.

The next morning Barbie sent his Gestapo officers to Montluc and selected five hostages from among the prisoners. One of them was Albert Chambonnet, the Maquis leader known as "Didier", who was forty-one that day; another was Léon Pfeiffer, an engraver, who was twenty-one and had been arrested for being in possession of a machine-gun clip.

Barbie had tortured Pfeiffer on discovering that he was a Jew, and had beaten him fiercely just the day before, adding the grotesque refinement of twisting a leather belt around his neck and hoisting him from the ground so he could beat his suspended body. A fellow prisoner who sought hospital treatment for Pfeiffer afterwards was told: "It's not worth it. There's nothing Pfeiffer is going to need any more."

At 11.30 in the morning of July 27, the Gestapo took Pfeiffer, Chambonnet and the three others to the street outside the Moulin-à-Vent. The Place Bellecour was full of people as a squad of German soldiers roped off the road and the pavement immediately in front of the restaurant. One of the Germans leant nonchalantly against a tree, cradling a sub-machine gun in his arms. A curious crowd gathered.

One by one the prisoners were pushed out of the grey Citroen *traction-avant* in front of the crowd, and as each one stumbled from the car on to the pavement he was shot through the head by an SS soldier. One of the prisoners, badly wounded but not yet dead, writhed on the ground in pain, but when a Red Cross nurse with others in the crowd tried to go to his aid, the SS forced them back. Finally the soldiers withdrew, leaving the French police with orders that the bodies were to be left in the hot afternoon sun for the next three hours as an example to the population. The orders were carried out scrupulously.

The next day Lyon newspapers were obliged to carry a report of the atrocity under the headline, "Rapid Punishment for an Attack".

It said that a swift operation had enabled the arrest of "five people who belonged to the terrorist group responsible for the attack. They were executed in the place of their crime, the same morning after the explosion."

For many among the people of Lyon, it was the first time they had been openly confronted by Nazi savagery, and they reacted with horror. Cardinal Gerlier went in person to Gestapo headquarters to deliver a written note of protest. But he was received with disdain by Werner Knab.

"It was a very stormy audience," said Monsignor Maury who accompanied the cardinal. "Colonel Knab pounded the table, upturning his chair. I wondered if we would leave alive." Eventually Gerlier was ejected from Knab's office, and his protest dismissed. He would be back with a far graver complaint less than a month later.

Just before dawn on August 15 American and French warships, ploughing through the Mediterranean towards the Riviera, turned their guns on the southern coast of France as bombers dived over German positions around Toulon and Marseille. The first Allied assault was launched mainly by American troops, but diplomacy dictated that they were led up the beaches by a small detachment of French commandos, who thus had the honour of being the first to land on the shores of Provence.

Two days later, on August 17, the US Navy Secretary James Forrestal was toasting Admiral Jean Lemonnier, French flag officer of the fleet, in the main square of St Raphael. That day in Lyon the Germans took fifty prisoners from the *baraque* that housed the Jews in Montluc and loaded them on to lorries.

The last of the cattle wagon trains had left for the east six days earlier. From now on, no more Jews would be deported, and in almost every other German-held town in France that meant the end of the persecution. But not in Lyon. Here, under the inflexible regime of Knab and his Gestapo chief Barbie, the "cleansing" would continue to the very end.

The Jewish prisoners that day were driven to the airfield of Bron in the suburbs of Lyon which had been seriously damaged by RAF bombing raids two days earlier, and put to work filling in the bomb craters on the runway. Otto Huber, a local cinema attendant, who was brought to Bron by the Germans to work as an interpreter alongside the work party, saw what happened next.

Towards noon [he says] one of the prisoners escaped. The German adjutant said that if the man was not found, his comrades would be shot. The Germans looked for the man, but in vain. At the end of work that evening the prisoners were getting back in the lorry that would take them back to Montluc when a major arrived and ordered the prisoners to be taken out of the lorry to another work site where nobody had yet worked.

That was the last Huber saw of them. Next morning he asked the German adjutant in charge of the party if the prisoners had worked late the evening before. The adjutant replied that it was none of his business. A few minutes later, the work detail from Montluc arrived, and Huber was surprised to see that there were only twenty-three of them – none were from the previous day's group.

The twenty-three prisoners were set to work. As they filled in the cratered runway, Huber noticed that one of them was injured. He told the adjutant that the man was unfit to work, at which the German turned to him, smiled, and said: "By this evening he will be feeling no more pain . . . do you understand now where the others are?"

At six that evening the adjutant asked for twenty soldiers to volunteer to accompany the prisoners. Huber says the soldiers stepped forward "eagerly", laughing and joking about going to "make music".

The prisoners were loaded on to a lorry with kicks and rifle blows, and driven off in the same direction as the previous group. A second lorry with German troops in it followed. Next day Huber returned to the airfield and, at around nine o'clock, was ordered to help bring a lorry-load of earth to a bomb crater in the area where the prisoners had been taken the previous evening. The lorry reversed, and the earth was tipped into the crater. Although Huber did not dare look in, he was certain that it contained the bodies of the twenty-three prisoners.

The following Monday, August 21, more prisoners were massacred at Bron, this time by members of the Milice. The craters were not discovered and excavated until after the liberation of Lyon in September, when 109 decomposing bodies, including one of a woman, were found in five craters around the airfield. Autopsies showed that they had been shot at close range.

There were now no more Jewish prisoners at Montluc. But there were still some eight hundred Resistance inmates housed in the main block and the two adjoining buildings. With German forces falling back in the face of a steady American advance from the south, the extermination continued. Even as the Jews were being killed, Resistance prisoners were picked out to be massacred. At 5 a.m, on Sunday, August 20, thirty-five members of the Lyon Gestapo with French auxiliaries in attendance assembled at Gestapo headquarters on the Place Bellecour. One of them was a French collaborator named Max Payot, who told a French war crimes tribunal after the war the story of that day's events.

A senior Gestapo officer approached him, rubbing his hands together, and said: "Aujourd'hui, belle affaire." At first Payot thought it was to be a police operation, but when they left in convoy for Montluc – "I understood it was a question of one or more executions."

At Montluc the Gestapo assembled in the courtyard 120 prisoners, including six or eight women, ordered them to face the wall, and bound their wrists behind their backs with rope. Then they loaded them in twos and threes on to two buses, one painted yellow, the other belonging to the Gendarmerie Nationale. The buses left the prison and sped through the town accompanied by six Citroens full of Gestapo men in civilian clothes. At 8.30 a.m. the convoy stopped at the Fort de Côte-Lorette, a disused building overlooking the town of St-Genis-Laval, south-west of Lyon.

Payot says:

The two buses entered the enclosure where there was an abandoned house which the Germans explored. Once this was done, the prisoners were taken out two by two from the buses and led to the first floor of the house where they were executed summarily with two bullets from a sub-machine gun – usually in the neck.

At first, Payot says, he stood guard at the corner of the house, but the Germans thought he was being squeamish, and brought him inside to the kitchen, from where he had to accompany the prisoners to the first floor.

At this point the prisoners were forced to climb on top of the heap formed by the mass of bodies of their own companions. Blood ran in torrents through the ceiling and I could distinctly hear the victims falling as they were executed.

The killing continued on the ground floor where around half the victims were in the same room in a pile of corpses about one metre fifty high. Sometimes the Germans were obliged to climb on the bodies of their victims to finish off those who were still quivering.

The bodies were soaked in petrol and set on fire; the Germans brought along phosphorus bombs to activate the combustion, as well as explosives.

During the fire we found, at the south side of the house, one of the victims who had been accidentally spared. She stood up at the window and beseeched mercy of her executioners. They responded with a hail of shots in her direction. At that moment, riddled with bullets and under the effect of the heat, her face set in a horrible vision. The temperature rising, her face melted like wax.

I also learned that two of the victims had jumped out of the window of the same room on the north side and were shot on the ground. Two of the butchers took the bodies and threw them into the furnace on the ground floor.

With the killing over, most of the Germans and French found their clothes drenched with blood and spattered with the brains of the dead. They returned in convoy to Lyon, leaving behind some Wehrmacht soldiers to dynamite the remains of the house.

The shooting of the prisoners took about ninety minutes, but it was only when fourteen huge explosions rocked the neighbourhood as the Germans dynamited the house, and human bones fell in gardens three hundred yards away, that the residents of St-Genis-Laval realised that something appalling had occurred. Empty bottles found on the massacre site afterwards suggested that the soldiers had toasted the successful conclusion of their butchery with champagne.

Evidence that Klaus Barbie ordered the massacre of St-Genis-Laval was assembled by French war crimes investigators after the liberation. Corroboration of his involvement comes from a number of sources including Barbie's French aides, among whom was a Corsican named Jean Baptiste Seta, who saw Barbie, Erich Bartelmus, and other Gestapo officers in the courtyard of Montluc as the prisoners were assembled and marched off for execution. Barbie was in command and issuing the orders of the day. Seta later heard Wehrmacht soldiers describing the operation in detail.

On August 24 Cardinal Gerlier went to Gestapo headquarters to deliver a letter of protest about the killings at St-Genis-Laval. He had been to the site itself, and his letter reflected his anger.

I am sixty-four years old, Monsieur le Commandeur [he wrote to Knab]. I fought in the war of 1914 and have seen in the course of my life many horrible sights, but I have never seen any which so revolted me as that which I witnessed only a short time ago ... I do not hesitate to declare to those who are responsible for this that they are forever dishonoured in the eyes of humanity.

At the same time, the Maquis, who held more than seven hundred German hostages, applied their own pressure by threatening to kill their prisoners if the massacres continued. At least eighty German soldiers were shot when the news of St-Genis-Laval came through.

The Wehrmacht seems to have refused to cooperate in any more massacres as they pulled back around Lyon; throughout the city the German army was in retreat, and by that evening the liberation of Montluc was at hand. At 9.30 p.m. on August 24, the commandant of the prison abandoned the building, handing over the keys to a Resistance envoy.

The prisoners assembled in the courtyard and joined in singing the Marseillaise. Next day, after being fed and washed, they went to say a mass of thanksgiving in a nearby monastery, with Cardinal Gerlier taking the service. The ordeal of Montluc was over.

The only detailed account we have of Barbie's last days in Lyon, and his escape back to Germany, come from his own mouth, and must therefore be treated with caution. According to his own "memoirs", he was assigned the task of capturing the commander of the Free French army, General Henri Giraud, who was approaching Lyon from the south-west. Barbie says that he and his men were ambushed on the road to Lyon on August 28 and he was wounded in the left foot and leg as well as his face and side.

German documents captured by the French after the war suggest that Barbie left Lyon earlier – on August 23, heading for Dijon. According to these scant records, he appears to have turned back early next morning, perhaps to join up with SS units who were fighting a rearguard action in the streets of Lyon; he was then caught in cross-fire and wounded on the evening of August 24 at Limonest, five miles north of Lyon. But the documents supply no back-up evidence, and the references are too brief to rely on.

Talking casually after the war to one of his American intelligence "controls", Barbie said that, some days after leaving Lyon, he returned with his men to "clean up the mess". By this he presumably meant to eliminate witnesses who would be able to give evidence later about the Gestapo's crimes.

As we have seen, at least one group of Frenchmen was gunned down by Barbie himself: Barbie revealed to Andrée Rivez during his bragging conversation with her in 1947 that he shot them personally after his men refused to carry out his orders. That killing most probably took place during the final return visit to Lyon. And perhaps it was then that he received his wounds. By the time Lyon finally fell to the Americans on September 3 Barbie had left, in no condition for fighting.

He was sent first to St Peter's Hospital in the Black Forest, then to Halberstadt, north-west of Leipzig, to recuperate. He was also promoted from lieutenant to captain, his citation proclaiming that "he has a definite talent for intelligence work and for the pursuit of crime".

CHAPTER SIX

Selection of a Henchman

On February 17 1945 Hauptsturmführer Klaus Barbie hobbled out of the gate of the military hospital at Halberstadt. He was by normal standards in no condition to fight. His mangled foot hurt intensely; the wounds in his face and side were hardly healed. But there were no normal standards any more.

The German cities were in ruins. Three days before, British and American bombers had obliterated Dresden. In the west, Allied troops had crossed the German border, their advance held back only by decimated armies whose generals knew they would collapse under the next onslaught. In the east, 170 Soviet divisions now stood almost on the Oder river, their leading tanks only forty miles from Berlin.

Barbie had orders to join the battle at Baranów on the Vistula, but the Russians had long since broken through there. Seeking new instructions, he made his way to Berlin and spent a few days trying to get some sense out of the Reichssicherheitshauptamt between air raids. All they could think of was to send him back to his old pre-war post with the SD at Düsseldorf. When he got there, the office had been evacuated to Essen, and when he reached Essen, he found that it had dissolved itself.

On April Fool's day 1945, Barbie joined up on his own initiative with the regular troops defending the Ruhr. But the Anglo-American offensive had resumed in March, and within a fortnight American tanks were grinding into what was left of Düsseldorf and Dortmund. Barbie and the rabble of soldiers about him realised they were surrounded; they buried their weapons, begged or stole civilian clothes and tried to melt into the landscape. Rounded up in the chaos by the Americans, Barbie managed to persuade them that he was a French "displaced person"; he was allowed to take a confiscated bicycle, and pedalled unsteadily off, his feet throbbing at every tread, to seek his family.

Kurt Merk had also reached Germany intact. He had been posted to a mobile intelligence unit with the 19th army in France. Knowing that his beloved Andrée faced almost certain death as a collaborator if she stayed in France, he had smuggled her with her mother across into Germany (where they narrowly escaped death in the bombing of Freiburg). The retreating army soon followed them into south Germany. On April 30 Hitler committed suicide in the Berlin bunker. On May 8 Germany surrendered. Eight days later, Merk was rounded up in Bavaria by the Americans. There he was variously and quite wrongly registered as an "SS officer" and a senior policeman. He was turned loose in August.

Merk joined Andrée and her mother at Oberstaufen in the Bavarian mountains. But on January 19 1946 he was picked up again. The American military censors had opened a letter to Merk from an old associate in the Abwehr at Dijon which revealed in a childishly transparent code that he was trying to make contact with other scattered survivors of the Dijon bureau. The censors noted "vague references to names and places, possibly concerning an underground movement". Merk was arrested at Oberstaufen by an agent of the US Counter Intelligence Corps (CIC) named Robert Taylor, and taken to the local prison for interrogation.

Once again, Merk's talent for inspiring trust brought him luck. Between the stout red-cheeked Bavarian with his small blond moustache and the imaginative young American who dreamed of becoming a writer, a deep chord was struck.

Taylor soon realised that Merk was not part of any dangerous Nazi conspiracy against the Allied forces of the occupation. He arranged for his release and then hired him as a CIC informant.

It was March 1946. Delighted to be back at his old profession, Merk settled down to the job of seeking out old wartime intelligence contacts and rapidly built up a network which spilled over the borders of the American occupation zone beyond the collapsed Reich and into foreign states to the east and west. Merk hired men with shady pasts and others with clean records; all that counted for him was professionalism. And a year later, on March 28 1947, Merk was standing on a station platform at Memmingen waiting for a contact when he saw a squat, shabby but all too familiar figure coming towards him. Klaus Barbie, on the run from the British, the French and the Americans, had heard that Kurt Merk was working for the CIC. He begged to be taken on board. And Merk, who had never liked Barbie but – typically – respected his gift for police work, agreed. The Memmingen CIC agreed too. In April 1947 the man whose name had been a by-word in Lyon for savagery and sadism began work as a paid employee of US intelligence.

Barbie's rescue was part of the growing Allied readiness to exploit the skills and knowledge of ex-SS officers and overlook what crimes they might have committed in the past. Although the Cold War encouraged this trend, the problem was far from new. Well before the war had ended, senior Nazis – including men from both the SS and SD – began to make approaches to Allied intelligence agencies, seeking to save their own necks and perhaps win a life of some comfort by selling the only commodity they had to bargain with: information.

These officers put the Allied military and political leaders in an ugly dilemma. Their wartime priorities were plain enough: the defeat of Nazi Germany and the prevention of a Nazi revival after that defeat. To make immunity deals with Nazis in possession of secret information might well advance both these aims. On the other hand, such deals were going to outrage public opinion throughout the world if they became known. In November 1943 Britain, the United States and the Soviet Union had announced that they would "pursue [war criminals] to the uttermost ends of the earth", and the Allies were committed to an ambitious (but hopelessly under-resourced) programme of arresting the guilty and purging German society of Nazi leadership at every level.

With the defeat of Germany the dilemma grew rapidly less painful, as the West became increasingly preoccupied with the threat presented by the Soviet Union. Nazi intelligence possessed priceless military and political information on the Soviet Union itself. Beyond that, the Gestapo and SD, especially, had spent years pursuing, identifying and suppressing Communist influence within Germany.

Faced with the almost inconceivable chaos left by the collapse of the Reich, the Allies were aware of their own limitations. The country was devastated; the economy had almost totally ceased to function. Millions of human beings were on the move: hordes of wandering soldiers, prisoners, and forced labourers pouring out of camps and hostels; the entire population of the eastern provinces acquired by Poland trekking westwards, the flood of Germans trying to escape from the Soviet occupation zone into regions controlled by the Americans or British. Without German collaboration, the control and policing of this wasteland – let alone its reconstruction – were unthinkable.

Entering Germany behind the fighting troops, Allied intelligence saw its job as a double one: the detection and smashing of any Nazi resistance movement, and the pursuit of Nazis and Nazi organisations classified as "guilty". It was assumed that there would be fanatical partisan war, especially from armed Hitler Youth guerrillas, long after Germany was occupied. The British and

Americans already had files full of information about the Werwolf movement, the subject of much desperate propaganda from Dr Goebbels in the last year of the war. Young Germans were to be given arms as the enemy approached and instructed to resurface behind the lines to murder Allied soldiers, blow up vehicles, and melt away again into the forests. Allied intelligence also took seriously the idea that large groups of SS and Nazi activists might organise passive resistance and sabotage, perhaps building up to an attempt to seize power again.

Few of these perils materialised. Here and there, a few Werwolf boys set off into the hills with bazookas and grenades. Most of them gave up within days, hungry and discouraged. The German people, totally exhausted by war and politics, thought only of survival: a kilo of potatoes or a piece of canvas to cover a shell-hole in the roof mattered more than dreams of a Fourth Reich. None the less, for the first two years after the surrender, Allied intelligence was still mainly concerned with seeking out war criminals (with very inadequate results) and with watching groups of SS and Nazi veterans suspected of preparing some form of clandestine organisation. As the Cold War began, however, and especially after the start of the Berlin blockade in 1948, the balance of emphasis steadily shifted towards the surveillance and suppression of Communism and the acquisition of intelligence on the Soviet Union and its satellites. At the outset, Allied intelligence agencies would hardly contemplate employing a German who was not prepared to denounce his own ex-comrades. By 1947, when Barbie was hired, this was no longer a crucial qualification and hired anti-Communist enthusiasm could compensate for many sins of the past.

Many senior Nazi intelligence men bought immunity and sometimes a new career in this way. Wilhelm Höttl, deputy head of the RSHA foreign intelligence department, offered his agents to the Americans and worked as an informant for the Counter Intelligence Corps in Austria. General Reinhard Gehlen, head of military intelligence on the eastern front, also turned over his files to the United States. American intelligence rebuilt the Gehlen organisation in an operation so secret that for the first years after the war, even the CIC were not informed about it; in 1949 Gehlen's team became the official espionage and counter-espionage service of the new West German state, under close CIA supervision.

Otto Skorzeny, the buccaneering SS officer who had rescued Mussolini from under the noses of the Allies, won immunity by denouncing his own comrades in American internment camps, and eventually settled in Franco's Spain. General Karl Wolff, one of the most senior SS officers to survive the war, won lenient treatment by surrendering the German forces in Italy without Hitler's permission. Friedrich Schwend, later to become a crucial figure in Barbie's life, was allowed to emigrate to South America after telling the Americans some of the truth about the SS treasure hoards.

All of these men had something to bargain with. But none of these enticing forms of collaboration seemed open to Klaus Barbie in 1945, pedalling slowly along country roads in search of a barn to sleep in. His only concern was to avoid identification and arrest. And although Barbie had been only a junior SD officer without access to major secrets, he had already been marked down as a man to be arrested. News about him had filtered back from Lyon to London during the war, and from there to Washington.

An index card on Barbie, apparently drawn up by SHAEF (Allied High Command) before the war ended, described him as "long a member of the SD ... a dangerous conspirator". Some other SHAEF cards, no longer available but quoted in a 1951 CIC document, describe Barbie's "brutal character hidden under a jovial exterior ... very cruel; shot French agents when they became useless"; these cards, too, seem to date from 1944 or even earlier.

In the spring of 1945 SHAEF began to compile a central register of suspected war criminals wanted by all the Allied nations. This master list, known as CROWCASS (Central Registry of War Criminals and Security Suspects) carried the name "Barbier" in its first edition of July 1945. The French had listed "Barbier" under two numerical codes, meaning that he was wanted for the murder of civilians and also for the torture of military personnel. The CROWCASS list for March 1947 contained the full and correctly spelled name of Klaus Barbie, mentioning that he was wanted by France for murder. A list published in London as early as 1945 by the War Crimes Commission also included Klaus Barbie as a war criminal.

Luckily for Barbie, the Allies had provided totally inadequate means to carry out their plan of bringing the guilty to justice. CROWCASS for a long time had no proper office or filing equipment and soon became a by-word for inaccuracy. Allied officers and civilians attempting to administer Germany also came to resent the "witch-hunt", seeing it as a further source of disorder. They were rapidly growing dependent on former Nazis to run local bureaucracies and police forces; the Allies might have preferred to use non-Communist "anti-Nazi democrats", but there were few of them – and fewer still with practical experience of anything but exile and imprisonment. Identifying wanted individuals among thousands of haggard, unshaven war prisoners was next to impossible, especially for junior Allied field intelligence staff who often spoke no German. And, as the months passed, the hunted men themselves began to devise their own ways of concealing their identities and keeping each other out of trouble.

It was into that underworld of men on the run, of conspiracies for survival, that Klaus Barbie was now drawn. But he had found his family again. Regine had left Trier in 1944, with her two-year-old daughter Ute and Ute's grandmother, Anna Barbie, when the town came under shelling from American tanks. They had ended up in Kassel, north-east of Frankfurt, where Barbie rejoined them; the town had been crushed to rubble by a single British air raid in October 1943, but they were able to find a lodging in the countryside nearby.

"My travels never seemed to end," Barbie recalled years later. "I had no job, and had to keep constantly on the move." He dared not spend much time with his wife and child, and in those first weeks did odd jobs in the fields or cleaning cowsheds. All ex-members of the SS, Waffen-SS, and SD were then in the "automatic arrest" category; he knew he would have to live by his wits to stay free, and by June 1945 – only a month after the surrender – he was in touch with a young man named Schneider and learning the art of forging identity papers. He was soon in touch with other clandestine groups of SS men and Nazi officials throughout the western occupation zones.

Much has been made of these groups – more than they deserve. At the time, and for years to come, the Allied intelligence services regarded these contact networks (some restricted to one city, some based on membership of a particular SS or army unit) as the germs of an aggressive Nazi revival. More recently they have been inflated into a whole genre of thriller literature about ODESSA, supposedly a world-wide underground league of old Nazis financed from South America with Nazi gold, which arranged the escape of Third Reich villains from Martin Bormann downwards and, with the secret assistance of the Vatican, smuggled them out of Europe to safety.

There is no doubt that something called ODESSA did exist. The CIC files for Germany covering the years 1946 and 1947 are full of queries about the association, whose initials stood for Organization der ehemaligen SS-Angehöriger (organisation of ex-SS members). But American and British investigations led again and again to disappointing results. Although the notorious Otto Skorzeny was often mentioned in connection with it, no evidence was ever found that ODESSA was anything like a single coherent network. The

CIC archives suggest instead that the numerous little groups of old SS comrades which sprang up often used the term, with its hint of remoteness and mystery, to lend themselves more importance than they possessed.

The real purpose of these groups was not to found a "neo-Nazi international", but to help their members to stay alive and evade arrest. They forged identity papers, without which nobody could hold a ration card, organised safe houses to hide fugitives, operated energetically on the black market, and occasionally and on a modest scale, helped their members to cross frontiers illegally. Certainly many prominent Nazis did escape down "underground railways" leading, usually through monasteries in Italy, to South America and the Middle East. But it does not seem that these routes were established by any post-war SS conspiracy; Nazi fugitives usually relied either on German or Austrian priests with violently nationalist sympathies, or used routes set up by others for their own purposes.

Between 1945 and 1948 nothing resembling a unified Nazi underground structure arose out of these scattered groups. They were certainly capable of building castles in the air; as Barbie was to find, some of their leaders still dreamed of that "natural" deal with the British and Americans which would restore an armed but sanitised National Socialist Germany as a partner in an anti-Russian crusade. But in the political context of those years, this was total fantasy.

In August 1945 Barbie and an ex-SS officer named Otto Ilgenfritz climbed out of a slow, overcrowded train and stared around them at the haunting landscape of rubble which had once been the port of Hamburg. Broad streets had been reduced to paths winding through mounds of collapsed ruins; block after block, gutted by the firestorm of the British air raids two years before, gaped roofless and windowless. The river Elbe was still choked with half-sunken shipping, masts rising crookedly out of the water. And yet in this devastation, human beings were swarming and struggling for food and shelter; queues formed as the first British-licensed newspapers went on sale, not because anyone wanted to read, but because this was the only source of paper in Hamburg.

On the doorways of burned-out apartments people had chalked up their new addresses. After a search Ilgenfritz was able to find a girl called Ellen Kühn who had been his secretary in those distant, luxurious days when he had worked in the Sipo/SD headquarters in Paris. The three talked and exchanged news about where other old comrades were to be found, about the trick of staying afloat in this post-war world. Barbie's circle began to extend; the next month he met two more young SS officers, Wolfgang Gustmann and Kurt Barkhausen, in the Kassel area near his home and teamed up with them to operate on the black market.

That winter, for reasons which are unknown, Barbie was arrested by the Americans and given a fourteen-day prison sentence at Darmstadt, just south of Frankfurt. But his captors failed to identify him and he was released. In January 1946 he enrolled as a student of law at the University of Marburg under the alias of "Becker".

Barbie remained an unrepentant Nazi who would never consider serving the Bolshevik arch-enemy. But in February that year he was invited to do so: in Hamburg he was introduced to an ex-colonel in the Abwehr who called himself Alexander Winter. Barbie met Winter and his friends in a bar; they were cheerfully drunk and boasted that they were selling information simultaneously to the British and the Russians – with a preference for the Russians. With uproarious toasts of "Heil Moscow", they invited Barbie to join them. But he found them an unimpressive lot and thought Winter a suspicious character; he left without committing himself.

Back in Kassel he still faced the problem of how to stay alive and feed his family. On April 18 1946 three men in raincoats turned up at the home of Baroness von Forstner in Kassel, and announced that they were from the criminal police; the baroness, they said, was suspected of illegal trafficking in diamonds, and must bring all her jewellery and valuables round to the police station. Protesting her innocence, the baroness collected her jewels, family medals and antique watches and gave them to the senior detective to hold, a rather squat man with a limp, while she looked for her identity card. When she returned the three "policemen" – who were Barbie, Gustmann and Barkhausen – had vanished.

Barbie's two accomplices eventually faced trial for the robbery in 1950; they were found guilty but released under an amnesty. Barbie was never brought to justice for the Kassel theft, although a warrant was issued for his arrest. But the baroness got back some at least of her jewels. They were handed to the German police late in 1950, not by Barbie himself, but by the US authorities in Stuttgart. By that time the Americans were Barbie's employers, and they wanted no trouble.

Barbie was now travelling about western Germany peddling forged papers, black market coffee and cigarettes. He was increasingly a "man to know", and he soon made contact with a variety of other groups of SS and SD veterans on the run. The circle of old comrades was growing fast.

Among them was a former German intelligence agent called Dr Emil Hoffmann. Although Barbie was quite unaware of it at the time, Hoffmann was working for British intelligence, and, as CIC archives noted, feeding his masters with information about SS fugitives. It was probably through Hoffmann that both British and American security services became aware of the circle to which Barbie belonged. The British code-named the group "Red Lilac".

Such operations in the American zone were handled by the CIC's 970th Detachment, whose task was, first, to "protect the US occupation against sabotage, espionage, disaffection, subversion and other acts", and, as secondary missions, to find and arrest war criminals, screen applicants for emigration, and speed up the secret programme for seizing important German scientists.

Divided into seven regions, the CIC was amazingly independent, answerable only to its own headquarters in Stuttgart. Its problem in those years was staffing; the heroic days when the CIC employed men like Henry Kissinger and the future novelist J. D. Salinger were over, and most of the talented and experienced agents recruited in wartime had been released. As the Cold War developed, the CIC in Germany was assigned more demanding tasks: the pursuit of war criminals was dropped, and the corps was required to carry out counter-espionage against Soviet and Czech agents.

But the CIC men of the late 1940s in Germany were often novices; there were a sprinkling of field agents who had emigrated to America from Germany before the war, but many of the others, especially in positions of command, spoke little or no German and were politically naive. Lack of experience, coupled with casual and erratic office procedure, made the 970th Detachment decidedly accident-prone.

It was the CIC which now infiltrated another informer, known by the cover-name of "Mouse", into the Red Lilac group. As often happens with agents on lone missions, "Mouse" embroidered the truth vigorously in order to inflate his own achievements: the CIC were soon hearing about an underground radio network, about "factories" in Munich, Dortmund, and possibly Kassel for producing false papers, about deliveries of cash and jewels from the Soviet zone authorities, and about an arms cache in an air raid shelter near Hamburg. (There is no evidence in CIC files that any of these things were later found, or, indeed, ever existed.)

The Red Lilac affair, with an American informer operating in the British zone, illustrates the ambiguous relationship between Allied intelligence services. In the main, the British and Americans cooperated and shared information. But at the same time there was surreptitious competition; the CIC was always suspicious that the British might be "turning" their own agents and informants, and both services paid for secret information about each other's activities, employees and techniques.

They were united, however, in mistrusting French intelligence. The British and Americans spied systematically on the military administration of the French zone. The reason was simple: they were convinced that French military intelligence was dominated by the Communist party and should be treated as a mere extension of the Soviet espionage system.

What the Red Lilac affair illustrated was not just the mutual suspicion that existed among the Allies, but the readiness of these so-called "fanatical Nazis" to sell each other out. As CIC papers reveal, Dr Emil Hoffmann, the Nazi-turned-British agent, was one example. Another was a young woman whom Barbie certainly regarded as a friend and one of the network, until one day in Marburg in late August 1946 he saw her sitting in an American CIC jeep and pointing at him. The Americans pulled him into the jeep, which set off down the street; at a corner, Barbie managed to jump out and run for it. One of the Americans banged off a few pistol shots, but he escaped.

Three months later Barbie and two friends were in Hamburg. Barbie told the CIC some years later that they had gone there to acquire fresh identity papers and to sell some (probably stolen) watches. More recently, however, he told an interviewer that he had also been looking for a doctor who could scrape out the tell-tale SS blood-group tattoo under his arm.

It was while he was in Hamburg that Barbie came across a former SD man and Waffen-SS cadet named Acker who said he was impatient to talk to him. They met in a café on the Gänsemarkt a few hours before Barbie and his two companions were due to catch a train to Hanover. Acker, Barbie found to his distaste, was a boastful type who dropped the names of mutual SD acquaintances and claimed to have blown up a French military headquarters near Stuttgart. He said that he might meet them all again that night as he too was travelling to Hanover.

On the evening of November 12 Barbie boarded a tram with his two friends to take him to the station at Altona in the Hamburg dockland. As it rattled along the street, he looked out of the window of the tram and saw a car with British police markings close behind. It kept pace with the tram, which was odd, yet he could not be quite sure that it was tailing them.

They arrived at Altona and boarded a train; as the three Germans sat waiting for it to start, four men in civilian clothes entered the compartment and arrested them. Barbie knew at once that they were from British field security, even before they were taken to face a British army captain who was waiting outside. The captain, clearly, was not only impatient to meet Barbie but had been well informed about his recent escapades. "Well, my friend," he said cheerfully, "we are not the Americans. You are not going to run away from us!"

As Barbie and his companions were driven off, he had time to speculate on what had gone wrong. Acker must have been an informer: what Barbie did not know was that Acker was "Mouse", the main American penetration agent who was reporting both to the Americans and the British. According to CIC documents, "Mouse" had reported that Barbie had an armed bodyguard, that he had planned three murders in Marburg and that the three men were about to escape to Denmark. It was the escape possibility that made the British arrest Barbie and his friends.

The three Germans were driven to a British safe house, a requisitioned villa beside the Alster lake in the centre of Hamburg. They spent two days in makeshift cells in the basement. Every half hour, two British soldiers would visit to check on them. But on the night of November 14 there was only one guard, a nervous young man who drew his pistol when approaching the cells and refused even to take the risk of escorting them to the latrine. He explained that he was on his own. Then he withdrew to an improvised guardroom on the floor above, and settled down to practising the flute.

One of Barbie's companions found an iron bar and a torch while exploring his cell; the three managed to lever off the padlocks on the cell doors, tiptoe upstairs, crawl past the guardroom to the accompaniment of trills and scales on the flute, and escape through a window.

They made their way to the house of the former SS secretary, Ellen Kühn, who could not offer them shelter, and then hid on the outskirts of Hamburg for a few miserable days until Kurt Barkhausen brought them fresh identity papers (Barbie filled his out in the name of Klaus Spier). Then they were able to return, angry and frightened, to their old haunts around Marburg and Kassel. Barbie never forgave the British for this arrest, and claimed afterwards that he had been physically roughed-up at the station. He said later to the Americans: "I lost all interest in the British, and all faith in their promises."

That December of 1946 Regine gave birth to their second child. Klaus-Jörg Barbie was born on December 11 in a Kassel clinic, with Barbie in attendance posing as a close relation of the mother. It was a painful and difficult birth, and Regine had to remain in the clinic for several months; when she came out, she was convinced that she was being followed. This was a threat not only to Barbie, but to what remained of their life as a couple, for Regine was not content to wait for her husband's furtive appearances whenever the coast seemed clear; she had taken to travelling about Germany in his company, leaving the little girl Ute in the care of relations or of her faithful grandmother Anna Barbie. If Regine had now been identified, she would be far easier to follow when she left the hospital with the new baby. The Barbies took a tough decision; they arranged to leave Klaus-Jörg behind, and for over a year he was dumped with one of the clinic nurses, fed on slops and milks (when fresh milk could be found), seldom seeing the light of day.

By now the British and Americans were growing alarmed by the spread of this "Nazi resistance group". The central figure appeared to be a certain Dr Kurt Ellersieck, an ex-SS officer whose political plan, according to the CIC, was

> to reorganise the Kameradschaftshäuser [university fraternity] groups within various universities as a legal front for an illegal organisation. The purpose . . . was the oft-repeated plan of offering the Western Allies a strong leadership group of former Nazis in order to build a strongly anti-Communistic Germany.

In the last months of 1946 the occupation authorities prepared a full-scale swoop on the "Ellersieck group" and its associates. Under the code name "Operation Selection Board", dozens of addresses were targeted and scores of agents deployed. The Selection Board raids began on the cold and rainy evening of February 22 1947, all over the British and American zones; over fifty men and women were arrested, and their preliminary interrogation led to the arrest of some twenty more. There was much publicity, designed partly to allay Soviet complaints that the West was displaying too little energy in the pursuit of Nazis. "This was the last large organised group of Nazis to be formed in the Western zones of Germany," commented a US army memorandum afterwards. "It was completely broken up . . . and its story now serves as a reminder to the German people of the futility of nationalistic action outside the scope of the existing democratic processes now in operation in Germany."

Only one major figure in the network, "Target Number Three" on the list, escaped the raid. He was described in the Selection

Board orders as leader of a cell which "concentrated on the establishment of an intelligence network throughout the United States and British zones, and possibly farther", responsible for "the procurement of money, radio equipment, printing presses, etc."

This was an absurd description of Klaus Barbie's real life in the underground; he had been reduced to the existence of a petty criminal, riding unheated trains and hiding in the lavatories to avoid conductors, sliding cartons of Camels under a café table to some ill-shaven contact who had once strutted in a smart black uniform, sounding out a farmer in some dimly lit kitchen to see whether he would look after a comrade on the run or send for the police. Barbie himself was an ex-policeman living the life of a crook, and his instinct for trouble was doubly sharp.

Perhaps it was a hint dropped, perhaps just a feeling at the back of his neck which made him leave his Marburg lodging that night of February 22. He went to stay with another Selection Board target named Fridolin Becker in Kassel. When the CIC burst into the front entrance, looking for Becker, Barbie ran into the bathroom and jumped out of the window at the back of the building. He landed safely in the garden, and vanished into the night.

Selection Board brought a whole phase of Barbie's life to an end. He was still free. He still had some friends and contacts who had escaped the sweep. But his time in the underground was clearly up. The British and Americans were on his track and closing the gap fast. Perhaps they did not yet know what he had on his conscience from the years in Lyon, but the French knew. If he was caught, it might be the beginning of a short walk to a court-martial in France and a firing squad.

From now on Barbie concentrated on the only chance of asylum close to hand: selling himself to his pursuers as an intelligence agent. A few months later, luck and persistence would provide him with that asylum in the shape of stout, good-natured Kurt Merk.

Robert Taylor, the CIC agent who had recruited Kurt Merk to work for American intelligence at Memmingen in 1946, was extremely pleased with his new employee. From CIC files he had learned that Merk was "considered one of the best counter-intelligence men in France during the German occupation", and from the start Merk had appeared to live up to his expectations.

The CIC records, however, indicate that Merk's first big score as an informant for US intelligence was one which was to cause a long chain of misunderstandings and disputes. After attending the birthday party of an unnamed woman in Stuttgart, Merk reported to Taylor the existence of a "possibly illegal" organisation of former members of the Nazi foreign intelligence service.

Merk was told to keep in touch with the group. He persuaded the birthday party woman (whose name the American government still refuses to release) to work for him as a CIC informant, and he soon began to receive invitations to join the group himself. What neither Merk nor Taylor realised was that Merk had stumbled not on an "illegal" grouping but on parts of what was later to become the Gehlen organisation, then being secretly put together under American supervision to spy on Russia. Its code name was "Operation Rusty".

So sensitive was the Gehlen operation that none of the CIC regional commands had been told about it. The result was confusion. Even when Taylor found out that the outfit was not another illegal grouping of old Nazis but was under American patronage, "Rusty" went on misleading the CIC by the unscrupulous methods it used to lay hold of Merk.

At one point Merk was even offered command of "Rusty's" counter-intelligence operations, and when he refused it, someone in the organisation circulated a memorandum which reached the CIC stating that Merk had indeed consented to join. Taylor questioned Merk and satisfied himself that this was sheer disinformation designed to shatter the CIC's confidence in their own agent, and inflate "Rusty's" success record. Taylor concluded that the approach was "a deliberate attempt to 'pad' the list of agents working for 'Operation Rusty'".

Using the name of "Walter Petersen", Merk now began to construct a network made up of Russian émigrés, female contacts in the Soviet zone, and an assortment of old and new acquaintances. The Bureau Petersen, under the cover of a business selling radio valves, soon spread its web beyond the local CIC region and outside the American zone. Taylor let Merk get on with his work, only occasionally travelling with him to meet his sub-sources at which times the tall American would pass himself off as a Hungarian displaced person.

But trouble and suspicions about Merk's operation kept recurring, made worse by the confusion in the CIC as many of its talented wartime agents were demobilised and replaced by men with far less skill and experience. The rows went on into the summer of 1947, and Merk was eventually obliged to "return" the birthday-party woman to the control of CIC Stuttgart.

Taylor says today that the documents describing these arguments fit his recollection of how the CIC operated in those years. "We had no real instructions on what we were supposed to do. Merk and I just made them up as we went along. It was really pretty chaotic."

He remembers much more about his personal relations with Kurt Merk. "We were friends . . . close friends. The friendship developed gradually as we worked together but it became quite warm."

Robert Taylor and his German girl friend Line (whom he had met when he tried to arrest her for illegal border-crossing) used to have dinner regularly with Kurt and Andrée Rivez, whom Taylor knew then as "Annemarie Richter".

Andrée and Line often spent the day together while their men were at work, and Line visited Andrée's mother at the flat in Oberstaufen, a place so small that Merk – so Taylor thought – felt ashamed to ask him there.

"When Bob and Line finally got married," Andrée recalled, "he was so poor, so badly paid, that he could not afford to give her a ring. My mother gave them one of her own, that she had brought with her from France."

This friendly group was now about to acquire a new member who would make the Kurt Merk controversies look positively mild by comparison.

Klaus Barbie had escaped the Selection Board arrests – but was it just because of his own sharpened instinct for danger? There is a hint in the Selection Board archives that the American agents were told to leave him alone. One CIC telex observes cryptically that "we are still not allowed to do anything overtly about Target Three" (i.e. Barbie). It may even be that somebody in the CIC itself tipped him off that he would do well not to be in his Marburg lodgings that night.

The first Allied intelligence service known to have taken an interest in recruiting Barbie, however, was not the American but the British. At Christmas 1946, while he was staying with Emil Hoffmann, Hoffmann revealed that he was working for "the English" and showed him letters from a British major named "Kruk" (perhaps a misspelling of "Cook"). Barbie objected that he had only escaped from British custody in Hamburg the month before, and would almost certainly be re-arrested if he approached them. Hoffmann promised to lay the problem before Major "Kruk" and early in 1947 he reported back to Barbie that the major was "very interested in obtaining his services". The major invited Barbie to meet him at Bad Godesberg, on the southern edge of the British zone. Still suspecting a trap, Barbie declined.

But if they did not initially approach Barbie, the Americans soon showed second thoughts about him. In March 1947, after Barbie's escape from the CIC raiders in Kassel, a CIC agent named John H. Derner urged that he be closely watched with a view to his arrest, but Derner also suggested that, left at liberty, he might become "a good source of information" on other Selection Board targets missed in February. Derner speculated that Barbie, "due to his background and experience with the German Intelligence Services", might be useful in penetrating a suspected centre of Soviet espionage.

Derner's idea was turned down, but the germ of the future American attitude towards Barbie had been born. Barbie was in any case now thinking desperately about offering himself to the Americans. He went to southern Germany to look for more old comrades with American connections and struck up an acquaintance with an exuberant businessman in the leather trade, one Walter Hirschfeld, another SS veteran. Hirschfeld claimed to be collecting information about Soviet espionage for US intelligence, and he introduced Barbie to one of his most prized collaborators, Dr Emil Augsburg.

Augsburg, who was to feature importantly in Barbie's life a little later, was an impressive figure – much the most senior Nazi intelligence survivor that Barbie had encountered in all his post-war wanderings. He had been chief Soviet political expert for the SS during the war, and one of the leaders of the "Wannsee Institute", the special SS Soviet research centre in Berlin. Born in Poland, with a wide knowledge of Slav languages and eastern European politics, Augsburg was potentially a big catch for any Allied intelligence outfit, and any group which included him was to be taken seriously.

Hirschfeld urged Barbie to join him. There was big money around, he promised – some from SS funds he had raided when Germany collapsed and more from the operations of his profitable leather business on the black market. He gave Barbie an accreditation as one of his leather salesmen. All this was alluring and when Hirschfeld offered Barbie a definite assignment – to penetrate a Soviet spy ring supposed to exist at Schwaebisch Gmuend near Stuttgart – Barbie accepted. But there remained something about Hirschfeld he did not trust. And, more important, he now had an even better idea of his own.

Earlier that month, he had heard from friends that his acquaintance from the French occupation, Kurt Merk, was working for the CIC in Memmingen. There were two attractive angles here. The first was that he knew Merk was good: a thorough professional, and honest into the bargain. The second was that, unlike Hirschfeld, Merk was directly employed by the CIC rather than as a freelance contributor. There is a German proverb which asks, "Why talk to the cat when you can talk to the tiger?" Barbie set off for Memmingen.

He failed to find Merk on his first attempt, and went back to Schwaebisch Gmuend to take a preliminary look at Hirschfeld's problem there. The reconnaissance completed, he none the less thought it worth trying Memmingen once more and had the luck to run straight into Merk on the railway platform.

They stared at each other, disagreeably aware that their roles had been reversed. In France, Barbie had been the man of power and reputation while Merk, as an Abwehr man and an anti-Nazi, had been obliged to step warily. Now it was a dishevelled Barbie who answered Merk's "What are you doing here?" with an agonised, "You must help me!"

Merk's first instinct, as he told Andrée later, was to say there was nothing he could do for Barbie. But he listened, and relented. The ex-Hauptsturmführer was a pitiable figure – Andrée, who met him a week or so later, found him still "absolutely on edge, extremely frightened. I asked why everyone had been so scared of this little fellow in Lyon. He seemed quite anodyne; he didn't have a dangerous air about him."

Merk told Barbie to wait for him in the Weinsiegel café, one of the few drinking places open in war-damaged Memmingen, and met him later for a talk. They met again that night at Merk's office on Kaiserpromenade for several hours of conversation about the past and about mutual acquaintances. It was plain enough what Barbie wanted. Merk sized him up, and told him to come back again on April 17 when "he might have some good news for him".

It is not clear exactly when Merk told Robert Taylor about Barbie's approach. Taylor wrote later that he was not told until April 10, when Merk confided that he had accidentally run into Barbie, an "old friend" who had "excellent connections to sources of CIC information". In a report several weeks afterwards, Taylor said that he had "immediately recognised" Barbie's name as that of one of the leading Selection Board targets still on the run.

It may be that Merk, who always felt privately that Barbie was an evil piece of work, simply hesitated. Rather more probably, he did tell Taylor at once, but the two men then spent a few days working out how to persuade their regional commanding officer at CIC Munich, Lieutenant-Colonel Dale Garvey, that it made sense to hire as a CIC informant one of the most hotly-pursued Nazis in the American zone. In the event, the CIC's own casual and chaotic style solved the problem. Garvey agreed, and simply failed to inform CIC headquarters that Target Three on the Selection Board arrest list, a man being industriously hunted by Garvey's own CIC colleagues all over the zone and who in theory he should at once seize and lock up, was now his employee.

Taylor went to see Colonel Garvey about Barbie on April 14 and 15 1947. In spite of the CROWCASS entries and the old SHAEF cards, there is no indication that either man even considered what crimes Klaus Barbie might have committed on SS and SD service during the war. Instead, Garvey agreed to the hiring of Barbie on two conditions. The first was that Barbie must sever all connections with the "Nationalist underground". The second, which blatantly reveals the mutual suspicions between the western Allies in Germany, was that Barbie must tell the CIC everything he knew about British efforts to employ Selection Board personalities as intelligence sources.

Barbie returned to Memmingen on April 17, as arranged. The next day, Merk introduced him to Robert Taylor who – perhaps touched by the nervous manner of the "little fellow" – told him to stop worrying: all that was required was a little chat.

Barbie then gave him what must have been a skilfully sanitised version of his wartime career in the Sicherheitsdienst, especially in its French episodes. Taylor still possesses a twelve-page essay written by Barbie, in a snappy, sub-Chandler style, on how he "turned" René Hardy and arrested Jean Moulin.

It's a cold February day on Munich's Stachus square in 1947. A bunch of human beings is hanging on the outside of the streetcar as it comes up to the halt. Jostling, cursing, yelling – the usual scene . . . Starving for news, I am reduced to buying a French zone newspaper. Strikes in France, inflation threat to franc, executions of traitors: these are the headlines. And suddenly I am not believing my eyes any more. I am reading the words: "Colonel René Hardy on Trial in Paris" . . .

Taylor is not sure of the date of this epic, but now thinks that Barbie may have written it for him in the first few days to convince him of his own skill at secret police work.

If so, Taylor hardly needed convincing. The CIC archives make it perfectly clear that at the end of that meeting on April 18 1947 he invited Barbie to work as a CIC informant and that Barbie accepted Colonel Garvey's two conditions. He said that he was happy to break his connections with the "Nazi underground", which had been "necessary only to retain his own personal freedom". And, to prove how enthusiastically he accepted Garvey's second condition, he produced as his first assignment a report about the British use of old SS men as intelligence informants (a report that, not surprisingly, given its sensitive subject and Barbie's striking malevolence about the British, is no longer to be found among the CIC records).

Taylor booked him a room at the station hotel in Memmingen, and Barbie settled down to await his next orders. His position was still irregular; he was now in a sense an American prisoner on a gilded form of parole rather than a free man. But for the first time in two years, he could feel solid ground under his feet again.

CHAPTER SEVEN

The Petersen Bureau

Though he never knew it, CIC agent Robert Taylor shared one experience with his new informant Klaus Barbie; both men had to fight a bureaucracy to get married. When he decided in the summer of 1947 to marry his German girl friend Line, Taylor knew that it would be the end of his career in American intelligence. The CIC rules insisted that any agent who married a German must return to the United States within ten days of the ceremony, and the marriage required advance permission from the CIC based on the partner's security clearance. Taylor waited impatiently for months while the necessary papers were shuffled until, on August 17 1947, he and Line were finally ready to face the mayor of Kempten and be declared man and wife, with the help of the amethyst ring which had belonged to Andrée's mother.

It was in several ways a poignant moment for Kurt Merk, Andrée, and her mother, the only witnesses in Kempten town hall that day. They were losing two firm friends: the next ten days were a succession of raucous farewell parties (at one of which Taylor remembers the appearance of Klaus Barbie) until Kurt and Andrée stood waving at the army jeep which carried Bob and Line away to Munich, on the first stage of their journey to America. But Kurt was also losing his patron, the man who had given him the chance of a fresh career and who had defended him loyally against all his critics as he built up the Bureau Petersen network.

In the last few months the net had expanded enormously – too fast, some CIC men would later judge. At the time Barbie was recruited, Merk ran ten to fifteen informants including a number of Russian, Ukrainian and other refugees from the east, and had contacts within the Soviet zone of Germany. Barbie proved an experienced, quick-witted collaborator and soon brought to Memmingen the impressive figure of Dr Emil Augsburg, the man who had been the leading SS authority on the Soviet Union. Merk reorganised the net and, with Taylor's approval, assigned Barbie an improbably wide range of targets. By May, only a month after he started work for the CIC, Barbie – according to a report by

Taylor – had "provided extensive connections to French intelligence agencies working in the US zone, to Banat German circles [i.e. refugees from the German minority in Yugoslavia], to high-ranking Romanian circles and to high Russian circles in the US zone." In all these giddy circles, there must have been some element of bluff – no agent starting from nothing could achieve so much in four weeks. Barbie later told American interrogators that Merk had required him, more generally, to penetrate Soviet-sponsored organisations and investigate Soviet intelligence operations in the American zone, France and eastern Europe.

By the time Taylor left in August, the Bureau Petersen had swollen to include sixty-five informants scattered all over Germany, Poland, Yugoslavia, Czechoslovakia, Switzerland and Greece. And this sprawling monster was still not enough for Merk. In June he had written an extraordinary prospectus in stilted English for Taylor, listing the achievements he claimed and proposing further expansion. "Already today we dispose of very good relations to the entire Russian zone which can easily be completed on the greatest scale . . . Already today we have relations to France which can be completed without great difficulties so that we can do intensive intelligence work in this country." He boasted of connections in Poland, all the Balkan countries, and Italy ("we can get into connection with the intelligence service of the Vatican"), and even the Soviet Union: "Having informants in Berlin we are able to establish intelligence relations to Russia using therefore the specialists working in Russia."

He proposed setting up a chain of "cover" companies, including a press agency and a firm ostensibly for building racing cars in Stuttgart, and suggested to Taylor that if this huge project was beyond the means of the CIC (whose main task, after all, was only preserving internal security within the US zone in Germany), it should be transferred to some other intelligence outfit, preferably the SSU. This was an alias for the covert-action units of the old Office of Strategic Services, which had survived under the auspices of the War Department in Washington.

Kurt Merk, in short, was out of control. There was something wonderfully crazy about the idea that a petty outstation of American soldiers in a small town in Bavaria was setting out to spy on the whole of Europe. CIC Memmingen had no permission to do this, no real idea why it was doing it, and above all, not the slightest qualification to process this sort of intelligence material. Merk, who was basically honest but well able to gallop through a stable door if it was left wide open, banked on the innocence and credulity of

the men he was dealing with. Robert Taylor was certainly intelligent, but very young and green as grass. And Merk had rapidly
understood how unlike the CIC was to the old Abwehr, no stiffly
disciplined corps of professionals but a slapdash, dislocated outfit
in which a few bright agents did their own thing by simply concealing their best schemes from the desk-bound dunderheads around
them. The Memmingen CIC seems to have reacted to Merk's
vaulting plans with a generalised "gee whiz!", followed by happy
dreams of how famous and successful they would all become.

Apart from Barbie and Dr Augsburg, Merk's team at Memmingen included a young Danish journalist named Christian Zarp
and Dr Franz Minnich, a Romanian-German who had worked in
Bucharest during the war. Both were friends of Dr Emil Hoffmann,
and between them they provided the net with information about
Romania. The result was that Barbie, whose ignorance of the
Balkans was total, acquired a reputation with the CIC as a
Romanian expert and a man able to operate a ring of espionage
agents in a Communist-dominated country. None of the Americans
in Memmingen was in a position to check the veracity of his
Romanian reports, but the CIC files show that they were taken
seriously.

Kurt Merk was not the only person to see the weaknesses of the
CIC. In early February 1947 Major Earl Browning had arrived in
Frankfurt to take over the job of operations officer ("S-3") at 970th
CIC headquarters. He saw how the quality of agents was falling as
the brightest wartime men returned to the United States. And he
saw how often the CIC outstations were being taken for a ride by
their German informants.

> Some informants were making a profession out of it [he recalls
> today]. They would get a piece of information – or even invent
> a piece of information – and sell it to everybody. You would get
> a report from Augsburg saying, "Something's happening, it's
> interesting." You'd get the same report from Marburg and think:
> "Now we're on to something!" But it's the same guy who is
> peddling the story, and it may not be true at all. Obviously we
> wanted to prevent this, so what we did was to require that all
> informants being used by the CIC in Germany should be regis-
> tered and controlled from my office.

Reform was on its way and down at Memmingen there were soon
signs that the Kurt Merk espionage balloon was about to be pricked.
A shrewd and sceptical agent named Camille Hajdu took over from

Robert Taylor as Merk's handler. It was a very much less warm relationship, and indeed Merk and Andrée seem never to have known Hajdu's real name, but always used his CIC alias of "Stevenson". Hajdu, with Earl Browning's new operating procedures in mind, looked at the Merk circus, the famous Bureau Petersen, and decided that it was time to prune it back.

One of the first things he did was to inform Colonel Garvey, the regional CIC commander in Munich, that Merk was using as an informant none other than a certain Klaus Barbie, the escaped "Number Three Target" of Operation Selection Board. It was now October 1947, and as Colonel Garvey had known this perfectly well for six months, Hajdu was putting him in an awkward position. Covering himself as best he could, Garvey informed CIC headquarters in Frankfurt that he had just discovered that Barbie was being used in Memmingen to "furnish information" (he did not reveal that the wanted man was in fact a salaried informant).

Earl Browning remembers the fury of his deputy operations officer, Jim Ratliffe, when he read Garvey's message. "Ratliffe came to me as mad as I've ever seen him. He says: 'This guy Garvey! You won't believe it! After telling us last winter to beat the bushes and find Barbie, Garvey now wants us to use him as an informant.' Ratliffe was terribly upset. He thought Garvey's behaviour was completely off the reservation."

Browning ordered Region IV (Munich) to arrest Barbie. "They said they didn't want to arrest him, and we said they had to arrest him." For a few weeks Munich went on whining and squirming, while Frankfurt alternated between reassurances and threats – at one moment promising that Barbie would probably be given back after questioning, at the next asking what Region IV thought it was doing organising spy nets within the French zone. Camille Hajdu, surprisingly, fought hard to keep Barbie at liberty: as Merk's assistant, he wrote in a memorandum, Barbie had "so far demonstrated exceedingly successful results . . . it is strongly recommended that subject not be arrested. It is further recommended that, inasmuch as the subject has in the past shown his willingness to answer any questions, subject's interrogation be conducted on a voluntary basis." But finally, on December 11, a frightened and very angry Klaus Barbie was taken into custody and carted off to the European Command Interrogation Centre (ECIC), an enormous internment cage at Oberursel just outside Frankfurt.

Barbie probably thought he would be identified as the Butcher of Lyon and handed over to a French court-martial and firing squad. Nothing could have been further from the truth. The CIC headquarters may already have known that he had been chief of the Gestapo in Lyon and that he was wanted as a war criminal: they certainly had a "central personalities index" card which told them so. Even the CIC in Munich knew vaguely that he had been an important SS agent of some kind in France. The point was that the CIC simply did not care. This was not the result of any pro-Nazi slant. It was essentially bureaucratic inertia, the unwillingness to create unnecessary problems. Barbie was arrested because he had been a Selection Board target, and the job of rounding up the remaining targets and questioning them about the supposed "Nazi underground movement" had to be completed. To have raised further matters about his past would have brought all kinds of other organisations into the process, generating much unwelcome extra work and fuss. And already, in the exchange of messages preceding his arrest, the point had been made that Barbie was a useful informant and that other intelligence services – the British were mentioned – would like to get their hands on him. That could never be allowed.

So Klaus Barbie was pushed into a bare cell containing nothing but a camp bed, a table and – as an invitation to confession – a typewriter. When he arrived at Oberursel, he told his captors: "You are not going to get anything out of me!" But in the six days and nights of silence and isolation that followed, interrupted only by mess-tins of food, his defiance leaked shamingly away. It was not even a matter of the biter bit; after all, nobody had struck him or – another of his Lyon tricks – threatened to arrest and torture his family. The fact was that Barbie was not good at being brave by himself. On the seventh day he sat down at the table and began to punch the typewriter keys.

It was the first of a series of autobiographies that he was to write for the American interrogators. And like all the succeeding ones, it cleverly sandwiched rashers of truth between wads of untruth. As far as his war past was concerned, Barbie admitted his membership of the SD but implied that he spent those years flitting about occupied France and even Italy without any precise assignment. His line was that he had belonged to Amt VI of the RSHA, the foreign espionage branch, rather than to the monstrously compromised Gestapo Amt IV. His chief questioner, Arnold Silver, noted briefly that he had been a captain in the Waffen-SS, as well as in the SD. Barbie had never been in the Waffen-SS, but these details mattered much less than Barbie thought. Silver was not interested in the past. Instead, as Barbie began to cooperate ("it is not believed that he has wilfully withheld information"), the questions centred on his post-war adventures and his contacts with other old Nazi intelligence officers on the Selection Board lists.

Barbie's arrest in December 1947 was a minor disaster for CIC Memmingen. Two months later, there was another. In February 1948 Colonel David Erskine, commanding officer of the 970th CIC, sent out a circular to all his regional offices by telex which announced that three CIC informants or contacts were wanted by the French authorities for "war crimes". They were listed as Kurt Merk, Andrée Rivez, and her mother (whose name CIC headquarters appeared not to know). The telex said nothing about the supposed charges against the three, but ordered that CIC headquarters in Frankfurt be immediately informed of their whereabouts.

On February 24, six days after receiving the telex, Camille Hajdu called Kurt Merk in for a little talk. But Merk was all injured innocence. The telex said that he had worked in the Stuttgart Abwehrstelle and he could protest truthfully that he had never served in that particular office in his life. Andrée Rivez and her mother? Never heard of them, said Merk stoutly. If thoughts of that pretty friend of Merk's with the strong French accent crossed Hajdu's mind, he did not commit them to paper.

The Merk crisis released swirls of conflicting anxieties within the CIC – conflicts to be repeated on a much bigger and more catastrophic scale the following year when the main Barbie crisis blew up. Nobody wanted to hand Merk over to the French. But motives for not doing so varied. Captain Max Etkin, CIC operations officer in Munich, revealed that his own colleagues were torn between the value of Merk's operations and the feeling that he had overstepped his limits and should be dropped. In a report to Frankfurt dated March 4, Etkin let slip the fact that Merk's net was now so widespread that CIC Munich (probably without Merk's knowledge) had begun to pass on his gleanings to the War Department Detachment, and that the WDD in return was paying some of the costs of the Bureau Petersen. The WDD, a cover name for the Central Intelligence Group, was the direct ancestor of the CIA.

This connection suggested that Merk should be kept on. So did a number of baser considerations to do with the mutual rivalry and suspicions of the Allies in Germany. "If he is dropped by this headquarters," agonised Etkin, "will not some other agency pick him up (the French for instance), and if he is picked up by some other agency, would he not take his net with him? Parts of his net are of extreme value to this organisation." Etkin leafed through the three options which arose if Merk was dropped: turning over his net to WDD, arresting Merk and sending him up to Oberursel to join Barbie for interrogation, or surrendering him to the French. The last was the worst option: "This point is suggested only as a last resort because, should the French use him, he would be an extremely valuable asset to their organisation." In other words, it was better to hide a possible war criminal from justice than allow him to work for the intelligence services of a European ally of the United States.

Camille Hajdu, meanwhile, was convinced that Merk should be removed. He blamed the problem on the unwise intimacy between Merk and Taylor, "mutual confidence extending into personal friendship". He added, priggishly but from the CIC perspective correctly, that "the relationship . . . gradually moved to the plane of a firm friendship established between two equals, rather than the relationship which should have existed between the American CIC agent and his informant." Hajdu proposed that the Bureau Petersen should be chopped up into three, and a new deputy to Merk appointed who could take over his job when the time came. All this was to be done gradually, in case – that old neurosis again – an alarmed Merk bolted with all or some of his net and gave away CIC secrets to somebody else. Merk, concluded Hajdu, should be taken to Oberursel "for a thorough and extended interrogation after his removal".

While waiting for this unkind plot to be approved, he was slashing back Merk's agent list from over fifty to about fifteen. In the report quoted above, which he wrote in March, Hajdu described a fresh row which had broken out over Merk's attempt to operate a secret radio station in Berlin without informing the local CIC. "The fact that he conceals these activities from this agent and many other small violations of principle and of orders directly given indicate without any doubt that Merk is not capable of adapting himself to a professional-like standard of work."

More French requests now arrived at CIC headquarters. Although they were for Merk and the two women, this development was also bad news for Klaus Barbie, still – in March 1948 – in solitary confinement at Oberursel. For it meant that the French courts and police had at last overcome the long interval of post-war chaos; they had pieced together a reasonably accurate account of what had taken place during the German occupation and were now ready to launch a new round of war crimes trials. Especially in Lyon, the tribunals had a long list of Germans and French collaborators to confront, as defendants or as witnesses.

The details the French supplied revealed that Charles Merlen, Andrée's uncle, and a married couple named Monniez, were on trial in Lyon charged with the betrayal of the "Technica" Deuxième Bureau network to the Abwehr in 1943. Merk, fairly plainly, was only required as a witness; nobody, then or later, suggested that he had behaved improperly. Jeanne Pecquignot, Andrée's mother, was presumably also wanted as a witness. But Andrée Rivez herself was in terrible danger. Before leaving France, she now says, she had told Charles Merlen to blame everything on her if he got into trouble over "Technica" after the war. He had evidently done so, and if she were convicted of collaboration before the Lyon court, she could face the death penalty. The French were aware that she had fled to Germany with Merk in 1944, and they seemed already to have known that Merk was working for the Americans. To call herself "Annemarie Richter" was a flimsy protection; she could be easily identified by a sharp-eyed French agent, and Andrée recalls today how Kurt Merk strictly forbade her to have her photograph taken in case prints or negatives fell into the wrong hands.

There was, in fact, a "Technica" old boys' network in Germany. Colonel Serre, who had commanded "Technica" in its early period, was now the French representative on the Quadripartite Allied Intelligence Committee in Berlin. And Colonel Bob Schow, the American officer who had been military attaché in Vichy until 1943 and whom Serre had supplied with copies of all "Technica's" daily reports, had also survived the war to become one of the deputies to the US European Command intelligence chief, General Edwin Sibert.

The Lyon trial had gone into recess on February 17 1948 to allow the necessary witnesses to be sought out in Germany. A week or so later Colonel Serre, in Berlin for a meeting of the Allied Intelligence Committee, dropped into the office of Colonel Peter Rodes, director of intelligence in the office of General Lucius D. Clay, military governor of the US zone of Germany. He brought with him a dossier on Merk, Andrée Rivez, and her mother. He had brought the affair to the very top of the American command in Germany, where it could not be ignored. As an extra precaution, on his way back to the French zonal headquarters at Baden Baden, Serre stopped off in Frankfurt to visit Bob Schow and ask for his help. He revealed to Schow that the case against Merlen – and against Andrée too – was based on the Abwehr reports on the operation, recording the names of their French informants and payments made to them, which had been captured intact in the Abwehr offices at Stuttgart at the end of the war.

From Berlin, Colonel Rodes wrote a memorandum on the case, which eventually landed in the CIC headquarters in Frankfurt.

With the office of General Clay himself on their tail, the CIC commanders did not dare to prevaricate. They at once ordered the interrogation of Merk and of another potential witness named by Serre, a red-headed young woman named Gertrud Burkhardt who had worked as a secretary in the Dijon Aussenstelle of the Abwehr. This was ominous. Gertrud Burkhardt had been famous in Dijon for three things: her affair with a married officer, her phenomenal memory for names, and her malice against Kurt Merk. In the Dijon days Merk had once warned Andreé against her: "ein gefährliches Biest", a dangerous little brute, was how he put it. And when the unwilling Gertrud was finally run to earth by CIC agents, she put the whole blame for the "Technica" betrayal on Andrée.

Merk was taken by Hajdu to Munich in May, and there confronted by two French officers, a Sureté man, and Lieutenant John Whiteway, a bilingual Canadian who worked for the French as their liaison officer with the CIC. Merk, who afterwards told Andrée that he considered that Hajdu had behaved unforgivably by taking him to Munich without telling him what was about to happen, boxed cleverly. He gave full and candid information about the raid on "Technica" and described the parts played by Merlen and the Monniez couple. When the French officers thrust under his nose evidence that Andrée had been one of his informants, he abandoned his initial statement that he had never heard of her and admitted that she had indeed worked for him at Dijon; it was through her that he had met Charles Merlen. But he insisted that he had no idea what had happened to her after the war, and they could not shake him.

Camille Hajdu, listening to all this, thought fast. He was now as sure as a hunch could make him that "Annemarie", Merk's mistress, was indeed Andrée Rivez. But he saw that his knowledge, and the desperate peril now facing Andrée, could be used to control Merk. If he said nothing to the French officers but let Merk know that he knew, he had his wayward informant in a perfect snare. After the interrogation was over he challenged Kurt Merk, who came disarmingly clean. He said, as Hajdu afterwards reported to his own masters in the CIC, "that he could hardly be expected to give away Rieves [sic] who had been his mistress for several years and with whom he was still in love".

Back in Memmingen, Hajdu typed out his idea.

It is felt that the agent who succeeds the undersigned. [Hajdu was about to be posted elsewhere] could greatly improve his control over Merk if it were positively ascertained that Rieves is his present mistress, who resides with him in Kempten. On the other hand, great care should be exercised not to allow Merk to believe that Rieves might be extradited to the French inasmuch as it is felt that Merk would not hesitate to escape with his mistress and to lend his services to any other power to avoid that Rieves be extradited to the French.

The CIC took this cynical advice to heart, and by July 1948 Erhard Dabringhaus, Hajdu's successor as Merk's handler, was reporting that "due to the French situation in which Subject [Merk] is involved by reason of his association with his present common-law wife, Subject can be easily controlled by offering him protection of the US Army".

The crisis over Merk proved to be merely a rehearsal for the infinitely more dangerous and scandalous affair which was now to arise over Klaus Barbie. In Paris the French authorities were preparing a second prosecution for treason against René Hardy, on the grounds that this supposed Resistance hero had betrayed Jean Moulin to the Germans.

Remarkably enough, they had just learned where Klaus Barbie was. Louis Bibes, a French counter-intelligence agent operating in Germany, knew the story of Jean Moulin's betrayal well. He also knew the name of Barbie, condemned to death in his absence in Lyon in 1947, who must clearly be the key witness. Bibes used to journey regularly to Munich in the American zone, treating the city as a gigantic flea-market for secret information which could be picked up from the émigrés and agents of a dozen European nations who had settled there. In the autumn of 1947 one of his Munich contacts, a Russian refugee whom Bibes had first met in Morocco during the war, mentioned that he had recently met a German who had told him he knew the whole story of the seizure of Moulin and his Resistance comrades at Caluire.

Commissaire Bibes, who now lives in retirement in France, remembers: "Naturally, I jumped at this opening. I told him to get more information. A week later he came back to me and said that he really did not know any more except that this man worked for the Americans in or near Munich. I told my boss, who informed Paris." Some time later the Russian gave more details, which allowed the French to be certain that they had stumbled across Barbie. "We came across Barbie by sheer chance. We were not actively looking for him, and my job was not hunting war criminals but counter-espionage."

Through the early months of 1948 Barbie remained in his cell at

Barbie in uniform – though not that of the SS. The pattern of the belt, cap and collar suggest the picture was taken while Barbie was still an NCO.

The children of Izieu, arrested by Barbie's Gestapo troops and deported to death camps on his orders. Below: The Barbie family in Germany after the war; (l to r): Klaus, his son, mother, wife and daughter.

(L to r): Barbie's SS portrait; Kurt Merk, his rival; Jean Moulin, the Resistance leader he killed. Below: the CIC officers in Barbie's life (l to r): Herbert Bechtold, Eugene Kolb and Colonel Jim Milano.

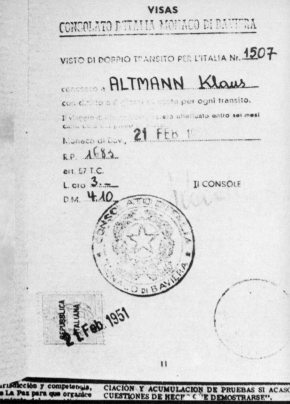

VISTO DI DOPPIO TRANSITO PER L'ITALIA Nr. 1507

consolato a **ALTMANN Klaus**

con diritto a 8 giorni di sosta per ogni transito.

Il viaggio di andata e ritorno deve effettuato entro sei mesi
dalla data di oggi.

Monaco di Bav., **21 FEB 1**

R.P. **1685**

art. 57 T.C.

L. cro **3.—** Il CONSOLE

D.M. **4.10**

REPUBBLICA ITALIANA **21 Feb. 1951**

II

FOTOGRAFIAS

DATOS QUE PROPORCIONA EL SOLICITANTE

; alemana PROFESION: mecânico

...onstadt, Alemania, el 25-10-1915.

...risdicción y competencia, ...e La Paz para que organice ...miento del ... CIACIÓN Y ACUMULACION DE PRUEBAS SI ACASO CUESTIONES DE HECE... 'E DEMOSTRARSE".

The Barbie file. Above, the visa form and, right, transit document that secured safe passage for the 'Altmann' family. Below: Barbie's Bolivian identity card showing him in the uniform of an honorary Lieutenant-Colonel.

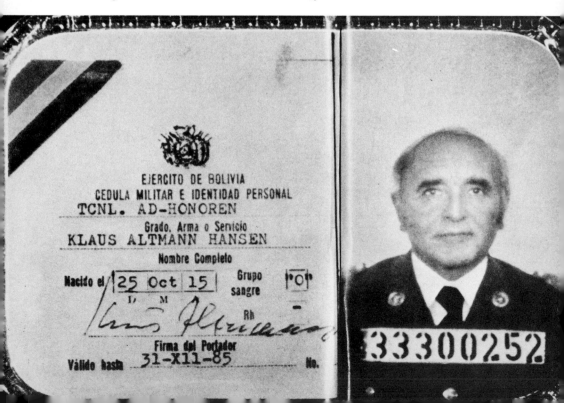

EJERCITO DE BOLIVIA
CEDULA MILITAR E IDENTIDAD PERSONAL
TCNL. AD-HONOREN
Grado, Arma o Servicio
KLAUS ALTMANN HANSEN
Nombre Completo
Nacido el **25 Oct 15** Grupo sangre **"O"**
D M
Rh
Firma del Portador
Válido hasta **31-XII-85** No.

333002 52

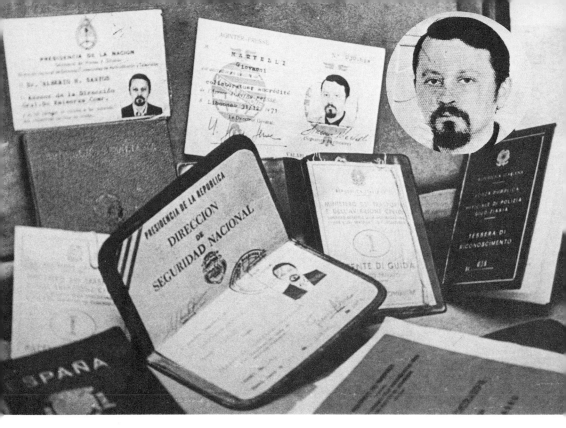

The ID cards of Stefano delle Chiaie, with (inset) his Aginterpress photo portraying him as a journalist. Below: The right-wing terrorist Pierluigi Pagliai close to death in Rome after his kidnap in Bolivia.

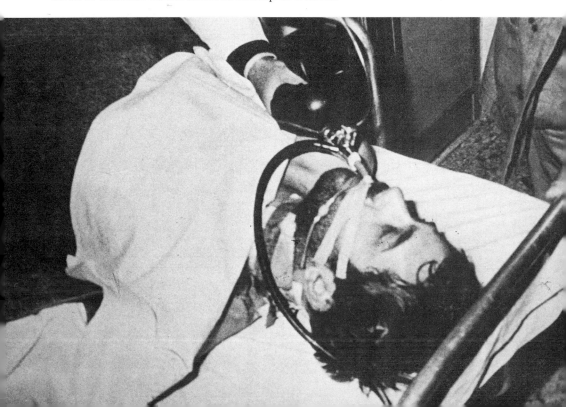

Above: Barbie celebrating with friends in La Paz. Below: The Fiancés of Death in Santa Cruz. Fiebelkorn is second right, top row. On his left, the lawyer Ustarez; on his right, the SS veteran Hans Stellfeld.

In Bolivia (l to r): General García Meza, Colonel Arce Gómez, and Barbie's friend, Alvaro de Castro. Below: in Peru, Klaus Barbie discussing tactics with his confederate in crime, 'Colonel' Friedrich Schwend.

Barbie, handcuffed, awaits his final departure from Bolivia, still unable to accept that the end has come.

Oberursel, while his American interrogators completed their dossier on his post-war links with other Nazi intelligence men and prepared to release him back to Memmingen. But now the French lodged a demand to be allowed to interrogate him themselves. At first, the Americans pretended ignorance. But Bibes had his own friends in the CIC – more wartime acquaintances from North Africa – and after a few months of arm-twisting he won permission to interview Barbie in the presence of American officers.

For the first time, Klaus Barbie now faced his French avengers. The meeting took place on May 14 1948 in the old office block of the IG-Farben chemicals firm at Hoechst near Frankfurt. The room was utterly bare except for a table and chairs. Two American CIC officers led Barbie into it. Bibes, who was accompanied by Lieutenant Whiteway, saw a "thin and extremely nervous man . . . he did not tremble, but he was very tense". He asked him if he was Klaus Barbie. The thin man denied it. "I told him we had incontestable proof that he was Barbie – birth documents etc. – but he continued to deny it. The atmosphere got very icy and sour. The Americans had warned us not to ask unauthorised questions, and they broke off this first interrogation after only ten minutes."

This was not good enough for Bibes. He saw quite well what the real situation was: Barbie had obviously been offered immunity by his American protectors if he went on working for them. He insisted on a second interview. In the next few days Barbie was released from Oberursel. Bibes met him again on May 18 in Munich, once more in the company of an American officer, Dick Lavoie. This second encounter lasted a full hour, but it was heavy going. Lavoie constantly interrupted to ban questions he did not like, above all any enquiry about where Barbie now resided and what he was doing. He did, however, observe that Barbie "is very important to the United States; he does dangerous things". A third meeting took place in the same CIC villa in Munich on July 16 1948. By now, Bibes recalls, Barbie was quite relaxed. He no longer disputed his identity and let it be understood that it was indeed René Hardy who had betrayed Jean Moulin at Caluire. "A tough cookie," said Bibes to Whiteway afterwards, impressed in spite of himself. He concluded that Barbie had now extracted cast-iron guarantees from the Americans, and that the French courts had little chance of getting hold of him. "The Americans would never have given him to us," he says now. "They had made a pact with him, and to have broken it would have been a betrayal of confidence that would have destroyed their relationship with other agents."

Gradually the CIC began to breathe more easily. Bibes seemed content with what he had found out, and the danger that France would demand the presence of either Barbie or Merk in a courtroom seemed to be receding. Barbie had been given a healthy fright by his spell in Oberursel and his confrontation with Bibes; Merk was subdued by the danger to Andrée Rivez if he misbehaved. In this new situation, the Bureau Petersen could be rehabilitated in its more modest form. From Frankfurt, Earl Browning set out the ground rules for its employment in future, demanding full details of assignments, targets and informants. Special agent Erhard Dabringhaus, today a retired professor of foreign languages in Detroit, had replaced Camille Hajdu as "minder" of Merk and Barbie. Dabringhaus had been born in Essen, but his family had emigrated to the United States before the war. He was assigned to move the Bureau Petersen to Augsburg, the graceful old city on the river Lech a little to the north of Munich. The move took place in June 1948. Dabringhaus remembers driving a three-quarter ton army lorry with a tarpaulin down to Kempten near Memmingen, to pick up the main figures of the Merk team: Merk himself, Klaus Barbie, and Dr Emil Augsburg with his secretary. Barbie, he recalls, was impatient. "He said: 'Hey, I'm waiting for you, Dabringhaus.' He knew my name. Who the hell gave it to him? I never saw him before. 'Hi, how are you? I heard a lot about you. I hear you're from Essen.' We were speaking German, of course. Then he starts introducing all the other people in the house." Barbie, now perkily self-confident again, insisted on sitting in the front seat beside Dabringhaus, while Merk and the others rode behind under the tarpaulin.

Merk and Barbie were settled in a solid detached house at Mozartstrasse 10, in the Augsburg suburb of Stadtbergen. The street was close to several huge American barrack blocks, and in 1945 the Americans had summarily evicted most of its inhabitants, forbidding them even to take the cutlery with them. Yugoslav refugees lived in several of the other Mozartstrasse houses, rendering the nights raucous with music, parties and the screams of women. It was not long before Barbie was allowed to summon his wife and daughter, who arrived from Trier and set up home. Andrée continued to live with her mother at Oberstaufen, but would come down to Augsburg for a few days at a time. Dabringhaus fixed up an office for the two men near the public swimming bath in Augsburg, equipped with a telephone and a German secretary. He would call round every morning at about nine o'clock, look through their reports and discuss future plans. "They would type, we would discuss certain things that they were following up, and they asked my opinion whether we should follow this particular story or whether we should cut this guy out . . ."

Barbie now had a secure post and even a family life again. But he was still frightened of the French, and one day Kurt Merk told Dabringhaus a little of the truth.

I heard from Merk that he [Barbie] had on occasion killed Resistance members that he'd caught and who wouldn't cooperate . . . I never heard of him killing any Jews or causing them to be deported. It is true that we recognised him as penetrating the underground primarily in France during the occupation, and it is for that reason that we felt pretty easy in using him. Had he been an Eichmann, I don't think we could have got away with it.

The French remained on Barbie's tail. Dabringhaus remembers a frantic telephone call from Captain Spiller, the commander of the CIC sub-region at Augsburg: "Spiller gets on the phone and says: 'Jesus, I haven't got time to tell you but there's two French agents on their way over. Get rid of the guys and tell them you don't know anything.' " Barbie and Merk vanished out of the back door of the office. "We had good exits there, that's what we used. I left the secretary there." When the two Frenchmen arrived, Dabringhaus earnestly assured them that he had never heard of Klaus Barbie, and five minutes later they left. Three or four weeks later, two other French agents interviewed Dabringhaus in Munich. He could hardly deny now that he had heard the name, but said he knew nothing about Barbie. "They were gentlemen. They didn't push me. They didn't say: 'Listen, you're working with a war criminal – why don't you cooperate with us?' No, they were very nice, talked about wine, and I told them I'd married a French girl and I tried my French on them . . ."

The affable French enquirers might have behaved very differently had they known that, in the reorganisation of Merk's network at Augsburg, Klaus Barbie had been assigned the target of "French intelligence activities in the French zone and their agents operating in the US zone". Underlying this move was that obsessive CIC idea that French security services were not merely a rival but so penetrated with Communists that they could be treated as a department of Soviet intelligence. To put Barbie of all men in charge of spying on the French was cheeky – and imprudent too. If Barbie was ever extradited to France or handed over as a witness, all this would presumably come out, creating an international scandal. The

CIC, by handling Barbie in this way, were digging their own grave.

Barbie's other assignment was more in tune with his talents and political views: the "penetration of illegal Soviet organisations" and of the German Communist party. He displayed much skill at infiltrating local party cells and groups, but the results were on the whole trivial: the German Communists were by this time no real menace to anyone. Dabringhaus remembers being taken along by Merk and Barbie one evening to a Communist meeting in the back room of a beer garden in Augsburg.

> I was dressed like a good German. I had my own Kennkarte, the German ID card, stamped with my de-Nazification on it. My name was Richard Holtoff and I was a laboratory worker from Essen . . . I never forgot that meeting. Because I put out a cigarette and left the butt in the ashtray. It almost blew my cover, and Merk kicks me in the ribs with his arms. And he looks at the ashtray. And I quickly grabbed the sonofabitch and put it in my pocket. Because at that time nobody ever threw a light [cigarette end] away!

They had gone to find out if the Communists were instigating a strike at the Augsburg gasworks, but all they discovered was that the gas workers were so badly fed that they were fainting in front of the furnaces they stoked. Dabringhaus reported that the strike was authentic, but, "that's of course the information nobody in higher headquarters wanted to hear. They wanted to hear that the goddam commies were doing this whole thing."

Those of Dabringhaus's reports which have survived tell the same story of haphazard little operations, disjointed and often leading nowhere very interesting. In July 1948, for example, Merk and Barbie reported that a "peace ring" in Stuttgart run by the publisher of a satirical magazine called *The Wasps' Nest* had been infiltrated by Communists. In August they were watching an association of Germans who had been prisoners of war in Yugoslavia, known as the "Winkler group", which was also suspected of Communist agitation. They kept track of the tortuous intrigues and feuds within the Ukrainian emigration: in September that year, the network reported that a Mr Siversky had been sacked by "the intelligence service of the Ministry of War of the Ukrainian Government in Exile" because the information he provided had turned out to be rewritten from Soviet newspaper clippings.

So, indeed, was some of the material served up as "intelligence" to the CIC. Dabringhaus once caught Barbie copying a Yugoslav news agency story, which he had already read in the morning paper. "I saw the damn article in the German newspaper and I said: 'Come on, Barbie, we're not paying you for this.' "

The only major "scoop" Dabringhaus can remember came from a contact of Barbie's who supplied information about the Russian-run uranium mine at Aue in the Soviet zone near the Czech border. "Jesus, that seems hot!" said Dabringhaus when he heard about it. The informant brought details of discontent and attempted protests by the enormous labour force digging out uranium for the future Soviet atomic bomb, and continued to supply reports about Aue to the CIC until well into 1949. But in fact this was not a scoop at all; although Dabringhaus did not know it, the British had been aware of the operations at Aue for many months already.

For the most part, the work at Augsburg was small beer, a far cry from Kurt Merk's continental spy ring based on Memmingen. And the pay was ridiculous.

In June 1948, West Germany had ended three years of hyper-inflation at a stroke by issuing the new Deutschmark, a rock-hard currency with real purchasing power. Yet the CIC went on paying its informants largely in cartons of American cigarettes, extra ration cards, and packets of groceries from the PX. Between August 26 and October 1, for instance, Dabringhaus paid to Merk DM 800, eighty packets of cigarettes, and six ration cards. Andrée remembers how angry this made Kurt Merk. "We had to sell the cigarettes on the black market to get any money for them, always with the risk of being arrested." They began to dream of working for some outfit which would pay a normal salary in proper money.

Dabringhaus moved on in October 1948 – this rapid turnover of handling agents was the curse of the Merk net – and was replaced by Herbert Bechtold, another German-born immigrant to the United States, who had worked in the US military police in Berlin after the war and then for the CIC in Munich. Bechtold reported to Captain Spiller, the CIC commander at Augsburg, for instructions, having been warned in Munich that Merk and Barbie had still not found their ideal role. "We have two cut-outs that have not been properly utilised; they are the best we have in the area and we want to make proper use of them." Spiller, however, was not much help. "Reporting to Captain Spiller was like reporting to the wall," recalls Bechtold. "He said they were shady characters. 'You can't trust them. I'll introduce you to them. But you've got to form your own opinions.' "

The CIC opinion of Merk and Barbie at headquarters in Frank-furt was again turning sour. Major Browning sent a note to CIC

Munich announcing that consensus in Frankfurt was that the net "should be dropped as such by this organisation". He gave three reasons: the worry that Merk's old agents, who had been pruned out by Hajdu, could now be working for foreign powers while maintaining contact with him; the contacts of the Merk group with a shadowy outfit of ex-SS officers known as the "Tetsch net" in Stuttgart (probably another embryonic element of the Gehlen organisation); and, third, the fact that "in order to continue employing subject net, we must protect an individual who is wanted by an Allied country for war crimes". This may refer to Andrée Rivez, but more probably it refers to Klaus Barbie.

Browning by now knew of Barbie's record in Lyon – or at least knew what he was accused of by the French – and after some procrastination he was eventually to order that Barbie be dropped as an informant. Many other American intelligence officers knew too. In Austria the 430th CIC was having problems of a similar kind; they had been employing Wilhelm Höttl, a former deputy commander of the whole foreign intelligence operations of the SD, and now, in October 1948, they were worried not only about his sinister war record but about his own private contacts. Major James Milano, CIC director of operations in Austria and Browning's opposite number, listed among these contacts a certain "Barbie, nickname, right name Beckert, member of the Merk intelligence group, formerly a Stapo [Gestapo] employee. He is on the French War Criminals list for shooting hostages." If the Austrian CIC headquarters not only knew that Barbie was working with Kurt Merk but roughly what he had done in France, it is difficult to believe that the CIC in Germany did not know as much and more by October 1948.

For the moment, Merk's defenders in the CIC regional headquarters at Munich were able to stave off the threat from Major Browning. They insisted that the net was producing valuable information, but promised to cut it down still further, halving its membership from twelve to six. Among the casualties was Dr Emil Augsburg, Himmler's old expert on the Soviet Union. It was Barbie who had brought him into the net, and Barbie who now threw him to the wolves; Dr Augsburg, he alleged, had been in private contact with members of the Tetsch net of old SS officers in Stuttgart and had kept secret the fact that his own brother was working with the net under an alias. So Dr Augsburg packed his bags and vanished. It was, in fact, a blessing for him in disguise. The Memmingen and Augsburg CIC had never had any idea how to use his enormous experience and knowledge properly. He was much better qualified to work in full-scale foreign espionage, and he was at once snapped up by the Gehlen organisation. There he enjoyed a long career, ending up as Gehlen's senior evaluator on Soviet affairs.

The Munich CIC continued to argue that Merk and Barbie were doing valuable work, above all in penetrating the local Communist organisations, and that "the danger of overlapping into other Regions has been almost completely cut out". They were now attempting to "seek out as many old Gestapo and SS informants as possible, especially those whose mission was penetration of the KPD [German Communist party] under the Nazi regime." Herbert Bechtold, their new handler, undertook yet again the job of inventing for the Merk net a task that made sense. "I think up to the time I arrived," he says now, "they were left more or less up to their own devices – what they wanted to do, the type of information they wanted to come up with, and so on. They were not channelled."

It was a polite description of the hit-and-miss Dabringhaus era. Bechtold's idea was to use the team not simply against the Communist party, which he seems to have regarded as a minor target, but on a variety of counter-intelligence targets within the region. Under Bechtold, Merk and Barbie found themselves hunting Czech spies around the American air base of Furstenfeldbrücke and up to the Czech border, snooping round the "America Houses" (centres for disseminating American culture and information) which, according to Bechtold, were "stocked with all kinds of left-wing literature", or studying the inner secrets of local politics at Augsburg.

Bechtold tried also to do something about the ramshackle system of rewarding his informants, a system which had once again broken down.

> Captain Spiller had absconded with the funds. You see, at that time the currency on which the pay was based was cigarettes. He had a German girl friend, although he was living with his wife in Augsburg. His girl friend took the cigarettes from him and her husband peddled them on the black market for him and he bought paintings, china – things that he could send home as household goods and reconvert into cash in the United States.

Meanwhile, Merk and Barbie were unable to pay their net, and had nothing for themselves. Bechtold had to resort to selling cigarettes himself, through a shady Ukrainian in Augsburg who operated on the black market, and passing the cash on to his two informants.

And the French still refused to go away. There was a request for yet another interview with Barbie, and in November 1948 Lieutenant Whiteway warned the Americans that the French authorities were considering the issue of a subpoena against Barbie to appear as a witness at the René Hardy trial. Unwillingly, the CIC now began formal talks on the Barbie problem, Whiteway representing the French and Joseph Vidal, Major Browning's "case control specialist" from CIC Frankfurt, speaking for the Americans. Vidal objected that if Barbie went to Paris, he would be interrogated "in the usual French manner and forced to not only reveal information pertaining to the Hardy case but also to reveal information pertaining to his activities with CIC and his connections in the French zone". Eventually a deal was struck: Barbie would not go to France, but the French would be permitted to question him again. Three more interviews, at one of which Merk was apparently present, took place in early 1949. Vidal was also worried about reports that British intelligence was again investigating Barbie. The British had been told that Barbie was forming a murder gang to assassinate their German informants. This was an improbable tale, but Barbie was interviewed about his attitude to the British by a CIC officer who reported that, although no such murder organisation seemed to exist, "he indicated . . . that he had an intense hatred for the British because he had been physically maltreated by them" at the time of his arrest in Hamburg.

Early in 1949 a new and energetic figure arrived in the CIC offices at Augsburg. Eugene Kolb had been working in Germany for the Office of Special Investigations, an élite but somewhat roughhouse air force intelligence unit set up by General Curtis LeMay (the man who twenty years later recommended bombing North Vietnam "back to the Stone Age"). While employed by LeMay, Kolb had struck a prisoner under interrogation, and had been dismissed from OSI; he arrived at CIC Augsburg with all the enthusiasm of a Russian official taking up a penal posting in Siberia. Kolb, none the less, was badly needed in Augsburg. A new commanding officer, Major Riggin, had been put in over the head of the erratic Captain Spiller, but had failed to master the growing chaos in the office, which was now expanding and gathering in far more information than it could process. Kolb, as Herbert Bechtold recalls, was brought in to "sift through the mess that Spiller had created, put it in order and start giving advice".

Kolb cast a cold eye over Kurt Merk and Klaus Barbie, still ensconced in their office near the swimming pool and still living in the Mozartstrasse house on the proceeds of black market cigarettes. He read himself into their activities with more care than his predecessors, and soon perceived the real truth about the two men: Merk, though much more likeable, was not doing well, whereas Barbie was the more reliable informant given the sort of work the team was now being asked to perform. That was, in fact, much closer to the policeman's talents than to the bent of a professional intelligence agent. Merk was prolific in the information he supplied, but much of it was inaccurate, uncheckable or simply stale; he was obviously bored and frustrated by the narrow confines of the Augsburg job. Barbie had also been accused of inaccuracy, but Kolb, reading through his files, concluded that he had always warned his superiors when he thought an informant was unreliable. It was Barbie's American handlers who had "hardened up" his reports before they passed them on and who then blamed Barbie when they turned out wrong.

When it came to this – that Klaus Barbie was held to be more useful and interesting than Kurt Merk – the end of the Bureau Petersen and of Merk's two-year connection with the CIC could not be far off. Kolb strictly forbade Merk to undertake espionage outside the Augsburg area and put both men back on the dreary, pedestrian task of gathering information about the Communist party in Augsburg. For a few weeks, the whole Bureau Petersen was applied to this work alone, code-named "Operation Happiness". But it was obvious that Merk was deeply unhappy. In the spring of 1949, the Bureau Petersen was finally disbanded.

It was suggested to Merk that he should carry on with "Operation Happiness" as an individual, working in harness with Barbie. But talking to a CIC agent some months later, Merk explained that "he would feel out of place and consider himself not used to the best of his ability". Barbie now regarded this sort of anti-Communist police work as his own patch and sharply resented Merk's "intrusion". Merk recalled that "his attempts to reconvert to political targets had led to misunderstandings with Klaus Barbie, who showed professional jealousy towards subject . . . Barbie had given him to understand that he was in complete control of all phases of political investigations and that he did not welcome his assistance". The agent noted: "Barbie is a self-centred personality who had demonstrated the same character traits to this agent."

Unknown to the Americans, personal relationships in the house on Mozartstrasse had already turned sour. Andrée detested Regine Barbie – and perhaps also resented the fact that Regine lived there while she remained with her mother and could only stay with Kurt for short visits. Once she arrived to find that the Barbies had finally rescued their small son Klaus-Jörg from his foster-mother in Kassel.

I went to look at the child; it was holding the cot sides and battering its head against the wall. I have never seen anything like it. Klaus Barbie didn't care. And she was worse than he was. She was even more dreadful politically, a Nazi to her soul. It was everything for her husband. She went on and on about what he had done or hadn't done: everything about him was wonderful. He had real support in that woman; no other woman would have been capable of living with him, knowing what she knew about him. He told her part of what he had done – but not all!

It was early in 1949 when the growing tension at Mozartstrasse finally exploded. "One evening we were sitting together playing cards," Andrée recounts. "Barbie was a chatterbox; he loved talking to make himself more interesting. He began to tell things – I couldn't stand it."

What Barbie had to tell – and his tone was that of a boast rather than a confession – was the story of how he had personally machine-gunned a group of Jews to death at the end of the German occupation of Lyon. Even today, Andrée finds it difficult to repeat his words without tears of horror. Her response was to go into the bedroom, pack her bag and walk out of the house.

I went to a hotel in Augsburg. Somehow Kurt found me there, although I hadn't told him where I was going. He asked: "What's up, what's all this nonsense then?" I said: "I can't bear ever to see those two again – that man, with blood up to his elbows! How can you go on living with him?" And Kurt said: "Look, I don't like them any more than you do. I'm going to leave anyway. I can't take them any longer and I have applied to join another intelligence service which is more my line."

Both he and Andrée had at last arrived at the end of the line. The CIC job had shrunk to little more than police work, offering nothing to Merk's restless imagination; he felt misunderstood and insulted, and with nothing to absorb his energies, the company of the Barbies had become insufferable. The CIC said goodbye to him, without too many regrets and on the understanding that he was moving to another intelligence outfit which was either American or under close American supervision; there should therefore be no question of Merk selling his talents and his dangerous knowledge of the CIC's methods and contacts to "a foreign power", whether Britain, France, or the Soviet Union. In May he left Augsburg on "sick leave", complaining of a long-standing glandular problem which needed treatment, and went to Munich. He saw Barbie only once again, in early 1951 when his old associate called round at Merk's flat in Munich to say goodbye. "He told Kurt that he was leaving Germany," says Andrée. "He had found a way. I went into the other room when he came in."

Merk's affliction may have been something of a diplomatic illness. His main concern was to find another intelligence job, and in October 1949 he was reported by the CIC to be "being utilised by another American intelligence agency". According to the "Merk" file released by the American authorities in 1983, he spent most of the next twelve months setting up and running a large "positive intelligence" (i.e. espionage) net in East Germany, collecting mainly economic information for the US Constabulary Forces. He spent much of his time in Berlin, exhilarated to be back in the "great game" he understood so well. In a letter written later to his old friends Bob and Line Taylor in America, he suggested – in a very transparent code – that he had started this assignment as early as the spring of 1949, immediately on his departure from the CIC. "On May 1 1949 I began work with a similar firm of a positive character in Munich, where I stayed until October 1950. I spent most of this time in Berlin, and might have been made an honorary citizen if the eastern town hall had not vetoed the idea. My Berlin period was very interesting and very, very exciting."

The files state that the net was closed down in the autumn of 1950 and Merk dismissed because the Constabulary was not entitled to undertake this sort of operation. But there is something strange here. The idea that the American military police – for that is what the Constabulary was – should on their own initiative launch a massive spying operation against East Germany is bizarre, and there is more than a hint that Merk was in fact working for the CIA or the Gehlen organisation or – given the intimate American control over Gehlen – for both. (It is known that the CIA have operational files on Merk, which are still kept secret.) He went on to take yet another intelligence post about which we know even less: "It's another concern which is part of the same firm and the work reaches very deep down and beyond the frontiers." Andrée Rivez today says that she does not know who his employers were, but that in the summer of 1951 he took up a permanent post with Gehlen at its new headquarters just outside Munich.

They thought they were very lucky. After ten years spent clinging to one another in the teeth of the gale, Andrée and Kurt seemed to have reached dry land at last. They decided to get married. And, precisely at that moment, their luck turned into grotesque, withering tragedy.

A fortnight before the wedding day, he and Andrée were together in a small house in the forest near the Starnberger lake. He was about to leave for work, but waited to have one more coffee. It was September 1 1951. Andrée tells the story with bleak economy:

> Suddenly he said: "Ach, a nasty beast has stung me!" I saw the wasp fall dead, after he had slapped himself behind the ear. I went into the kitchen to get vinegar to put on the sting, but when I came back he was lying down in the bedroom. He said to me: "It's all up, I can't breathe." Ten minutes later, before a doctor could get there, he was dead.

Kurt Merk, the man who could be trusted in a world of lies, was only thirty-six when he died of a lung embolism brought on by a wasp sting. The Americans provided a massive oak coffin for him, which was too big to fit into the family tomb outside the little church at Fleinhausen. An old peasant woman who was there remembers that, as well as the family and friends from the village, there was a tall foreign woman standing by the grave – Andrée. After she had seen him laid to rest, Andrée left Bavaria with only twenty-five Deutschmarks in her purse, and after great hardships, made herself a new life elsewhere under another name. Andrée lived with her mother until the old lady died in 1983. She never married again and never returned to France. On her wall there hangs a miniature portrait of a sturdy, fair-haired young man with a small blond moustache.

On May 14 1949 the smouldering French discontent over Klaus Barbie suddenly exploded. The daily *Paris-Presse: l'Intransigeant* announced:

> The Resistance members of the Jura are scandalised . . . Klaus Barbie, who in 1944 was a commissar of the German SD at Lons-le-Saunier is free. During the occupation he burned his victims with an oxy-acetylene torch to make them confess during interrogations which lasted more than forty-eight hours . . . His activities extended also to the Franche-Comté, where deaths totalled more than five thousand.

The detail about the oxy-acetylene torch seems to have been pure invention, while the paper's remark that Barbie was now "a peaceful businessman in Munich, US zone" was equally wide of the mark. But the fat was now in the fire.

If the finger was not yet pointing straight at the CIC, it was pointed in the general direction of the American authorities in Germany – whose commanders still had no idea that Barbie was a paid CIC informant. In the CIC headquarters at Frankfurt, Joe Vidal sat down hastily and wrote a memorandum suggesting that Barbie should be interrogated about the newspaper story. He allowed, warily, that the headquarters was "inclined to believe that there is some element of truth in the allegations, since a mass reaction such as that indicated in the clipping would hardly stem from naught or from behaviour in accordance with the rules of land warfare". On the other hand, he went on, the CIC had no hard previous evidence that Barbie was a war criminal or a barbaric monster.

> Although it was known to this headquarters that during the German occupation of France subject had performed several successful missions and had been responsible for the arrest of a number of French Resistance personnel, his actions from a professional point of view were interpreted by this headquarters as mere performance of his duty. It was not, however, known that such barbaric methods had been employed by subject to obtain confessions from his victims.

The CIC was now admitting, although so far only to itself in an internal memorandum, that it was probably employing a man guilty of atrocities. Vidal certainly realised that Barbie was becoming a liability. He ended his letter by instructing the CIC office at Augsburg that Barbie "be dropped administratively as an informant but that relations with same be maintained as in the past until necessary action is dictated by the State Department and/or Department of the Army".

But Augsburg, now upgraded to a full CIC region of equal status to Munich, protested. Captain Kolb, the new operations officer at Augsburg, wrote back, vigorously defending Barbie.

> Subject has been interrogated on four (4) occasions by French authorities regarding his activities in France and regarding l'affaire Hardy. French authorities know where subject is located, know where he can be reached, and probably know what his activities are here, yet no attempt has ever been made to extradite subject, nor has any formal charge of war crimes ever been made.

If French authorities were interested in subject as a war criminal (and if his alleged crimes were as barbaric and well-known as the newspaper claims, they certainly should have been), it is almost certain that subject would have been extradited by now.

There was some justice in this. Kolb was wrong about the lack of charges (Barbie, after all, had been on the CROWCASS wanted lists and condemned to death by a French court immediately after the war). But he was correct in seeing that French behaviour was inconsistent. The reason was one which a CIC officer should have been quick to grasp: that the bureaucratic right hand had failed to inform the left hand what it was doing. French military intelligence in Germany knew where Barbie was and more or less how he was employed, and it is probable that some officials of the Ministry of Justice involved in preparing the second René Hardy trial had unofficially been told as well. But they had questioned Barbie about the Hardy affair, not about his own crimes. And the judicial authorities in Lyon were left in ignorance.

Kolb was sceptical about the accusations.

The operations officer of this region as well as the handling agent of subject have frequently watched subject interrogate certain suspects. Based on these observations, it is the belief of both that subject is intelligent and skilful enough to accomplish a successful interrogation by use of his head and consequently did not require the use of his hands.

He concluded, in his memorandum written on July 20 1949, that "while charges against subject may possibly be true, they are probably not true ... Subject is now considered to be the most reliable informant this headquarters has."

Barbie was not the only German with a sinister past employed in the Augsburg CIC office. Herbert Bechtold recalls that a certain Herr Müller worked there as "our administrative chief". Müller had been the Munich special prosecutor in charge of the interrogation of Hans and Sophie Scholl, the two young students who had led the "White Rose" resistance group against Hitler during the war, and who were executed in 1943 after distributing anti-Nazi leaflets in Munich university. In its way, the hiring of Müller is even more shocking than the hiring of Barbie. The CIC can at least argue that Barbie's true past was unknown to them when he was engaged in 1947. Exactly the opposite seems to be true in the Müller case.

The French quest for Barbie was coming up against an ungainly square-dance of evasions, as one office after another professed ignorance and passed the buck to the next. On the American side, there was real ignorance and ignorance that was faked. The American military government in Germany genuinely had no idea where Barbie was, because the CIC and its own intelligence division had never told their military commanders that Barbie was an American paid informant. The CIC of course knew very well where he was. It had now dug two lines of defence: initially all knowledge of Barbie could be denied; but if that were exposed as untrue, then it could be said that he had been dropped as an informant and CIC no longer had any trace of him. Here was the outline of the grand cover-up that was later developed. If General Lucius D. Clay, as head of military government in the US zone, had known about Barbie, he would almost certainly have ordered his delivery to France. But he did not, and the anxiety of the CIC to see that neither he nor the French found out what had been going on led the CIC to dig its trench of mendacity deeper and deeper until – in the end – it could not climb out of it.

A coalition of Resistance veterans' groups in Lyon now added their letter to the protests snowing down on the desk of the American ambassador in Paris. They offered more gruesome recollections about Barbie's crimes, and asked why he was living at liberty in the American zone of Germany. The Embassy, as ignorant as they were, was inclined to ask the same question. Then the French consular office in Munich wrote to the Office of the Military Governor in the US zone (OMGUS) in Frankfurt, asking where Barbie was and – if he were found – how he could be turned over to France. OMGUS asked the German police in Munich if they knew Barbie's address. They replied honestly that they did not. OMGUS passed this reply back to the French, who then put the same question to the local headquarters of OMGUS in Bavaria. They in turn passed the query back to the Munich police, received the same reply, and sent it to the French, who reported their failure to Paris. (The matter of Barbie's exact address was important. Under General Clay's extradition rules, issued in 1947, no request for extradition from the US zone could be considered unless the suspect's precise address was supplied. Louis Bibes, the year before, had never been allowed to know where precisely Barbie was being kept by the Americans.)

None of these futile manoeuvres affected Barbie himself. The awkward questions from the State Department or the Department of the Army foreseen by Joe Vidal did not materialise. Barbie was officially "dropped" from the books of the Augsburg CIC, as a precaution, but carried on working as an informant much as before. His handler and partner on operations remained special agent Herbert Bechtold. And the work he was now required to do, penetrating and combating German and foreign Communist organisations, suited his narrow police talents as much as it had confined and frustrated Kurt Merk.

The game of ping-pong between France and the American military government in Germany went into another set, as the French Ambassador in Washington delivered a formal request to the State Department on November 7 1949 for the surrender of Klaus Barbie. The note named him as the former head of the SD in Lyon, and observed that "despite repeated requests, American occupation authorities in Germany have not to date arrested and surrendered this war criminal". The successor to OMGUS, the office of the US High Commissioner in Germany (HICOG), retorted that no official request for Barbie's extradition had ever been received and suggested that any such application should be sent to HICOG by its French equivalent, the French High Commission in Baden Baden.

The ball was back in the French court, and they slammed it at the Americans from an unexpected direction. The allegations against Barbie himself had obscured the earlier interest in what he knew about the Hardy affair, but in 1950 René Hardy surged back into the headlines. Fresh evidence had emerged suggesting he had perjured himself in his first trial about his relationship to the Gestapo, and a second trial was about to begin. Lieutenant Whiteway, the Canadian who acted as liaison officer (and honest broker) between the French and the CIC, transmitted to the CIC a request for Barbie's appearance in person as the star witness in the second Hardy trial. Whiteway offered his own personal guarantee that Barbie would be returned to American hands after his testimony. Uneasily, the CIC agreed.

But still nobody had broken the awful truth about Barbie to HICOG. When the French High Commission wrote bitterly in March 1950, recalling that Barbie had been interrogated in American hands in 1949 and warning of violent popular reaction in France if he were not brought to trial for his own crimes, several HICOG officials wrote blithely innocent minutes, mocking the French lack of evidence about Barbie's whereabouts and remarking that "the allegations of the citizens of Lyon can be disregarded as being hearsay only".

This innocence was about to be rudely and permanently violated. René Hardy's trial opened in April 1950, with the French press stoking all the furnaces of political scandal and patriotic outrage.

On April 28, as the prosecution began to read Klaus Barbie's damning testimony against the accused, the proceedings were furiously interrupted by Maurice Garçon, Hardy's lawyer and one of the most theatrical advocates in France. Garçon tried to have Barbie's statement withdrawn: it was "scandalous", he said, that the American military authorities were protecting "for security reasons" a man who "had taken pleasure in torturing French patriots and who had often executed them with his own hands". Barbie, he went on, had taken part in reprisal massacres at Chambéry and Aix-les-Bains, and had thirty people shot in front of him near Die while serving as head of the Lyon Gestapo. "At another place, he watched the agony of 120 Frenchmen, and it was he who ordered five patriots to be shot in the Place Bellecour at Lyon to give an example of his repressive methods." The judge insisted that Barbie's statement was admissible, but described him as "a sinister torturer and war criminal".

A pack of French journalists now descended on the press office of the US army at Heidelberg. The press office tried to stem the onslaught with a routine "No comment", while it sought frantically for guidance, but this was taken as a form of admission that Garçon's charges were true, and the furore grew. Meanwhile Lieutenant Whiteway, that much tried honest broker, rang CIC headquarters at Frankfurt and told them frankly that, after Garçon's speech, Barbie would be arrested if he appeared in person at the Paris trial. He could no longer stand by his personal guarantee and agreed with the CIC that the idea of letting him testify should be abandoned.

The CIC were now falling back on their second line of defence – that Barbie had indeed once worked for them but had been dropped. Joe Vidal, the case supervisor at CIC headquarters, wrote to the army admitting that Barbie was an "ex-informant of this organisation" who had worked for the CIC from May 1947 to May 1949. He had known that Barbie had been "chief of the Gestapo at Lyon", but after reviewing Garçon's accusations had concluded that they "are considered by this headquarters in view of the known facts in the case to be a malicious distortion of fact". The same day, May 3 1950, Vidal wrote a much less confident internal memorandum to Colonel David Erskine, commander of the CIC in Germany, suggesting that it might now be safe to allow Barbie to be extradited "by virtue of the fact that this headquarters has had time to liquidate the net operating in the French zone" of Germany. However, he pointed out that neither a written request for extradition nor written evidence that Barbie really was a war criminal had been received from France. "Prior to May 1949 this headquarters had no indication that Barbie was wanted by the French for war crimes but had always gone on the assumption that he was wanted merely as a material witness against Hardy."

For the CIC the long-delayed moment of decision had arrived. On May 4, the day after Vidal's letter was written, five senior CIC officers gathered in Colonel Erskine's office: Erskine himself and his deputy Lieutenant-Colonel Eckmann, Major Wilson the new operations officer who had succeeded Earl Browning, Wilson's assistant Major Daniels, and Joe Vidal. They had essentially two choices. The army now knew that Barbie had been a CIC informant in the past, but of course had no idea that he had continued to function as such for over a year since being officially "dropped". The first option was to surrender Barbie to the French and permit him to be tried for war crimes. But Klaus Barbie, before he was taken to the guillotine or the firing-squad, would be certain to try to take the CIC's reputation with him. He would reveal not only that he had been spying on the French on American instructions, but that his 1949 "dropping" had been a fraud designed to deceive the American military commanders in Europe. Heads would roll at CIC headquarters, Colonel Erskine's no doubt among them.

The other course was to hang on to the second line of defence until the bombardment stopped – to continue to protect Barbie and, above all, to protect the inner secrets of his employment by the CIC. This created its own problems. The CIC would have to lie consistently and perhaps continuously to its own supreme authorities, army command in Europe and the US High Commission in Germany. It would be consciously committed to protecting a war criminal from the legal authorities of a friendly state which was a full member of the Atlantic Alliance. And, if the CIC could maintain the deception, Barbie would have to be kept under close supervision; it would no longer be possible simply to "dispose" of him by turning him loose in Germany or letting him seek work with some other intelligence outfit. (One ex-CIC agent, Gene Bramel, claims that at some point the idea came up of disposing of Barbie with a bullet, but there is no independent confirmation of this.) The CIC would be stuck with Barbie, for better or for worse.

The five men in Frankfurt did not take long to reach a decision. A handwritten minute of the meeting, taken by Vidal, has survived in the CIC archives: it was resolved that "Barbie should not be placed in the hands of the French, contrary to opinion expressed by me."

Who else knew? Vidal recorded in another memorandum that

two unnamed colonels at European Command army headquarters concurred in the decision.

The storm blowing in from France continued to rise, and alarm grew both in the American Embassy in Paris and in the US High Commission in Germany. On May 10 a French senator declared that the American answers to requests for Barbie "do not give, to put it as mildly as possible, the impression of perfect uprightness". The minister chairing the debate replied that the French government would not "recoil before any step necessary to obtain the surrender of a war criminal who deserves to be punished". The legal attaché to the French High Commission in Germany sent the US High Commission a letter detailing what was known about Barbie's relationship with the CIC and including photographs and a schedule of the dates on which he had been interviewed by the French agents in the presence of CIC officers. The Resistance organisations in France continued to protest in Paris and Lyon. The honorary president of the Confédération Nationale de la Résistance wrote to the American consul in Lyon complaining that "all police forces may use bandits as informers, but the employment of this one, famous as a torturer and murderer, causes a veritable scandal in Lyon. I ask you in the name of the entire French Resistance to insist to Washington that this individual be delivered to French justice." A public dinner in Lyon ended in turmoil when a French general turned to the American consul, one of the honorary guests, and bitterly reproached him over the Barbie affair.

HICOG, headed by John McCloy, tried feebly to deflect the tempest. By now, of course, HICOG knew that the French were probably telling the truth both about Barbie's crimes and about the fact that he had been employed by the CIC in the past. The McCloy policy was to appear helpful and placatory towards the French, but not to ask penetrating questions of the CIC or to demand a manhunt. Perhaps it would all blow over in the end. HICOG drafted letters offering to help the French find Barbie and admitting that it had some "clues" to his whereabouts, but then decided not to send them. Instead, James D. Riddleberger, a senior HICOG official, was sent to Paris to consult with the American Embassy there. He certainly managed to frighten the Embassy, which cabled the State Department that he had brought "secret information" indicating that the Barbie case "has highly embarrassing possibilities, to put it mildly". The Embassy begged the State Department to stall any French enquiries about Barbie which might arrive in Washington, but complained to HICOG that in spite of Riddleberger's visit, "we should very much like to have some word of advice from you as to how to handle this kind of protest, for it seems obvious that the matter is not dying down". It certainly was not, and John McCloy himself now decided to step in. A stiff French note had been delivered in Washington, and when the State Department cabled HICOG on May 26 asking for "guidance" in drafting an answer, McCloy ordered his staff to "smoke out EUCOM (the US Military Command in Europe) on the matter and see how far they would go in helping to find this character, and to get more details as to just how embarrassing it would be to them [CIC] if he were turned over to the French".

This was the first real test of the cover-up decision. On June 16 1950 Benjamin Shute, who was McCloy's director of intelligence, travelled to Heidelberg to meet General Robert Taylor, the army's chief of intelligence in Germany. Taylor and Major Wilson of the CIC, one of the five men present at the May 4 decision, sat down with this personal representative of McCloy and lied to him like troopers. They went over the old ground of Barbie's "former" employment with the CIC, giving Shute a few extra details, but then assured him that on May 24 1949 Barbie's attachment "had been discontinued, following publication in France of charges that Barbie was a war criminal". Since then they had not used Barbie, "although they did keep in contact with him until late April 1950", as Shute recorded in his notes. They added that the CIC had "not been in touch with him since late April 1950 and does not know his present whereabouts".

With this pack of deliberate lies the CIC finally burned its boats. If the truth came out, the first victim would be John McCloy himself, who from now on would be telling enquirers on his personal authority that Barbie had not been used by the Americans for over a year and had since vanished. Second place in the casualty list lay in a dead heat between Barbie himself and Colonel David Erskine, commander of the CIC in Germany.

Comforted with this false information, Benjamin Shute flew to Washington. He advised the State Department, now confronted with a full French dossier on Barbie's atrocities in wartime Lyon, that it was safe to allow extradition proceedings to go ahead. Green lights started flashing all the way down the hierarchy: the State Department told HICOG to go ahead, HICOG sent an extradition clearance request to EUCOM, and EUCOM passed on the same formal request to the CIC headquarters in Frankfurt. The speed of all this took Colonel Erskine by surprise; the CIC had not realised how eager Washington was to clear away the Barbie problem. He and Joe Vidal wrote anxiously to their confidants in EUCOM's intelligence division, reminding them of the secret decision on May 4 not to give up Barbie to the French.

Early in September 1950 the intelligence division officers consulted Erskine and Vidal by telephone: what should EUCOM say to McCloy's HICOG enquiry about extradition? They agreed to go on lying. A certain Colonel Hardick from EUCOM confirmed this in a secret cable to Colonel Erskine, who must have been a deeply relieved man to read the words: "Further propose that HICOG be notified informally that Barbie is no longer under control of any agency of this division." HICOG would be told that the CIC had no objections to the extradition papers being made out.

But if Barbie was to be extradited, he had first to be found. This, as Colonel Erskine must have pondered, was now the real danger confronting the CIC. For the moment, he could rely on the ineffectiveness of the quest. On November 17 1950 a HICOG lawyer reported that "after diligent search, the arresting agencies have not found Barbie", but on January 31 1951 the US High Commission again assured the French at Baden Baden that "continuous efforts to locate Barbie are being made". As long as Barbie was in Germany the risk of his discovery – and the exposure of the CIC's lies to its own superiors – would remain and grow.

CHAPTER EIGHT

The Good Father

In December 1950 Captain Walter Unrauth, a young American officer attached to the CIC 66th headquarters in Stuttgart sat down to write a long and devastating report for his superiors on the Klaus Barbie affair. It is evident from the controlled passion behind Unrauth's clipped official prose that he was shocked by what he was describing. His opening paragraph, sparse as it was, set out something that the CIC had succeeded in concealing from its command headquarters, and perhaps from itself, for the past three years:

> Klaus Barbie has been an informant of this organisation since 1947, operating in the Region XII area [it began]. Barbie was formerly a high official of Gestapo in Lyon, France, and during his period of service is alleged to have tortured and killed many French patriots. Because of these alleged acts, Barbie is wanted by the French for trial as a war criminal.

Unrauth went on to set out in clinical detail the steps taken by various officers at different times to withhold Barbie from the French; he listed them individually by name and he indicated that along the line deliberate lies had been told by those who had protected Barbie while claiming that the CIC was no longer connected with him.

Unrauth was wise enough, however, to see the difficulty now confronting the CIC: if Barbie was picked up by any other power he could cause "a great deal of adverse publicity to CIC in particular and to the armed forces in general". He could expose the CIC for employing him in the first place, he could reveal its secret operating methods, blow the cover of its informants, and further blacken its name by pointing out the identity of other "unsavoury personalities" protected and employed by the organisation. Barbie, in effect, was a man who knew too much. Nevertheless, Unrauth's recommendation was that the 66th CIC should get rid of him immediately – something that "should have been done a long time before . . .

Subject is a professional intelligence man," he pointed out, "who is very capable and qualified to take care of himself – unless this organisation persists in remaining his guardian angel."

It was not going to be quite as simple as that. Barbie was holed up in his CIC safe house on the Mozartstrasse in Augsburg; but there was nothing at all safe about his position. He was now on the wanted list of both HICOG's public safety branch and the German police. He might be picked up at any moment for the most minor offence and immediately exposed. He might be betrayed or even kidnapped by agents of the French Sureté who were known to be in the US zone; according to Unrauth he was "living in constant fear of being apprehended by the French".

For once Barbie's natural arrogance had deserted him. He was trapped by his dependence on the CIC and neither he nor his wife could see a way out. "They were entirely at our mercy," said Herbert Bechtold, his case officer at the time. "They didn't know what was going to happen to them and it played constantly on their minds. Barbie resented it deeply that he was not master of his destiny. He was anxious, insecure, depressed. He felt he had no future to look forward to. He was living from day to day."

At the same time there were disturbing upheavals within the CIC which was coming to the end of its natural role in Europe. Within months it would be disbanded, and by early 1951 the personnel at Augsburg had begun to change rapidly. Bechtold was told he was to be transferred to Bonn, and Barbie would acquire a new "baby-sitter" – Leo Hecht, a fluent German speaker who was also a Jew. The change did nothing to improve Barbie's morale.

But then, quite unexpectedly, a ready-made escape route presented itself, appearing to offer at a stroke a convenient solution both to Barbie's problem and to the CIC's.

The way out had first surfaced in December 1950, just about the time that Walter Unrauth was writing up his report. It was perhaps as well that Unrauth himself knew nothing about it since he would doubtless have detected that it was every bit as corrupt as the CIC's relationship with Barbie. The escape route was known, not for nothing, as "the Rat Line". It had been opened up in Austria four years earlier by the 430th CIC, whose headquarters were in Vienna, and its mastermind was a brilliant US intelligence officer, Lieutenant-Colonel James Milano, who had served as an under-cover agent in Italy during the war and had been decorated with the OBE by the British for his exploits.

In 1945, as the Russian zone was established in Austria, he was sent to Vienna as CIC operations officer. He found himself plunged into the twilight city of *The Third Man* – a place teeming with desperate refugees and double agents, where identity cards or safe passes acquired the value of hard currency and changed hands at blackmail prices. The 430th CIC's offices were on the third floor of the Allied Insurance building facing the Vienna University hospital, and it was here that Milano and one of his top lieutenants, Paul Lyon, confronted the urgent problem of rescuing from the Russian zone those undercover agents who had worked for the Allies during the war and now found themselves trapped behind a rapidly descending Iron Curtain.

At first, escape was relatively simple to organise. Passes, forged or bought on the black market, were supplied to take agents as refugees through the Soviet zone to Salzburg, where the American zone began, and where they could take their chances with the flood of "displaced persons" heading west. The forging of passes was done in the CIC's offices in Salzburg. "Forgers weren't hard to find," recalled Milano. "We always found good ones among the locals. French, Austrian, German – all of them were good. Sometimes we even brought them into the official photo labs – but only at night."

But as relations between the Americans and their former Allies deteriorated, the Russians began more careful checking on the trains leaving Vienna in an effort to stop the flood of refugees heading west and it became clear that a more sophisticated operation was needed by the CIC. The Rat Line was conceived by Milano and Lyon in late 1946. "It was born in my office one night," is how Milano described it. "I was sitting there with Paul Lyon and a couple of others and we just decided we needed a rat-line to Latin America."

The concept of South America as a haven was not simply conjured out of thin air. In Vienna, as elsewhere in Europe after the war, representatives of South American states were combing refugee camps for skilled workers. Countries like Argentina, Chile, Peru, Brazil and Colombia needed them to help rebuild their post-war economies.

While the British, the Americans, the French and the Russians competed with each other for top German scientists and engineers, South America was more down to earth: it needed plumbers, mechanics, builders and electricians. Each country had strict quotas for immigrants in each category, and the CIC made sure it was extremely well-informed about who needed what.

Milano and Lyon fitted would-be escapers to the particular job category that happened to be open at the time. Thus, if Argentina was looking for plumbers, Milano's men would introduce refugees to the arcane mysteries of plumbing, calling on local talent for instruction if necessary. At the same time the refugees were given a crash course in Spanish or Portuguese, as appropriate.

The CIC had devised a system for selecting genuine informants with a real need to escape from those whose claims were bogus.

> We investigated the hell out of them [recalled Milano]. I was not interested in anyone from the SS. I hated them – and traitors. If we knew someone was a member of the SS we wouldn't take him. For every one sent through, one was turned down. We also interrogated them to make sure they weren't Soviet agents. The final decision was based on two main principles: did they make a contribution to the Allied cause? And did they risk their lives?

The fact that this system was not able to detect Klaus Barbie when he went through was hardly Milano's fault, since by 1951 he himself had left the Rat Line in the hands of his successors.

By then it had had three remarkably successful years in the course of which around a hundred agents and their families had escaped by using it. The scheme was never officially condoned. Milano had not sought approval for it, "except for a quiet word in the ears of G-2 (the intelligence headquarters in Austria) who had to approve the finance", but he is equally certain that "the generals" knew perfectly well what was going on.

None of this could possibly have worked without an intermediary who could cross borders with impunity and help the refugees on their way to South America. The CIC's discovery in 1947 of an extraordinary go-between called Dr Krunoslav Draganovič was crucial to the success of the Rat Line.

But in employing this deeply flawed intermediary the Americans were involving themselves in a relationship at least as damaging as the one they had established with Klaus Barbie.

Draganovič was a Croatian priest and scholar who worked for the Croatian Red Cross. He was secretary of the Confraternity of San Girolamo in Rome – a Croatian religious institute – and he was a man who enjoyed the patronage of the Vatican. The fact that he was also a Fascist, wanted for questioning about war crimes, and an active supporter of a regime whose atrocities had matched and often outstripped those of the Nazis themselves was judged irrelevant. In all other respects he was ideal.

"Paul Lyon found Draganovič," Milano recalled. "He came to me and said, 'Jeez, there's a priest who works for this refugee

organisation and is getting hold of all these Red Cross documents.'
I never met Draganovič myself. Paul Lyon handled him. He was
really well positioned for our needs. We called him 'The Good
Father'."

The procurement of Red Cross passports was a critical factor.
They could be used for crossing frontiers or to help establish
someone's identity in a Europe swamped with stateless people.
They could also be cynically exploited. In 1947 an American
undercover agent in Italy drew up a revealing report for the State
Department to show just how easy it was. The agent, Vincent la
Vista, demonstrated how the Vatican and the Red Cross were
helping many Nazis and Fascists – as well as deserving refugees – to flee to South America with false passports.

> The justification of the Vatican for its participation in this illegal
> traffic is simply the propagation of the Faith [he reported]. It is
> the Vatican's desire to assist any person regardless of nationality
> or political beliefs, as long as that person can prove himself to be
> a Catholic. The Vatican further justifies its participation by
> its desire to infiltrate not only European countries but Latin
> American countries as well with people of all political beliefs as
> long as they are anti-Communist and pro-Catholic Church.

La Vista demonstrated how easy it was to get Vatican sponsorship
by taking two men posing as Hungarian refugees into the offices of
a Vatican priest in Rome, where they spun a false story about
having escaped from the Russian zone after losing all their papers.
The priest listened sympathetically, then asked only for an affidavit
which would establish the fact that they were both good Catholics.
After swearing one, they filled in a form which he signed, testifying
to the fact that they were genuine Hungarians. This was enough to
allow them to apply for the vital Red Cross passport. "Both informants were Italian," added la Vista, "neither ever having been
outside Italy." He listed those Vatican organisations known to
help suspect refugees. Among them was the Confraternity of San
Girolamo, whose Secretary was Dr Draganovič.

By 1951, however, the Red Cross had tightened their procedures
considerably, and the CIC was lucky to find Draganovič, a man
who was still prepared to exploit the system to its limits under the
double protection of the Red Cross and the Vatican. Most of his
attention was given to fleeing members of the Croatian terrorist
organisation, the Ustase, rather than specifically to Nazis, and it is

perhaps for this reason that, in the intense debate over the Vatican's attitude to the Nazis, his role has been overlooked. Yet the Ustase, and a few of the Croatian priests who supported them, committed war crimes so terrible that even today, in the full knowledge of the Nazi holocaust, they have a deep capacity to shock. Under the leadership of the puppet dictator Ante Pavelič who established the "independent" Fascist state of Croatia in 1941, with its capital in Zagreb, the Ustase carried out a calculated campaign of genocide against more than two million Serbs of the orthodox faith.

Their aim was spelled out with brutal precision by Dr Mile Budak, Pavelič's Minister of Education who spoke in 1941 of the necessity for killing one third of the Serbs, expelling one third, and forcing the remaining third to embrace the Roman Catholic religion: "Thus," he said, "our new Croatia will get rid of all Serbs in our midst in order to become one hundred per cent Catholic within ten years."

Pavelič himself set his stamp on the campaign when he addressed Ustasa troops in Zagreb, and, in the course of a manic speech, announced: "A good Ustase is one who can use his knife to cut a child from the womb of its mother."

From June 1941 bands of Ustase roamed the countryside of Bosnia with knives, bludgeons and machine guns, slaughtering men, women and children. Whole village populations were massacred. Death camps were set up in which prisoners were kept in conditions so appalling that they died of dysentery or other diseases within days of arriving. In one camp prisoners were bound to each other by wire and taken to the edge of a precipice where one of them would be pushed over, dragging the others with him. Then hand grenades would be lobbed down on to the broken bodies.

Pavelič's instructions were often obeyed to the letter, with guards attempting to outdo each other in the savagery of their executions and the desecration of bodies. There was often no burial at all following a massacre. Even German officers who had seen extermination camps in Poland were horrified by what they witnessed. One who was taken round the camp at Zemun, where a prison population of seventy thousand had been reduced to twenty thousand in a matter of weeks, was told by the camp commandant: "We Ustase are more practical than you. You shoot, but we use hammers, clubs, rope, fire and quick lime. It's less expensive."

Some of the atrocities were carried out by, or under the supervision of Catholic priests, with the Order of the Franciscans often among the worst offenders. They included a Franciscan who was commandant for six months at the concentration camp of Jasenovac where tens of thousands of prisoners died, and another at Alipasin Most where a massacre of 180 Serbs was recorded.

The only alternative was forcible conversion to Roman Catholicism. Often whole villages would be received into the Church by a single priest, with armed Ustasa guards looking on. But occasionally, with redoubled horror, a congregation of newly-converted Catholics would be hauled from the church and shot anyway. The bishop of Mostar, reporting directly on these atrocities to the head of the Croatian Church, Archbishop Stepinac, in Zagreb, said: "They go to mass; they learn the Catholic catechism; they have their children baptised. And then . . . while the new converts are in church attending mass, they seize them, young and old, men and women, drag them outside, and send them to eternity in droves."

This then was the regime that Draganovič represented in Rome. That he was a fervent Croatian nationalist is not in doubt. Though his background was that of the scholar-priest – he had edited the general register of the Catholic Church in Yugoslavia in 1939 and was, at the same time, a director of oriental studies at the University of Sarajevo and secretary to the archbishop there – his role in Rome assumed a strong political slant. He had become an ecclesiastical adviser to Pavelič's regime in 1941, then went to Rome in 1943 where the Croatians hoped that his close contacts with the Vatican would be useful in the promotion of the Croatian cause and the boosting of the uncertain reputation of Pavelič himself.

In this he may have been at least partially successful; although the Vatican kept the Pavelič regime at arm's length in its diplomatic relations, Pope Pius XII never uttered any direct condemnation of Croatian atrocities, restricting his statements to general observations on human rights. When the British Minister to the Vatican, in private audience, ventured to draw his attention to events in Croatia, the pope referred to Pavelič as "a much maligned man". The British Foreign Office, to whom this was reported, reacted by saying that "this is really carrying Christian charity a little too far" and instructed the minister to draw His Holiness's attention to the reality of Pavelič's violent career.

As the war ended and Croatia collapsed, Draganovič came into his own. Using his cover as chief representative of the Croatian Red Cross, he offered sanctuary and safe passage to streams of Ustasa agents. He visited the many refugee camps set up in Italy, identifying Ustasa supporters and issuing them, where necessary, with fresh identity cards.

Stephen Clissold, a young British liaison officer with the Special Refugee Commission in Rome, made a study of Draganovič, and included it in a manuscript account which has never been published.

> In the summer of 1945 [reported Clissold] Draganovič made a personal tour of the camps where ex-members of the Ustasa armed forces and political organisations were housed, and established contact with leading Ustasa representatives . . . This led to the formation of a political intelligence service which enabled San Girolamo to collect reports and data on political trends among the émigrés. The territorial immunity enjoyed by San Girolamo . . . also provided safe asylum for the émigrés most in danger of arrest by the Allies.

A CIC report on Draganovič in 1947 estimated that at the time of writing there were twenty named and wanted Ustasa war criminals within the walls of San Girolamo, though Draganovič had denied any contact with Ustasa personnel. The same report referred to a list of 115 Croats who had been shipped by Draganovič out of Italy to Argentina. They had all been "fed, clothed, housed, and otherwise provided for by the Institute of San Girolamo".

Another CIC report in the same year, based on interviews with Draganovič, concluded that "his sponsorship of the Ustasa cause stems from a deep-rooted conviction that the ideas espoused by this arch-nationalist organisation, half logical, half lunatic, are basically sound concepts". Draganovič apparently tried to draw a distinction between his support of the Ustase and the war crimes they had committed. "I am a Ustase," he said. "However, I disassociate myself from all other attributes of the Ustase."

His contacts in Latin America, which were now to be so useful to the CIC, had helped some of the most notorious Croatian war criminals to escape, including almost certainly Ante Pavelič himself who slipped through the hands of the British after the war, and fled to Argentina. Stephen Clissold, whose job it was to detect Ustasa war criminals and bring them to justice, had to watch in frustration as scores of them disappeared virtually under the nose of the Special Refugee Commission. The Vatican, which might have brought pressure on the authorities of San Girolamo, refused to act. Indeed the pope signalled his support for Draganovič when he received a two man delegation from the institute in 1946; both men were close friends of Draganovič. Clissold even suspected that some of the Croatian refugees were being helped on their way with funds provided by the Vatican's charitable organisation, the Assistenza Pontifica.

It was small wonder, then, that Paul Lyon of the 430th CIC, who met Draganovič in Trieste in 1947, thought he had struck gold. Tall, dark and saturnine, dressed always in a cassock and long flowing cloak, with a broad-brimmed priest's hat, Draganovič was a striking figure. But not everyone liked the look of him. "There was about him a strange oily manner which I found very off-putting," recalled one of those who encountered him in Rome at the time. "He had snake-like eyes that shifted constantly. I did not take to him at all."

Milano called for a thorough investigation of Draganovič when Lyon reported back to him. He does not now remember the results of this inquiry, but he believes it was not "excessively damaging". In any event, he gave the Draganovič project his personal approval. "I made the final decision to employ him as an integral part of the Rat Line," he said. "He was only interested in honest Catholics. He wasn't a spy."

But Milano can have been under no illusion about Draganovič's background by 1950 when Lyon drew up a confidential report on the Rat Line. "Draganovič is known and recorded as a Fascist, war criminal etc," he wrote, "and his contacts with South American diplomats of a similar class are not generally approved by US State Department officials."

He was also grasping when it came to money. He demanded $1,000 to $1,400 per defector, a considerable sum in those days, and Lyon noted that he was "unscrupulous in his dealings . . . it is not entirely impossible that he will delay one shipment for the organisation to benefit another organisation who pays higher prices".

Somewhere along the line the CIC appears to have given the "Good Father" an undertaking that they would be prepared to help any fleeing Ustase in return for his help with Rat Line customers. But apart from funding the Draganovič operation, there is no evidence that the CIC extended direct assistance to Ustasa war criminals. Reflecting on his long association with Draganovič, Milano saw no reason to regret it: "We were taught, and we honestly believed, that the end justified the means," he said. "I thought it was a very worthwhile thing to do. I was very proud of it."

Klaus Barbie and his family were to be among the last of the Rat Line's customers. When Lieutenant John Hobbins, a close CIC colleague of Walter Unrauth, travelled to Vienna in December 1950 to see whether the Rat Line might be suitable for the evacuation of

Barbie, he noted that "in order to keep the established channel open for their own use, [the Rat Line] must be used frequently . . . at present they do not have enough of these cases to ensure that the channel can be kept open against their contingencies". The 430th CIC in any case was not budgeted beyond June 1951, and "some time in the undetermined future, the CIA will assume responsibility for evacuations".

Hobbins returned to Augsburg to brief his fellow officers on what the procedure would be. Barbie, he said, would be supervised by George Neagoy, a CIC officer from Landsalzburg in Austria, who would travel to Augsburg to interview him and determine his "special needs". He would then begin making the arrangements. The process might take anything from six to sixteen weeks.

Barbie required an assumed name under which he would be provided with travel documents obtained by the 66th CIC from the Combined Travel Board (a branch of the Allied High Commission for Germany) in Munich. These would enable the family to travel through Austria to Italy, accompanied by Neagoy. Thereafter Draganovič would take over.

> Upon arrival in Italy [wrote Hobbins] the emigrant will be placed in a hotel, and, on a day to day basis, provided with sufficient funds to live until embarkation. Upon embarkation, the emigrant is given $50 in greenbacks. He is given no further assurances, and is strictly on his own. From the beginning of the processing, the 430th tries to create an atmosphere which leads the emigrant to believe that he is being treated with great consideration; that everything within reason is being done to provide for his own welfare; that he is entitled to nothing further, and has no right to ask or expect further assistance after boarding ship.

Back in Augsburg, the news that a way out had been found for Barbie was greeted with enormous relief. By late January 1951 permission had been sought and obtained from EUCOM to use the 430th CIC's escape route, and by February Barbie's new case-officer Leo Hecht was reporting that the whole Barbie family was learning Spanish in preparation for their new life. Barbie himself was full of expectation about the prospects in Bolivia. His trade was to be that of mechanic, and his adopted name the one which his wife and children had been using ever since they had come to live in Augsburg – Altmann, the name that Barbie had stolen from the old rabbi of Trier.

A long and totally spurious reference for the "mechanic" Klaus

Altmann was prepared by the CIC and translated into Italian for the benefit of the Bolivian consulate in Genoa. It stated that "Il Signor Altmann" had been born in Kronstadt, and had worked from 1945 to 1948 as a mechanic in Dortmund. His fictitious employer testified to the fact that he had been "molto diligente, molto volenteroso, e molto conscienzioso" – diligent, willing, and conscientious. He had worked in difficult circumstances, helped build up the business after the war, and had given every satisfaction.

The original idea had been to send the Barbie family to Argentina, but Draganovic had suggested Bolivia instead. There were two reasons for this: Bolivia was currently encouraging the immigration of skilled mechanics; and Draganovič had an old colleague, a Croatian priest like himself, Father Roque Romac, who would act as guarantor for Barbie when he arrived in Bolivia. In fact, of course, Father Romac of the Franciscan community of Sacaba, near Cochabamba in Bolivia, had never even heard of Barbie let alone met him, but Draganovič knew he could rely on him. For Father Romac was also a fugitive. His real name was Father Osvald Toth, born near Varazdin in 1905, and he was wanted for questioning by the Yugoslav government of Marshal Tito. He had been interned in Italy after the war and had only narrowly escaped being handed back to the Yugoslavs. Draganovič had found him a passport belonging to Father Roque Romac, an older priest who had just died. Armed with this new identity Toth had escaped, first to Patagonia, then to Bolivia – he was in no position to ask any embarrassing questions.

In late February Draganovič cabled him in Sacaba and informed him that a family called Altmann was on its way to Bolivia with his name on their visa application as sponsor.

Back in Augsburg, the CIC was determined that nothing should go wrong – the papers must be impeccable. Region IV of the CIC, in Munich, was asked to apply for a temporary travel document and Augsburg hastened to assure them that this was a top priority case. "Subject mentioned above and his family are of definite interest to Uncle Sugar intelligence," they cabled. A scrupulous check into the family's background had revealed "no derogatory information" about them.

Region IV seems to have entered into the spirit of the thing. On February 21 1951 they forwarded a "Temporary Travel Document in lieu of passport for stateless persons and persons of undetermined nationality", numbered 0121454 – the first, but by no means the last piece of paper, to give Klaus Barbie the status and identity that would be his for the next thirty-two years. A second travel document for Regine and the children accompanied it, as well as a transit visa for Italy issued by the Italian consulate in Munich, and a military entry permit for Trieste which was, at this stage, given as the destination.

There was one last matter to be taken care of: Klaus Barbie had to say goodbye to his mother who was still living in Trier. It is clear that the CIC were extremely worried about arranging the rendezvous. They thought it quite likely that she was being watched – by the German police or by French agents – and so they arranged an elaborate operation with Region XII whereby Barbie's mother would travel alone by train to Augsburg; there she would be met by Leo Hecht in an undercover Volkswagen with special licence plates and driven to a prearranged spot outside the town. Careful instructions were given to Hecht on the art of spotting a "tail" and getting rid of it once spotted.

In the event the meeting went off smoothly, if emotionally. Barbie was saying goodbye, probably for ever, he thought, to the woman who, more than any other single person, had shaped his life.

The "Altmann" operation had now achieved the status of a high-priority intelligence mission. On February 28 the Intelligence Division of EUCOM in Heidelberg notified their office in Salzburg that "subject" was ready. Lieutenant-Colonel Jack Dobson, Milano's successor with 430th CIC, instructed his agent George Neagoy to carry on with the job. Accompanied by another agent, Jack Gay, Neagoy travelled to Augsburg to begin the final preparations.

On March 9 "Klaus Altmann, mechanic", his wife Regine Wilhelms, his nine-year-old daughter Ute Maria, and his four-year-old son Jorge, left Augsburg by train for Salzburg and freedom. Leo Hecht watched them go. Augsburg, he reflected, felt quite empty without Barbie: "He'd made such an enormous contribution."

The Rat Line worked smoothly. The Barbies stayed for two days in a CIC "safe house" in Salzburg, then left by train for Trieste and Genoa. Barbie himself recalls a dramatic incident on the Austrian border. A customs official, he claims, spotted something wrong with the travel documents. For a moment it looked as if everything was going to end in disaster. Then, Barbie says, he shouted: "Look, I've got children." To which the customs officer shouted back: "Get going, and I don't want to see you again." Barbie replied: "You can be sure of that."

In Genoa the family booked into the Hotel Nazionale at Via

Lomellini 6, and met for the first time the tall stooping figure of Draganovic, who had already made approaches on their behalf to the Bolivian consulate. According to Barbie, the two of them hit it off instantly.

Their first task, on March 15, was to call at the offices of the International Red Cross. There Draganovic, in his official capacity as head of the organisation's Croatian section, assisted the "Altmanns" in their application for travel passes.

For stateless refugees the Red Cross travel document was almost as good as a passport, though officials of the organisation were insistent that it was merely to be used to get from one place to another and should be immediately returned on arrival (the Barbies never got around to this). Without Draganovič standing by to vouch for them, the family would never have acquired the documents. That same day, in addition, they acquired medical certificates testifying to their mental and physical health and their capacity for work.

On March 16 they went to the Bolivian consulate to secure their visa. Barbie's qualifications as a mechanic were produced, and his resources were put at $850. (In fact the CIC had seen to it that he had nearly ten times this amount.) There was also a moving testimonial prepared by Draganovič on Klaus and Regine's religious background. Apart from his own signature, appended as secretary of the Confraternity of San Girolamo, the application was signed by the rector, Monsignor Junaj Magjerli. It stated that the couple were "well known to them both from first-hand acquaintance and from reliable sources of information". They were "good practising Catholics, convinced Christians and anti-Communists, alien to all sinister tendencies". Draganovic had also brought from Rome a form secured from the Justice Department of the Ministry of the Interior to show that the "Altmanns" had clean records in Italy. The visa was duly issued.

Three days later the family applied for, and were granted, transit visas for Argentina, and then, on March 22, armed with third class tickets, they boarded the liner *Corrientes* which was flying the Argentinian flag and bound for Buenos Aires via Naples, Las Palmas, Rio de Janeiro and Santos.

Agents Neagoy and Gay reported back to their intelligence chiefs that the "complete operation was without incident". The 55th CIC headquarters breathed an official sigh of relief and commended everyone involved for the extremely efficient manner in which "the final disposal of an extremely sensitive individual had been handled". It concluded its message: "This case is considered closed by Intelligence division, European Command and this detachment."

There is an intriguing postscript to be added on the subsequent career of the "Good Father". Soon after the Barbies had departed Dr Krunoslav Draganovič left the Institute of San Girolamo and took a private apartment in Rome. He was still a wanted man in Yugoslavia and he maintained a low profile. Then, on November 11 1967, he disappeared after travelling in the direction of the Yugoslav border. The rumour that went round Vatican circles in Rome was that he had been kidnapped and almost certainly executed by agents of Tito's secret police, the UDBA. But that was not the case. In fact he had returned voluntarily. A local paper reported that he had crossed the frontier at Sezana of his own free will after writing to the public prosecutor in Sarajevo, and had undergone examination under Article 118 of the Criminal Code concerning hostile propaganda. Although he was under surveillance, reported the paper, he had some freedom of movement and had even visited his sister in the Sarajevo area.

Draganovič had purchased his freedom with information. The threat posed to Yugoslavia's internal security by Croatian terrorists was, and is, a major concern of the authorities, and UDBA was keenly interested in Draganovič's enormous knowledge of Croatian exiles, their whereabouts and their political activities. After lengthy interrogation (though no torture), Draganovič was allowed to resume his old work. Under the supervision of the archbishop of Sarajevo he became chairman of a committee preparing a new edition of the general register of the Catholic Church in Yugoslavia, and by 1974 it was completed. The volume was the first new edition to be published since the one he had himself prepared back in 1939. The introduction did not explain the long gap between publication dates.

In Church circles his reputation was clouded by controversy over his Ustasa associations and he was regarded with some distaste. One summer he travelled to Zagreb where he bumped into a priest who had known him in the old days. The priest began to question him about his return to Yugoslavia, and asked him about the circumstances in which it had occurred. Draganovič fell silent. His face flushed a deep and unnatural red, then went pale: "When anyone has been through what I've been through," he whispered, "then you are too deeply affected to talk about it."

Right to the end he was watched by the secret services, for although he had been fully interrogated by UDBA on his return, he had never been entirely cleared. In the summer of 1983 he fell ill. On July 6 his house in Sarajevo was raided and the contents turned over by police officials who even searched his bedroom as he lay ill.

Whether they found anything is not known. Whether they knew what they were looking for is uncertain. Whether the house still held any great secrets may never be ascertained. But that night, following the raid, Draganovič died.

INTERLUDE

When Klaus Barbie left Europe he was thirty-seven years old. By the time he returned finally, to face judgment for his crimes, he was a sick, elderly man of sixty-nine. His life in South America was thus to last more than twice as long as his service with the SD and the CIC put together. He was to make full use of it.

These years tell the story of a man unable to resist the pull of his old profession. When Barbie was hustled down the Rat Line and out of Europe, he knew that he was one of the lucky minority of Nazi criminals who had been given the chance of a new and anonymous life in a distant country – and for a while he was thankful to accept it. But gradually his itching ambition and his unyielding political beliefs tempted him back towards his old trades of secret policeman, spy, and counter-insurgency expert.

His career in South America began, as it had in the ruins of post-war Germany, with crime – larceny, fraud, forgery and blackmail – then spread into the more profitable trades of arms-dealing and freelance espionage, before launching into the jungle of high politics.

Here Barbie thrived. For although at first he found the continent of Latin America utterly strange, it was, in one fundamental respect, familiar. His career had been founded and built around the existence of war: the war of repression waged by the Nazis against their enemies at home and abroad, and then later the Cold War against Communism. In Latin America too there was war. In every country he visited, Barbie found all about him a merciless struggle being waged between ruling oligarchies and the populations they governed, a struggle sometimes carried out by routine police terror and repression, sometimes by the direct use of armed force, sometimes by the enforcement of a poverty so terrible that it held a whole people in hungry passivity.

This was a situation which Barbie recognised through the political lens of his own Nazism. Here, on one side, stood the rulers, committed to the same ideology of force and order in the name of a nation, that Barbie had long since made his own. There, on the other side, were sullen masses, generally of "inferior" race, their cause supported by international Communism. It was simple. In South America there was a job to be done. And Barbie knew how to do it.

He was not alone. There was a new generation which understood the continent in this way too, who saw it not only as the last world stronghold of Fascist ideals, but as the future battlefield between Marxism and European values.

This new generation of Fascists had grown up in Europe under the decrepit regimes of Franco in Spain and Salazar in Portugal. But it was in Italy that it had come closest to seizing power. There, with the tradition of Mussolini's Fascism still a powerful memory, a young man, Stefano delle Chiaie, grew up to espouse the cause of right-wing terror as a weapon with which to weaken and then attempt to overthrow Italy's democratic government. He came within an ace of doing so.

Delle Chiaie was much younger and more vigorous than Klaus Barbie, and he was to bring to the struggle a fiercer view of Fascism. But in Bolivia where they met and worked together, first to overthrow a government, then to serve the harsh military dictatorship that replaced it, they recognised a common goal: to transplant the ideals and the ruthless methods of Fascism into the New World. Those ideals and methods found fertile soil. The right-wing dictatorships of Argentina, Bolivia and Chile and the secret police they employed, adopted and exported them to Central America – to El Salvador and Guatemala, where the death squads which are the weapons of dictatorship can be seen in operation today. That is the true legacy of Fascism.

To understand how Klaus Barbie came together with this younger generation, and to grasp the force and danger of the neo-Fascist migration to Latin America, it is necessary to leave Barbie's career briefly, and to bring into focus the man he was to work with in Bolivia, the most dedicated and dangerous of European right-wing terrorists – Stefano delle Chiaie.

PART TWO

The New Order

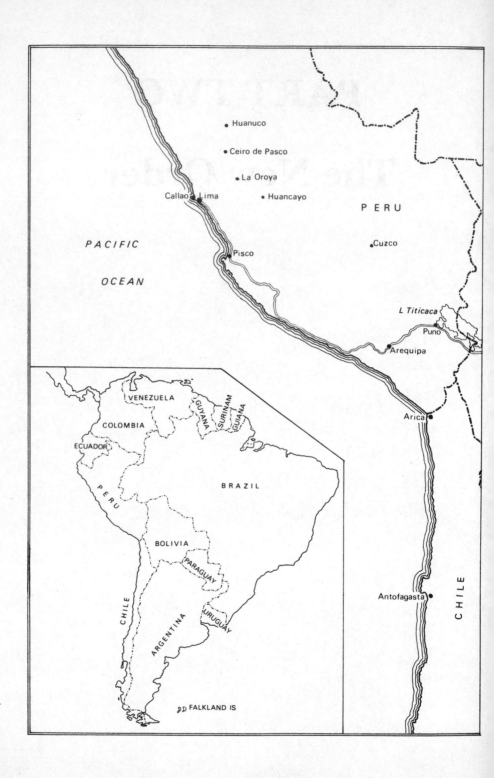

0   200 Miles

0   300 Km

B E N I

• Santa Ana

B O L I V I A

B R A Z I L

• La Paz

Cochabamba

• Cesaba

• Oruro

A L T I P L A N O

L Poopo

• Santa Cruz

• Sucre

• Potosi

• Tarija

PARAGUAY

• Salta

A R G E N T I N A

CHAPTER NINE

Black Terror

On most days during the summer months, an erect and energetic old man may be observed on the promenade at Torreblanca, a sprawling resort on the Costa del Sol in southern Spain. His stride is purposeful, his manner authoritative, and there is little sign of diminishing stamina, although he is now in his eighties.

Léon Degrelle is a survivor. For thirty years after the war he was Belgium's most wanted Nazi collaborator, condemned to death *in absentia* for treason, remembered with loathing as Hitler's confidant, the object of several kidnap attempts by Nazi-hunters. Until recently he avoided the limelight, hiding his identity behind a Spanish name until his death sentence had expired.

But now Degrelle lives openly, willing and eager to expound his unrepentant views on Nazism, and to recall his close friendship with Hitler, the man he calls "the greatest genius, the greatest leader of this century".

For any ex-SS officer who likes to remember the old days, Degrelle is an essential port of call. His circle of friends in Madrid has included Nazis such as Colonel Otto Skorzeny, the man Hitler called his "special commando", and General Karl Wolff, SS chief in Italy and sometime head of Himmler's personal staff.

Among his humbler visitors was Klaus Barbie, who came to Spain twice on business from his adopted country of Bolivia and paid his respects both to Degrelle and Skorzeny, though neither of the great men thought much of him:

"Ce n'était qu'un capitaine . . ." sniffed Degrelle.

"A captain – that's the least you can do in wartime," said Skorzeny.

Far more important, and flattering to Degrelle was the steady stream of younger visitors who came to sit at his feet in the 1960s and 1970s. There was, he discovered to his delight, a new generation of right-wing zealots ready to pick up the torch of Fascism and carry it forward. They were eager to listen to his Nazi views. Far from being repugnant, Degrelle's Fascist convictions appeared to accord perfectly with their own. He found himself invited to address rallies of the extremist Fuerza Nueva party of Spain, where thousands of youngsters would raise their arms in the Fascist salute and cheer him to the rafters. The reception he encountered did not surprise him. "The young have always needed to fight for an idea," he said.

Among them all, one young man made a specially deep impression on Léon Degrelle. Stefano delle Chiaie, an Italian neo-Fascist, was introduced to him in 1970 by an old friend, Prince Valerio Borghese, one of Mussolini's most brilliant wartime commanders. Delle Chiaie, said Borghese confidently, was a man of action, a "zealot" in the cause of the right, and "one of the few men capable of putting things in order in Italy".

The way delle Chiaie had chosen to "put things in order" had been a singularly violent one. His career, first as gang-leader, later as right-wing terrorist on the streets of Rome and Milan, had begun in the 1950s, at more or less the time that Klaus Barbie was sailing from Europe to pick up the threads of his new life in South America.

It is not too fanciful to draw parallels between the careers of the two men. Both believed in the use of counter-intelligence, infiltration and ruthless methods in dealing with Communists and the left. Both received assistance from intelligence agencies working for right-wing governments. And both wound up working together in Bolivia, the young Fascist and the old Nazi, each with his special skills. The routes by which they arrived there, however, were very different.

Delle Chiaie had grown up in the bleak post-war years of a defeated Italy, his home a faceless apartment block in Appio Latino on the outskirts of Rome. He was an unsuccessful student of social sciences, and later an even less successful insurance salesman. Small and wiry – only just over five feet tall – he was nicknamed, insultingly, "Il Caccola" (Roman slang for the sniveller). His face was instantly forgettable, the kind that was easily absorbed in a crowd, though later he grew a small goatee beard which became something of a trade mark on the identity cards supplied to him by intelligence agencies in Europe and South America under a series of aliases.

The looks were deceptive, for delle Chiaie was a natural leader. From his schooldays on, he developed a single-minded ambition and an extraordinary capacity for organisation which he used to further his violent political aims.

One of those who remembers him from the early days recalls the anger and frustration delle Chiaie and his little right-wing gangs felt in a Europe where the drift seemed steadily towards the left, and where even the Communists seemed likely to take part in government: "We didn't give a fuck for ideology," he said, "we were just angry. We set out to wreck Communist party branches, destroy the memorial plaques of the partisans who had murdered Mussolini, violate Jewish cemeteries, set fire to union offices . . . anything to hit back."

While delle Chiaie was still a teenager in the early 1950s he had joined the Italian Fascist party, the MSI. But he had soon found that organisation too stuffy for his liking, and in 1958 at the age of twenty-two he switched to a new and more extreme group founded in Rome two years earlier, called Ordine Nuovo, the "New Order". Its emblem was a two-edged battle-axe and its slogan was that of the Nazi SS: "Our honour is our loyalty." Ordine Nuovo had set out to restore Mussolini's brand of Fascism – the "pure Fascism of our origins", as the Duce himself had termed it, and it was prepared to condone violence as a means to achieve it.

Within a year of joining Ordine Nuovo, however, delle Chiaie had left to found a smaller and even more militant group, the Avanguardia Nazionale which, under his leadership, would be responsible for some of the most bloody acts of terrorism in post-war Italy. "We are for man-to-man engagements," said one of Avanguardia's leaflets. "Before setting out our men are morally prepared, so that they learn to break the bones even of somebody who kneels down and cries."

Small as delle Chiaie's organisation was, its achievements were spectacular. Throughout the 1960s it took part in attacks of growing violence against student and Communist groups, breaking up street demonstrations and attacking the homes of left-wing activists. But delle Chiaie himself was more than just a street-fighter. He believed in forging links with organisations similar to his own throughout Europe, and, if possible, beyond. Travelling to Spain, Greece and Portugal, he made contact with various Fascist organisations to compare notes and discuss political aims. As the activities of these groups came more and more to the attention of the outside world, they acquired the title of the Black Orchestra, and a whole series of unexplained acts of terrorism was ascribed to them. On the books of Interpol, as time went on, it would become increasingly hard to distinguish between the violence of the left-wing Red Brigade and their right-wing counterparts in the Black Orchestra.

Apart from delle Chiaie himself, another formidable figure in the Black Orchestra was a tough French paratrooper called Yves Guérin-Serac, a veteran of the French Secret Army Organisation (OAS) which had taken part in the vicious war against Algerian nationalists in the 1950s. Guérin-Serac ran a right-wing propaganda agency called Aginterpress which numbered amongst its correspondents Stefano delle Chiaie, masquerading under the name of Roberto Martelli. Aginterpress was no ordinary press agency. It acted as a cover for an espionage bureau used by the Portuguese secret service; a centre for the recruitment of mercenaries in Africa; and a coordinator for a small clandestine army of mercenaries known as the Organisation Armée Contre le Communisme International. Its patron was the old Nazi veteran, Colonel Otto Skorzeny.

It was during lengthy discussions with Guérin-Serac that delle Chiaie and his comrades began to develop a new political theory known as the "strategy of tension". It was not, perhaps, the most original idea of its time but it was later dressed up as something profound – a serious contribution to the ideology of the right. The idea was that if acts of terrorism were carried out and then blamed on left-wing groups, they might gradually lead to the kind of instability that threatened the democratic state. If this continued long enough, the army might finally be encouraged to step in and take over, thus laying the ideal breeding-ground for Fascism – a military dictatorship.

"Our belief is that the first phase of political activity ought to be to create the conditions favouring the installation of chaos in all the regime's structures . . ." read one of delle Chiaie's favourite passages. "In our view the first move we should make is to destroy the structure of the democratic state under the cover of Communist activities."

In Italy he began to organise the infiltration of left-wing groups, encouraging his Fascist colleagues to grow their hair long and join anarchist groups which would then be encouraged to stir up trouble. Initially, at any rate, the tactics seemed to succeed. In April 1969 explosions at Padua University and later at the Milan industrial fair organised by the right were immediately blamed on left-wing anarchists.

On August 8 1969 ten bombs were placed on trains running from several main-line stations in Italy. Eight of them exploded, though since the trains were half empty, only ten people were injured. Again the left was blamed, and something like hysteria began to creep into media coverage of what was seen as a well-organised campaign of subversion.

Then, on December 12, a massive explosion ripped through the foyer of the Banca del Agricultura on the Piazza Fontana in Milan, just a few steps away from the great cathedral of the city, killing sixteen people. In Rome, twenty-five minutes after the Milan explosion, another bomb went off wounding fourteen passers-by, and half an hour after that, again in Rome, two more bombs exploded in the Piazza Venezia, causing great damage but no casualties.

The bombings were greeted with horror in Italy and throughout Europe. Coming as they did in the wake of the student demonstrations of 1968, they were seen as evidence that the left would stick at nothing to achieve their ends. But within three days a significant arrest had been made: Pietro Valpreda, a former ballet-dancer and leader of a left-wing anarchist group, was picked up by the police and charged with having organised the Piazza Fontana bombing in Milan. Over the next few days about 150 anarchists or anarchist suspects were hauled in for questioning by police.

The arrest of Valpreda and his comrades was a perfect illustration of the "strategy of tension" in action; for unknown to any of the investigators, all the bombings, from the Padua explosion to the outrage at the Piazza Fontana, had been the work of right-wing groups organised by delle Chiaie and his friends. Valpreda had been "framed".

It would be thirteen years before the Italian courts were finally able to determine that Valpreda was innocent and to issue warrants instead for the arrest of delle Chiaie and other members of the Avanguardia Nazionale. But oddly enough there was one discreet organisation which did know right away. The Servizio Informazione Difesa, or SID, Italy's main secret service agency, had already noted that delle Chiaie seemed to have close connections with the police and had recorded him as being "an informer of the Rome central police" with contacts in the Ministry of the Interior.

Five days after the Piazza Fontana bombing, the SID circulated a note to their branch offices stating flatly that delle Chiaie had organised all the attacks and that the man who had actually planted the bombs was delle Chiaie's closest lieutenant, Mario Merlino, who had also infiltrated Valpreda's anarchist group. It then went on to note delle Chiaie's links with Yves Guérin-Serac, in a report which concluded that Merlino and delle Chiaie "committed the attacks in order to place responsibility on other groups".

It may seem strange that these suspicions were not immediately passed on to the Italian judiciary. If they had been, the career of a dangerous "black" terrorist could have been brought to a swift conclusion. But it is now clear that the SID considered delle Chiaie extremely useful, both as a source of information on the Left which he had successfully infiltrated, and as an agent provocateur. Just as Klaus Barbie was valued by the American CIC for his experience in counter-intelligence and his ability to recruit informers, so delle Chiaie was a man to be kept quietly on the books rather than turned over to the law.

But there was nothing quiet about delle Chiaie's life, for in 1970 he took on an assignment which was the most ambitious of his career – the attempted overthrow of the Italian state.

The coup d'état was organised by a man who had by now become delle Chiaie's patron – Prince Valerio Borghese, friend of Léon Degrelle and known by all his right-wing comrades as Il Commandante. It was planned for December 7 1970, a date deliberately chosen because it marked the anniversary of Pearl Harbor. It was code-named "Tora Tora" in memory of the Japanese attack, and the man placed in charge of its most spectacular action was delle Chiaie.

At the head of a commando group of thirty men – the toughest veterans of the Avanguardia Nazionale – delle Chiaie led a night-time raid on the Ministry of the Interior in Rome. The building was deserted as the squad forced its way into the armoury and seized two hundred machine guns. At midnight delle Chiaie telephoned his commander, Borghese, and announced that the ministry was in his hands. By then other squads were ready to seize the radio and television stations, arrest left-wing politicians and announce that they were in control of the machinery of government.

But at the last minute Il Commandante announced that the coup was to be called off. The troops, he ordered, should stand down; the operation was aborted. Everyone was stunned. Borghese's second-in-command stormed into his office to demand an explanation. But the old man was implacable. "I have obeyed superior orders," was all he would say.

There has never been a satisfactory explanation of who those superiors were, though there has been no shortage of rumours, including the suggestion that the coup had the secret backing of the US government which had stationed warships off Malta, ready to sail towards Italy as soon as the coup was announced. Borghese himself refused to divulge the secret, even to his close friend Léon Degrelle, and he went to his grave without ever revealing why the coup, which might have changed the course of Italian history, was so suddenly thrown into reverse.

Delle Chiaie pulled his men out of the ministry building as efficiently as he had led them in. He replaced 199 machine guns, keeping just one as a souvenir, and then, in the early hours of December 8 he slipped out of Italy for exile in Barcelona. His departure was carefully monitored by the ever-vigilant SID.

His career from now on would concentrate less on the affairs of his homeland, where he could only return clandestinely, and more on Spain and South America where right-wing governments were open to his ideas and interested in his unusual skills. Over the next three years delle Chiaie kept a diary which was later discovered by Italian investigators, and it records the astonishing ease with which he was able to travel freely from country to country, although he was an internationally wanted man.

In Spain, a country which was effectively still run as a police state, he never once had to apply for a resident's permit; his name did not appear on the list of foreigners held by the Spanish police; and when he opened an office and a restaurant in Madrid, neither was entered on the commercial register as required under Spanish law. The police and the intelligence agencies, who were perfectly well aware of his identity, simply turned a blind eye.

Yet the company he set up dealt in arms, and the restaurant El Apuntamiento was a regular thieves' kitchen, patronised by right-wing terrorists. Scarcely any of those who ate or worked at the restaurant had residence papers, nor were the cooks and waiters regularly employed. Many of them were on police records as Italian right-wing extremists on the run.

On most nights, unless he was on missions abroad, delle Chiaie, dressed in a khaki shirt or a light safari suit, would preside over the establishment with his wife Leda, an Italian ex-school teacher. Fights were common as the evenings wore on, and delle Chiaie would have to step in and break them up. Sometimes he himself was the focus of resentment, particularly from those of his colleagues who nursed grave suspicions about his contacts with the Italian authorities.

Delle Chiaie's diary says nothing about what he was really up to in Spain beyond speaking vaguely about "meetings", "operations" and "missions". But evidence which emerged later, after the death of Franco, shows that not only did delle Chiaie import his "strategy of tension" into Spain in an attempt to shore up support for the right-wing, he also waged a remarkable clandestine war against the Basque Separatist movement ETA, an organisation which posed a running threat to the Franco regime.

From 1973 to 1976, operating permanently outside the law, yet on behalf of the Spanish authorities, delle Chiaie helped organise a series of raids against ETA both in Spain and across the border in south-west France. On one occasion two ETA terrorists, hiding in France, were found dead in mysterious circumstances. Later it emerged that their murderer, a twenty-eight-year-old Sicilian, Luigi

Concutelli, had been brought to Spain by delle Chiaie, provided with papers and commissioned by him to carry out the killings. On another occasion delle Chiaie actually had himself photographed with members of an anti-ETA death squad after a raid in which two pro-ETA demonstrators were killed. This, however, was unusual. In general he preferred to stay in the background: delle Chiaie was an organiser, not a hit-man.

The gangs used for his raids were referred to by delle Chiaie himself as Commandos de Acción. To those who watched their activities and wondered just who they answered to, they were known as "Los Incontrolados", the Uncontrolled Ones. But their operations were not simply freelance. In Spain delle Chiaie was recruited to carry them out by the Spanish police through their secret service agency the Brigada Central de Informacion. He reported regularly to the Brigada's headquarters in Madrid, and he was supplied with the favoured Spanish police weapon, the Ingram machine gun. This weapon, manufactured in America and purchased in bulk by the Spanish police, provides the hardest evidence against delle Chiaie of his involvement at this time in terrorist activities. Not only was it a familiar part of the armoury of his death squads, it was used in July 1976 to murder an Italian magistrate, Vittorio Occorsio, who had single-mindedly pursued investigations into delle Chiaie and his activities ever since the Piazza Fontana bombings in 1969.

Delle Chiaie once told a television journalist that he had wept only once in his life – on the day in 1973 when he learned of his mother's death in Italy, and realised that he would be unable to attend her funeral. "Cursed be those who oblige me, after three years on the run, to be still far from my mother," he wrote in his diary. "I will find no peace until I have found my revenge. I shall find no peace until I have torn from their lurid faces the masks they wear of justice-makers of society."

The man he blamed for these "limitations on my liberty" was the magistrate Occorsio, who was by now building up such a formidable case against him on charges of terrorism that delle Chiaie could not risk the trip to Italy. Some time in the summer of 1975, therefore, he decided that Occorsio should die. He told members of Ordine Nuovo and Avanguardia Nazionale that Occorsio was a proven enemy of Fascism. His death would be a political act which would remind the Italian people that the movement was still a force to be reckoned with.

The man delle Chiaie chose to carry out the assassination was

Luigi Concutelli, the Sicilian who had already taken part in ETA killings in Spain. Concutelli travelled to Italy in Easter 1976 carrying a large bag containing the disassembled parts of an Ingram machine gun with the serial number – 2/2000381 – filed off. At 8.30 a.m. on July 10, as Occorsio brought his Fiat to a halt at the cross-roads leading out of the Via Giuba in Rome, Concutelli approached the car on foot, holding the Ingram machine gun in front of him, and sprayed the windscreen with bullets. Occorsio made a desperate attempt to flee, but only managed to open the car door before collapsing. Concutelli walked calmly up and dropped several leaflets on the body. Each one bore a double-headed axe – the insignia of Ordine Nuovo.

Concutelli was not picked up until January 1977, but when he was, police found the Ingram machine gun in his Rome flat. Despite the absence of the serial number, ballistics experts managed to trace the weapon back to its factory in Marietta, Georgia, from where it had been shipped in a batch sold to Spanish police before being passed on to delle Chiaie. When asked how a weapon of theirs had got into the hands of a known terrorist, the Spanish police preferred not to comment.

Delle Chiaie himself, when confronted by the evidence in the course of an interview, denied it: "I never gave the machine gun to Concutelli," he said, "nor did I give the order to murder Occorsio. However, I do approve of it, and don't condemn it."

By the time of the murder he was approaching the end of his sojourn in Europe. The political stage on which he had operated all these years was beginning to shrink alarmingly. Portugal's dictator, Salazar, was dead; in Greece the right-wing colonels had gone; and in November 1975 after a long and lingering illness the Caudillo of Spain, General Franco, finally died, bringing to an end a dictatorship that had lasted for thirty-six years. It was plain to delle Chiaie that he would soon have to move on, and there was no doubt in his mind that the place he would be heading for was South America.

His links there were already strong. Among his friends in Spain he had numbered José Lopez Rega, an Argentinian ex-police corporal who had been secretary to Argentina's charismatic leader Juan Peron during Peron's exile in Madrid. Lopez Rega had returned with the dictator to Argentina in 1972 and there he had founded the right-wing death squads of the Argentine Anticommunist Alliance.

Lopez Rega – nicknamed El Brujo, the sorcerer – had held long discussions with delle Chiaie before going to Argentina; then, when Peron died and Lopez Rega returned to Spain, he brought several

AAA members with him. They swiftly found employment operating alongside delle Chiaie's own squads of anti-ETA killers.

There were other contacts: among delle Chiaie's friends in Madrid was the right-wing ex-president of Bolivia, Alfredo Ovando Candia, who had been expelled in 1971 for plotting against the government. He had once served on the board of one of Klaus Altmann's companies. The name Altmann may not have meant much to delle Chiaie at that stage, but later he would form an intimate relationship with the man, work closely with him, and eventually learn his real name – Klaus Barbie.

Delle Chiaie had made his first trip to South America in 1973, travelling on behalf of Guérin-Serac's Aginterpress to Panama, Curaçao and Colombia under the alias Mario Fiore. Later in the same year he went to San José in Costa Rica under the name of Giovanni Martelli, though at some point he acquired a police identity card under yet another name, Francisco Alonzo. But the picture on the card, the anonymous face with the goatee beard, remained the same.

Then in April 1974, along with his patron, Il Commandante, Prince Valerio Borghese, he travelled to Santiago, Chile, where, on April 29, he was ushered into the presence of General Augusto Pinochet, head of the military junta that had overthrown President Salvador Allende the year before. It was a crucial meeting, for among those attending it was Colonel Jorge Carrasco, head of police intelligence, which would soon avail itself of delle Chiaie's services. Delle Chiaie later recorded his impressions of the Chilean president:

> The meeting with the general was of the highest interest: the man is bluff but intelligent. His few words have given me a clear impression that he wants to help us. I hope that this is not another of my over-optimisms. [Of Carrasco he noted]: He is very close to us. We understood each other immediately. I am sure that we will hear from him again soon. In this case we will have a true and determined ally.

Another useful contact in Chile was Michael Townley, an American-born agent of the Chilean state security service, DINA. Townley was impressed by the size of the organisation delle Chiaie claimed to represent. He was, noted Townley, a man who could "think big", and the two would cooperate on some of the international operations which DINA was planning – mostly to hunt down exiled members of the Chilean opposition. Delle Chiaie was given the code name "Alfa" and he was handed a DINA document marked "Secret" which outlined the aims of the Chilean regime.

Just eighteen months after that first meeting with Pinochet, the Townley-Alfa axis pulled off its first coup – a cold-blooded assassination attempt. In August 1975 Townley was in Europe under instructions from DINA to eliminate the Chilean socialist leader Carlos Altamirano. Delle Chiaie, whom he consulted, pointed out that Altamirano, who lived in Germany and had an armed escort, was a very difficult target. Instead, he proposed killing another Chilean in exile, Bernardo Leighton, the ex-vice president and a founder of the Chilean Christian Democrat party. He was a far easier proposition, delle Chiaie pointed out – he lived in Rome with his wife Anita, and had no bodyguards.

Townley sought advice from Santiago and approval was given. On the night of October 6 1975, as Leighton and his wife were walking back from a dinner engagement with friends in Rome they were passed by a tall thick-set man. As they walked on, two muffled shots rang out and Leighton slumped to the ground; Anita swung round in time to look the gunman in the face, then she too was shot.

The attacker was Luigi Concutelli, delle Chiaie's hired assassin. "I left them for dead," Concutelli told his colleagues later. But the Leightons had survived. A bullet had entered the back of Bernardo's neck and had come out on the left side of his forehead. Following long drawn-out surgery, he recovered. Anita's spine was damaged by a bullet, and she is confined to a wheel chair. She has since identified Concutelli. "I thought they were gone," Concutelli had told his friends. "It was the only mistake I made."

Within six weeks of the attack, delle Chiaie was able to report directly to General Pinochet, who arrived in Madrid on November 20 1975 to attend Franco's funeral. They met in the Madrid hotel where Pinochet was staying; among those in attendance were Townley and the infamous head of DINA, Colonel Manuel Contreras.

By this time the attraction of Spain for delle Chiaie was fast disappearing. Everywhere the talk was of El Destapo, the liberalisation of the country. Franco's death would hasten the process. Then, in the summer of 1976, a Spanish journalist discovered delle Chiaie's restaurant, El Apuntamiento, and soon dozens of pressmen were crowding into the dimly lit dining room, plying delle Chiaie with questions.

"Just forget about us," he murmured. "We're all long since out of violence."

It wasn't true of course. But it was clear that the honeymoon was over. Quietly El Apuntamiento was closed. The time had come to move on. Delle Chiaie was about to take the route that would lead him to Bolivia, a route that Klaus Barbie had ventured down exactly twenty-five years earlier. They were to meet very soon.

CHAPTER TEN

In the Service of the State

Unlike Stefano delle Chiaie, Klaus Barbie stepped on to unfamiliar territory when he first landed in South America; the family which arrived in Buenos Aires on the *Corrientes* on April 10 1951 betrayed distinct signs of nervousness. Queuing among the other, largely Italian passengers, the Altmanns chose to register their entry to Argentina separately. Klaus went through Customs first and declared himself unmarried, while Regine, who came two names behind him in the immigration records of Buenos Aires port, contradicted him by stating that they were man and wife. She recorded the names of their two children as Jörg, aged five, and Maria, aged nine.

Their nervousness, though understandable, was unfounded. The busy immigration officials paid little attention, and the family, in any event, was only in transit through Argentina. Some days later, the Altmanns caught a train to La Paz, arriving on April 23.

The Bolivia which Klaus Barbie encountered was to be scarcely more peaceful than the Europe he had fled. Over the years this small mountain republic had earned itself a reputation as one of the most unstable and turbulent states in the world.

Since the days of its founder-president, Simon Bolivar, in 1825, Bolivian political life had developed a character of its own, in which racial tensions exacerbated geographical divisions. The people of the lowland east tended to look with more favour on their neighbours in Paraguay than on the overwhelmingly Indian population of the great plateau of the Altiplano, whom they despised. Among the small ruling class, intimately linked by ties of kinship, there were deep ideological differences; the struggle for power, backed by the corrupt and ambitious armed forces, was bitter. There were at least forty political parties, whose splits, quarrels and shifting alliances owed as much to blood relations as to doctrine. Political posts, widely accepted as a means of self-enrichment, were shared among the dominant clans. In Bolivia, who you knew was just as important as who you claimed to represent.

The country itself, small, mountainous and landlocked, spread across the slopes and plateaux of the Andes, could not have been more different from the Europe Barbie had left, and it was, according to his friends at the time, a difficult period of adjustment.

Neither Klaus nor Regine spoke Spanish well, despite their training in Augsburg; and Bolivia, although cheap to live in, lacked many of the civilising comforts of Europe. There were few major cities. The formal capital, Sucre, was a beautiful sleepy relic of colonial days. The real capital, La Paz, clinging to the slopes of a canyon on the edge of the Altiplano, drops from a height of 14,000 feet down to the suburbs at 10,000 feet, where the better-off inhabitants live; it is one of the few cities in the world where the upper social classes live at the bottom of the city, with the slums of the poor at the top.

At the time the Altmann family arrived in Bolivia, the stranglehold of the ruling industrialists – the tin mining oligarchy – was beginning to break down, but the country lacked any real middle class ready to step into the breach. The majority population, descendants of the conquered Indian peoples, eked out an existence of grinding poverty, ruled by a tiny, Spanish-speaking élite who considered themselves "white".

According to Alvaro de Castro, a Bolivian businessman and later Barbie's friend and bodyguard, the family began their life in La Paz in the Hotel Italia. It was not very grand, but what stuck in Barbie's memory that first night was something different.

"He used to describe how he went out to buy some soap," said Alvaro de Castro. "He just went into the first shop that was open and it wasn't until he was inside that he realised it was a Jewish shop." Barbie hesitated momentarily, but went on to buy his soap. This, after all, was to be a new life, and though he was never fully able to overcome his prejudices, he was nothing if not a realist.

The Altmann family were by no means the first Germans to make the long journey from Europe to Bolivia. There had been a sizable and prosperous German community there since the beginning of the century; it was noted for its hard work and efficiency, well respected and tolerated. "It was always considered a sign of success for a daughter to marry a German," recalled one early immigrant.

In the late 1930s a fresh wave of immigrants began to arrive. Some were political refugees, others were fleeing the persecution of the Jews in Hitler's Germany. For by 1938 the only two places in the world which still remained open for desperate German and Jewish refugees were the unlikely havens of Shanghai in China, where the British concession adopted a "no visa" policy, and Bolivia, where visas were required, but could still be bought.

This bizarre pocket of safety in the Andes had been guaranteed in 1938 by the then Bolivian president, German Busch, who declared that Jewish immigration to Bolivia, previously subject to special restrictions, should be open: "In Bolivia, we should not make ourselves co-participants in the hatred or the persecution of the Semitic elements in European countries."

This open-hearted gesture, however, was shortly to suffer from the time honoured Bolivian practice of corruption. In 1939 the Bolivian consul-general in Paris was discovered to have enriched himself by routing all applications for Bolivian visas through the Paris office, where a large fee was levied. Immigrants from that time recall that the price was two hundred dollars per visa. It was a seller's market. In the year before war broke out, ten thousand Jews were to slip out of Germany and make their way to Bolivia.

Once there, the welcome was not particularly warm. Most of the visas were given for agricultural work and most of the immigrants were middle-aged intellectuals. Even doctors were told that they must work for five years in the remote countryside and requalify through Bolivian examinations before they could set up practice in town. It was not surprising that most of the Jews moved on, the lucky ones through the good offices of relatives and friends in the US.

Others had to rely on a more risky and more dramatic route to safety: a now prosperous Bolivian businessman who preferred for the purposes of an interview to be known simply as "René", recalled that as a boy of thirteen working in a trucking company he had taken several men disguised as mechanics over the border to Argentina. "The price for acting as an escort was $150 in those days," he told us.

What they were fleeing was not only an inhospitable economic climate. In Bolivia, as in other countries of Latin America, the Third Reich had launched a huge propaganda effort, and most of Bolivia's established German community was heavily pro-Nazi. The German ambassador in La Paz was Himmler's brother-in-law, and there were close ties between the Bolivian and the German armed forces; in the 1930s the chief adviser to the Bolivian army had been Ernst Röhm, later SA chief of staff, murdered by Hitler in the "blood putsch" of 1934.

Many of the Jews who stayed in Bolivia during the war encountered the kind of attitudes which had been responsible for their flight from Germany in the first place. One immigrant recalled going into the German Club in La Paz on his first visit to the capital and finding a sign saying "Dogs and Jews not allowed".

There were three German clubs in La Paz – one Nazi, one frequented by Communists, Jews and Social Democrats, and a third for the German Protestants. For anyone holding an official post, membership of the pro-Nazi club was virtually compulsory. "They treated us like bootboys," complained one anti-Nazi German teacher at the time.

Many of the new arrivals, driven out of their homes in Germany, were determined to continue the fight against the Fascists. For them, a key challenge was to persuade the Bolivian government to side with the Allies and they ran their own small propaganda effort: "We used to poison German dogs, put cement in the keyholes of Nazi businesses and paint anti-Hitler slogans on the walls," recalled a member of the group.

The group also published a German-language newspaper, *Rundschau von Illimani*, named after the Illimani mountain which towers over La Paz. Its most important action was covert – compiling information on Nazi activities in Bolivia both to identify to the Allies Nazi sympathisers and agents and to serve as evidence to persuade the Bolivians to join the Allied side.

Their efforts met finally with success when, in December 1941, the Bolivian government announced its support of the Americans following the attack on Pearl Harbor; in January 1942 it broke off relations with Germany, Italy and Japan; and at the same time it passed anti-subversion laws designed to suppress the active fifth column. Known Nazi agents were rounded up and deported to internment camps in the United States, where their activities were carefully monitored by the ever-vigilant anti-Nazi group.

With the ending of the war, however, many of these German refugees were to return to Bolivia where they resumed their positions as respected members of the community. And after 1945 came new waves of German refugees, most of them with a past to disguise: the escaping Nazis.

In the closing months of the war as the Third Reich crumbled, those in Germany who saw the future all too clearly began quietly to transfer money from Germany to Latin America. Those countries with large German communities, sympathetic dictators, and bribable officials had been organised as potential places of refuge, and in 1945 the Bolivian "René" – who as a boy of thirteen had smuggled Jews to Argentina – found himself at the age of nineteen ferrying some very different customers.

One in particular sticks in his memory: "He was a nervous German who asked to be known as Erik, a curious figure, muffled up with a heavy sweater in spite of the heat." Under his clothes he wore a Long John suit with pockets in the top and bottom halves from which he drew out cash and documents. "He never took that suit off, even in bed."

Only years later, long after "Erik" had been smuggled out to Argentina, did René discover his customer's true identity. "I was sitting in the café, eating a salteña, when suddenly I saw a photograph in the newspaper. I just stared at it . . . I couldn't believe it. Adolf Eichmann had been kidnapped in Buenos Aires . . . and it was Erik."

The Altmann family, with its new identity, had opted to travel the other way – from Argentina into Bolivia. Once in La Paz, Barbie was quick to notice that, in some small respects at least, Bolivia brought back memories of home. Although the most conspicuous Nazis had been deported during the war, their influence had taken root in two important Bolivian political parties. Principal among these was the Movimiento Nacional Revolucionario (MNR), a populist party which was both revolutionary and neo-Fascist in style. The MNR signalled its allegiances when it adopted as its headquarters the empty pro-Nazi German Club in La Paz.

The second openly pro-Fascist grouping was the Bolivian Falange, founded in exile in Chile in 1937. It was the sight of Falange supporters which lifted Barbie's spirits during those difficult early days. Recalling that moment later, Barbie said:

When I arrived in Bolivia in 1951 I had, by chance, a comforting vision: a procession of the Bolivian Socialist Falange with their uniforms, identical to ours. The leather belt, the armband, the Fascist salute. Later I even had an opportunity to become intimate with members of the party and to get to know its philosophy in depth. I thus confirmed my sympathy for the movement. I always helped those people whenever I could.

It was not quite true, as Barbie claimed, that he knew nobody on his arrival in Bolivia. In the documentation so helpfully supplied in Italy by Father Draganovič, he carried his Bolivian visa bearing the name of Father Roque Romac, guardian of the Franciscan community in Sacaba, a small town some twenty kilometres outside the important centre of Cochabamba. Father Romac's church is still there, dominating the dusty square, though the Franciscan community itself abandoned Sacaba in the late 1950s.

In 1951 Father Romac was a powerful figure in Sacaba, and is remembered still as a leader of the staunchly anti-Communist

Croat community around Cochabamba. His sympathies for Barbie must have been fortified not only by their coincidence of political views but by the fact that Romac too was a man with something to hide: his real identity, as we have seen, was that of Father Osvaldo Toth – wanted for questioning by the Yugoslav government in connection with war crimes.

In the Franciscan monastery of the nearby town of Cochabamba there is an ancient ledger where Father Romac's name is lodged, and where his true identity is still remembered by the priest who runs it. And in Austria, in the Franciscan monastery of Hall, there is an old monk called Father Motsch who remembers Romac well: "He was a good priest," said Father Motsch, "and a good member of the Order. He loved Croatia and he was a true patriot. One can see nothing wrong in that . . ."

Through the good offices of Father Romac and others, Barbie quickly established some contacts. He deemed it prudent, however, to live for a while in decent obscurity. He got a job working in a sawmill in the tropical Yungas region of Bolivia. Again, he had to make some mental adjustment: the sawmill was the property of a Jew called Ludwig Kapenauer (whose liking for Barbie remained a mystery to many of his friends). Barbie worked diligently. As he later described it, in a highly idealised version of his life, his Teutonic discipline and capacity for hard work stood him in good stead in surroundings he and his wife found trying. "They did social work, really, among the Indians," said Alvaro de Castro. "Those people knew nothing – not even how to keep themselves clean. The Altmanns taught them to wash; Frau Altmann taught them to read."

Barbie himself has put it more briskly: "I had to decide whether I should shout at them Prussian-style or say nothing because I couldn't speak Spanish." He decided to keep quiet altogether and instead set them a good example by working hard, instituting what he called "some of our good National Socialist ideals".

To the casual observer the Altmanns appeared to live the lives of model citizens. By 1954 the diligent Klaus had achieved partnership in the business. A year or two later he set up on his own and, by 1956, aided by his contacts in the German business community, he was able to move his family from the tropical heat and mosquitoes of the Yungas to the more moderate climate of La Paz. There he opened a wood yard which also undertook simple carpentry. He appointed a manager in the Yungas for the wood business while he himself ran the retail side in La Paz.

His friend de Castro is at pains to emphasise the family's humble beginnings and early struggles in Bolivia. But even then, the German connection was useful. In the 1950s a major customer for his wood business was a local German-owned canned food factory to which Barbie supplied crates. This was to lead later to a lucrative contract with the massive and powerful Mannheim pharmaceutical company Böhringer, to whom he supplied *quinquina* (the tree bark from which quinine is extracted). Barbie's connections with Böhringer were to span more than a decade, and were to be sufficiently close for the company to offer his daughter a job when she began looking for one in the mid-1960s.

The Altmann family became well known figures in the capital. To visitors the main feature of La Paz is its altitude: the thin atmosphere makes breathing difficult and calls for several days of adjustment. The recommended pace of life is slow. Frau Altmann wandered round the shops of La Paz with her Indian maid, arguing about prices. Klaus maintained the image of the genial businessman, never able to walk more than a hundred yards through the streets without stopping to exchange pleasantries with an acquaintance. He was a regular figure in the Club La Paz, a spacious, slightly run-down café at the top of the steep main street, opposite the war memorial.

The Club La Paz is the hub of La Paz's social life, a place of regular ritual. At 11 a.m. it fills up with customers eating salteñas, a local delicacy of meat-filled pastry. The conversation is lively until lunch time, when the clientele scatters, returning in the afternoon to linger over cups of coffee until about six o'clock. "The Fascists sat at one side, the Communists at another and in a corner, the ex-presidents," joked one of Barbie's admirers. Barbie's own regular table was in the far right-hand corner from the entrance, where he would consume cup after cup of strong black coffee. He was on good terms with the proprietors and even had some of his mail directed there.

The Altmann family was establishing itself in Bolivia against a background of momentous political upheaval. In April 1952 the MNR had been brought to power by a popular revolt against the military government. Victor Paz Estenssoro, its leader, flew in from exile in Buenos Aires to assume the presidency and embarked on a series of radical measures which turned Bolivia upside down; he nationalised the mines, instituted land reform and permitted the foundation of a trade union organisation, COB, which was to play a vital role in Bolivia.

Paz Estenssoro was a man of contradictions: while carrying out far-reaching social reforms, he still maintained some of his old Nazi sympathies. His opponents divided their political insults almost equally between accusations of Communism and Fascism. The MNR movement, in fact, contained elements of both. Its government, popular with many, was perceived by others as little short of a Fascist dictatorship.

One bitter enemy of Paz Estenssoro, Cespedes Rivera, a newspaper editor and leader of the Bolivian Democratic Front exiled in 1954 in Venezuela, wrote a long memorandum to the United States ambassador in which he accused Paz Estenssoro's government of using the services of a series of former Nazis:

> Paz Estenssoro has hired a number of totalitarian experts . . . to achieve control of the masses and perfect his methods of repression. We might mention among them, Heinz Wolf, a former member of the Gestapo and one of Himmler's lieutenants; he arrived in Argentina after the WWII and is now working in the Government Palace of La Paz, as chief of the Political Department . . .

He went on to list several others, whose links had been with the Third Reich and with Vichy France. Although there is no mention here of Barbie himself, it is clear that his connections were already sound. On October 7 1957, on the basis of his false documentation as Klaus Altmann, he was granted a prize of inestimable value, and one which would protect him for the next twenty-five years – Bolivian nationality. It was not, perhaps, one of the world's most sought after citizenships, but, for a Nazi on the run, any nationality provided security against expulsion or extradition. The Altmann family had taken a major step, from hostages of fortune to secure citizens.

The man who signed the vital papers was the vice-president himself, Hernan Siles Zuazo, who was at this stage part of the bizarre balancing act between left-wing populism and Fascism which made up the Paz Estenssoro government. He was inclined to favour the application for citizenship of a sound German who appeared to be a pillar of the new Bolivia. Those who spoke for Barbie in support of his case were German friends who described him as a model citizen and a credit to his newly-adopted country.

Many of Barbie's friends in La Paz still argue that he had shed his Nazi politics and that he betrayed no anti-Semitic sentiments during his years in Bolivia. It is clear, however, that he had by no means renounced his Nazi views. In correspondence with friends and sympathisers at this time, his disparaging references to Jews, his ferocious anti-Communism and his sentimental memories of the glories of the Third Reich were regular themes.

The anti-Nazi group, whose evidence on Barbie's early life in Bolivia is a crucial part of the story of his rise to power, soon noticed that the man known as Altmann seemed to have a past to hide. "I was working in the Cerveceria Boliviana, the main brewery," recalled one of the group who made it his business to compile careful notes throughout the period. "The boss had been deported as a Nazi and had apparently repented, but working as head brewer was SS Obersturmbannführer Fritz Hahn, who still wore his SS boots and overcoat. Altmann quickly became a friend of his, and when they got drunk they would sing Nazi songs."

To his friends at this time, the businessman Klaus Altmann was the epitome of the courteous German gentleman; but after a few too many of a fierce Bolivian cocktail known as *chuflai*, his gentlemanly exterior would slip, to reveal traces of the Nazi bully underneath. As late as 1968 he caused a scandal in La Paz's German Club, by giving a Nazi salute and shouting "Heil Hitler!" in the presence of the German ambassador, to the fury and embarrassment of the members. He was expelled and the club president, in his letter of apology to the embassy, assured the ambassador that Altmann did not represent the views of the majority of the members. In several other bars in La Paz he was remembered for offensive remarks about Jews, which occasionally, even in the tolerant climate of La Paz, led to ugly scenes with other customers.

Within his trusted circle, Barbie made no effort to disguise his views. One journalist, a friend of Barbie's in the 1970s, recalled the night he appeared on her doorstep, bearing a bottle of champagne. "It is the anniversary," he explained, "of the day that the Führer made me a member of the SS. Will you help me celebrate?"

Remembering the impression he created, a Jewish refugee who watched his activities in Bolivia closely over the years remarked: "There were many Nazis who came to South America, settled and lived out their lives quietly and uneventfully, content to forget the past. Others never forgot and never gave up. Klaus Altmann was one of those." But despite checking Ministry of Interior records, and even obtaining his fingerprints from a wine glass, the anti-Nazis were unable to discover Altmann's real identity.

In spite of his new citizenship and the remoteness of his hiding place, Barbie had grounds for nervousness. In 1960 the Zentralstelle in Ludwigsburg, West Germany, the centre of prosecution of Nazi war crimes, launched an investigation into his whereabouts. Aware that he had been in Kassel after the war, they sent his file to the Kassel prosecutor who opened a case against him and issued an arrest warrant.

In 1961 the Kassel police questioned a woman named Frau Bouness, living nearby at Sandershausen, who proved to be Barbie's cousin. The tale she told was extraordinary: Barbie, she said, had worked for the American CIC after the war and had then been smuggled to Bolivia, from where he wrote regularly. What is more, his wife Regine and the two children had returned to Europe on a visit in 1957, and had stayed first with Barbie's mother in Trier, then with Frau Bouness herself in Sandershausen. No one had lifted a finger against them.

All this information was passed from Kassel to Augsburg, which was Barbie's last known place of abode; from there the file went to Munich where it lay, gathering dust, in the prosecutor's office.

Then in 1963 a French inquiry began, rather closer to home. A Bolivian, who was owed money by the apparently respectable businessman Klaus Altmann, began making his own enquiries into his background, and finally managed to establish that Klaus Altmann and Klaus Barbie were one and the same man. The Bolivian promptly informed the French Embassy in the hope that they would bring pressure on Barbie to pay his debt. The matter was referred back to France, where the police managed to establish that Barbie was in correspondence with his mother in Trier, but it was never pursued, and the dossier simply remained in the Embassy files. Clearly, however, Barbie was in need of better protection.

That protection was soon to be assured. In the early 1960s the always volatile politics of Bolivia shifted again. Paz Estenssoro had been re-elected president, but, under increasing economic pressure had moved away from his radical stance, and begun to creep rightwards. He had chosen as his running mate a colourful and ambitious air force general called René Barrientos, a man whom Barbie had met and cultivated. It was a useful friendship: the power of the armed forces, which had been all but abolished after the 1952 MNR revolution, was rapidly and systematically restored in a burst of military spending.

Barbie's personal friendship with Barrientos was a shield against the ever-present danger of French justice. Barrientos was a man of whom even his political enemies spoke with a certain admiration. He was renowned for his physical courage – a daring pilot who enjoyed the reputation of a man of the people, with a strong personal code of honour. In 1964 he became even more useful to Barbie when, in a military coup, he overthrew Paz Estenssoro's MNR government. With the backing of the peasants against the miners, he established a dictatorship which ushered in a period of military rule destined to last, almost unbroken, until 1978. But his regime still faced a violent struggle to establish its power securely, and Barbie, expert in "counter subversion" from his days in Lyon, had something to contribute. He swiftly offered Barrientos his services in the struggle against subversive elements and his offer was equally swiftly accepted. He was established in the Ministry of the Interior, where he had the use of an office. But his work was increasingly carried out with the army, whose Department 4 was the intelligence section, concerned with monitoring the activities of political opponents. As time went on, Department 4 became increasingly concerned with countering subversion, or "enemies of the state" as these dissident elements were known. A report prepared later for the Bolivian government showed that by the mid-1960s Barbie was regularly advising Department 4 on anti-guerrilla tactics, interrogation, and, as we shall see, torture.

From this point on, Barbie began to prosper. His friends noted the difference: he was no longer the humble wood yard proprietor, making crates for a German canned food factory; he was now a man of some standing, with a distinct, though unspecified, place in the government hierarchy. His powerful contacts and his own plausible manner gave him credibility and status. As the initial enthusiasm for the Barrientos coup began to wear off and the regime took on the characteristics of a brutal dictatorship, so the skills of Klaus Altmann became more central to the maintenance of power.

It was not, however, as interrogator or informer that Barbie first came into the public eye. Instead he emerged in the surprising role of "marine engineer". That was how he described himself to Gaston Velasco, a prosperous La Paz businessman driven by one patriotic ambition: to restore to Bolivia her access to the sea. Ever since the war of the Pacific in 1887, when Bolivia lost her coastline to Chile, the restoration of naval status had been a constant preoccupation in the landlocked mountain republic. Even today the La Paz telephone directory carries on the spine the legend, "Bolivia demands her access to the sea". Velasco was the driving force behind La Cruzada del Mar, a great crusade launched in 1966 to raise funds to buy a boat for Bolivia.

The navy, which defends Bolivia's rivers and the beautiful Lake Titicaca, although a small body of men, counts several admirals among them. They lent enthusiastic support to the scheme. Prominent among the participants were men with whom Barbie shared a common political outlook. They included an eccentric admiral who had once announced that Bolivia was doomed to mediocrity because of the high proportion of Indians in the population, and who counted himself racially inferior because of the Indian blood in his veins; and the éminence grise of Bolivian Fascism, Federico Nielsen Reyes, who numbered among his achievements the translation into Spanish of *Mein Kampf*.

The uncharitable might suggest that it was merely the scent of money and the prospect of power which drew Barbie to the cause. He himself, and his faithful defender, Alvaro de Castro, maintain that it was a desire to contribute to the national good. "One day," says de Castro, "his contribution will be recognised." That view is, as yet, a minority one. By most Bolivians Barbie's intervention is recalled more as a national débâcle.

The collection for the boat was a great success, raising $450,000 by public subscription. And Velasco, the originator of the scheme, was delighted when the "marine engineer" Klaus Altmann offered to help organise, not only the actual purchase of the ship, but the foundation of a shipping line to be known as Transmaritima Boliviana. Velasco still remembers the party: "We stood around drinking champagne. Everyone was there, Barrientos, Altmann . . . we toasted our success and the future of Bolivian shipping."

Several years later, Barbie himself gave evidence to a judge in La Paz about the circumstances in which he first became involved in Transmaritima. He had received a proposition, he explained, from a shipping company in Hamburg, which then sent a delegation to Bolivia to discuss it. Present at the meeting were several senior military officers, including one who was a future president of Bolivia – General Alfredo Ovando Candia, then commander of the armed forces.

Barbie maintained to the judge that he had only wanted to negotiate the formation of the shipping line and take a commission for himself, but he was pressed, he said, to accept the managership also. Of Transmaritima's stock, fifty-one per cent was owned by the government. The remaining forty-nine per cent was split between a Bolivian engineer, Alfonso Fernandez, who also acted as technical manager, Barbie himself, and a Captain William Ayers, an American businessman from New Orleans. Funds collected from the public, and deposited in the Central Bank, were to be used to purchase a ship which would operate out of the Peruvian port of Callao.

Conveniently, among the board members of Transmaritima Boliviana were the head of the navy, the chief of the joint chiefs of staff and, significantly, the head of Department 4, the army intelligence section, by which Barbie had been covertly employed since the Barrientos coup.

Captain Ayers, the American partner, who still operates a shipping business in New Orleans, understood from Barbie that he had been a major in the German army (a significant promotion), and he was impressed by his apparent standing in Bolivia. As far as Ayers was concerned, Transmaritima was a promising business investment. In his later statement to the La Paz judge, Barbie explained that Ayers had been approached after another potential investor in America had pulled out.

The investment settled, the company was formed. Offices were found in central La Paz and Barbie was installed as general manager. Being a semi-state operation through the participation of the navy, the company had every reason to succeed. The government had decreed that half of Bolivia's exports must, by law, be carried in Transmaritima ships, and business was expected to be heavy.

Instead, it was a financial disaster. Gaston Velasco to this day nurses his fury about what happened: "No boat was ever purchased," he said. "Four boats were leased and painted with Bolivian colours to make people think that Bolivia had a merchant fleet, but not a single Bolivian sailor was ever involved . . . the thing was a farce." Captain Ayers arranged two cargoes of flour, but eventually withdrew his participation when he saw that there was not enough business. In addition, Velasco charges, Barbie flagrantly milked the organisation, setting up branch offices which he staffed with relatives and friends. His son Klaus became representative for a time in Hamburg.

By virtue of his position as general manager, Barbie was furnished in 1966 with an official passport which permitted him the privileged travel of a government representative. Between 1966 and 1968, despite still being listed as a wanted war criminal, he visited Spain, Portugal, France, Brazil, Mexico, the United States and Peru.

In Spain he saw his son Klaus, who was half-heartedly pursuing his studies in Barcelona and scratching a living selling postcards, before moving to Hamburg. On the same trip he paid his respects both to Léon Degrelle and Otto Skorzeny in Madrid.

He also met Jordi Mota, secretary of the Spanish neo-Fascist organisation, CEDADE, and struck up something of a friendship. Mota remembers Barbie's visits well. "We spent two days together. I showed him the countryside and we talked about many things. He told me he had been to Paris and laid some flowers on the tomb of Jean Moulin." This bizarre exercise does seem to have taken place. Barbie showed pictures of the episode to Mota, and boasted about it several times to sceptical journalists.

The resounding failure of Transmaritima was blamed by Barbie years later on unfair hostility from other shipping companies and on lack of government support. But a far more realistic explanation is that Barbie was not particularly interested in Transmaritima's legitimate business. He had discovered that the company provided him with the perfect cover for something far more lucrative than shipping flour, but which never showed up on the Transmaritima accounts – dealing in arms.

The military dictatorships of Latin America needed weapons and armour, both for external defence and for their internal campaigns against political opponents and guerrillas. Not all this equipment could be openly purchased, and any dealer prepared to operate without asking too many questions was a welcome figure, not only in La Paz, but in Lima or Santiago or Buenos Aires.

Klaus Barbie became one of these – and something more. In the course of his many deals, he was to learn much about the military regimes of Latin America. He cultivated the officers he met; he collected documents; he kept his ears open. And everything that he stored away now was to serve him in good stead in the years to come.

When the truth about the Transmaritima books was finally discovered, Gaston Velasco, the Bolivian patriot who had set out with the most idealistic of motives, could trace no benefit at all to Bolivia, but a great deal to Klaus Barbie.

Much of Barbie's business had been conducted with the help of a circle of Nazis who themselves had acquired influence in various Latin American governments. Among them were the ex-Nazi officer Frederick Schwend in Peru, with whom Barbie was to form an extraordinary partnership; and Hans Ulrich Rudel, the former Luftwaffe air ace, who had developed a close personal and business relationship with President Stroessner in Paraguay and was later to become a friend of President Pinochet in Chile.

Barbie was also greatly assisted at various times by his friend Alvaro de Castro who was the agent in Bolivia of the Austrian weapons firm Steyr, Daimler and Puch. Barbie himself had dabbled in the arms business since the early 1960s when he had set up a company called Estrella, ostensibly dealing in quinquina bark. Although no records exist in the public registry in La Paz, at least one Bolivian arms dealer still remembers it as a weapons trading company.

Transmaritima, however, soon rendered the use of other companies obsolete, and over the next few years Barbie dealt widely throughout South America, mostly in small arms. By no means all of his transactions came off. Some of the most extravagant remained simply as figures on pieces of paper. But by 1968 Barbie was in a position to pull off a real and spectacular coup. The customer, ironically, was Israel.

Following the 1967 war, the state of Israel, facing an international arms embargo, approached Bolivia's ambassador to Spain, Alfredo Alexander, and proposed a three-way arms deal whereby a consignment of Belgian and Swiss arms, ostensibly destined for Bolivia, would be diverted on the high seas to Israel. The company involved in transporting them would be Transmaritima; and its general manager Klaus Altmann, together with the military officers approached, were to receive substantial commissions.

The proposal went right to the top. Among those who gave their whole-hearted approval was the president himself, General Barrientos, and that useful member of the Transmaritima board, Army Chief of Staff Ovando Candia. Barrientos had a special reason for enthusiasm: he was on a ten per cent commission, and the deal was valued at fifty million dollars.

The first of three shipments went through in March 1968, without difficulty, but the deal later turned sour. In 1969 Barrientos died in an air crash, leaving Ovando to become president, and Alfredo Alexander, the ambassador at the centre of the deal, found himself recalled from his diplomatic post in Spain. On his return to Bolivia he made the grave mistake of threatening to publicise the arms deal unless he received a share of the commission. Another man in possession of evidence about the deal was a leading Bolivian journalist, Otero Calderon, editor of the daily newspaper, *Hoy*.

Neither of these two was given a chance to use the information. On February 17 1970 Calderon was found dead in his office in circumstances which have never been explained. The only thing missing after his death was the documentation relating to the arms deal. A month later, on March 15 1970, a young man arrived with a package at Alexander's home in La Paz and instructed the porter to deliver it to the former ambassador. Alexander's wife accepted the package and carried it to her husband. A few minutes later their house was all but destroyed by a powerful explosion which killed them both.

One deal that particularly enraged Gaston Velasco involved a clandestine shipment of arms to Bolivia's historic enemy, Chile. In March 1971, flying a German flag, the Transmaritima ship *Birk* docked in Valparaiso to unload a cargo of 40.5 tons of small arms. The men who gained from the deal were Barbie and his friends on the Transmaritima board. The real losers, in Velasco's view, were the people of Bolivia who had contributed towards the setting up of Transmaritima.

But despite this secret trade, the company ran steadily into debt. By 1971 it owed a million dollars, and when, that year, foreign creditors issued writs to seize its assets, they found there were none. In 1972 Transmaritima was forced to cease trading.

Barbie's arms dealing introduced him to senior intelligence officers, not only in Bolivia, but in Chile too. As early as 1967, two years before Barrientos's death, there is evidence to suggest that he planned to extend the circle even further. That year, Barbie arranged a meeting in Santa Cruz between Barrientos and his old friend, the Nazi air ace Hans Rudel, whose connections by now extended well beyond the borders of Paraguay. The purpose was to discuss an arrangement whereby Rudel would keep Barrientos informed of Communist activities in Latin America. It was an ambitious operation with a suitably imposing title, Interamericana, but like many of the plans of these Nazi exiles, it does not seem to have been especially productive; Barbie himself later admitted in a letter to a fellow Nazi that it never came to anything – "at least not officially".

There was another initiative at this stage, however, which very nearly did reach fruition: joining forces with US intelligence in Latin America in its fight against "Communist subversion". The evidence for this extraordinary alliance comes from US army documents.

In February 1965 the police in Augsburg, West Germany, still sporadically pursuing the Barbie case, asked the US army high command in Germany if they could supply any information on Barbie. The army passed on the request to the CIA.

The CIA replied in March 1965 with a detailed memorandum listing Barbie's wartime activities and his post-war collaboration with US intelligence. They had, they said, no current operational interest in him, nor did they know his precise location.

But later that year the US army, stepping up its intelligence activities in Latin America, found out all about Barbie's life in Bolivia. Their enquiries stemmed from renewed interest in America about Barbie's wartime career, and Washington's continuing trauma about the march of Communism in South America. They made a discreet approach to the CIA and asked whether they knew of any former German intelligence officers in South America who might help monitor guerrilla movements. A routine trawl produced Barbie's name as a likely informant, though the CIA hastened to make it clear that they had no operational interest in him. The army then asked the US Embassy in La Paz to discover Barbie's whereabouts, and received tentative confirmation that a man called Altmann who seemed to be Barbie ran a wood business in La Paz. Shortly afterwards the US army in Europe, who had also been approached, produced Barbie's name and details of his flight to Bolivia.

There were clearly disadvantages to employing Barbie, but by 1967 there was a new urgency to the army's search. In the mountains of Bolivia a guerrilla campaign had begun, which, though hopelessly romantic and ultimately doomed, was to capture the imagination of the radical youth of the 1960s.

It was in November 1966 that Ernesto (Ché) Guevara had launched his attempt to start a rural guerrilla movement in Bolivia. From that small base he hoped to spread his revolution throughout the continent. It was not a well judged venture: the Bolivian peasantry had enjoyed the mixed blessings of land reform in the early 1950s and were being cultivated by the Barrientos regime as a weapon against the militant miners. It was, however, a sufficiently serious attempt to set alarm bells ringing in Washington and to attract the attention and collaboration of US army intelligence in trying to stamp it out.

Suddenly the suggestion from the army in Europe that Barbie might be useful began to look more interesting: their report in December 1966 had mentioned that "Klaus Altmann claims to number many high ranking Bolivian officers among his friends." Two months later the assistant chief of staff for intelligence in Washington made the army's second approach to the CIA, asking for any information they had, "prior to re-establishing contact with subject for purposes of an assessment of his present capabilities".

The work for which Barbie was being considered would have suited him ideally. His connections in Bolivia and his anti-Communism would have equipped him well for the fight against Ché Guevara's guerrillas. The US army was clearly tempted to take him on; but it was, interestingly, the CIA, conscious of the potential for bad publicity which Altmann's past offered, who were eventually to dissuade them from employing him directly. On April 5 1967 the CIA held a meeting in Washington with army intelligence to discuss the agency's findings and to seek an assessment of the merits and demerits of using him.

The CIA summarised Barbie's ostensible activities in Bolivia, including the carpentry business on the Calle Pedro de la Gasca in La Paz. But, according to the record of that meeting, the CIA officers went on to stress that employing Barbie carried grave risks. The war criminal charges, they said, were serious and the agency would have to be convinced that his help was extremely valuable before taking the risk of knowingly employing a Nazi war criminal. The CIA had an important say in the matter because any operation would be a joint one between them and army intelligence.

The CIA's doubts about the wisdom of employing Barbie would have been confirmed beyond doubt had they seen a letter he wrote to a fellow Nazi three weeks after the date of that Washington meeting. "With nostalgia I paid respects yesterday to the Führer's birthday. If he had been a little more patient until we 'young men' had got to the top, he would certainly have been celebrating his own seventy-eighth birthday."

And they would have had further cause for hesitation had they known that employing Barbie meant buying information not just from one ex-Nazi, but from a whole group of ex-Nazis who collected and exchanged intelligence for their own purposes. As Barbie wrote to his Nazi friend in Peru, "There's one good thing, in a few days we'll get another cabinet, composed exclusively of the military . . ." Barbie and his friends were already working on the problem of the guerrillas; as he wrote in the same letter: "The guerrilla band affair is guided from abroad, as has been established without room for doubt."

The army checks on Barbie continued through the summer of 1967, but by October, Ché Guevara and his little band were dead. The immediate problem was therefore deemed settled and in April 1968 the army notified the CIA that their interest in reactivating Altmann/Barbie was terminated.

By this point Barbie had other more personal things on his mind. On June 5 Klaus junior, his son, now aged twenty-two, with whom Barbie had had a difficult relationship, offended him further by choosing to marry a beautiful young French woman. Barbie was later to quote this as an example of his broad-minded tolerance of the old enemy, but friends testify to his fury and distress at the time. The marriage was to bring other unwanted consequences. When it was registered at the French Embassy in La Paz, a sharp eyed vice-consul, Dominique Colombani, noticed a strange similarity between the names and birthdates of the Altmann parents and son and that of the long hunted Barbie family. He informed the ambassador, Jean Louis Mandereau, who in turn notified the French government. There was, however, no immediate reaction.

Barbie seemed determined that one of his children, at least, would marry someone he could approve of. A few months later he arranged, through a contact in Switzerland, a friendly reception for his daughter Ute, who was sent to Germany – as her father put it – "to look for a man". The trip, in fact, was to inch Barbie a little closer to discovery. When Ute contacted the German Embassy in La Paz to arrange her residence permit, it was the turn of the German authorities to notice, as the French had done, the curious similarities between the Altmanns and the long-lost Barbies.

The German authorities were sufficiently interested to pursue inquiries, and on September 20 1969 the Ministry of Foreign Affairs in Bonn sent a secret report they had received from their Embassy in Bolivia to the Federal Ministry of Justice. It read: "We recommend a very careful inquiry because Klaus Altmann has extremely good relations in government circles and with former Nazis like Fritz Schwend in Lima. I enclose a photograph of Altmann with a group, published in a Bolivian newspaper."

The report went to the Munich public prosecutor, Dr Wolfgang Rabl, who had taken over Barbie's case from the Augsburg authorities. When Rabl examined the file he concluded that it was unlikely that a successful case could be brought against Barbie and, in spite of the fresh evidence of his whereabouts, recommended the matter be dropped.

Meanwhile in Bolivia the Altmanns prospered. The potential setback of 1969, when Barbie's protector President Barrientos was killed in a helicopter crash had been smoothly weathered: his friend and business partner, Ovando Candia, eventually succeeded to the presidency.

In some ways Ovando's government was more liberal than that of Barrientos, but his was still a militant right-wing regime; under it Barbie maintained his standing as a well connected businessman, with his secret role as military adviser well concealed from all but a few close friends. He himself lightly dismissed any suggestions that he was other than a harmless businessman. His favoured image was that of a genial and civilised bon viveur, who liked nothing better than to sit down and hold an agreeable discussion on politics or the passing scene in La Paz with anyone who dropped into the cafés he frequented. What none of those acquaintances knew was that anything of interest they said was rapidly reported either to army intelligence or to the secret services of the Ministry of the Interior.

But there was another dimension to Klaus Altmann's life, one which went hand in hand with his intelligence role, and which was to extend his activities to a third country, Peru. This was his role as confidence trickster, swindler, and blackmailer.

These were not crafts which came unnaturally to him. Ever since his hand-to-mouth days in Germany after the war, Barbie had found crime a perfectly acceptable way of life. And in Bolivia, where official posts can be bought and political corruption and bribery are endemic, Barbie was in his element – it was part of the normal business of survival. As a Bolivian saying puts it, "The stupid ones work, and the clever ones live off the stupid."

Just as Barbie's secret arms deals had introduced him to military intelligence, so the practice of fraud and blackmail gave him the capacity to use that intelligence for his own ends. The role of secret agent was thus subtly reversed; the government departments which employed him were, in their turn, being exploited – in Barbie's hands, intelligence picked up in the course of work became a lucrative commodity to be used to make money or gather a little more power.

Barbie could have achieved little of this, however, without the help of an old acquaintance who was to be his mentor, working partner, and closest confidant for fifteen years.

It is difficult to appreciate the career of Klaus Barbie in South America without some understanding of the Byzantine character of SS Colonel Friedrich Paul Schwend, of the 3rd Panzer Division (retired). Since most things recounted by Schwend turn out on analysis to be lies, it is worth stating at the outset that Schwend was neither a colonel, nor SS, and certainly had nothing whatsoever to do with the 3rd Panzer Division.

CHAPTER ELEVEN

Klaus and Fritz

Friedrich Paul Schwend's progression from humble car mechanic in the small German town of Gemmingen to international confidence trickster in Europe and South America had been achieved with barely a stumble.

His first step up the ladder had come in 1929 when, in the teeth of family opposition, he married into the local aristocracy. The baroness of Gemmingen-Guttenberg was a niece of the then German Minister of the Exterior, Baron von Neurath, and through his new family connections Schwend became administrator for the personal fortune of his wife's aunt, a member of the extremely wealthy Bunge family of Argentina.

His pre-war income from this job alone was fifty thousand dollars a year and it was not his only source of income. Schwend himself recorded that in the early 1930s he also dabbled in arms dealing, acting as agent to the Balkans for the firm of Lemm Daimler, and sold Belgian weapons and Junkers planes to China.

When war came to Europe, Schwend's first thought seems to have been to make money out of it. He moved to Italy to take advantage of the black market exchange rate for dollars and lived comfortably on the fortunes of his aunt by marriage until America entered the war and the money stopped flowing. Soon afterwards Schwend's marriage was dissolved. Undaunted, he quickly married again, this time the daughter of a wealthy Austrian engineer.

In 1941 he was arrested in Italy, allegedly for spying for the Allies. After three months of investigation in Germany, he bought his way out of gaol and promised to work for his own country. Returning to Italy, he used his talent for manipulating currency as purchasing agent for the Wehrmacht, the SS and the SD.

But it was the development of Operation Bernhard in early 1943 that gave Schwend his greatest opportunity. This has usually been described as a Third Reich attempt to ruin the British economy by flooding the market with forged Bank of England notes. More likely its real objective was to generate sufficient capital to transform the SS into an independent economic power. In 1944 Schwend was put in charge of the "Special Staff Group of the General Command of 11 Germanic Panzer Division SS". This impressive title concealed a special unit devoted to "laundering" the forged notes by exchanging them for genuine currency and valuables.

Acting under the orders of Ernst Kaltenbrunner, the head of the SD, Schwend travelled extensively during the war in Europe, finding the means to exchange the forged banknotes for genuine ones, which were then deposited in banks in both Spain and Switzerland.

The fate of the Bernhard millions remains one of Europe's greatest post-war mysteries. As the war turned against Germany, the funds became a personal life raft for those SS officers who knew how to divert them; but huge deposits simply vanished or remained locked in numbered accounts in Switzerland. This tantalising fortune was never forgotten by those close to the operation and Schwend was later to join a secret consortium of ex-Nazis whose aim was to recover the Bernhard fortune.

At the end of the war, like Klaus Barbie, Schwend worked for the Americans before escaping to South America. US documents reveal that after passing into the hands of the 44th CIC Detachment he was used as an informant by American intelligence agencies in Austria, the Austrian Tyrol and Meran, North Italy.

He was, however, wanted for murder. On August 26 1944 Theophil Kamber, an SD agent who had allegedly tried to abscond with Bernhard funds, was found dead in mysterious circumstances. Schwend and two others were suspected and US documents contain lengthy details about the charge which was listed as a war crime. This does not appear to have deterred the Red Cross or the American authorities who employed him throughout the latter half of 1945 and early 1946, when Schwend decided that the time had come to pull out of Europe. He and his wife travelled to Rome, where they acquired Croat identities, almost certainly thanks to the circle of Croatian exiles, among whom was the "good father" Dr Draganovič who would later help Barbie. Equipped with Red Cross passports which described them as Wenceslas Turi, agronomist, and his wife Hedda, the Schwends travelled to Barcelona, where they arranged papers for emigration to Venezuela. They left Spain in early December 1946.

The initial intention appears to have been to settle in Venezuela, but the Turis soon moved on to Lima, Peru, where they stayed. By the early 1950s, their false identities were abandoned and they lived openly in Lima under their own names. Schwend even took the precaution of establishing his credentials with the Jewish community and became a staunch member of the Anti-Defamation League.

In those years, too, Schwend made contact with Klaus Barbie in Bolivia. Schwend was later to say that they had first met during the war, but since he added that Klaus Altmann was nothing to do with Klaus Barbie, the Butcher of Lyon, his remarks must be viewed with caution. Whatever the truth, the two men maintained a regular and frequent correspondence, a close friendship and a highly lucrative partnership throughout their time in South America.

The parallels between their careers are striking. Like Barbie, Schwend established a respectable business – in his case raising chickens; like Barbie he set up a company dealing in arms; like Barbie he worked secretly for government agencies, and like Barbie his respectable front represented only a fraction of his activities: as early as 1953 US records show him offering his services as a "trained saboteur" to an exiled Bolivian group trying to mount a coup against the Paz Estenssoro government, and then, a few months later, describing himself as a consultant in "anti-Communist activities" to the Peruvian army.

The business objectives of this apparently modest chicken farmer were the enrichment – through arms dealing, the sale of state secrets, blackmail and extortion – of Friedrich Schwend and his circle of "Kamaraden": former Nazis like himself and Barbie who had won the confidence of a series of Latin American governments. At the same time they built up considerable political power in their respective countries, by virtue of the information they collected.

How much benefit Schwend, Barbie, and the Kameraden actually brought to the governments they advised is best summed up by a Peruvian judge, Santos Chichizola, who was to investigate their activities twenty years after and who took possession of the voluminous Schwend archives. At the end of a lengthy interview, during which he described in some detail the astonishing careers of the two men, he concluded: "As I went through the documents, it became clear to me that Peru did not have a single military secret left. Schwend and his friends had sold them all."

The Schwend papers, currently held in a Lima vault, and still the object of enormous interest among Nazi historians, open up a fresh area of Barbie's life and document the involvement of the Nazi network in South America in arms-dealing and counter-subversion. Only by gaining access to them has it been possible to compile the detailed account that follows of a unique and unscrupulous partnership.

The primary business of Schwend and Barbie – arms trafficking – was carried on through two German-based firms, Merex and Gemetex. The two Nazis acted as agents, negotiating purchases not only on behalf of the Bolivian and Peruvian governments but, through their friendship with the Nazi Hans Rudel, sales to Paraguay and Chile and, through Colonel Otto Skorzeny in Spain, further deals in Madrid.

From Merex alone, as Schwend's correspondence reveals, they proposed buying M14 tanks "for Herr Skorzeny", twenty MAX 13 tanks, "for a general here", Mercedes military vehicles, and six power boats. The sources of the equipment were impeccable. As Merex wrote to Schwend in 1966:

> We are cabling you the prices of "birds" being enquired about, sending specifications. What do you mean by "exceptional things"? . . . find a secure way to tell us, perhaps via courier through Peruvian embassy in Bonn. Our common friend Colonel R [Rudel], who also works for us, will be coming out soon; he could take a message. We must be paid in cash for official German or American equipment.

In the same period, Schwend and Barbie's dealings with Gemetex included ground to air rockets, coastal patrol boats, 20mm air cannon ammunition, modern machine guns for aircraft, armoured cars, ground to air and ground to ground rockets. At the same time, the delighted Gemetex reported to Schwend that "on your suggestion, our naval department is getting in touch with Herr Altmann in La Paz", with the idea of selling him ships for Transmaritima. On April 21 1969, they wrote: "Here is our offer of 20 mm ammunition – is it for Oerlikon or Hispano Suiza cannon? You will get ten per cent commission. Anyone there interested in Noratlas transport aircraft or Sycamore helicopters from Bundeswehr stocks?"

On this occasion the deal failed to come off, but Schwend's correspondence reveals not only the scale of the deals he and Barbie put together, but the way in which they often went hand in hand with offers of assistance as "security consultants". Both the governments of Honduras and El Salvador were approached in August 1969, with the suggestion that they might be in need of specialised military advice or "end-user" certificates to help with arms supplies, though there is no evidence that in these two cases the offers were taken up.

Barbie also developed a profitable sideline trafficking in Bolivian government credentials, which he procured from his contacts in La Paz – a trade which also bought protection. Possession of official government papers, distributed at a price by Schwend and himself, enabled them to conduct their arms dealing under the convenient cover afforded by diplomatic immunity.

Typical of such deals was the sale of the Bolivian consulship in Geneva to an arms dealing contact, Eugen Albert Huber. On June 9 1965 Schwend wrote to Huber in Zurich suggesting that he might like to purchase the general consulship in Geneva for a "neighbouring country". As reassurance, he added: "The country concerned is *absolutely rightwing* – or at least, its government – and is very skilfully ridding itself of previous leftist influences . . ."

Huber was delighted with the deal and the business partnership flourished. Not only did Huber try to negotiate shipping deals with Transmaritima Boliviana but, in spite of both his and Schwend's much proclaimed antipathy to Communism, a few months later they were deep in discussion of a dubious three-way operation to ship oil to Cuba, a deal to be financed via the Soviet Woschod Bank in Zurich. There were personal favours too. When in 1969 Barbie decided to send his daughter Ute to Europe, Schwend wrote to Huber:

This summer, the daughter of my business friend Klaus Altmann is visiting Europe, at her father's request, to look around for a man. The father is a strong business partner of Böhringer, exported over one million dollars' worth of chinin bark to Germany for Böhringer. Also put through a petrochemical plant and a sulphuric acid plant for Bolivia, the first project worth about thirteen million dollars. If you have any projects for Bolivia, you can write to Altmann using my name. The man is OK . . . I have given Altmann's daughter your address and suggested she call on you in Zurich . . .

Huber was, of course, delighted to oblige.

Not all of Schwend and Barbie's deals went so well. In 1966 a Nazi contact, Johann Hieber, wrote from New York expressing interest in buying Bolivian citizenship, with passport, and becoming the Bolivian delegate to the World Health Organisation in New York and Geneva. He actually received a Bolivian diplomatic passport and the consulship in Lugano, in Switzerland, for which he promised to pay forty thousand dollars in cash. But when, instead, he forwarded shares in his company, Malto, and the shares turned out to be worthless, a furious Barbie informed Schwend that he was arranging for the diplomatic passport to be withdrawn so that they could report the defaulting Nazi to the police.

As Schwend and Barbie developed the gentle art of exploitation, so they learned to manipulate not only their victims, but the intelligence agencies with which they worked. One method was to keep their employers in a high state of alarm about the extent of subversion in their countries. Schwend's main protectors in Peru were the Peruvian Intelligence Police (PIP), who had been persuaded by Schwend's impressive military contacts to take him on as an adviser.

In this role, Schwend kept up a steady stream of "reports" to PIP on subversive activities in Peru, some genuine, others highly coloured, and yet others thinly disguised character assassinations of individuals who had the misfortune to stray into his sights. He also used his new status as a supporter of Jewish interests in Peru to keep a dossier on Jewish groups and Nazi-hunters; if a Nazi-hunter arrived anywhere in Latin America, details were quickly passed round the group.

In some cases where Schwend and Barbie did pick a genuinely subversive target, they made sure that they extracted maximum benefit from it, both in terms of prestige and in financial gain. One group in Peru which came to Schwend and Barbie's attention was a small guerrilla movement financed, Schwend claimed in a 1965 report, by both the Soviet Union and China. Using their contacts in the arms trade, Schwend and Barbie negotiated a deal to sell them weapons, then informed the security services where they were. In a letter written to "Rudi" – one of Barbie's code names – Schwend laid out the proposition, which first of all involved an elaborate "scam". The letter is a supreme example of the Schwend-Barbie style – deeply corrupt, seedy and vindictive:

Dear Rudi
    In this country lives a man who from a confirmed source has money available . . . The money is in Switzerland, or in Monte Carlo. I now have the following ideas. You write to the man's address, a few lines, saying not very much, roughly going like this . . . "I was advised to let you know that our friends here and I in particular would gladly furnish you with equipment of any sort for expeditions. I can transfer the goods to you here or, of course – and that is important to you – at any port of yours or at any agreed point that can be reached by lorry. Wishing you all the best, I would hope to hear from you directly or through friends and I would be glad if I could help our project." Address is Sra de la Puente Uceda, Av Arequipa no. 2984 Lima, Peru.

What do I want? Well, to get into contact. You can sell the man anything you want and let it be known that the goods can be handed over in the interior of the country. Logically the prices would then go up. You can stick stones in the packing cases and take the money for the goods – as long as I know exactly what really has been handed over etc. My name must never be mentioned, or all trust will be lost. I would advise you not to use your own name. On the other hand, the affair must be so solid and watertight that we can cash the money by using our names. Maybe you or [. . .] have an acquaintance, with a red tinge, to whom you can tell a fairy tale and who will function as a man of straw . . . So think the affair over and let me know in writing how you want to weave the web . . .

The operation, according to Santos Chichizola, the Peruvian judge who later investigated Schwend and Barbie's activities, was successful. Santos described how the consignment – not, in fact, of stones but of useless weapons – was delivered to a destination near Lake Titicaca. The next stage was to notify the Peruvian security forces who rounded up the unfortunate guerrilla group as they prepared to take delivery of the consignment. Not only had they been thoroughly taken in, they were now prisoners.

There was nothing, it seemed, which could not be turned to the advantage of Schwend and Barbie – or Fritz and Klaus as their friends called them. Even their common Nazi past could be a source of revenue, and provide a certain amusement at the expense of journalists eager to track down the more notorious criminals of the Third Reich.

For one ambitious young German journalist, Herbert John, "Colonel" Schwend had at first seemed the ideal source. But like many others who imagined they enjoyed Schwend's trust and friendship, John soon felt the ground give way under his feet. Counting on the free-spending German magazine *Stern* to take the bait, Schwend began to hint to John that he could help him pull off the scoop of the century and find the most hunted war criminal of all, Martin Bormann. Constructing an elaborate set of "security measures", Schwend gradually led John into the trap. He put him on to his friend Klaus Altmann in Bolivia who, he said, would make the final connection with Bormann; but at the same time, having secured his advance of several thousand dollars, he tipped off PIP in Peru that John was a cocaine dealer. John only narrowly escaped arrest. Warned by friends of what was happening, he rapidly fled the country.

So fruitful was the business partnership between Schwend and Barbie, that in 1970 Barbie began to divide his time between Lima and La Paz, driving between the two capitals in his Volkswagen. Later he bought a house for himself in Lima near the spacious compound owned by Fritz Schwend. Although at first his trips were strictly for business purposes, later in the year a coup in Bolivia, this time by a left-wing general, persuaded him to ride out the unwelcome interruption in the relative safety of Lima.

A major attraction for Barbie was the increasing importance of Schwend's connections in Peru. As well as his close relationship with PIP, he had, some years before, secured a useful job in the office which monitored the correspondence of the unfortunate citizens of Peru on behalf of the security police. The job was found for him by senior military officers for whom he had done favours himself over the years. For a man who dealt in information about other people's lives it was a gold mine.

The success of Barbie's Peruvian operations depended on two factors: his and Schwend's own plausibility and the essential respectability of their victims. Schwend, an apparently impeccable chicken farmer and his friend, Klaus Altmann, an equally eminent and well connected businessman, behaved at all times with the courtesy and rectitude which befitted their respective pasts as German officers. Their victims were, on the whole, citizens with a reputation to maintain who were helped and encouraged to circumvent state regulations of a relatively minor nature, then blackmailed with the threat of exposure. But in the early summer of 1970, the two old Nazis finally encountered a man who fought back, and in doing so began to dismantle the elaborate structure of protection that both men had built up over the years.

The story that Volkmar Johannes Schneider-Merck has to tell about Schwend and Barbie is not only a remarkable first-hand account of two supreme confidence-tricksters at work, it provides the crucial link between Barbie's freewheeling life in Lima and his swift departure back to La Paz where the richest part of his career was to begin.

In those days, Johannes Schneider-Merck was a young and ambitious German businessman, without too many scruples himself, who had been living in Lima for eighteen months. By the end of 1969 he was assistant manager of the powerful Peruvian-German Chamber of Commerce, an organisation devoted to furthering trade between the two countries.

His relationship with "Klaus and Fritz" began, as he recalled it, one day in February 1970 as he sat in his office. A visitor was announced, who presented a card bearing the legend:

Colonel Federico Schwend
ex-Chief of Staff
8th Panzer division

The scholarly and distinguished-looking gentleman who confronted Schneider-Merck looked more like an antiquarian bookseller than an ex-SS officer, with his beak-like nose and his gleaming bald pate. But his confident and authoritative manner was impressive, and when the colonel invited Schneider-Merck to drop in for a drink that night on the way home, he accepted.

The conversation at that first meeting revolved around the prosaic subject of milking machinery: Colonel Schwend, in his role as agricultural engineer and chicken farmer, was always interested in the latest agricultural equipment. As Schneider-Merck recalled, the contact seemed a valuable one: "He talked about all the people he knew – and he did seem to know a lot of people, not just in Peru but throughout Latin America. He was very helpful – any problems I had at the Chamber of Commerce, he told me, I should call him. He would always be able to help, through his contacts."

Over a drink that evening in Schwend's sprawling house, some fifteen kilometres from central Lima, Schneider-Merck met the rest of the Schwend family, and some close friends who were visiting from La Paz – Regine or "Gin" and Klaus Altmann. Schneider-Merck liked Altmann, who was introduced to him as a Bolivian businessman of German descent, and was fascinated by Schwend, who told him stories of a glamorous past which included the legendary Bernhard affair and the romance of a dashing wartime career.

The relationship developed pleasantly enough: Schneider-Merck's house was a few kilometres further along the Carretera Central from the Schwends' and he passed that way every night on the way home. "I got into the habit," he remembered, "of dropping in and having coffee, to talk about what was going on . . . It was a big house, with a big verandah and a long table. We would all sit around it, Schwend, Altmann and I, drinking a glass of Peruvian red wine. It was a very pleasant relationship in the beginning."

Schneider-Merck found ways of repaying the favours: Klaus Altmann was looking for a new car, so Schneider-Merck sold him one, and when he decided to buy a house in Lima, Schneider-Merck put him in touch with a German friend who was planning to sell. Altmann bought the house and became a neighbour.

243

In 1970, when the Peruvian government suddenly clamped down on foreign currency regulations, Schneider-Merck was deeply impressed by Schwend's sang-froid. Decree number 818275 caused considerable resentment among the freewheeling foreign business community in Lima. At a stroke, it outlawed the holding of foreign currency either inside Peru or outside. Within fifteen days, it said, all such holdings must be repatriated and no further export of currency was permitted. Since the local currency, the Peruvian *sol*, was considered extremely unstable, and everyone with any money held US dollars, there was panic. Even private safe deposit boxes were sealed and the dollars inside forcibly converted to *soles*.

Schwend was quite unperturbed. "There's no problem," he told Schneider-Merck. "Whenever you have some money you want to get out, just come to me. I can fix it." It was not long before Schneider-Merck, in spite of the potential penalties involved, began providing customers. "I do not regard dealing in currency as a crime," he later insisted.

Schwend's method of avoiding the currency regulations was ingenious. Altmann, as manager of Transmaritima, needed a large amount of Peruvian currency to pay the port expenses of various cargoes arriving at and leaving Peruvian ports. Anyone who wished to export currency would give Altmann the Peruvian currency and receive a receipt from him for "loading charges" which they could recover in the port of destination for hard currency. Using this system, several deals were satisfactorily concluded. Of course, there was a mark-up on the money, with Schwend and Barbie taking a handsome rake-off for exporting the cash. And there was, naturally, a small commission for Schneider-Merck too.

The system worked, and as the government changed the regulations, so variations were developed. The first hint Schneider-Merck had that things were beginning to go wrong came with a transaction carried out in October 1970 in which the promised deposit abroad of ten thousand dollars failed to appear.

Schwend was quick to reassure him. The money, he said, was in the hands of a Seventh Day Adventist priest, Father Aaron Silverstein, who would shortly make the dollar deposit. He had even left shares as guarantee for the money. But the priest somehow failed to materialise and, as Schneider-Merck discovered, the shares – in the defunct company, Malto – turned out to be dud holdings.

Reconstructing the sequence of events later, Schneider-Merck came to the conclusion that the succession of catastrophes which were now to befall him had been, from the beginning, devised by

Altmann and Schwend. But in late 1970, when the two men proposed a way in which he might earn enough to refund the ten thousand dollars to his "customer", he gratefully accepted.

The proposed solution was that Schneider-Merck should redouble his efforts to earn commissions by passing on to Barbie more customers who sought to export even larger sums of hard currency. But the next deal too went wrong, and Schneider-Merck found himself listening as a smooth-tongued Schwend explained that, unfortunately, the Peruvian *sol* had dropped badly on the markets. In La Paz, Klaus was seriously out of pocket on the deal. There would, alas, be no commission available.

Schneider-Merck was beginning to find the bluff Klaus Altmann less and less congenial. There was, he noted, behind those blue eyes a distinctly cold and unprepossessing air about him.

The deals, however, multiplied through the early part of 1971. Schneider-Merck continued to supply "customers" whose identity he concealed, even from Schwend. By June he had earned enough commission to repay three-fifths of his original debt.

Then one day towards the end of June 1971, Barbie told Schneider-Merck that a major opportunity was coming up. Barbie would shortly require a large amount of Peruvian currency to pay for a consignment of wheat. If Schneider-Merck could collect the equivalent in hard currency, he would get it out of the country. Schneider-Merck still had a list of willing customers, suffering under the ever stricter currency laws.

> I collected together . . . about half a million German marks, a kilo of gold that I had bought myself, several letters to my bank and the letters which explained where the money was to be deposited on behalf of the customers. I bought a fine pigskin leather suitcase with two double locks and the three of us went to the Bolivian Embassy in Lima. There the suitcase was sealed with diplomatic seals and labelled an official package.

Barbie, with his official Bolivian passport, was to carry the bag to La Paz, change the money and forward the funds to the appropriate destinations.

"I had no reason to believe anything could go wrong," says Schneider-Merck. But after a week of silence he grew nervous and tried to telephone Barbie in La Paz. There was no reply. It was not until July 16 that he had news from his diplomatic courier. "Mr Schwend sent one of his cronies to my office to bring me a letter he had received from Altmann. I read the letter and I was completely stunned."

Writing under the code name "Emilio", Barbie announced to Schwend that he, in turn, was appalled by the misfortune which had overtaken him. The Barbie style, honed under the tutelage of Fritz Schwend, was unmistakable:

> To tell it briefly, the little black case went missing with all its contents in the customs hall of the airport on Saturday, 3rd July. Since then I have been racking my brains to see how it could have happened. I took the briefcase from the plane into customs. There I waited for my big case, which took some time. There was quite a bustle, as the Braniff plane was due and on the Lloyd aircraft there was an American youth group (musicians and actors). I put my briefcase on the counter.
>
> As the passengers' heavy baggage arrived, including mine, I had to go and look for it as the whole checking system here is very disorganised. The briefcase must have gone during this confusion ... There is the possibility – and I have thought seriously about this – of a deliberate, planned act, as recently there have been a series of such thefts and robberies, including opening mail sacks. It's thought that it may be an ELN [a left-wing guerrilla group] action, aimed at certain private persons ...

Barbie explained that he himself had become a target of kidnapping threats and mysterious burglaries. "I have now become known here as a 'Fascist'," he complained, hinting of the difficulties this unfortunate affair could bring him. "Nobody is to blame," he adds, "and not I, as such things do happen. One really should not go in for that sort of transaction in which we have no experience."

As if that was not galling enough for Schneider-Merck, Barbie even attached as "evidence" a statement he had made to the police at El Alto. But the real menace, in addition to the catastrophic loss of funds for which Schneider-Merck was morally responsible to his "customers", lay in the hints about discovery. "Most disagreeable to all," wrote Barbie, "are the letters which were in the case which Volkmar gave me. I put them on the top of the contents."

The letters, of course, contained the names of Schneider-Merck's customers, as well as implicating Schneider-Merck himself. The penalties for infringing the Peruvian currency laws were savage: not only was the money automatically confiscated, but a fine of ten times the amount was payable and the culprit was liable, in addition, to a term of imprisonment. Clearly, all Schneider-Merck's customers would be most anxious to prevent the documents coming to the notice of the Peruvian authorities.

Dazed, Schneider-Merck telephoned his contacts with the bad news. Then he went to see Schwend, who was full of regrets, but, for the first time, without a helpful suggestion. Over the next few weeks, Schneider-Merck was to realise the extent of the web which had been spun around him, and the importance of Schwend's many friends – in intelligence, the fiscal police and the military.

Once Schwend had the names and addresses of his customers, all well-heeled potential blackmail victims, Schneider-Merck's usefulness was over. All that remained was to neutralise him. Schwend notified the German Embassy, in his capacity as patriotic German, that the fiscal police were in the process of investigating a massive currency ring operated by the young deputy manager of the German Peruvian Chamber of Commerce.

Don Federico had no need to spell out to the alarmed ambassador that the scandal would do grave damage to Germany's image. As proof, he showed to the Embassy copies of the correspondence from the famous vanishing suitcase, appropriately stamped "secret and confidential" – a clear hint that they were already in the hands of the security police. "He used to stamp them himself to make them more convincing," said Schneider-Merck. "He had a collection of stamps hidden in his house."

When Schneider-Merck saw the correspondence, he lost the final shred of illusion about his benefactors. "I knew there was only one place the tip-off could have come from," he said. "From that moment, I resolved to fight." After a confrontation with his superiors at the Chamber of Commerce, Schneider-Merck took an unscheduled holiday in Colombia to await developments.

While he was away, Schwend, still trying to save Germany's image and avoid a scandal, sold the originals of the documents to the Chamber of Commerce for twenty thousand *soles* and ceremonially burned them in front of the distraught manager. He also wrote a series of letters to the absent Schneider-Merck urging him to stay away while he, Schwend, sorted out the problem. On hearing that Schwend had produced the documents, Schneider-Merck decided he had enough proof. He returned to Lima, ready to do battle.

Klaus Barbie meanwhile had other things on his mind. An old friend of his, General Hugo Banzer, a ruggedly-built Bolivian officer of German extraction, to whom Barbie had been introduced some years earlier, and with whom he was now on close terms, had come to power in yet another military coup. Banzer had been helped by the Santa Cruz sugar tycoon Erwin Gasser, who had raised money for the coup from the German business community, remarking: "You can't make a revolution with hamburgers."

The Banzer coup was particularly good news for Barbie. Not only were the right-wing of the MNR party incorporated into the new government, but it marked the beginning of a period of power for his old friends in the Bolivian Socialist Falange. The news immediately went round the network. "Klaus is in La Paz," wrote Schwend to a Nazi contact in Chile, "living the wonderful revolution. Hugo Banzer's declaration that this time it is an anti-Communist revolution has meaning for and will influence the entire continent. Let's hope it happens soon in Chile, too."

Banzer immediately re-employed Barbie as security adviser, with duties which included informing on the comings and goings of eastern bloc visitors. Barbie's role in the security apparatus was kept discreet, and he was paid partly out of Banzer's special "reserved" funds and partly by Department 4 (later Department 7) of the army, now responsible for psychological operations, from its base in Cochabamba.

The return of good friends to the government of Bolivia was a stroke of fortune which came just in time. For unknown to Barbie, a series of events was now in train which was to bring him to within an inch of retribution. And the wheels of justice in this endeavour would be liberally oiled by the now bitterly vengeful Schneider-Merck.

CHAPTER TWELVE

The Nazi-Hunters

Johannes Schneider-Merck's relations with Schwend and Altmann had degenerated severely in the months following the "loss" of his precious briefcase. While maintaining apparently civil relations with Schwend, he waited for Barbie to reappear from Bolivia where he had been helping General Hugo Banzer to mount his coup.

As soon as he had returned, Schneider-Merck went to see him. "I said I didn't want to discuss what had happened, but that I was shattered that a former German officer would behave in such a way."

Taken aback by the virulence of his accusations, Barbie suggested that they both go and discuss the matter with Schwend.

"There was a lot of bluster," said Schneider-Merck, "and Schwend threatened to call the police, but I told them that whatever it cost, I would never let the matter rest."

Barbie favoured a conciliatory line. Carefully insisting that he accepted no responsibility or guilt, he agreed to pay Schneider-Merck the one third he had asked for. Schneider-Merck took the payment as a sign of good faith, but a few days later came retaliation from the indefatigable Schwend.

"I was at home, late one night, when there was a terrible hammering at the door. It was the police – the PIP – coming to arrest me. I opened the window, took my pistol and started firing into the air, screaming and cursing at them. They must have thought I was crazy, but they left in a terrific hurry."

From then on, it was war. Schneider-Merck resigned from his position at the Chamber of Commerce, and withdrew to his house to prepare his campaign.

I decided to write down everything I could remember about them [he said]. I had known them for eighteen months and, as I sat there thinking, details began to come back to me – like the night at Schwend's house when I said that the idealism of the German people had been betrayed by Hitler – I can still see, to this day, Altmann's face. He went bright red and he jumped up: "In my

249

presence," he shouted, absolutely furious, "nobody says anything against the Führer." I was laughing, then I saw he wasn't joking.

As Schneider-Merck remembered such incidents, he in turn became convinced that Barbie was hiding his past.

It was very unusual, for instance, for any German to give up German nationality for Bolivian nationality. If you are respectable, it's a great deal easier to go round the world with a German passport. And why had he lived in the Yungas all those years? That's a hell of an uncivilised place to live. As I thought about it, I suddenly realised – that bastard really must have something to hide.

His memoranda complete, Schneider-Merck sent them, via a friend in Switzerland, to Simon Wiesenthal, doyen of Nazi-hunters, to see if he could identify Klaus Altmann or Friedrich Schwend. Some weeks later came the reply: Schwend, yes, was a legendary figure, but there were no records of an Altmann.

"I thought, 'Bingo!' " said Schneider-Merck. "I knew he had been a German officer. He had even shown me his medals. If he didn't appear in the records, it meant he had changed his name."

Determined to uncover the secret of Altmann's past, Schneider-Merck collected all the details and photographs of Altmann he could, and sent them to Wiesenthal.

If Wiesenthal did not know about Altmann, Altmann certainly knew all about Wiesenthal. In the letter he had written to Schwend on the occasion of Hitler's birthday in 1967, he remarked of Wiesenthal: "Couldn't we get him over here . . .? He certainly wouldn't get out of my hands again!!!" It was one of Wiesenthal's friends, Barbie went on, who had "invented" the figure of six million Jews murdered by the Nazis.

It was not, however, Wiesenthal, but another formidable Nazi-hunter who was to make the key break-through in identifying Barbie. Beate Klarsfeld was herself German and had spent her childhood and adolescence amidst the partitioned ruins of Berlin. She had grown up a stern judge of the apparent indifference of her parents' generation to what had happened under the Nazis, and once said of her mother and father that they had neither forgotten nor learned anything from the great disaster which had overtaken them.

Her dedication to the pursuit of Nazi war criminals had begun when she met and married Serge Klarsfeld, a young French lawyer and a Jew who, as a child, had crouched hidden behind a partition while his father was dragged out by the Gestapo to be gassed in Auschwitz.

The Klarsfelds' quest for Klaus Barbie, as Beate recounts it, had begun on July 25 1971 in the Contemporary Jewish Documentation Centre in Paris, when she came across a report of the decision taken one month earlier by the Munich prosecutor, Wolfgang Rabl, to drop the case against Barbie, both for lack of evidence and because of the long lapse of time. Reading Rabl's report, the Klarsfelds realised that the Barbie case risked vanishing completely – a dangerous precedent for many similar cases – and resolved to fight to have the decision reversed.

Within a few days of Rabl's decision, Beate and Serge had compiled and distributed to the press a large dossier on Barbie. On July 28 the Lyon newspaper *Progrès*, denounced the Rabl decision in the course of a long article, and in September Beate, along with the mother of three children who had been at the orphanage at Izieu, staged a protest at the prosecutor's office in Munich. But it was the Klarsfelds' own research that produced the most important new evidence on the Barbie case.

They had succeeded in tracing the witness who had heard, at second hand, Barbie's damning remark about the Jews whose deportations he was supervising: "Deported or shot – there's no difference." If authentic, it clearly indicated that Barbie was aware of the fate of the deportees.

Beate had extracted from the Procurator-General of Munich, Dr Manfred Ludolph, a promise that, if the Klarsfelds could find the direct witness to Barbie's remark, the case would be reopened. Less than two weeks later, her husband Serge had found Raymond Geissman, the former head of UGIF in Lyon.

Geissman was by now living in Paris, a lawyer in the Court of Appeal. Of course he remembered Barbie, he told the Klarsfelds. "I remember seeing Barbie frothing at the mouth when he talked of his hatred of the Jews," he recalled, "and the phrase 'deported or shot, there's no difference' is certainly his. He said it in front of me . . ."

Beate returned to Munich on October 1, and Ludolph, as promised, reopened the case. He also handed her three photographs: two of Barbie taken in 1943, and one of a group of men seated round a table. The third photograph, he explained, had been taken in La Paz in 1968 and was of a man suspected, but not proved, to be Barbie. "You have demonstrated yourself to be effective," said Ludolph, "help me to identify this man."

Towards the end of 1971 Ludolph again contacted Beate, this time to ask her if she was willing to be put in touch with a German called Herbert John, now living in Lima and working for a newspaper belonging to the Peruvian fish-meal magnate Banchero Rossi.

John had survived Schwend and Barbie's attempts to destroy him, but he had never forgotten or forgiven; when his opportunity for revenge came, he seized it. He had long suspected that the man he knew as Klaus Altmann had some sort of Nazi past, and when he saw the 1943 photograph of Barbie in a copy of a German newspaper he notified the Munich prosecutor that he knew him.

On December 28, through a contact in Munich, John sent the Klarsfelds the name Klaus Altmann – and an address care of Schwend in Lima. Thus, by the end of 1971, Beate had not only identified, but located Klaus Barbie.

On New Year's day 1972, however, events in Peru were given an unexpected twist. That day, Luis Banchero Rossi, the Peruvian millionaire and former employer of Herbert John, was murdered in his luxury villa outside Lima. He had arrived there in the company of his beautiful secretary, Eugenia Sessarego, for an amorous visit. The PIP who investigated the case arrested her and a young man called Juan Vilka, the supposedly half-witted son of a neighbour's gardener. Within a few hours Vilka had been charged with the murder.

Almost immediately, however, rumours began to circulate that there was more to the Banchero Rossi murder than met the eye. The thirty-four-year-old probationary judge, Santos Chichizola, was appointed amid a blaze of publicity to investigate the case, and rapidly found himself caught up in a welter of outlandish allegations, among which the names of Klaus Altmann and Friedrich Schwend began to figure insistently.

The allegations stemmed from Herbert John in Lima, who saw the opportunity of putting Friedrich Schwend behind bars by suggesting that Banchero Rossi had been murdered by an international Nazi network which included Schwend and Altmann. "I thought it was a work of fiction myself," confessed Santos. But he began to investigate it nevertheless.

John added to the complexity of the case by producing evidence of Schwend's illicit currency dealings and blackmail, which the judge could use to order a search of Schwend's house. But he warned that it would be no easy matter. The house itself, he said, was guarded by fierce dogs, and in the basement was a gang of savage Croat terrorists, the men who had probably carried out the murder of Banchero Rossi on the instructions of Schwend and Altmann.

As the judge pondered these matters, John produced another witness – Schneider-Merck. "I had got to know Herbert John and had told him what had happened," said Schneider-Merck. "He was very excited by my story and persuaded me to come and talk to the judge. He would give me all the protection I needed."

On April 12 1972 Schneider-Merck testified before the judge on the dealings of Altmann and Schwend: "I gathered together all the documents, gave all the names and told him all about it." His evidence took five hours to get through, but by the end of it, Judge Santos felt he had enough justification to move. He immediately ordered a raid on Schwend's house.

Forcing an entry, the Guardia Civil encountered, not a pack of savage guard dogs, but a single, bemused Dachshund. Through a window they could see Schwend in his pyjamas, hastily burning papers in a ground floor office. "We impounded the documents," said Santos, "some of them slightly charred." A search of the house revealed, under a rug in the kitchen, a trap door to the cellar. "We were looking for that, because Herbert John had told us the Croats lived in the cellar," said Santos, "but we didn't find them. Instead there was a huge collection of files laid out on wooden shelves." These – the Schwend archives – were impounded by the judge. He also arrested the master of the house.

Schneider-Merck saw the scene as he was driving home that night. "I saw the whole place was surrounded by police with guns, and searchlights going. They took Schwend to the HQ of the Guardia Civil which is in the same compound as the PIP."

Four hours later, at 6.30 a.m., Schneider-Merck's house was raided by the PIP, who arrested him, claiming they were doing so on orders from the judge. In the small hours of the following morning, Santos managed to locate him in a secret PIP prison and have him handed over again to Guardia Civil custody. The atmosphere all round was thoroughly tense.

There were several attempts, the judge claims, to have Schwend released.

At one point, the German Ambassador turned up, but I had a copy of the Brown Book of Nazis, and I found his name in it. I asked if he was making his representations in his capacity as ambassador or as a former Nazi. I showed him the book with his name in it. He shook hands very correctly, and left without saying another word. I then prepared myself for the interrogation.

In spite of Schneider-Merck's help and a mass of circumstantial evidence against Schwend and Altmann now in his possession, Santos still felt himself in a delicate position. "There was a writ of habeas corpus served by Schwend's lawyer who was accusing me of arbitrary detention," he recounted, "and I still had no real evidence to link him with the Banchero Rossi case, which was the one I was investigating. I couldn't really hold him for long."

The judge determined to plunge into the world of German Nazism and equip himself to deal with Schwend and his friend Altmann. "I had some help from Jewish friends in Lima," he said, "but I also read a lot. I read everything I could find about the SS, about ODESSA and about the SSS." (The "SSS" was a wild figment of somebody's imagination, but the judge took it quite seriously: it was, he said, the homosexual branch of ODESSA.)

"I also read *Who's Who in the CIA*," continued Santos, "and I became a fan of Frederick Forsyth." He might have been less impressed by his reading had he realised that the author of *Who's Who in the CIA*, a notoriously unreliable work of reference, was the East German Dr Julius Mader, a correspondent of Schwend's, and that Schwend himself had contributed to the Latin American section of the book.

His mind reeling from this crash course in Nazi history and mythology, the judge felt he was ready for his adversary. He told Schwend that there were no formal charges against him, but that he would like to talk to him. Afterwards, he would be free to go. Schwend agreed.

"In general," said Judge Santos, "Schwend had a low opinion of Peruvians, but I think he met his match."

The truth is that Judge Santos emerged from that twenty-three hour interrogation little the wiser on the subject of the murder of Banchero Rossi. But he knew a great deal about Schwend and Altmann's extraordinary financial activities in Peru – especially after the helpful Schneider-Merck, still languishing in a Guardia Civil gaol, had translated all the German documents he had impounded.

The evidence of extortion and blackmail was clear, and the documents revealed other hidden aspects of Schwend's life: his close relationship with the PIP, for instance, as well as his many intelligence connections. The worst thing, the judge found, was that all the time that the Peruvians and the Bolivians were protecting Barbie and Schwend, the two Nazis were busy selling those countries' secrets to whoever was in the market for them. Santos explained:

Altmann would give Schwend Bolivian information, Schwend would investigate exiled Bolivians in Peru for Altmann and give him Peruvian intelligence. Others supplied material from Chile, Argentina and Paraguay. Because of the arms dealing and their connections, they learned a lot about the state of the armed forces everywhere. Schwend used his Nazi friends as agents, throughout the continent. He helped to organise the Peruvian external intelligence service, on the strength of having worked with the Americans, but at the same time he kept up connections with intelligence organisations behind the Iron Curtain.

Evidence that the papers Judge Santos had examined did indeed contain information along these lines was confirmed by the actions of Peruvian army intelligence who impounded large sections of the Schwend archives, and hold them to this day. Reference to it was prohibited at the eventual trial on currency charges of Barbie, Schwend and Schneider-Merck, on the grounds of national security, and the trial judge refused any access to the material.

But now, after examining many of the most revealing papers from the archive, and the testimony and documentation of Johannes Schneider-Merck, it is possible to go a long way towards confirming the findings of Judge Santos.

Staggering as they were, none of these revelations implicated either Barbie or Schwend in the murder of Banchero Rossi. Reluctantly, Santos decided he could hold Schwend no longer. He made a formal accusation against both men for currency speculation and handed over the evidence to another judge for prosecution.

By this time the publicity which had accompanied the Banchero Rossi affair and the efforts in Germany of Beate Klarsfeld, had prompted Klaus Barbie to put himself beyond the reach of Peruvian justice.

One day in late January 1972 a television crew from Peru's Channel 4 was interviewing neighbours of the late Banchero Rossi and asking them what they knew of the murder case, when they came across a courteous old man with a slightly foreign accent who spoke to them cheerfully enough, even if he did not have much to say.

When the interview was broadcast that evening, the face on the television screen matched that of the wanted war criminal, Klaus Barbie. Word was immediately sent back to Paris and a telex was dispatched to Albert Chambon, the French ambassador to Lima, who had been an inmate of Auschwitz and had a keener interest than many other diplomats in the hunt for missing Nazis. Within half an hour of receiving it, Chambon had asked the Peruvian Ministry of the Interior to make a preventive arrest, in anticipation of a French extradition demand. In this, as in other diplomatic initiatives, the Peruvian government was curiously slow to react.

Barbie's first warning of these moves came on the afternoon of January 20, when Albert Brun, the Lima correspondent of Agence France Presse, and his wife and colleague, Nicole Bonnet, acting on a tip from their Paris office, rang the bell of Barbie's luxurious home.

"I said in French that I wanted to speak to Klaus Barbie," said Albert Brun, "and the voice over the intercom replied in Spanish that there was no one of that name there. Altmann said he had just got out of the swimming pool and didn't want to open the door." Brun and Bonnet went to Schwend's neighbouring chicken farm and rang the bell.

I gave my name in French and they let us in almost at once. Perhaps he thought we wanted to buy some eggs. We went straight to the point over a whisky which Don Federico kindly offered us. He said there was no problem in seeing his friend Altmann and invited us to return at six p.m. the following day. I had the impression that Schwend was the boss and if he said Altmann would be there, he would.

The next day the journalists returned and Altmann was indeed waiting for them. The conversation was relaxed and cheerful as the two men explained that it was all a tiresome case of mistaken identity. The following day Altmann again kept an appointment with the two journalists, this time for a photographic session in central Lima. "He was extremely relaxed and cordial," remembered Brun, "and he totally convinced me. I was on his side and thought what a mistake everybody was making."

The Peruvian and French press, however, did not share Brun's certainty.

Suddenly I opened a newspaper [recalled Schneider-Merck], and all over the front page was the headline "War criminal Klaus Barbie in Lima". Wiesenthal had made a statement claiming to have known all about him and giving several aliases that I had supplied him with. They included the name Martin Lauer, which was one they used in the currency dealings.

That night, Schneider-Merck saw Barbie driving home in the car he had sold him. Barbie spotted Schneider-Merck, stopped and got out, furious. "How did they get that name?" he yelled. "Only three people knew that name."

I replied that he himself had told me that the suitcase had been stolen and his post box opened. And anyway, frankly, I didn't give a shit how they got the name. As far as I was concerned, he had betrayed a comrade and in my book you deserve the death penalty for that. That was the last time I saw him.

It was indeed one of the last occasions on which Barbie was to be seen in Peru. By his own account, the publicity resulted in a call to his house, asking him to visit the PIP headquarters. There he was told that the PIP had orders to investigate him. "An Inspector Vargas interrogated me," Barbie recounted later. "I answered all his questions."

But in the small hours of the following morning, to Barbie's indignation, Vargas returned to his house and asked him to accompany him to see General Richter, a minister in the military government. Barbie refused, but the police delegation returned at seven a.m. Then, Barbie claims, he was informed that an attempt on his life was being planned and the authorities deemed it wise that he should leave Peru on the next flight.

"I said I would go, but I would go in my own way," said Barbie. "I wanted to pack and I wanted to drive."

Barbie's own account of sang-froid in the face of danger does not accord with the recollection of others about his rapid exit from Peru. Judge Santos, who says he had been asked by Ambassador Chambon to help detain Barbie, went to his house that evening and found it deserted.

"There was no reply and the neighbours said they had seen Barbie leaving that afternoon with his suitcases, driving off in a Land-Rover," said Santos. "I immediately ordered the Guardia Civil to mobilise, but I suspect my orders were not carried out."

On January 26 Beate Klarsfeld, hurriedly preparing to depart for Peru, heard on the radio that Barbie had already left and was believed to be heading for the Bolivian frontier. She immediately flew to Lima, where, with the help of Herbert John and Albert Brun, she explained her mission to the Peruvian press.

By that time, as a contingent of pressmen staked out the airport, Barbie was well on his way to the border, accompanied by a

Peruvian police escort which handed him over to the care of the Bolivian authorities.

"At the border," Barbie later claimed, "there was a message that the expulsion order had been rescinded and I was free to return to Lima if I chose. But then I heard that the French had demanded my extradition from Peru, so I thought it wiser to continue to La Paz."

The news that Barbie had crossed the border reached the French Embassy just as Beate Klarsfeld was handing over to Ambassador Chambon the file of evidence she had brought with her. Thwarted of her quarry in Peru, she decided to follow him to Bolivia.

Back in La Paz Barbie had immediately been assigned a police guard. "I stayed in a hotel and used a false name for a few days," he said. "The Bolivian authorities explained to me that they appreciated that I was an honourable Bolivian citizen with all the rights that implied. They were afraid of an Eichmann style operation to kidnap me."

In case the bodyguard was not enough, the Bolivians had made it clear that Beate Klarsfeld was less than welcome. After she had spent three days of fruitless lobbying, they threw her out of the country. The reason for her expulsion was "violation of a tourist visa". She returned to France to regroup her forces.

The French government – belatedly, in the Klarsfelds' view – now asked formally for Barbie's extradition from Bolivia. On February 11 President Georges Pompidou wrote a personal letter to President Hugo Banzer in support of the extradition request, a letter which was politely fended off with reassurances of the independence of the Bolivian judiciary. There were several legal objections to the extradition, not the least of which was the absence of firm evidence that Barbie and Altmann were one and the same person.

Three days later, President Banzer received a letter from Lima, Peru. It read:

Esteemed Mr President
Circles pursuing their own interests, evidently for vindictive reasons, have exaggerated the case of Klaus Altmann.

I knew Altmann in the first years of WW II as a German soldier who did his duty and never was involved in guerrilla cases like that of Jean Moulin in France. Bolivia has also suffered from the consequences of the presence of subversive elements, and the French guerrilla Debré, who now is at liberty, not only involved himself in the affairs of a foreign country but is also responsible for the deaths of many Bolivians.

The fact that the French Minister Debré is in charge of the Altmann case is a serious provocation against Bolivia. In the name of all the soldiers who fought, under oath to their fatherland, I beg you respectfully, Mr President, to do justice to the old soldier Klaus Altmann, and give him the protection of Bolivian law.

Yours etc

Federico Schwend

Former Commander of the Special Staff in the General Command of the German Third Armoured Forces.

This moving appeal seems to have struck a more receptive chord in Hugo Banzer than the request of his fellow head of state, Georges Pompidou. He may well have been influenced by Schwend's reference to the French journalist Régis Debray (misspelled in the letter), who, as Banzer well knew, had been captured in Bolivia after lending support to Ché Guevara's guerrilla movement. Schwend appears to have confused him with the French Foreign Minister, Michel Debré.

Meanwhile, as a posse of journalists combed La Paz, Barbie had disappeared from public view. He was, in fact, in prison. By his own account he had been taken in for questioning on February 4, when a Colonel Palma telephoned him and asked him to call at the Ministry of the Interior. On arrival, said Barbie, he noticed that a French television team was installed and a young Bolivian reporter from the evening newspaper *Ultima Hora* asked him if he was prepared to be interviewed. He refused the invitation.

He was then told that he was under arrest for a debt of four thousand dollars to the Bolivian Sugar Corporation. Barbie claimed, improbably enough, that he did not have the wherewithal to pay up, but as he sat in the ministry building, musing on his dilemma, the solution came to him: to grant an interview to the French television reporter and charge him the equivalent of the sum demanded.

Hasty negotiations followed. The reporter finally settled for two thousand dollars and got his interview – which, when broadcast in France, added considerably to the public pressure for Barbie's extradition. Barbie himself, however, remained a prisoner; he was taken to the San Pedro gaol, a huge, fortress-like building in La Paz.

Behind its high walls and impressive gate, the San Pedro gaol can be a comfortable place of refuge. For the privileged, there is always a room with television, and if the prison food is not appealing enough, meals can be sent in from outside. Barbie locked himself in with his own key and remained behind bars until February 12, when he was quietly released.

A week later the indomitable Beate Klarsfeld set off again for La Paz, this time accompanied by a sixty-eight-year-old woman, Itta Halaunbrenner, whose husband had been shot by Barbie in Lyon, whose eldest son had been deported by him to Auschwitz, and whose two younger children had suffered the same fate after Barbie's purge at Izieu. Beate hoped that the effect of Madame Halaunbrenner's story on Bolivian public opinion might still secure Barbie's extradition. In fact, it was a fruitless journey.

After lobbying officials in La Paz and holding a press conference, the two women chained themselves to a bench in the Prado, La Paz's main street, opposite the Transmaritima offices. The gesture produced banner headlines, but under a military dictatorship public opinion counts for little. That evening they abandoned the inhospitable atmosphere of La Paz and left Barbie to the slow and corrupt machinery of Bolivian justice.

He did not seem unduly troubled at the prospect. In May 1972 the French Embassy in La Paz, which had been documenting France's extradition request, handed over lengthy files of evidence on Barbie's identity and crimes to the Supreme Court in the ancient colonial capital, Sucre. Barbie chose that moment to receive a Brazilian journalist, Dantes Ferreira, and give a long series of interviews which were to be published under the headline "Memoirs of Klaus Altmann/Barbie".

The interviews scarcely served as historic truth, but they did reveal the extraordinary confidence which Barbie had in the security of his position. He even told Ferreira that he had dropped the pretence of his identity some time ago and claimed that the Bolivian authorities had long known who he was. Some years earlier, he said, he had received a visit from a government delegation which had included an old friend of his, the Under Secretary of the Interior, a Dr Elio. The delegation had been sent to establish the truth about him.

"Are you Altmann or Barbie?" they had asked. "Were you really head of the Gestapo in Lyon during the war?"

Barbie explained gravely to Ferreira that as soon as the question was put he had realised it was the moment to tell the truth – a decision aided, perhaps, by his confidence in Dr Elio:

It wasn't simply a case of a government representative doing me justice, but also a man for whom I felt great sympathy because of the coincidence of our philosophies. I knew him as a member of the Socialist Falange and for his tenacious anti-Communism. I am an old National Socialist, and I have not changed my views, although my personal battle is over . . .

He had, he implied, conceded the case that Altmann and Barbie were indeed one and the same person, an important admission in view of the French extradition attempt.

The long interview with Ferreira drew parallels between Barbie's "struggles" against French subversion during the war, and the battle which Bolivia had fought against the guerrilla Ché Guevara: "What Bolivia did in 1967 to defend herself against a coup by Ché Guevara was also condemned in many parts of the world as a crime," he said. The current campaign against him, he added, was a well-organised Jewish conspiracy.

It was a conspiracy which Friedrich Schwend in Peru claimed already to have detected. He turned once more to his Baby Hermes typewriter to pass on his findings on the subject:

To the President of the Republic of Bolivia, Colonel Hugo Banzer.
The Sureté agents BRUN and Secretary Nicole BONNET, resident in Lima, acting under the cover of being representatives of the French press, are now in La Paz, together with Herbert John, an agent of a foreign country. They are trying to influence the legal proceedings by subverting important officials. Brun and Bonnet were the organisers of the commando operation which liberated Debray. Brun and Bonnet have considerable sums of money at their disposal.
Respectfully yours
Colonel Schwend

In La Paz, too, Barbie had his defenders. His long-standing lawyer was Constantino Carrion, an elderly, bird-like man, a consti-tutional lawyer who had been temporarily inconvenienced himself by a brief imprisonment on a fraud charge. He was supported by another lawyer who was later to play a prominent and sinister role in Bolivian affairs – Dr Adolfo Ustárez, dapper, fast-talking and supremely self-confident. Finally, as dog's-body, fetching and car-rying papers, travelling frequently to Sucre to attend the court, was the man who would play the role of friend, shadow and bodyguard for the next ten years, Alvaro de Castro.

The judicial process, never exactly a speedy affair in Bolivia, ground on. In September 1972 there was added to the French extradition request, a Peruvian demand that Barbie should return to Lima to face questioning on currency fraud. Neither case seemed to make much progress.

At this point the Klarsfelds decided to mount a daring kidnap, seize Barbie, and bring him back to France to face trial, a plot which did indeed involve the French Marxist journalist, Régis Debray, whom Schwend had so eagerly identified as a security risk in his letter to President Banzer.

In the late summer of 1972 Debray and Serge Klarsfeld, Beate's husband, made contact with Bolivian guerrillas on the Chilean border and concocted a plan which involved grabbing Barbie, drugging him, then shipping him out to France via Chile. The scheme, however, depended on the cooperation of Chile's Marxist president, Salvador Allende. In early 1973 Chile was plunged into the crisis which would end with Allende's death. The kidnap mission was called off.

This was not the only freelance attempt on Barbie in Bolivia. On two occasions, he was confronted face to face by men bent on vengeance. Both times his challengers lost their nerve at the last minute. But the incidents were a forcible reminder of how fragile his position was – despite his own self-confidence.

The first was Barbie's former Resistance prisoner, René Hardy, whom Barbie had accused of betraying Jean Moulin. Hardy had been stung by Barbie's claims, and in July 1972 he had travelled to La Paz with a journalist from the magazine *Paris Match* to confront his accuser.

It was, as it turned out, a somewhat absurd confrontation. The two Frenchmen accosted Barbie in the street, but, Barbie claimed, Hardy failed to identify himself and Barbie did not recognise him. Hardy made an appointment to see him later that day at his office, but when he arrived he was refused admittance by a police guard. Soon afterwards Hardy returned to France.

The second incident occurred much later, in 1975, when a young Jew called Michael Goldberg resolved to assassinate Barbie. Goldberg travelled to Bolivia from France and located him, but after several encounters with Barbie, he finally failed to pull the trigger, reasoning that the brief pain of a fatal bullet was no recompense for the agony Barbie has inflicted on others.

Not all the visitors drawn to Barbie were hostile. One was a Californian woman who turned up in La Paz claiming to have been married to him. "We didn't really know what to do with her, so we all had dinner in the Club La Paz," said Alvaro de Castro. "Klaus had never seen her before in his life. It was all very funny, but most odd."

Nevertheless, Barbie was never again to be seen on the streets of La Paz without a "shadow". Increasingly uneasy about the attention they were attracting, the Barbie family bought an elegant house in Cochabamba, two hundred kilometres from La Paz, where outsiders rarely came.

In March 1973 the Barbie/Altmann case swung into action again. That month, Barbie was summoned for interrogation by the Fiscal (prosecutor) of La Paz, Dr Gaston Ledezma, whose lot it was to establish Barbie's true identity. Despite the bravado he had displayed the previous year, Barbie had clearly decided that the hour of truth was over:

"My name is Klaus Altmann Hansen," he told Ledezma. It was a dismal and uncertain performance. Barbie stopped narrowly short of open contempt of court, but the record of the interrogation shows that he lied steadily and unconvincingly. He claimed to have acted in Lyon under the name Klaus Barbie, a pseudonym which he had taken "under orders from above". He continued to insist, however, that he was not the person of that name wanted by the French and that, in any case, those crimes were not recognised under Bolivian law. His children, he said, were not Ute and Klaus Barbie, born respectively in Trier and Kassel, but Ute and Klaus Altmann, both born in Kassel.

Why, the clearly exasperated Fiscal wanted to know, was there no record of the Altmann marriage, or the births of the Altmann children, while the Barbie family was, by contrast, meticulously documented? "Germany," Barbie explained, "was heavily bombed in the war and millions of documents were lost." It was, he admitted, a bit of a coincidence that *all* the Altmann records had been destroyed, but, as he explained helpfully, "life's like that". He failed, however, to point out that Germany was not noticeably bombed after Klaus junior's birth in 1946.

Barbie's insolence stung Ledezma into pressing him further. Barbie twisted and turned, denying all knowledge of the person sought by the French, then shifting to the familiar, "I was only obeying orders", and finally, "This all happened thirty years ago."

"To sum up," said Ledezma, "you are the same person, Klaus Altmann and Klaus Barbie."

"Yes," Barbie finally replied, "because during the war I was the same person."

It was, unsatisfactory as it may have sounded, a crucial statement, which appeared to remove one major objection to the French extradition request.

Ledezma promptly ordered Barbie's detention, and he returned to the familiar surroundings of San Pedro prison. The Fiscal's report concluded that Altmann was indeed Barbie.

But behind the smokescreen of the legal proceedings the political reality was unchanged: Hugo Banzer was president and Barbie was a friend of Banzer's. The Supreme Court, which was now actively considering both the French extradition case and the attempt by Peru to charge Barbie for currency offences, squirmed under the pressure of conflicting expectations. In April they rejected the Peruvian request on the grounds that, although there was a treaty of extradition between the two countries, there was not enough evidence to consider the case. In July the Supreme Court accepted a habeas corpus demand from Barbie's lawyer, Carrion, and ordered Barbie's release, pending a decision on the French request.

The news was brought from Sucre to La Paz by Barbie's friend de Castro. "I came here with the release order," he said, "and went straight to the prison. Everybody was very happy of course, and the prison governor called Klaus in to congratulate him on his exemplary conduct through those difficult months."

But then came a countermanding order: "He was just collecting his belongings together to go home when a messenger arrived from the High Court ordering his detention again for the Peruvian matter," said de Castro. "It was all a plot against Klaus . . ."

By October the Supreme Court had thought up a new excuse to release him. The Peruvian affair, they said, was not extraditable – this time because the alleged crimes did not constitute an offence in Bolivia. Once again de Castro rushed to the prison with the news. Finally, doubtless after renewed congratulations from the governor, Barbie was released. In December of the following year, under threat of dissolution by Banzer, the Supreme Court rejected the French extradition request on the grounds that there was no extradition treaty.

The decision did not go down well with the French government which immediately cancelled twenty million dollars' worth of industrial credits and a scheme for military aid and scholarships planned for Bolivia. Barbie, as might be expected, saw the matter differently. In a letter published in a Bolivian newspaper he thanked the Supreme Court for its honourable and just decision. He had been, he added, "a German citizen who had only complied with his patriotic duties in wartime like any other citizen".

The Schwend saga has, not surprisingly, an unexpected dénouement. After numerous attempts to fend off Peruvian justice, including the comprehensive slandering of his main accuser, Herbert John ("The son of a German washerwoman . . . Jew . . . failure . . . seller of authentic and false information . . . bounty hunter . . . agent for the Germans, the French and the Israelis . . . 'turned' by the Czechs as a Communist agent", etc, etc), he and Schneider-Merck, with Barbie *in absentia*, were eventually put on trial for currency speculation. All were found guilty, and Schwend and Schneider-Merck were expelled from Peru to return to Germany.

Judge Santos finally completed his investigation of the Banchero Rossi murder and handed in the file. Both the young gardener, Vilka, and Banchero's secretary, who had been arrested with Vilka, were found guilty and sentenced, though later pardoned. Santos was never confirmed in his post as a judge and is today a lawyer in Lima. He still speculates on the possibility that Schwend and Barbie murdered the fish-meal magnate for his missing millions. "I could never prove it, though," he admits sadly.

Back in Germany, Schwend was imprisoned again while the ancient case of the Italian murder was investigated. Typically, he claimed – successfully – both legal aid and social security from the West German government on the grounds of poverty.

The murder charge, however, was not pursued and Schwend returned to Peru in the late 1970s after the expulsion order for both him and Schneider-Merck had been lifted.

In 1980 Schwend died in Lima. "I remember sitting in a hotel in Hong Kong and reading that he was dead," said Schneider-Merck. "I thought, you old bastard – I don't believe it."

CHAPTER THIRTEEN

Fiancés of Death

There is, in the hands of the Ministry of Defence in La Paz, a lengthy internal report, commissioned during the period of democracy ushered in by President Hernan Siles Zuazo in 1982. It is the best and most authoritative evidence available on the work which Klaus Barbie carried out for the Bolivian government during the 1970s.

The details that follow, beginning with Barbie's work for the military dictatorship of General Hugo Banzer, are drawn from that report. But they are supplemented by the first-hand evidence of those who knew Barbie during this period. These include a former senior Interior Ministry aide who witnessed Barbie's steady rise in the hierarchy of power, and then later, following the arrival in Bolivia of the Italian terrorist Stefano delle Chiaie, his participation in the most spectacular of all Bolivia's coups.

From the moment of Banzer's accession to power, Barbie was continuously employed by two organisations: Department 7 of the army in Cochabamba, a department notorious for what were euphemistically known as "psychological operations"; and by the Ministry of the Interior. For the former, according to the Defence Ministry report, Barbie undertook the restructuring of Bolivia's repressive apparatus. That work was vital for a government which had relied increasingly on the use of terror to maintain itself in power.

Barbie's work was recognised and rewarded. He was given the rank of an honorary colonel in the Bolivian army and provided with an army pass which bore his picture showing him in a Bolivian uniform. Barbie was inordinately proud of this and, in later years, would show it off to his friends in La Paz. It was, perhaps, some small compensation for the lowly rank of captain which was all he had managed to achieve in the SS.

The Banzer regime had begun with a measure of civilian support and included, at the beginning, representatives of the right-wing Falange party and the MNR. In 1974, however, they were expelled, and with them went the last important civilian influence. From this

266

point on, it was an undiluted military dictatorship, in which the role of repression increased as consensus diminished. Conditions were ideal for the steady growth of Barbie's influence.

One of the most important aspects of Barbie's work was advising Banzer on how to adapt the army effectively for internal repression rather than external aggression [said the Interior Ministry official]. Many of the features of the army which were later to become standard were first developed by Barbie in the early 1970s. The system of concentration camps, for instance – there had been a few under Paz Estenssoro, but under Banzer they became standard for important military and political prisoners.

The interrogation methods of Bolivian intelligence too were to benefit from Barbie's guiding hand. Having learnt perhaps one lesson from his own handling of Jean Moulin, Barbie – according to the official – brought a subtler touch to the use of torture in Bolivia than had been standard: "The Bolivians used simply to beat people up. Under Barbie, they learned the use of techniques of electricity and the use of medical supervision to keep the suspect alive until they had finished with him. Barbie used to tour the camps, giving lectures."

There is testimony about Barbie at this time from a very different source: one victim from this period, Mirna Murillo, recalls vividly the time Barbie came to deliver a lecture in her prison: "One night, in the prison, most of the guards disappeared. When they came back, they were talking about a lecture they had just been to, given by Mr Altmann. I used to wonder, after they had tortured me, what he had taught them."

Mirna, now an elegant woman in her late thirties, talks calmly of the tortures she endured in the early 1970s. She is one of the few surviving members of the ERN, the National Revolutionary Army, a small and not very accomplished guerrilla movement which began in Bolivia in 1970. She spent two years in prison, under constant torture, but survived to go into exile. None of those arrested with her lived.

Barbie's instruction went beyond the interrogation cell. "In strategic matters, he advised the army on the disposition of forces away from the frontiers and round the major population centres to deal with civil revolt," said the Defence Ministry official. In weapon purchases, too, for the usual commission, Barbie proffered his advice. "They began to buy smaller calibre weapons – bullets which would wound a guerrilla rather than kill, armoured cars which were useful in city streets."

Barbie was well paid for his expertise. According to the Defence Ministry report, his salary never dropped below two thousand dollars a month, in addition, of course, to the commissions he received for his weapon purchases.

For the Ministry of the Interior, Barbie continued his role of informant and internal spy, handing on, among other more significant information, details gleaned from the endless conversations over small cups of black coffee in cafés in La Paz, Cochabamba and Santa Cruz. One regular visitor at the ministry was the wife of a political activist: "He was always around the building," she recalled. "I was there myself a lot because my husband was in prison and I used to see him going into his office on the fourth floor. Barbie behaved as though he owned the place."

It would be wrong, however, to suggest that Barbie was too senior to attend to the more menial responsibilities of the security business. Bolivia is a small country, and not everything can be delegated – in particular the crucial job of controlling who enters and leaves the country.

From 1974 Barbie was seen increasingly in person at the airport, working in a small and dingy office in the immigration service, keeping an eye on suspicious travellers and compromising documents.

It was a problem for us [remembered a Bolivian human rights worker]. We were constantly trying to get evidence of human rights abuse out of the country, but none of us could safely carry such documents. I remember one occasion when we had given papers to a visiting Lutheran minister and warned him not to put them in his luggage. Barbie was at the airport that day and our friend's luggage was picked out and searched. He stopped just short of a personal search of the minister.

There is something both seedy and sinister in this picture of Barbie, a top adviser on security to the Bolivian army, sitting in the customs office at La Paz airport checking immigrants, opening suspicious baggage, inspecting documents, occasionally singling out a suspicious arrival who would then be hustled off for more intensive questioning. But it was almost certainly through his own choice that he did it. Barbie, at heart, was a policeman. It was a business he understood perfectly, and the knowledge he gained at first hand in his little office at the airport undoubtedly stood him in good stead as political opposition to Banzer mounted.

It is clear from other documents, however, that Barbie was playing the security game at several different levels. The old lesson he had learnt from Fritz Schwend was that information equalled profit; you could sell it to make money or as insurance; you could bank it and cash it in later; you could use it against your enemies or your friends; and, given the nature of the commodity, you could invent it.

One of the recipients of Barbie's somewhat dubious currency at this time was the United States which maintained a close relationship with the Banzer regime. General Banzer himself was in the classic mould of pro-United States, anti-Communist dictators whose doctrine of national security was held to justify repressing dissent in the interests of stability throughout Latin America. While Barbie collaborated closely with the Bolivian Ministry of the Interior, the ministry for its part liaised with the CIA.

One Bolivian official, who served under Banzer's government as administrative head of the Ministry of the Interior and was its main contact with the CIA, remembers passing on information which Barbie had supplied specifically for the Americans; and on one occasion, as CIA records show, Barbie offered the agency an extraordinary document which listed the names of every KGB agent operating in the southern cone of South America. Barbie is specifically named as the source. The record reveals that the CIA not only knew the list came from him, but also believed it to be accurate.

Another CIA report at this time records Barbie as housebreaker: in 1976, says the document, Barbie master-minded the burglary of the Peruvian Embassy in La Paz. Acting on behalf of the Banzer government, he photographed the files and handed over his findings to Bolivian officials. Whether the agency itself was allowed to examine the documents is not recorded.

Finally, as if to emphasise the many levels on which Barbie was now operating, a CIA report shows that the agency approved a meeting, organised by Barbie in 1977 in the tropical Yungas region of Bolivia, between representatives of the Chilean and Bolivian intelligence services. Barbie himself attended it.

According to a Bolivian official who was there, the discussion centred around coordination between the two services, and the promotion of Condor, a system of mutual aid between right-wing regimes in Latin America, promoted by the US to unify their anti-subversion activities. Condor is one of those shadowy organisations that are mentioned from time to time in US intelligence reports on South America in the 1970s, but it is never fully documented. It appears to have been used more as a system for exchanging information than undertaking joint activities. It would have suited Barbie's conspiratorial instincts admirably.

There is no record of what came immediately from the meeting. But, as later events in Bolivia were to demonstrate, the intimacy established at meetings such as these between the intelligence services of Chile, Argentina and Bolivia in particular, was to affect directly the internal affairs of many countries in South and Central America – and beyond. Argentina would send agents, trained in its "dirty war", to help mount a military coup in Bolivia; Chile's secret service DINA would train assassins, whose work was then carried out as far afield as the United States or Europe; El Salvador would later recruit the men and the expertise for its death squads among those who had learnt their trade in all three countries – Argentina, Chile and Bolivia.

A senior US intelligence official who specialises in Latin American affairs, has pointed out that the influence of these shadowy groups went far beyond their actual organisation:

> Actually, their organisation never worked that well to begin with. They held a lot of meetings and talked, but it was always very nebulous.
>
> Then, in the mid-1970s, they began the coordination of the military regimes, and these people became very useful. In the dirty war in Argentina, for instance [where thousands of political opponents "disappeared"], they were in the front line.

The problem was that because their organisation was so nebulous no one could be entirely certain who was running whom. "In Argentina they went out of control," said the US official. "They worked across international lines. There was a lack of consensus in Argentine society about what was legitimate in terms of repression, and this meant that some groups just went rogue." And that experience was to be repeated in Bolivia two years later.

By the time Barbie organised the Condor meeting of 1977, the Italian terrorist Stefano delle Chiaie was already an employee of DINA in Chile. He would shortly commit himself full-time to his work in South America, move to Argentina and thence to Bolivia. It was at the executive level of intelligence, where he and Barbie both operated, that their partnership would be established.

If accounts of Condor at this time are vague, the CIA is very specific about another business in which it believed Barbie was involved.

The Bolivian drug industry, with its rich and sinister blend of crime and politics, was to become an important element in Barbie's life. It would boost his standing in Bolivia, sustain his career, and vastly extend the range of his influence. But more important than that, it would be Barbie's reason for recruiting a band of unscrupulous adventurers from Europe – young neo-Fascists and neo-Nazis whose political instincts were as hard-line as his own. And it would be the catalyst for the climax of Barbie's Bolivian career: the military coup of 1980. Here Klaus Barbie and Stefano delle Chiaie would be central participants. They would not, however, have been drawn together in the first place had it not been for the ferocious demands of Bolivia's multi-billion dollar cocaine industry.

Cocaine was not new to Bolivia. The coca leaf had been a vital part of life on the Altiplano for several thousand years. To the Inca it was a ritual drug. For their conquered and enslaved descendants, it became a means of survival: packed into a wad in the corner of the mouth and chewed, the coca leaf enabled the miners and peasants of Bolivia to endure prolonged periods of exhausting physical labour without food and at bitterly low temperatures.

But it was only when cocaine began to be a fashionable drug in the United States and Europe that it became a truly giant business. A kilo of cocaine paste, sold in Bolivia for five thousand dollars, yields a fine white powder which, by 1980, had a street value in the United States of between forty and sixty thousand dollars. The profits, for the cocaine barons who knew how to exploit the business, were enormous.

The capital of Bolivia's drug trade is Santa Cruz de la Sierra, some four hundred miles east of La Paz, once a sleepy frontier town, now a booming industrial centre. From Santa Cruz fortunes have been generated which corrupt all they touch and which were, and are, defended with ruthless violence by Bolivia's newest class, the narco traficantes.

The almost legendary "capo" of the drug barons was Roberto Suarez, sixty years old, silver-haired, with the looks of a genial father-figure. In 1978 Klaus Barbie became security consultant to Suarez, and provided him with a small and vicious private army of desperadoes.

The wealth of Roberto Suarez is legendary. By the mid-1970s it was estimated at three hundred million dollars. Suarez himself has boasted that he was able to equip his army with modern sub-machine guns and vertical take-off aircraft.

In the still primitive Beni region, Don Roberto distributes the sizable crumbs of his wealth by building clinics, roads and schools, luxuries which no government has ever provided. In return, he is regarded with the respect due a feudal lord, a man who has counted among his friends such figures as the former president of the republic, Hugo Banzer.

It was through the tight German circle in Bolivia, to which both Banzer and Barbie belonged, that Suarez first came into contact with Barbie, a man, he quickly discovered, who was excellently placed to advise him on the delicate matter of protecting his drug-runners from the Colombian dealers who were a constant threat to the traffic. Barbie's contacts in the underworld of crime, as well as his intimate knowledge of Bolivia's security apparatus, were by now formidable. After some discreet enquiries, he produced for Suarez a twenty-eight-year-old "minder" called Joachim Fiebelkorn.

Fiebelkorn has been variously described as pimp, strong-arm man, murderer, drugs dealer and neo-Fascist thug. A native of Frankfurt, he had deserted from the West German army and then, by his own account, served in the Spanish Foreign Legion. In the mid-1970s he went to Paraguay, where his frequently drunken style got him into more and more trouble.

The climax, according to Fiebelkorn himself, came in 1978, when he challenged an old SS officer, Adolf Meinike to a game of Russian roulette after a drinking bout. Meinike lost, and Fiebelkorn deemed it advisable to leave Paraguay in a hurry.

An opportunity for work opened in Bolivia where, Fiebelkorn himself claims, his first job was with military intelligence, in Santa Cruz. "My cover name was Pedro," he explained several years later, when his past had caught up with him and he found himself on trial in Frankfurt for assault. "My number was P0147."

But according to the evidence of a colleague of his in Bolivia – a young and distinctly nervous drug-racketeer who asked to be known simply as "José" – Barbie had spotted Fiebelkorn's potential earlier than this:

Roberto Suarez was expanding his business and was having trouble with the Colombian dealers [said José]. He had plenty of men, but he needed someone he could trust to organise and train them and to help him fight the Colombians. Klaus Altmann brought Joachim over from Paraguay to work for Suarez, and I became his right-hand man. I never left his side while he was in Bolivia. Joachim worshipped Hitler and I worshipped Joachim.

Fiebelkorn was certainly obsessed by the Nazis. His house in Santa Cruz was bedecked with Nazi posters and swastikas, and he owned an SS uniform in which he would swagger about, singing Nazi songs. To serve under Klaus Barbie, a man who was the genuine article, marked the summit of his ambitions.

Roberto Suarez, while professing distaste for Fiebelkorn's extravagances, recognised his value. After lengthy discussions, in late 1978 he commissioned Barbie and Fiebelkorn to assemble a group of men who, for a substantial payment, would give him absolute loyalty.

The squad recruited by the two Germans – the elderly battle-hardened Barbie, and the dedicated young neo-Nazi Fiebelkorn – was as unpleasant a group of para-military thugs as has ever been put together. They were christened by Fiebelkorn, who had an instinct for the melodramatic, the Fiancés of Death. Jose recalled some of the members:

There was Manfred Kuhlmann, a Rhodesian mercenary, who came in from Paraguay with Fiebelkorn and Fiebelkorn's wife, Linda. He was Fiebelkorn's favourite. Hans Stellfeld, a former SS man and old friend of Klaus Barbie. Then there was Ike Kopplin, an old Nazi and a sadist who enjoyed beating prisoners with the butt of his revolver. Ike liked living in the wilds. He was a tactical genius in open country. He was a Nazi too.

And then there was Napo – Jean "Napoleon" Le Clerc – who used to think everybody was a Communist and would talk about killing all the time.

Le Clerc, a fugitive from French justice, later detained by the Bolivian authorities, claimed, in the course of a long interview in a La Paz prison where he faced charges of murder and drug-dealing, that he did not come to Bolivia specifically to join the Fiancés of Death. He had left France in a hurry, he said, after a "misunderstanding" ended his brief career as a security guard. He fled to South America and arrived in Bolivia where he was spotted and recruited by Fiebelkorn. His job, as Le Clerc described it, was essentially riding "shotgun" for the cocaine traffic – guarding Suarez's fleet of light aircraft which flew from any one of the more than six hundred clandestine airstrips in the department of Santa

273

Cruz; and making sure the Colombian dealers, to whom the cocaine paste was supplied, paid up.

"During our time with Suarez," said Fiebelkorn, "there was always trouble with the Colombians." At one point, according to a former member of the group, they placed bazookas along one airstrip and fired at the Colombian dealers waiting to take delivery of the drug. "We didn't have much trouble after that," he recalled.

Another duty was to provide a bodyguard for Suarez himself. "He always had a guard of ten or fifteen people equipped with machine pistols," said Fiebelkorn. "Wherever he landed, there was an enormous reception, as if the president of Bolivia was arriving. I tramped along, immediately behind him, with my machine pistol."

Barbie himself was rarely seen in the company of drug dealers. But his advice was crucial to their organisation, and Fiebelkorn consulted him regularly. "Fiebelkorn looked up to Barbie," recalled José. "He always said that he wished he had had the chance to do what Barbie did. He would telephone Barbie or Barbie telephoned him almost every day. Fiebelkorn always took his advice."

In June 1980 Fiebelkorn was prosperous enough to buy a corner bar in the centre of Santa Cruz. Renamed the Bavaria, it became the social centre for the neo-Nazis who gathered there to give Fascist salutes and sing Nazi songs. "It never made a profit," said José, "because nobody paid. But that didn't matter." Money was no object. "Fiebelkorn," according to Napo Le Clerc, "would spend up to a thousand dollars a night in the Santa Cruz nightclubs."

The Fiancés of Death were greatly in demand, not only by Roberto Suarez, but also by the "drug suppression" authorities in Santa Cruz who were always looking for freelance strongmen to seize supplies. There was a certain ambiguity in their attitude to drug dealing: in 1979 Le Clerc was caught at Santa Cruz airport with a bag containing seven kilos of cocaine. He was taken into custody, but instead of being put on trial for drug smuggling, he was invited to take on assignments for the narcotics police.

The Fiancés of Death might have been nothing more than a group of petty criminals with neo-Nazi fantasies, had not the fortunes to be made from drugs attracted the attention of a group of senior military officers.

Official involvement in the cocaine business was nothing new – even some members of General Banzer's own family were commonly supposed to have been part of the smuggling network. But with the arrival on the scene of Colonel Luis Arce Gómez, a cousin of Roberto Suarez, and his close friend General Luis García

Meza, soon to become commander of the armed forces, the matter took on a completely new dimension. Both these men, unscrupulous and ambitious, used the money and power which the drugs trade afforded to usher in a military dictatorship universally regarded as one of the most vicious and squalid that even Bolivia had ever seen. And at the right hand of Colonel Arce Gómez in his moment of triumph would be Klaus Barbie.

Arce Gómez was a pot-bellied thug who affected the traditional dark glasses of the stage dictator, and combined characteristics that were both sinister and absurd. He also had an over-weening sense of his own importance: on a visit to Washington once, he demanded, as a member of the Bolivian army, to be allowed to place a wreath on the tomb of the unknown soldier; when this was refused, he jumped over the fence one day and hastily deposited his wreath anyway, to the consternation of the tomb's guard of honour.

Arce Gómez combined a military career with a highly profitable sideline in drugs. In 1975 he set up an air taxi business transporting cocaine – a business so profitable that within five years he was operating eight aircraft.

Then in 1979 he became head of Department 2 of the army – the section which was in overall charge of intelligence – a position from which he quickly moved to take control of Bolivia's entire internal security machine. He did so in fairly brusque style by raiding the offices of the only rival intelligence organisation in Bolivia, that of the secret police. Holding up the Minister of the Interior at machine-gun point, Arce carried off the secret police records to Department 2.

Among the documents he removed were the narcotics files. The combination of these, and the skilled intelligence operators he brought over at gun point from the Ministry of the Interior, gave him a virtual monopoly of power within Bolivia's security apparatus. To complete his team, he invited Klaus Barbie to join him.

Arce Gómez later denied that his relationship with Barbie was a close one. "He was an old man," he insisted to a Uruguayan journalist who interviewed him later. "He was out of date." That was not, however, his story at the time. Introducing Barbie to another journalist in 1980, Arce Gómez said: "This man is my teacher."

For Arce Gómez, Barbie provided two things that he needed badly to maintain his position. One was Barbie's expertise in counter-intelligence, the other was the information he supplied on the drug trade. Henceforth, Barbie would concentrate on work for Arce Gómez's Department 2. "Presidents come and go," remarked an Interior Ministry official. "Only the security apparatus never changes."

Some changes, however, did now begin to take place under Barbie's patient instruction. In 1979, in the course of a meeting in Santa Cruz, attended by both Arce Gómez and his friend General García Meza, Barbie pointed out the potential of the Fiancés of Death.

"García Meza and Arce Gómez were in the drug trade up to their necks," said José, who was also at the meeting. "García Meza saw the troops that Joachim was training for Roberto Suarez and he was impressed. He asked Suarez if he could borrow some men. He borrowed about forty, but he only kept the German group."

This power base in Santa Cruz was being constructed with a clear goal in view: García Meza and Arce Gómez, with a weather eye on the political state of the country, were preparing their own bid for power.

The eight-year regime of General Banzer had seen a steady deterioration in Bolivia's economy under an increasingly corrupt regime. By 1978 there was widespread unrest, with demonstrations and hunger strikes held in protest against his all-military government.

Banzer attempted to defuse the opposition by calling elections, and though he himself did not run he endorsed a favourite son, General Pereda. When, in spite of Banzer's backing, Pereda looked like losing, the elections were simply rigged.

The public protest was immediate and widespread, so much so that the rigged results were annulled. In response, Pereda fell back on the more traditional route to power and staged a coup, but by summer 1979 new elections had been called, and in spite of attempts to prevent the return of opposition candidates to the country by stationing para-military groups at Santa Cruz airport, the right-wing lost ground heavily. Hernan Siles Zuazo, the man who had once endorsed Barbie's application for Bolivian citizenship but was now on the left of the political spectrum, secured the presidency by a narrow margin. It was not, however, quite enough. In the Congress there was still a right-wing majority. The resulting stalemate could only be resolved by handing over the interim presidency to the leader of the Senate.

Fresh elections were planned for July 1980. It was obvious, however, that the votes of the people held no promise of support for the right-wing, and in the absence of any better idea, in November 1979 the army launched yet another coup. Brutal in its first impact, it aroused such massive popular resistance that it failed after just fifteen days.

Watching what happened, Arce Gómez and García Meza learnt a vital lesson. If the next coup was to succeed it would have to be better planned. A great deal of advance intelligence work, and some ruthless pre-emptive strikes would be necessary if another fiasco was to be avoided.

Klaus Barbie echoed that view – though for different reasons. The French extradition request was dormant for the moment, but the French ambassador was renewing his plea for support with each new head of state, and one day, one of them might agree.

Dividing his time between Santa Cruz, his elegant house in Cochabamba and his apartment in the Edificio Jazmin on Calle 20 Octubre in La Paz, Barbie shared his views about the coup with a small group of neo-Fascists whom he met regularly. To them he would explain that their plans should be seen in a far broader context than just Bolivia. It was, after all, part of the battle against Communism, he said, a battle which should have been fought forty years earlier in Europe, but was now more important than ever.

For the Fiancés of Death in Santa Cruz the preparations for the coup, according to a former member of the gang, came with a visit from Barbie:

> One day, Klaus Altmann came to see us. "The moment has come," he said. "We have to overthrow this government before Bolivia becomes another Cuba. With the other foreign comrades, we are getting together a security service. You have to cooperate, but first you must be tested."
>
> We began to follow the union demonstrations, to keep files on the opposition, to threaten and punish subversives. We worked well. We even had a private prison for the torture, which we left, however, to the Bolivians.

Their political adviser was Barbie's lawyer, Adolfo Ustárez, who used to address the gang with the words, "We must kill all the Communists." To which the group's commander would reply, "Count on us. We are ready for everything."

In La Paz Barbie kept in touch with developments through a new friend, Emilio Carbone, an Italian neo-Fascist in his thirties, who had left Italy rather suddenly in 1970. After a period in Spain, Carbone had arrived in Bolivia where he started publication of a Fascist magazine which he also sent back to his old contacts in

Europe. His connections with senior military officers in Bolivia were impressively close.

Through the young Italian, Barbie began to learn more about the neo-Fascist groups in Europe, their links with South America, and their somewhat tortuous ideology. The two would meet regularly in the Café la Paz, together with other contacts. Both men had realised that if the planned coup was to succeed, they would need expert help. Arce Gómez had expressed the view that they needed someone ruthless: "Bolivians are not hard enough," he said.

In late November 1979 Carbone was able to announce that help was on its way. "Two Italian friends," he said, "are in Central America. They will be here in a few days." Within a week they had both arrived in La Paz – a young man calling himself "Mario Bonone" and a somewhat older man, very small in stature, with a pointed goatee beard, who said he was "Alfredo Modugno".

Bonone it emerged, was a twenty-five-year-old neo-Fascist whose real name was Pierluigi Pagliai. And Modugno was Stefano delle Chiaie.

There was little doubt that the two Italians were a valuable addition to the team. Both knew Latin America well – and they knew the right people. Delle Chiaie's contacts dated back to Spain and his work with Lopez Rega of Argentina's AAA death squads. From 1976 he had helped DINA, the Chilean secret police, to locate and "neutralise" Chilean exiles; and here too had gone into the "news agency" business with a DINA-financed outfit called AIP, along similar lines to Guérin-Serac's Aginterpress. By mid-1977 he was so well established inside the Chilean security apparatus that he claims to have persuaded many DINA officers to wear the Ordine Nuovo insignia – the double-headed axe and its SS-inspired motto: "Our Honour is our Loyalty".

In 1978, however, delle Chiaie had to move somewhat rapidly to Argentina. A scandal had broken in Chile following the murder in Washington of Orlando Letelier, former ambassador of President Allende of Chile. It emerged that the murder was the work of the American-born DINA agent Michael Townley, a close friend of delle Chiaie, carried out on the orders of Manuel Contreras, head of DINA and delle Chiaie's protector. As Contreras' position weakened, delle Chiaie slipped quietly out of the country.

He took with him the twenty-five-year-old Italian neo-Fascist Pierluigi Pagliai who, like him, had fled from Italy after a right-wing terrorist attack. Argentina was a natural choice as their next base. The military dictatorship which had seized power in 1976 offered delle Chiaie in particular similar opportunities to those he had enjoyed in Chile, and he already had friends in Buenos Aires. But even so, it was not easy to gain a foothold.

"When they first arrived in February 1978," said one right-wing activist from that time, "they didn't know many people. They asked me to help them make contacts in military intelligence." A few introductions followed, but progress was slow.

This was frustrating, for delle Chiaie had ambitious plans. He dreamed of making Buenos Aires a neo-Fascist centre, with its military regime a model to be applied throughout Latin America. At the beginning of 1979 he began to travel, visiting other right-wing regimes on a journey which took him first to Paraguay, then to the troubled region of Central America, already a potential gold mine for those offering "security services".

It is here that the threads of delle Chiaie's past begin to be drawn together with those of the violent present. For there is strong evidence that the lessons he had learnt in Spain and Italy, and which had been reinforced in Chile, were to be applied practically in Central America; the next step would be Bolivia.

In El Salvador the aspiring nationalist politician, Major Roberto D'Aubuisson, listened enthusiastically to delle Chiaie's account of the men and the expertise he could provide. He invited him to contribute his views on how the Salvadorean army should cope with guerrillas and subversives, and delle Chiaie responded with a paper written in his inimitable leaden style. The document, signed with delle Chiaie's code name "Alfa", was included in a June 1980 analysis of the Salvadorean military from the private files of a group working closely with D'Aubuisson. It is clear, on reading it, that delle Chiaie's views had not changed. The battle should still, he argued, be fought outside the normal conventions:

> The military operations of the armed forces now are more effective and they are attacking the neurological points of the enemy, destroying important sections of their organisational structure. Finally, the Salvadorean army is making battle outside the framework of conventional war . . .

Delle Chiaie returned, full of enthusiasm, from El Salvador to Buenos Aires, where he gradually convinced the Argentine military that he really did have something to offer. His most obvious asset was his ability, through his European network, to monitor the activities of exiled opponents of the Argentine regime in Spain, France and Italy.

He and Pagliai began travelling to Europe in pursuit of their duties. They held Argentine passports and were paid by the Argentine military in dollars. Soon they were performing a similar service in Nicaragua and El Salvador, transmitting information back to Buenos Aires on left-wing exiles and passing on arms, equipment, and finally men for the Salvadorean death squads. Delle Chiaie was an efficient recruiter of European labour. He telephoned his unemployed friends in France, Germany, Italy and Spain and negotiated trial contracts which rarely paid less than $1,500 a month.

Towards the end of 1979 Argentina's military leaders began to look anxiously at the deteriorating political situation across their northern border, in Bolivia. Argentina was just emerging from its devastating internal "dirty war", in which up to thirty thousand people had "disappeared", and the military leadership was deeply concerned about Bolivia's trend to the left – a trend which could easily cross the border and refuel resistance to the military in Argentina.

An Argentine intelligence officer, Major Hugo Raul Miori Pereira, whom delle Chiaie had got to know well during his time in Central America, was appointed by the military high command in Buenos Aires to maintain close liaison with right-wing Bolivian officers. It was in Miori's fashionable apartment on the Avenue Libertador in Buenos Aires that delle Chiaie first came into contact with a series of prominent Bolivians – including General Hugo Banzer.

As a result of those meetings in late 1979, delle Chiaie and Pagliai, travelling in the guise of the Argentine officers, Modugno and Bonone, moved discreetly to Bolivia via Central America. They had come to offer their support in mounting the military coup which Klaus Barbie and his friends were by now actively preparing.

The arrival of delle Chiaie in Bolivia marked the beginning of a new and ruthless phase in the run-up to the coup.

Delle Chiaie was now forty-four, his enthusiasm for the cause undimmed by his many setbacks. He saw the Bolivian crisis as an essential part of a right-wing movement which he hoped would roll back Communism and left-wing governments everywhere in South America.

I decided that I had to contribute to the creation of an international revolutionary movement [he told a Spanish magazine interviewer in early 1983]. I was thinking then, as I think now, that it is not possible to carry forward revolutionary action in one country without a global vision of political events and a common strategy . . . So when the proposal of a national revolution presented itself in Bolivia, we were there, collaborating with our Bolivian comrades. We were neither torturers nor drugs terrorists, but political militants.

Despite this high-sounding language, delle Chiaie was there to do an essentially practical job. Arce Gómez placed him in Department 2 to work alongside Klaus Barbie.

Barbie was sixty-seven, hardened and cynical. For him the coup would be primarily an act of self-preservation, though he could argue the case against Communism with the best of them. But he admired delle Chiaie's inflexible approach – it struck a deep chord in his old SS heart.

It was not the first time the two men had met. Alvaro de Castro, Barbie's shadow and bodyguard, recalled a trip delle Chiaie made to Bolivia in 1978: "He came to Bolivia from Argentina with Pagliai," he said. "I met them, with some others, to discuss the possibility of publishing a magazine in La Paz." The two Italians held long discussions with Barbie and de Castro. The bond then struck between them was to last. "They were good people," said de Castro disingenuously. "We liked them."

What Barbie was able to offer delle Chiaie when he arrived in November 1979 was unrivalled local knowledge. He could explain the intricacies of Bolivian politics, the strengths and weaknesses of the security apparatus, and the importance of the drug mafia. Delle Chiaie was impressed to find that the kind of para-military squad he had always used himself was already in existence, organised by Barbie. He set about organising his own to supplement it.

The hit-squad assembled by delle Chiaie in Bolivia, like the Fiancés of Death, was an unsavoury collection of neo-Fascist mercenaries. In delle Chiaie's case, however, they were mostly Argentines and Italians. He called them, with a characteristic touch of melodrama, the "Phoenix Commando".

The reality scarcely matched the hyperbole. Among the civilians, Mario Mingola was a fairly standard case. An Argentine who had tried, at one time or another, every religion, from training for the Catholic priesthood to joining the South Korean-based cult of the Moonies, interspersed with clandestine operations in Central America, Mingola had finally opted for neo-Fascism in Bolivia.

"We identified sixteen international terrorists in Bolivia at this time," said a US intelligence official. "Most of them had been brought in via Argentina."

The presence of these bizarre foreigners did not go entirely unnoticed in La Paz. José Fajardo, an eccentric Uruguayan bookseller living in the Bolivian capital, was sufficiently alarmed to attempt to infiltrate the group around Klaus Barbie in order to find out more about them. He then made strenuous efforts to warn both the Bolivian press and trade unions about them.

"But they thought it was all too fantastic," he said, "and they never listened. I tried to get messages to Europe through visiting tourists, but it was like putting messages in a bottle."

Fajardo described the relationship between the very different members of the group:

> Barbie was the moral authority, a sort of oracle and ideological director. He gave them advice and contacts, and he helped them organise their false documents. He was always careful not to be in the forefront of the action. Carbone was important for the international connections . . . He was a coward, though. They once gave him a rifle to hold and he could hardly stop trembling. Delle Chiaie was the other ideological guide and a great organiser. He was a poor physical specimen, but very brave. His lieutenant, Pagliai, was a real man of action.

Bolivia, according to Fajardo, was attractive to the group for several reasons:

> They had a tremendous contempt for the Bolivians themselves for racial reasons – they regarded them as something akin to the missing link, and they certainly didn't think they could build a race of supermen here. But it gave them a refuge when they were on the run. They could count on the corruption of the military officers. It was easy to get papers and easy to influence the Fascists in the military.

In a bizarre echo of Ché Guevara's analysis, they also saw Bolivia as a strategic location – if they did not stop Communism there, they argued, it would spread throughout the continent.

The Argentine military dictatorship provided essential back-up, supplementing the Bolivian credentials supplied by Barbie with Argentine army papers. They also increased their military mission in La Paz to seventy, including in their number several notorious veterans of Argentina's dirty war.

As Bolivia limped from crisis to crisis in the early months of 1980, delle Chiaie and Barbie worked intensively together. Over the next few months the two men, holding regular discussions with García Meza, Arce Gómez and their military cronies, put together the essential ingredients for a military coup that would serve their common purpose: the restoration of a dictatorship in the Fascist mould.

A new element of terror was proposed by delle Chiaie as part of the build-up. It was one he had learnt in Argentina: key opposition figures must be picked off early; they should either be murdered or kidnapped, always using unmarked vehicles. To avoid the hostility against a new regime that actions like this might attract, the work should be done, not by uniformed soldiers, but by "unofficial" elements – hooded para-military gangs. The Bolivians were not entirely convinced about this:

> There were diverging views about the form and degree of repression, both before and after the coup [said a former associate of delle Chiaie]. Delle Chiaie argued that the enemy had to be completely beheaded – which meant the elimination of Hernan Siles Zuazo, Juan Lechin the trade union leader, and the rest of the leaders of the political opposition. The Bolivians, on the whole, hoped for a less drastic solution.

Delle Chiaie seems to have won at least some of the arguments: in February 1980 the office of the left-wing newspaper *Aqui*, a persistent critic of the involvement of prominent Bolivians in the cocaine trade, was destroyed by a bomb; in March its editor Luis Espinal, a Jesuit priest, was kidnapped and tortured to death by a para-military squad, acting, it emerged later, under orders from Department 2.

As rumours of coup preparations circulated, there were conciliatory gestures from the commander in chief of the armed forces, General Reyes, towards the powerful trade union organisation COB; they signed a pact to "respect each other" and to back the elections, planned for June.

But by May there were ominous signs of dissent: García Meza, who had been promoted head of the army, described the "pact" with COB as no more than a "dialogue". By June the atmosphere was electric. On June 2, Siles Zuazo's vice-presidential candidate narrowly escaped death when the aircraft on which he was travelling was sabotaged. Four leaders of the coalition group he represented died in the crash. The plane, it transpired, had been hired from a company owned by Arce Gómez.

The world outside began to take a close interest. The United States put out a statement in defence of the electoral process and was swiftly denounced by the military high command; the US ambassador to Bolivia, Marvin Weissman, was declared *persona non grata*.

On June 29, however, the general election went ahead. The result, as expected, was a victory for Siles Zuazo's coalition. There was no doubt about the outcome: on August 6 Bolivia would have a new constitutional government in which, among other groups, the Communist party would participate.

It was a signal for the plotters to move.

CHAPTER FOURTEEN

Coup d'État

They moved on July 17 1980. At dawn that day, Bolivians woke to the announcement of a military rising in Trinidad, the capital of the Beni, where mutinying soldiers were calling for Colonel Luis Arce Gómez to "lead a national revolution". The one hundred and eighty-ninth coup in Bolivia's history had begun.

As the news came through, an emergency meeting was called in La Paz at the headquarters of the trade union organisation, COB. Key members of the Committee for the Defence of Democracy assembled, along with trade union and human rights leaders, among them Marcelo Quiroga Santa Cruz, a primary target for the coup leaders.

What happened next was a grim demonstration of delle Chiaie's strategy; he was later to boast that the bloody events at the COB headquarters that day were not only supervised by him, but that he took part himself in the killing. According to Ministry of the Interior sources, the plans for the raid and the attacks on radio stations that day had been devised by a small group consisting of Barbie, delle Chiaie and Pagliai, with a Bolivian officer, Guido Benavidez acting as liaison. Those plans had been directed from Department 2 of the army. But delle Chiaie was later to boast that he took a personal hand in the COB raid.

At 10.30 a.m., news reached the COB meeting that the main square in Santa Cruz had been taken by the rebels and that military units in Cochabamba had joined the coup. Quiroga quickly proposed a general strike, a proposition unanimously accepted. As the strike call was being drafted for immediate release to the radio stations, the sound of automatic fire outside interrupted the debate.

Inside the COB building it was at first assumed that the firing was meant simply to intimidate. But this coup was different. As the windows began to shatter, the members realised they were under attack. Noel Vasquez, an official of COB, remembers what happened then.

We all hit the floor . . . Moments later they burst in – hooded civilians with automatic weapons . . . they were very ferocious.

They ordered us outside. They took the leaders out first. And as we were going downstairs one of them ordered Marcelo [Quiroga] to stay behind. He refused, but they pushed the others on in front and fired a burst of automatic fire at him. They killed another comrade, too. I saw his body in the angle of the stairs, with Marcelo lying on top of him. I lifted Marcelo's head and he was still alive, but bleeding heavily. Later we heard he was dead.

What happened next bears all the characteristics of the brutal tactics delle Chiaie had been proposing to his Bolivian hosts. The survivors of the COB raid were taken to the headquarters of the joint chiefs of staff, where they were beaten and tortured. The women among them were repeatedly raped. From army head-quarters the group was taken to the offices of the secret police, and a week of torture and beating followed. "We spent days in a cement cell, without food, living in our own excrement," said Vasquez. "We were tortured by hooded para-militaries with Italian or Argentine accents."

As the COB leadership was led captive away, steps were taken to crush the strike. An armed para-military squad launched a heavy attack on a Catholic radio station, Radio Fides, and silenced it. Over the next twenty-four hours, about twenty trade union leaders were to die, while the leader of the peasants' union, Simon Reyes, was so brutally tortured that he never walked again. The strike call was effective only in the mines, where some miners held out for two weeks. But with its leaders rounded up or killed, resistance crumbled.

In Santa Cruz, things went equally smoothly. Barbie's lawyer Ustárez organised Fiebelkorn's gang, now impressively renamed the Special Commando Group, to which he had recently presented an armoured car. "The day of the coup was not very laborious," said a former member of the group. "Our job was supposed to be to take the revolutionaries' positions with the assault car. We were destined for important positions, not very bloody ones and we didn't have to use the assault car."

Ustárez's armoured car did, however, feature that day. The group took a commemorative photograph in front of it, dressed in battle fatigues and holding automatic weapons. Strung across the car was a banner reading, "Long live Free Bolivia", and prominent in the back row, dressed in battle fatigues, an ammunition belt strapped round his waist and sub-machine gun in his hand, was Ustárez himself.

July 17 had gone well for the ring-leaders of the coup. By the end of the day in La Paz, the Presidential Palace and the university were under military control and every radio station but that of the army was silenced. Outside the capital, the miners' radios continued for a few days until they too were attacked. On July 22 the union leader Juan Lechin, captured in the first assault on COB, went on television to call off further resistance as useless.

García Meza, who had supervised the initial rebellion in Trinidad, returned to La Paz for the swearing in of the junta on July 18. Sporadic resistance continued, in spite of more than five hundred detentions in the first twenty-four hours, but over the next few days massive arrests mopped up those who had not managed to reach the security of a foreign embassy or go underground. In operations reminiscent of the Chilean coup of 1973, detainees were herded into sports stadia, from where selected groups were taken out and shot. By July 18, with the borders closed and the country declared a military zone, the coup had, in the short term at least, been a success.

For the citizens, things looked less encouraging. "It became clear who was helping very quickly," recalled one Bolivian. "I was watching television and suddenly found myself watching a string of Argentine soap operas. The shooting was still going on in the streets." One diplomat said: "Overnight it became the weirdest place imaginable, with creeps with carbines running around and everybody normal off the streets. It was as though the Mafia had taken over in downtown Washington." The famous Argentine technique of making people disappear into innocent looking vehicles was much in evidence. "For a while," said a young Bolivian student, "every time you saw an ambulance, you ran like hell." The exact number who disappeared is unknown, but one estimate put the dead, by mid-August, at five hundred and the wounded at two thousand.

With García Meza installed as president, Arce Gómez became Minister of the Interior and ran the country's security machine. A law of National Security was introduced giving him swingeing powers, and he set an unmistakable stamp on the new regime when he announced: "All those who violate the law will have to walk around with their last will and testament under their arm."

Meanwhile the coup had left the little team in Department 2 in privileged positions. Barbie and the Italians were given command functions in state security under the new Minister of the Interior.

Barbie himself, with the rank of honorary colonel in the Bolivian army, continued to supervise internal intelligence. Alvaro de Castro was suddenly to be seen at the airport, monitoring the arrival and departure of interesting foreigners. Mario Mingola became an adviser to Department 2 in psychological operations. From his room in the Sheraton Hotel, he would indulge his taste for disguise, his mission being to infiltrate potential resistance and report on dissent. Pagliai worked directly under Barbie, specialising in disinformation.

One of delle Chiaie's roles was to be in international propaganda. Argentina and South Africa had quickly recognised the new government, but others were less enthusiastic. The Organisation of American States roundly condemned the coup, and the United States, with whom relations were already strained, began a campaign against the new regime which was never to let up and which accounted, in large part, for its eventual downfall. The ambassador, whose residence had also come under attack, was withdrawn, as was all military and economic aid. Delle Chiaie was assigned the task of winning back some international support.

He was quick to show off his new credentials. On September 2, he travelled to Buenos Aires for the opening of the Fourth Congress of the Latin American anti-Communist League, accompanied by García Meza's personal delegate. There he arranged several meetings in the Hotel Plaza between Major D'Aubuisson of El Salvador and senior Bolivians, at which D'Aubuisson sought and obtained their help in sending weapons and money to his "anti guerrilla" forces.

D'Aubuisson was impressed by the advice he received from delle Chiaie and his comrades. "They are professionals," said one Salvadorean who went to Buenos Aires with him. "They can teach the Guardia Nacional how to do things."

In October, delle Chiaie was given an advance of fifty thousand dollars with which he travelled to Lausanne in Switzerland to set up the Europe-Bolivia Association, followed later by branches in Paris, Rome and Madrid.

Back in Bolivia the death squads were in operation, and there was a more or less permanent curfew in La Paz. Barbie, delle Chiaie, Pagliai, de Castro and the rest of their associates carried special credentials from the Ministry of the Interior which permitted them to operate after the curfew hours. If an over-zealous Bolivian patrol made a mistake, they quickly paid for it.

José Fajardo remembered one such incident, when Pagliai's brother-in-law was arrested by a Bolivian patrol after curfew hours. He instructed the patrol to drive to the house of the Argentine military attaché where Pagliai himself came out with a pistol in both hands and an Argentine behind him with a sub-machine gun. "Stinking Indians, Bolivian scum!" he screamed at them in the authentic tones of the Fascist. "How dare you arrest my brother-in-law?" The Bolivians melted away.

But there was more than just privileges to enjoy – there was big money. As the internal repression continued, the conspirators moved swiftly to profit from their victory and to bleed the drug business.

"For the first time in history," one US official remarked, "the cocaine trade had bought itself a government."

The principle under which García Meza intended to operate was laid down at a meeting in the Ministry of the Interior towards the end of 1980. Klaus Barbie summoned Fiebelkorn and two of the Fiancés, Kuhlmann and Kopplin to attend; the minister, he told them, had something important to discuss. Arce Gómez handed Fiebelkorn a list of 140 of the smaller Santa Cruz dealers who were to be "suppressed". None of the big five drug barons, including Roberto Suarez, was on the list.

"The generals were no longer satisfied with a percentage of the trade," said one of the Fiancés later. "They wanted to control the business. The government wanted to begin a clear-out of the small and medium-sized pasta dealers so that they could concentrate on the big ones afterwards."

The "suppression" had another purpose: the new regime was under heavy criticism already from the United States for its close involvement in the cocaine trade, and some show of narcotics suppression had to be mounted. The Fiancés would have a key role to play in it, though the campaign they were now to launch would be a model of hypocrisy.

· Once again, Barbie was in control of the squad, handing down instructions to Fiebelkorn, and reporting back on the activities of the Fiancés to Arce Gómez. Increasingly, as the group became more arrogant, he found himself relaying horror stories about their excesses. A monster had been created, which would be hard to tame again. But Arce Gómez was untroubled: the monster was making him a great deal of money.

Licences to transport the coca leaf, available only from the Ministry of the Interior, cost $1,500. For a plane to take off un-molested by the authorities could cost $30,000. And, of course, there were direct profits to be gleaned from that section of the traffic which Arce Gómez and García Meza controlled directly. There

was more than enough for everybody, as a member of the gang
remembered:

> The García Meza regime put us into the money. We transferred
> our general barracks to a building near the airport, surrounded
> by trees and a two metre cement wall. On the terrace, we installed
> two machine guns. The generals in the government had decided
> to take the drug traffic into their own hands, going round the
> dealers and intermediaries. It was a big affair – $2,000 million
> worth.

In November, playing out his public role, Arce Gómez announced
publicly that drug trafficking in Bolivia would be punishable by the
death penalty, under a forthcoming internal security law. More
secretly, in the course of another meeting in La Paz, García Meza
told the Fiancé leadership, "We have to operate in a convincing
manner."

The key to García Meza's plan lay in a secret report headed
"Plan 001-FRGE", an unassuming plain white document, prepared
for him by "Special Intelligence Group Number 2" of the army. It
is clear from the criticisms it contains of Department 2 that this
remarkable document was prepared by a rival section within Arce
Gómez's organisation, but some of its warnings about the excesses
of the Fiancés echo precisely what Barbie had already begun to
pass on to the minister. The report began:

> Fulfilling your instructions, Colonel Camacho [a senior intellig-
> ence officer] put the Special Intelligence group in touch with
> the principal exporters of cocaine. The great majority of those
> interviewed showed great enthusiasm for Your Excellency's plan.
> In order that we might perfect the plan, they facilitated visits for
> us to several factories that we might observe the various processes
> and gave us samples of the finished product.

The report is a fascinating and detailed account of the business
conducted by the major traffickers, the favoured and most profitable
export routes, the maximum "tax" the traffickers would pay in
protection money and the problems the traffickers currently faced –
high on the list were the excessive demands for protection money
from government officials; these should be controlled, said the
report. "For the success of the plan, the exporters consider essential
the suppression of individual and workshop production. It is

necessary to guarantee the functioning of industrial plants which have a potential capacity of 5,000 kilos a month."

This was the task assigned to the Fiancés of Death. All the cocaine seized was to be handed over to the Ministry of the Interior; the rest of the confiscated property would be counted spoils of war. And, as Joachim Fiebelkorn later testified in the course of his Frankfurt trial, the man who ensured that the special police passes were issued, and who ironed out any problems that arose was Klaus Barbie. He was also responsible for paying the Fiancés, which he did every month, using a Major Luis Cossio as the go-between. Cossio had once worked for the drug suppression agency, but had switched sides, so he was a useful and knowledgeable intermediary.

The leaders of the Fiancés returned from their meeting with García Meza in high spirits, and threw a party in Santa Cruz. "Fiebelkorn was splendid in his SS uniform," recalled one member of the group. "The women from the Women's and Mothers' National Front gave us flowers. The party ended with shouts of 'Heil Hitler'."

But there were also, had García Meza cared to take notice, these warning remarks contained in the report:

> The need urgently to bring under control the para-military groups which have taken to assaulting producers and harvesters has been pointed out. Many of them played an important role in the revolution of July 17, but faced with their libertinism nobody has removed the arms and credentials supplied to them by Department 2. With these arms and credentials, they are terrorising many people.

Already there had been trouble in Santa Cruz. On October 22 Fiebelkorn and Manfred Kuhlmann had been arrested by the Santa Cruz police for carrying weapons, but by the time the long suffering German consul arrived at the police station they had been released. The following month one of the Fiancés, known throughout the bars of the small town for his wild drinking, was found dead on the street. Among his effects handed in to the consulate, were Fascist and neo-Nazi membership cards.

On December 16 the group was further depleted by the mysterious death of Hans Stellfeld, the ex-SS soldier and friend of Klaus Barbie. He was found in his Santa Cruz home with gunshot wounds in his head. Two young Germans who had been living with Stellfeld reported his "suicide" to the consulate and rapidly left for Paraguay.

Stellfeld was given an elaborate funeral at which the main tribute was offered, in suitably rhetorical style, by Adolfo Ustárez, Barbie's lawyer, now promoted under the new regime to comptroller-general of the republic. "Valiant soldier," said Ustárez, "you defended a great nation and, undismayed in the face of unequal defeat, you undertook a new life, always maintaining your spirit of discipline and obedience. Now that Moscow and Peking have formed a new front, you defended Bolivia against terrorists and anarchists . . ."

Undaunted, the Fiancés continued to make life a misery for the ordinary citizens of Santa Cruz. Periodically, the Italians would go to Argentina to bank their money, then return to celebrate. There would be a boisterous round of the local night clubs. They were guaranteed good service, though at a cost, as one restaurant proprietor remembered.

We nearly closed down at that time, rather than have to stand it. Ordinary people stopped going to bars and restaurants because they never knew when they might run into them. They would come in here, sometimes bringing their own musicians who would play Nazi songs. If you didn't like it, you just had to get out.

The group was causing embarrassment even to the military. As the army report spelled out:

Concern is being caused by the continued presence in the country of South African and German mercenaries, all of whom have credentials from the Ministry of the Interior and Department 2 . . . Their high remuneration and their behaviour makes things very uncomfortable for all who have to pay and deal with them.

Had García Meza heeded these signs, it is possible that his extraordinary regime might have lasted longer than it did. Instead, he and Arce Gómez confirmed the Fiancés in their role as masters of Santa Cruz, able to raid houses, confiscate property and kill with impunity. In three months, according to one of the gang, the group seized twenty luxury cars, and over $300,000 in cash.

José, Fiebelkorn's faithful admirer, remembers the penalties paid by those who ran foul of the group: "Everybody who was in the traffic had to pay ten per cent to Arce in an office on the eighth floor of the Edificio Santa Cruz. Whoever didn't pay, died." José said that in the course of three months, fifteen men in Santa Cruz broke the rules and paid with their lives.

José also recalls pay day. Fiebelkorn received $100,000 a month which was brought in cash by Major Cossio. "Barbie would always telephone to say the money was coming," he said. García Meza could afford to pay well; the potential yield of his plan had been spelt out in the December report:

> Even before initiating the campaign of concentration of production, you could collect, without difficulty, around $200 million annually, on the basis of a tax of $2,000 per kilo, which all the exporters were willing to pay, as a single tax. If we can guarantee all the industrial process and the suppression of the intermediaries, without prejudicing the interests of the peasant producers of the leaf, this sum could rise to $600 million annually.

There was, of course, the occasional mistake: for instance, the Fiancés arrested Sonia Atala, who was a major trafficker but also a mistress of Luis Arce Gómez. "She was furious," said José. "She immediately got on the telephone to the president and gave him a terrible earful." Sonia was soon released with fulsome apologies, and the group was rebuked for "misinterpreting orders".
Increasingly, there were tensions further up the hierarchy.

> García Meza and Arce Gómez didn't always give the same orders [said José]. Whenever Arce Gómez gave an order, Fiebelkorn would call Barbie to discuss it with him and to ask for advice. Barbie always knew everything that was going on and Joachim always followed his advice. Arce Gómez visited a couple of times, but the closest contact was with Barbie. He would arrive in Ustárez's car, with Alvaro de Castro, or sometimes we went to see him in La Paz.

But, as Barbie and the army report had warned, the extraordinary anarchy in Santa Cruz contained the seeds of its own destruction. Very soon it would be brought to an end.
In February 1981 CBS television broadcast a devastating programme in its "Sixty minute" series. It accused the Interior Minister of Bolivia, Luis Arce Gómez, of direct participation in the narcotics traffic.

A few days prior to the broadcast – on February 26 – Arce Gómez quietly resigned as Minister of the Interior and was redesignated Head of the Military Academy, but his new appointment caused deep resentment within the armed forces. In March, following a mutiny by a hundred cadets, García Meza was forced to remove him from the Military Academy to give him time to organise a defence against allegations by the American Drug Enforcement

Agency and news organisations, that he had been trafficking in cocaine.

García Meza redoubled his public relations effort, dispatching General Banzer to Washington for private talks with Department of State officials. But even in Bolivia itself his regime was seen as having gone too far. Civilian resistance was mounting, fomented by the clandestine trade union activists who had secretly returned to the country, and even the right-wing was beginning to protest.

In April 1981 García Meza finally yielded to pressure from dissatisfied army officers and began a clean-up of the Fiancés of Death. Fiebelkorn was handsomely paid off and warned by García Meza that he should leave the country.

García Meza then appointed as head of the army in Santa Cruz one of Bolivia's most famous and popular army officers, Colonel Gary Prado, whose task, which he swore publicly to fulfil, was to root out the Fiancés. The end was not long in coming, though, as José described it, corrupt habits die hard:

> The police came and installed two machine guns behind the house – they called for us to surrender, but we said they would have to kill us, we would never surrender. They sent a captain to talk to us, who said we could carry on working for them, if we wanted to. Then they gave us three hundred dollars and told us to go home.

Most of those in the house slipped away, but that night the police returned.

> Napoleon [Le Clerc] telephoned the house and some stranger answered. I went past on my motorcycle and I couldn't see the two dogs we had. I thought it was suspicious, and I phoned from the house on the corner. Somebody answered and I asked to speak to one of the women. She wasn't there. I never went back.

None of the Fiancés was detained long in Santa Cruz. José still lives there, anxious, short of money and dreaming of Fiebelkorn's return. Le Clerc moved to La Paz where he was arrested under Siles Zuazo's government and eventually expelled to France. The silent killer, Ike Kopplin, is still in Bolivia, though not out of trouble: he hit the headlines again in Santa Cruz a year later when, in the course of a night out, he shot the manager of the Playboy Bar in Santa Cruz and rifled his safe. Arrested by the police, he was released on the grounds that he worked for the security police. He is still free and recently sent a message to the German consul in Santa Cruz asking for his German passport to be renewed.

Fiebelkorn himself headed for Brazil. A few days later, Brazilian police arrested his group of eight crossing the Bolivian frontier with three kilos of cocaine. As well as the drugs, the group was discovered to be carrying a collection of Nazi pamphlets, military uniforms, arms and membership lists and ID cards for two neo-Nazi groups. The lists revealed Joachim Fiebelkorn to be the commander of the Special Commando Group. After questioning, the eight were released. Later Fiebelkorn returned to Germany, but was subsequently arrested there and charged with assault on a young girl – a charge relating to his violent times in Bolivia.

The extraordinary reign of the Fiancés of Death was thus over. Only those who had run the group for their own profit and advantage – García Meza, Arce Gómez, and Klaus Barbie – remained, so far, untouched, while the Italians, too valuable to lose, continued their intelligence work unharmed.

In La Paz, García Meza turned the break-up of the group to the best advantage he could, announcing publicly that a dangerous ring of para-military terrorists had been successfully smashed.

"He always was a treacherous bastard," said José.

The ignominious departure of the Fiancés of Death might have served as a warning to Klaus Barbie that the regime he had helped to install was rotting from within. But, by the time Fiebelkorn was packing his bags, Barbie's attention was distracted by personal tragedy.

On May 1 1981 the Altmann family went for a day out in Cochabamba to watch Klaus junior compete in his latest sporting passion, hang-gliding. At midday, strapped into his hang-glider, Klaus kissed his mother and launched himself off the cliff. But instead of gliding out over the valley, Klaus was caught by a wind and dashed almost immediately against a rock. Barbie tried to give his son mouth to mouth resuscitation, but Klaus's injuries were swiftly to prove fatal. He died an hour and a half later.

Klaus junior's wife Françoise and their three children, at home in Santa Cruz, were unaware of the tragedy. "It was my father-in-law who told me over the telephone," said Françoise, "he was in tears, although he was not a man who cried easily."

Father and son had frequently disagreed: Barbie never forgave Klaus for abandoning his law studies, regretted that he had never shown any signs of developing a career, and was irritated when he insisted on marrying against his advice. "He had more social ambition for his son than his son had for himself," said Françoise.

Nevertheless, Françoise insisted, it was a close and loving family. For Regine, Barbie's wife, the blow was devastating. No longer could she bear the elegant villa in Cochabamba where she had to keep the curtains of the living room closed against the view of the spot where her son had died. In spite of the discomforts of the high altitude, the Barbies were henceforth to spend more and more time in La Paz.

As they recovered from their private tragedy, political developments in two countries were taking place which were to have a decisive effect on Barbie's life. In France that May, a Socialist government had been elected. Meanwhile, in Bolivia, the García Meza regime was disintegrating.

There were several armed protests against the regime. In May an army rebellion was slapped down, only to be followed by another in June, defused by a combination of force and the payment of "loyalty bonds". García Meza promised to resign his power on July 17, the anniversary of his coup, but failed to keep his promise.

His final moments came on August 3, when a new rebellion began in Santa Cruz and rapidly gained support in other regions. Delle Chiaie, aware of the personal risk of a change in the regime, tried to persuade García Meza that the rebel leader should be assassinated, but it was too late. García Meza attempted to marshal support amongst his senior officers, but one army commander, who rapidly became a popular hero, refused to mobilise his regiment against the rebels and told the president to resign instead. Enraged at his insubordination, García Meza began to belabour him about the head, to which the commander responded by kicking García Meza in the groin and menacing him with a pistol, thus bringing his unhappy regime to a close.

That night, García Meza went on television to announce his own departure: "Above any reasons of pride or vanity," he said, "comes the fatherland."

Delle Chiaie later gave a more lengthy, if similarly high-flown, explanation for García Meza's departure. In an interview in a La Paz newspaper, he blamed his fall on those of his advisers who "lived more for the moment than for the future of Bolivia, and deceived the general with lies and manoeuvres. One of these, specifically, caused the departure of the Minister of the Interior, Arce Gómez." He charged the Carter administration in Washington and "international capitalist interests" of interfering with García Meza's radical programmes.

Of Arce Gómez, he said: "I was his adviser . . . much has been said against him, and I believe there is a desire to destroy the prestige of one of the pillars of the anti-subversive struggle. I consider myself his friend . . ."

With the resignation of García Meza, three of his branch commanders hastily formed an interim junta. But Bolivia by this time was teetering on the edge of disaster: in July the Central Bank had run out of dollars, foreign lenders had cut off credit, payments on the foreign debt had stopped and ten million dollars worth of government cheques, written against an empty account in the New York branch of the Bank of Nova Scotia, bounced.

The new junta lasted only a month. In September 1981, an "internal readjustment" elevated to the presidency one General Celso Torrelio, who had replaced Arce Gómez as Minister of the Interior.

In spite of these changes at the top, the work of Barbie, delle Chiaie and Pagliai continued and was to continue through two further changes of presidency. Barbie's job was perhaps a trifle less distinguished than it had been. He no longer had an office at the Ministry of the Interior; instead he made regular deliveries to the building, bearing photocopies of his internal intelligence reports. Officials noted that he was careful never to leave the originals.

His protection, however, remained intact, as two *New York Times* journalists, Maria Isabel Schumaker and Peter McFarren, discovered when they were arrested after ringing the bell of Barbie's house in Cochabamba and soliciting an interview. They were taken to the local headquarters of the intelligence service, and grilled and threatened for several hours before being released.

"Anyone else might have called the police," said McFarren. "Barbie demanded, and got, the secret service."

Barbie continued to be seen regularly at the headquarters of the armed forces in La Paz, where he was an honoured guest at ceremonial occasions and a discreet participant in meetings. When, in August 1982, General Vildoso took over the crumbling government in La Paz, journalists at the government palace were astonished to observe that, on the first day of his presidency, he received Barbie and his shadow, de Castro. And, as one photographer discovered, curiosity about Barbie still did not pay: he was beaten up for recording Barbie's exit from the palace.

But by now Barbie was in need of more than strong-arm protection. America had renewed diplomatic relations with Bolivia, and the new US ambassador was no friend of old Nazis or new Fascists. His reports to Washington would cut the ground from under

Barbie's feet when the time came. But first he intended to clear up once and for all the matter of the Italian terrorists.

The ambassador, Edwin Corr, was a tough, trouble-shooting career diplomat with long experience of Latin America. It had been clear, even before his arrival the previous November, that he and the Italian terrorists were going to clash.

"Edwin Corr," delle Chiaie was to remark, "behaves as though Bolivia were a province of the United States." Corr held equally strong views about delle Chiaie. "He's like a fictionalised version of Carlos the Jackal," an aide reports him as saying.

Corr was even more appalled by delle Chiaie's friend, Pagliai. As one diplomat put it: "When we first heard about Pagliai, we couldn't believe it."

Pagliai, it emerged, concealed behind his film-star good looks and cultivated manner the personality of a sadistic torturer with almost theatrical tastes. He regularly appeared for torture sessions wearing ballet tights, stripped to the waist, and with his torso oiled. He found especially entertaining a version of electric shock torture known locally as La Diablada after a Bolivian dance: it consisted of flooding the floor on which the victim lay and passing an electric current through it as the victim's body jerked convulsively.

The US Embassy took seriously the regular death threats made against Ambassador Corr and he was assigned a massive body-guard of fourteen armed Bolivians and ten US security agents. The confrontation, at times, came into the open. One diplomat remembered a reception in Santa Cruz at which both Corr and Pagliai were present, each with a large contingent of armed men: "The scene was unbelievable. The two groups circled round and round each other, each trying to get the drop on the other – it was like something out of *West Side Story*." The ambassador resolved that something had to be done.

There was more to the Americans' interest in the Italians and in Barbie than the mere desire to get their own back. In 1980, when the administration of President Reagan came to power, it made clear publicly that it intended to launch a crusade against terrorism; there were strong speeches from Secretary of State Alexander Haig about the international threat that terrorism posed, and defence and intelligence agencies were instructed to gather information on terrorists and prepare plans for dealing with them.

Although the crusade was directed mostly at leftist groups, the CIA decided that it should take an interest in right-wing terrorism as well. At least part of the reason was that at the same time an international war on drugs had been proclaimed, and the two went hand in hand.

By 1982 the two Italians in Bolivia – delle Chiaie and Pagliai – had become subjects of special interest at the agency's headquarters in Langley, Virginia. There are extensive operational files on both men, though enquiries under the Freedom of Information Act have failed to have them released. Selective files that have been elicited show that Pagliai in particular was closely watched for most of 1982.

However, even the ambassador of the United States in Bolivia, backed by the resources of the CIA, cannot simply remove undesirable elements without a good excuse. In September 1982 such an excuse presented itself.

For over two years the Italian authorities had laboured over the investigation of one of the bloodiest terrorist outrages post-war Europe had seen: the bombing in August 1980 of the railway station at Bologna, which caused the death of eighty-four passengers and staff caught by the blast in the second-class waiting room, and left two hundred wounded. In September 1982, after a long and often frustrating investigation, a Bologna magistrate, Claudio Gentile, issued warrants for the arrest of five men on suspicion of the bombing. They were: Joachim Fiebelkorn, Stefano delle Chiaie, Pierluigi Pagliai, Maurizio Giorgio (a long-standing friend and associate of delle Chiaie), and Olivier Danet, a French rightist.

Gentile's warrants were based on the confessions of Elio Ciolini, who had been among Fiebelkorn's Fiancés of Death from January to April 1981. In 1982 Ciolini, in prison in Switzerland for fraud, bartered his information with Gentile for twenty-five thousand dollars, the price fixed for his bail. In his evidence Ciolini testified that Pagliai and Fiebelkorn had travelled from Bolivia to Bologna in August 1980 to supervise the Bologna bombing, which had been planned by delle Chiaie. The Bologna magistrates had, almost from the start, suspected the involvement of delle Chiaie, but this was the first break they had had. The arrest warrants were immediately issued.

The Italian intelligence service, SID, had been aware of delle Chiaie and Pagliai's whereabouts for three months before the warrants were issued. Delle Chiaie's friend, Maurizio Giorgio, who had been with him throughout his work in Latin America, was arrested in Italy. From Giorgio's address book and his reluctant confessions, the Italians discovered contact numbers in both Argentina and Bolivia for delle Chiaie, and Pagliai's Santa Cruz address.

The Italians swapped notes with their opposite numbers in the CIA. An Italian secret service report, dated May 7 1982 and sent to the Bologna magistrate, acknowledges American intelligence reports and describes Pagliai as "a well known torturer, responsible for the greater part of the violations of human rights in Bolivia in the past two years".

The Americans, for their part, had traced Pagliai to a well-fortified house in Avenida Grigota, Santa Cruz, belonging to a Captain Larea of the intelligence service of the Bolivian army; it was equipped with heavy steel shutters and a variety of weapons. US agents followed with interest the meetings which took place inside.

They had also spotted an extremely interesting connection. A cable from the CIA station in La Paz, one of the very few CIA documents on this period that has slipped through the net, records that on July 16 1982 three men were seen together at the Café La Paz. They were Klaus Barbie, Pierluigi Pagliai and Emilio Carbone, Barbie's neo-Fascist friend.

The cable makes no comment on the meeting beyond recording it. However, the fact that Barbie was in communication with a man currently on the wanted list for the Bologna bombing rang alarm bells with the Italian secret service when it was passed on to them. The possibility that Barbie had himself been involved in the Bologna plans was widely canvassed within SID, before being dismissed for lack of evidence.

In July 1982 Edwin Corr decided it was time to move. In a secret visit to Italy he persuaded the authorities there that a daring *coup de main* was the only way to secure their prize. Pagliai and delle Chiaie, he argued, would never be handed over officially by the military, and to wait until the civilian government was installed would simply give them time to escape.

Corr argued persuasively for an entirely novel approach: on the very day that Bolivia was to celebrate the inauguration of the democratically elected government of Hernan Siles Zuazo, he said, a joint US-Italian operation should be mounted to capture the two terrorists. The idea was astonishingly bold. If it came off, it would be one of the most ambitious covert operations since the plots against Lumumba in the Congo, or Castro in Cuba.

Delle Chiaie was later to claim that, through infiltration of both the American and Italian intelligence services, he knew in advance of the plans which were being laid; but there is little sign that Pagliai appreciated the danger he was in. Almost to the end he continued to work for various branches of Bolivian intelligence, even taking on new assignments, among them a practical demonstration which made one spectator, himself a hardened member of the Bolivian military, sick with horror.

Using one of his many aliases, "Mario Bonone Sicario", described as "Major of the Chief of Staff and Military Attaché of the Argentinian Armed Forces in La Paz", Pagliai gave a series of seminars before an invited audience in a safe house at 271 No. 3 Street, in Obrajes, La Paz. The audience was by numbered invitation and from September 7 to 16 talks were given on various aspects of "counter-subversion", ranging from "Methods of repression of organised delinquency" to "A plan for the training of personnel in anti-narcotics operations". It was during the longest session, on Monday September 12, billed as "Interrogation techniques, physical and psychological aspects of coercion: practical demonstration with lie detector", that Pagliai killed two people in front of his audience. During the practical "demonstration" of torture, which included the insertion of red-hot needles into the ears of the victims, two Bolivian peasants, one a suspected cocaine trafficker, died in agony.

By now the Americans were selecting a small contingent of Bolivian police to cooperate in their planned operation. Secrecy was paramount, but even so, rumours began to leak out that, on October 10, the day of Siles Zuazo's inauguration, a kidnapping involving foreign agents was planned.

Four times during September it reached the ears of Klaus Barbie and Alvaro de Castro that there was a kidnap attempt in the offing. But the rumour received was slightly wrong: it was said to be an attempt to seize Barbie and return him to France. Barbie was less concerned than de Castro. "I have done nothing wrong in Bolivia," he insisted, "they will never hand me over. I know this government, they are friends."

But the warnings were insistent and well sourced – one came from a former Minister of Finance. With the fourth and most detailed version, de Castro felt it prudent to double-check. "I went to see the Head of Military Intelligence," he said, "and asked if he could check to see if there was any basis to it." Barbie's connections were still excellent and the intelligence services at his disposal. A few days later, de Castro returned to see if there was any news. "You don't talk about that sort of thing on the telephone," he explained. "He told me he had investigated and there was nothing to it, that Klaus did not need to worry."

In the short term, this was true. The operation planned for October 10 did not concern Barbie. But, as the return of democracy approached, the French government too was laying plans which, after more than thirty years, were to bear fruit. For both generations of Fascists in Bolivia, the shadow of their European past was shortly to reach the sanctuary they had thought invulnerable.

CHAPTER FIFTEEN

The Past is Present

Klaus Barbie had not been looking forward to the weekend of October 10 1982. Military rule had always been good for him. But October 10 and the inauguration of a civilian president would bring it, definitively, to an end.

There had been disturbing rumours, too, that something dramatic was going to happen on inauguration day itself. As preparations were laid in La Paz for national celebrations Barbie announced to Alvaro de Castro that he considered it both pleasanter and more prudent to spend the weekend in Cochabamba.

"He tried to persuade me to go with him," said de Castro, "but I get bored in Cochabamba, so I stayed here and he went alone." Both men devoted the day to their families: de Castro took his young daughter to the cinema and Barbie spent a pleasant day out in the country with his daughter-in-law Françoise Croisset and her two children. It was not until late afternoon that he got back.

Soon afterwards he received a telephone call from an agitated de Castro. Something dramatic had, indeed, happened: an event which grazed the security of Barbie's comfortable existence and which was to be the first and clearest warning of his own downfall. The news was confused, de Castro told Barbie, but it appeared that Pierluigi Pagliai had been kidnapped in an Interpol operation. "He was very calm when I told him," recalls de Castro. "I begged him to leave the country, but he simply repeated: 'I have done nothing wrong in Bolivia, why should I have anything to fear?'"

Versions of Pagliai's capture which appeared in the press the next day were deeply confusing. It was hardly surprising, for the Pagliai operation, planned for months by the American and Italian secret services, was so startling that even in Bolivia it seemed incredible. Had it gone smoothly, it might have passed almost unnoticed. But, almost from the start, it went terribly wrong.

Shortly after Corr's visit to Rome to recruit the help of the Italian Ministry of the Interior, two Italian secret service agents had flown out to help prepare the operation. Then, in September 1982, fresh warrants were issued for the arrest of the Italians and in a last attempt to persuade the Bolivians to cooperate, the Italian government had asked them formally to expel them. The response was not encouraging: "These people," said the Minister of the Interior, "could not be located."

In early October, following a conference in La Paz, attended by Corr, and US and Italian agents, the Italians were asked to fly in a small plane from Rome on the day of Siles Zuazo's inauguration, when the country's attention would be fixed on events in La Paz. The new Interior Minister, whoever he turned out to be, would be approached to sign an expulsion order for the two terrorists, and the US Embassy would pick a force of around thirty Bolivian police from those it considered trustworthy.

The military would not be informed: they were considered too close to the intended targets to be reliable. The Americans would clear overflying rights with the necessary neighbouring countries and keep a close watch for international complications.

Barbie and de Castro were not the only people in La Paz who viewed the imminent accession of Siles Zuazo with unease. An Argentine official in Bolivia, who identified himself only as "Pedro", an intimate friend of Arce Gómez and García Meza, was deeply concerned as well.

"I wasn't worried for myself," he said, "but I thought something would happen to the boys." The "boys" were delle Chiaie and Pagliai. "I went to Santa Cruz to try to warn them. By a stroke of good luck, I bumped into Pagliai at the airport and I told him he had to leave. He said he would leave within a few days, but there was some business he wanted to clear up . . . a debt to collect." Delle Chiaie needed no further warning, however. He slipped out of the house in Santa Cruz and went to Cochabamba.

Pedro was still worried enough to remove from Pagliai's house all the documentation which compromised the Argentine government through its secret connections with the drug trafficking terrorists. "The documents left the country for Argentina on a military plane the next day," he said. His duty done, Pedro retired discreetly to Los Tajibos, a luxury five star hotel on the outskirts of Santa Cruz, where he spent the next day sunbathing.

Meanwhile other people had a less than tranquil day. Dr Freddy Terrazas, chief neuro-surgeon at Santa Cruz's Petrolera Clinic, had planned a quiet Sunday, and had gone home at 10 a.m. after completing his shift. It was only an hour later that his bleeper warned him of an emergency case. "I live quite close," said Dr

Terrazas, "and I drive quite fast." It took him eight minutes to get back to the clinic. "I found a young man in emergency. He was lucid and conscious, but had quadraplegia from a bullet wound in his throat, on the left. He talked with an Argentine accent and he said his name was Alberto Costabruno." Costabruno, Terrazas was told, had been dumped at the hospital lodge a few minutes earlier by a group of men who had hastily driven off.

Costabruno was another of Pagliai's aliases. His condition, as he was unceremoniously dumped at the gate of Santa Cruz's best hospital, was only one of the things which had gone wrong with the elaborate operation.

The Bolivians had supplied only fifteen men instead of thirty, scarcely enough to stake out Pagliai's house, let alone storm it, so the decision had been taken to seize the young Italian in the street.

Pagliai was a creature of regular habits. "He got up early in the mornings and went to the office, just like a normal person," remarked an intelligence officer. But that Sunday, October 10, he rose late, unaware that at nine the previous evening the Alitalia jet, "Giotta da Bondone" had taken off from Rome's Fiumicino airport with a team on board bent on kidnapping him. The Bolivians were appalled by the size of the plane, and by its route. The "Giotta da Bondone", far from being the small aircraft the Americans had requested, was a vast DC-10 – the largest ever seen in Bolivia. And it was meant to go straight to Santa Cruz, not La Paz.

The Italians had picked a formidable squad of secret service agents, who had flown in radio silence via Recife in north-eastern Brazil to La Paz, where the pilot requested emergency landing facilities. It was the morning of Sunday, October 10.

At 10 a.m. air traffic control at Santa Cruz airport received a call from La Paz, asking for information on their runway. The next message from La Paz announced that an aircraft was to land at Santa Cruz for a technical stop to take on fuel. Its final destination, the message said, was Lima. The plane arrived an hour later, touching down without much difficulty on the runway at Santa Cruz. The airport official whose job it was to check the plane's documentation looked at the flight plan: instead of flying on to Lima, he discovered that the DC-10 planned to return to La Paz without refuelling. He checked whether it had had permission to enter Bolivian airspace, found that it had, and went back to his office and closed the door. "It doesn't pay to be too curious over things like that," he said.

The DC-10 taxied off the runway and parked on the apron, some yards from the airport cafeteria. Instructions were issued not to approach the plane and nobody got off. Inside, the thirty occupants were growing increasingly restless. They were late, the ground operation had gone ahead without them, and by the sound of it, things had not turned out well.

Pagliai, leaving the house at 9.30 a.m., jumped into his light grey Toyota jeep and drove down Avenida Grigota in the direction of the airport. Three blocks away, as the jeep approached the Plaza de Nuestra Senora de Fatima, a white Lada police car eased out of a side street and as the jeep approached pulled out in front of it. Pagliai twisted the wheel of the Toyota and it skidded to the side of the road. Three police agents, one a tall blond man, leaped from the car and surrounded the jeep.

What happened next is a matter of dispute. The Bolivian police officer who commanded the operation claims that Pagliai reached for his gun. A Bolivian officer, he then says, tried to wound him by shooting him in the shoulder, but Pagliai twisted round and the bullet entered his neck.

Eye-witnesses, however, and there was quite a crowd, claim that Pagliai had already surrendered when a policeman smashed the right hand window of the jeep, leaned over and deliberately shot him. Above all, the identity of the tall blond man is a mystery. Both the Americans and the Bolivians insist there were only Bolivians in the detail, but later a secret ten-page CIA report on the incident alleged that Pagliai was actually shot by an Italian; and the two Italian secret agents who had travelled to Bolivia three months earlier were certainly part of that morning's disastrous operation.

Pagliai was dumped into the police car and driven at high speed to the Petrolera Clinic, where he was abandoned at the gate. The police then returned to the house on Avenida Grigota to search it for two missing items: Stefano delle Chiaie and the documentation. They found neither.

Meanwhile at the hospital Dr Freddy Terrazas was confronted with his seriously wounded patient. "I ordered him to be taken to emergency X-ray, before he went upstairs to the intensive care unit for the operation," he said.

He nearly failed to get as far as the operating table.

"While he was in X-ray," said Terrazas, "a group of about eight men turned up. They said they were friends of the patient and they wanted to take him to Cochabamba, to his wife. They said they had a plane leaving at 12.30 p.m. and asked me to hand him over immediately."

Terrazas very nearly complied. "The patient was conscious at the time, so of course I asked him whether he wanted to go. He became very agitated – he said he had no wife in Cochabamba and begged me not to hand him over. It was pure chance that he was lucid, otherwise I might well have done so."

The "friends" it emerged were led by Captain Larea, the Bolivian intelligence officer, though Pagliai had no means of knowing this. Larea later paid the hospital bill at the Petrolera Clinic. Larea's attempt to extract Pagliai from the hands of his captors was not the last which would be made.

Terrazas ordered his patient to be taken upstairs to intensive care as he scrutinised the X-rays.

We found a lesion of the lamina at the level of the fourth vertebra. The bullet was lodged in the muscle and doing no further damage. He could just move his arms and legs, although it was painful, so we decided to operate immediately. If he had lost all movement, there would have been no hurry. We decided to leave the bullet where it was – you usually do more damage trying to dig it out.

The operation took three hours and the patient came round about two hours later. "He had lost a lot of blood during the operation," said Terrazas, "so I authorised a transfusion of 1,500 cc."

It was while their patient was recovering in the intensive care ward that the bemused hospital authorities had their next surprise.

"A group of men came to see me," said Dr Raimers, the hospital director, "claiming to be from Interpol. They said that Costabruno was not Argentine but Italian and they produced a warrant from the Italian Ministry of the Interior. They demanded that we hand him over immediately."

Terrazas refused. "He was in no condition to travel. My concern was medical, nothing to do with police business, and I refused to authorise his discharge until I judged him fit," he said. "Police jurisdiction stops there," he said, pointing to the door. "Inside, the jurisdiction is medical."

The police settled down to wait.

Back inside the stranded DC-10 the atmosphere was growing heated. The airliner was surrounded by military cadets, and it was by no means clear whether it would be allowed to take off again.

It was 11.30 p.m. before Terrazas decided that Pagliai's blood level was sufficiently high for him to be transferred safely. "He was lucid and conscious when he left," Terrazas remembered.

Pagliai was rushed to the airport in the company of a Bolivian doctor who had been brought in from La Paz, and loaded on to the waiting plane, but it was not until 1.18 a.m., thirteen hours late and with the operation in ruins, that the DC-10 managed to surmount the endless bureaucratic delays that had by now set in. A US agent, later decorated for his efforts, stepped in to clear the flight, and the plane was finally allowed to take off for La Paz.

It was during that long afternoon of waiting that de Castro first heard of the affair. "I had a sixth sense that something was going to happen," he said. When he got back home in the afternoon, his telephone rang. "It was an Italian friend. He said, 'Something's happened.' I said, 'Is it Klaus?' 'No,' he said, 'they've taken Pagliai.' I telephoned Klaus immediately to give him the news. He was very calm; he just said, 'That young man was asking for trouble.' "

Another interested party received the news with outward calm. Pedro heard about it by the Los Tajibos swimming pool. Clearly delle Chiaie was in danger. "We had a prepared emergency procedure in case something serious happened," he said. "It swung into action and went like clockwork." In the next few days a small group of men made their way on foot through the thorn scrub on the Bolivian side of the Argentine border, sleeping by day and walking by night. "There were five of us, delle Chiaie, me, and some helpers. We got over the border to Salta and there some of our people took delle Chiaie. From there it was easy – they took him to Buenos Aires." The chief target of the elaborate plan, one of Europe's most wanted terrorists, had made his escape.

In La Paz things were going less smoothly. Pagliai had been rushed to the Clinica Santa Isabel where he was being attended to under heavy guard. His condition, stable in Santa Cruz, had begun to deteriorate. The US authorities, desperate to get him out of Bolivia in a condition in which he could still talk, began to hear rumours that plots were being devised to "rescue" him; the new Minister of the Interior, Mario Roncal, was showing himself strangely reluctant to sign the necessary papers.

On the morning of October 11, the chargé d'affaires of the Italian Embassy contacted the Bolivian Ministry of the Interior and went round to collect the signed expulsion order, which, after considerable delay, he eventually obtained. Eight copies were made and left in the ministry. Italian officials found it odd that, when the news of the affair caused a political row in Bolivia, not one of the eight copies could be found.

At 4 p.m. Pagliai was taken to the airport and put on the plane. Again the delays seemed endless. Airport fees were demanded. The scene at the airport was becoming chaotic. An increasingly furious pilot alternated between rage at the airport authorities and anxiety lest his plane be sabotaged. It was not an idle fear. As the argument boiled inside the terminal building two men were observed close to the undercarriage of the aircraft. The security officers gave chase, but the two men vanished.

By this time the US ambassador, Edwin Corr, who had kept discreetly in the background, was losing patience. Arriving at the airport at 5 p.m. to see off William Middendorf, US ambassador to the Organisation of American States, who had attended Siles Zuazo's inauguration, Corr noticed the DC-10 still parked on the tarmac. Once his visitor had left, he swung into action.

"He was furious," said an onlooker. "He went straight into the VIP lounge and got on the telephone. He rang up Roncal and actually ordered him to authorise the departure of the plane." It is unorthodox, to say the least, for an ambassador to issue an order to a minister of his host country, but it worked. Roncal reluctantly ordered the plane's release.

It was not, however, until 11 p.m. that the demoralised occupants found themselves rolling down the long La Paz runway, bound for San Juan in Puerto Rico.

There are, as it happens, no scheduled Alitalia flights from La Paz to San Juan, and details about the DC-10's flight had been kept to a minimum. There was only one obvious assumption and the San Juan authorities made it: the word hijack spread through the airport like wildfire. Their worst suspicions seemed to be confirmed when a request came from the approaching airliner for analgesics.

The plane's occupants were mortified to observe, as they landed at San Juan, that the entire runway was lined with ambulances, police cars, television crews and reporters. "We thought it was a hijack," explained an apologetic airport official. At 2.13 a.m., after taking on forty thousand litres of fuel, the DC-10 took off again, bound, finally, for Rome.

At Fiumicino airport at 3.40 a.m. the embarrassing scene of San Juan was repeated: flocks of police cars, their lights flashing, ambulances and crowds of reporters lined the runway. Without stopping to open its doors the plane was towed into a hangar where an ambulance stood waiting. By the time he was wheeled into Rome's San Camillio hospital Pagliai was receiving oxygen, the pipe plastered to his mouth, while a nurse held a drip attached to his arm. That evening doctors announced that he was unconscious and paralysed.

Pagliai survived for twenty-five days but, by the official account at least, never spoke again.

Back in La Paz there was an unholy political row, which brought neither Barbie nor de Castro much consolation. "ALTMANN NEXT", screamed the headlines, as the newspapers elaborated the theory that the Pagliai operation was a rehearsal for a similar exercise to rid Bolivia of one of her most notorious citizens.

Rumours spread that Barbie too had fled Bolivia. But in spite of the urging of his friends, he had not gone.

"I used to argue with Klaus about it," said de Castro. "My mother used to ring me and say, 'Go to Paraguay, the United States . . . anywhere.' But we didn't. I wanted to, but Klaus got very stubborn those last few weeks."

The truth was that Barbie had grown tired. The prospect of being on the run again did not appeal. He was approaching his sixty-ninth birthday and was beginning to feel and look his age. He suffered from an old man's anxiety about his health and complained of cramps in his legs. His wife Regine had fallen ill and the prognosis was not good. It was not a time to move. In any case, Bolivian politics are a volatile commodity. Perhaps the fall of the military and the capture of Pagliai were only setbacks.

For the French Embassy in La Paz the inauguration of the new president had involved a routine duty. Every president since Hugo Banzer had been asked to accede to the French request for the extradition of Klaus Barbie. The answer was always the same. Each president promised "to see what he could do", none had done anything. The French, however, had reason to hope that this government might be different.

The ambassador, Raymond Césaire, knew the intricacies of Bolivian politics well. He had been in post during the coup of 1980, and had given refuge to many of Siles Zuazo's supporters. His action had saved several lives at the time. But in May 1982 a new complication had arisen. The West German government, as a result of the renewed labours of the Munich prosecutors and the file Beate Klarsfeld had forced them to reopen in 1972, had asked for Barbie's extradition on a charge of the murder of Joseph Kemmler, leader of the St Claude Resistance. As one of Barbie's former Gestapo officers was prepared to swear, Barbie had beaten Kemmler to death.

The German request was pursuing the well-trodden route through the Bolivian Supreme Court. As the last two presidents had pointed out, the German matter would have to be resolved before the French request could be dealt with. At first, Siles Zuazo's reply was much the same. His presidency had opened with a monumental parliamentary row over the botched Pagliai operation and, for the time being, Siles was content to let justice take its stately course. Although the government took office in October, the Supreme Court was not nominated until December and judgment on the German request was not due until February 1983.

But two things were against Klaus Barbie. The first was that Siles Zuazo himself was quite determined that somehow or other he would be made to leave Bolivia. A few weeks earlier he had told a reporter from *Newsweek* magazine of his intention to "solve the Barbie problem".

The other circumstance was the American attitude. As the stream of messages from La Paz to Washington at this time demonstrate, the United States was prepared to throw its weight behind extradition. The administration did not want to see any accusations that it was once more obstructing French justice; furthermore the State Department now knew of the links between Barbie and Pagliai, and believed that his neo-Fascist associations made him a legitimate target for extradition.

Barbie was aware of the German request, but the weeks following the change of government were once more dominated by personal matters: his wife Regine was suffering severe abdominal pains and her condition appeared to be deteriorating. She entered the German Clinic in La Paz where Barbie visited her several times a day. "She was clearly getting very ill," said Alvaro de Castro. "She had intestinal obstructions and three operations were performed – they would remove the obstructions, but the trouble would start up again somewhere else."

Regine's illness was finally diagnosed as cancer and, as her condition worsened, Barbie telephoned his daughter Ute in Austria and told her she must come to Bolivia. Nine days before her mother died, Ute arrived. Regine died just before Christmas and was buried in the German cemetery in La Paz. "Klaus was very affected by her death," de Castro remembered. "He began to get ill too. He developed a hernia and he began to suffer from tremendous pains in his legs."

After a brief period of absence following the death of his wife – an absence which quickly gave rise to rumours that he had left – Barbie was once again to be seen on the streets of La Paz. He paid his daily visit to the Café La Paz, where he received a weekly copy of *Newsweek* openly addressed to "Klaus Altmann-Barbie, SS Hauptsturmführer" – possibly a practical joke, but one he no longer cared to object to. Those who greeted him noticed that he looked older suddenly, depressed by the loss of his wife.

"I used to meet him on the street," said Mery Flores, a Bolivian journalist and friend of Barbie's. "I used to tell him not to walk around like that, but he said, 'Why worry any more?' He had been very afraid of being kidnapped while his wife was ill, but he just lost heart after she died."

Barbie maintained his old friendships in the military, but his contract as adviser had been terminated in December 1982. Many old friends had already taken the prudent route: two days after Siles's inauguration a man in sunglasses, accompanied by three bodyguards, made a last minute dash for the midday Lloyd flight to Buenos Aires. Ex-President García Meza told bystanders that he planned to be away only for a week. Nobody believed him. Arce Gómez, too, had felt the climate of Buenos Aires would be more congenial. Barbie was scarcely left friendless, but the watchers at the French Embassy began to calculate that his old protectors might feel his usefulness had diminished and the embarrassment of conspicuously defending him might be too great.

De Castro, still trying to persuade Barbie to follow his friends to a more secure haven, took it upon himself to establish the progress of the German extradition request.

> I went to Sucre to try to find the papers, so we could prepare a defence – there was never any direct communication with us about it and the only way of finding out what was going on was to go there. Klaus wasn't really worried about it, he thought it would be all right, as it always had been.

Barbie's confidence was not entirely misplaced. As the interested diplomats realised, the Supreme Court judgment was unlikely to go against him. Although the presidency was politically sympathetic to the idea of getting rid of Barbie, it was the Congress, predominantly right-wing, which appointed the Supreme Court judges. But as Barbie waited confidently for that judgment, trouble came from another quarter.

"It was such a small thing when it began," said Alvaro de Castro, "a ten thousand dollar debt which dated back years."

The debt in fact dated back to September 1970, when Bolivia's state mining corporation COMIBOL paid to Klaus Altmann, manager of Transmaritima Boliviana, ten thousand dollars to ship minerals to various European ports. The cargo was never shipped and, since then, COMIBOL had begun an action to recover their money.

When Barbie was called to give evidence on the debt, on July 22

1982, it must have seemed nothing more than a tedious irritation; a close friend of the president had little to fear from such a minor matter. In his defence, Barbie confidently argued that he personally had no obligation for the debt and that, in any case, he had lost money on the deal: through a series of misfortunes, he claimed, it had cost him over twelve thousand dollars to get the cargo as far as Callao, in Peru.

But when the matter came to judgment in December 1982 the political situation was very different. On December 30 the sub-comptroller of the republic, Dr Jaime Urcullo, issued a mandate instructing Barbie to pay his debt within five days. If he failed to pay, he would be under arrest. "We didn't know anything about it until January," said de Castro. "Then somebody rang me up to tell me they had heard that judgment had been given against Klaus."

Barbie and de Castro made their way up the steep streets to Dr Constantino Carrion's tiny office in the corner of a dilapidated courtyard. Carrion, Barbie's defender for so many years, was eighty-six and was shortly to die himself. He was still waiting, he said, for notification of the case so he could present a further defence. His attention to Barbie's affairs was clearly slipping.

Carrion sent his devoted daughter and assistant to the comptroller's office to try to determine whether judgment had been given. She returned furious and without information. "I went round there myself," said de Castro. "There was a mountain of documents which one old man shuffled through and eventually produced a piece of paper. I was right, judgment had been given. It was already January 24, which meant there must have been a warrant out for Klaus's arrest: it's automatic in these cases."

When de Castro telephoned him as usual the next morning, Barbie was not feeling well. "I told him to go to the clinic, but he said, 'My wife died there three weeks ago. How could I go there?'" De Castro hoped to persuade him to see a doctor and arranged to meet Barbie for coffee in the Café La Paz. "He had a meeting with the chiefs of staff in the morning, and when we met, he said he had already had coffee. He wanted to go and see the lawyer and get this debt problem sorted out." The two men visited the aged Carrion and, in the afternoon, Barbie rang de Castro in some excitement. "He said he had found a statute which would help us – which allowed him to repay the debt in pesos. He wanted to go immediately to the comptroller's office and sort it out."

De Castro was nervous but allowed himself to be persuaded. "I told him I would go – I said they would arrest him if he went, but he wouldn't listen." It was getting late by the time they reached the comptroller's office and there was a long queue of people. The interview, with a junior functionary, did not go well and, exasperated by Altmann's arrogance, he ordered his arrest. "I turned around," said de Castro, "and there were two men on either side of him. I was furious, it was all so unnecessary."

Dr Urcullo, the sub-comptroller, took a different view: "People said afterwards that we had planned it with the French, but that was not the case. There was a warrant for his arrest for debt and we arrested him. I was quite upset by what happened later."

News of Barbie's arrest had apparently taken even the Bolivian government by surprise. As the Foreign Minister Mario Velarde left his office in La Paz that day, he was besieged by journalists demanding to know what the government intended to do with Barbie.

"Has Barbie been arrested?" asked Velarde. "What for?"

"Fraud," a journalist replied.

"If they start putting people in prison for fraud," responded Velarde, "half of Bolivia will be in gaol."

Barbie was taken to the familiar surroundings of the San Pedro gaol, but this visit was to be very different from his previous imprisonments. As soon as rumours of the arrest reached the German Embassy, the staff telephoned the Ministry of the Interior to ask if it was true. An official confirmed the news. What was more, he told a startled German diplomat, if nobody minded they planned to put him on a Lufthansa flight and expel him to Germany.

> They were proceeding from the assumption that he was German [recalled the diplomat]. After all, they reasoned, if his Bolivian papers were obtained under false pretences, he was not Altmann the Bolivian, but Barbie the German. I explained that if they expelled him, they would have to take him to Germany themselves. If they granted the extradition, then Germany would pick him up here. They had to think about that.

The Ministry of the Interior, where grasp of international protocol is hazy, listened to the German explanation of the problems of simply putting Barbie on a plane. "They didn't realise that the captain, for instance, could refuse to take him." The Germans telephoned the French Embassy with the news. "They didn't believe it," the diplomat recalled.

De Castro, meanwhile, grew suspicious. "They filmed him being taken to San Pedro," he said. "The French TV cameras were there. I visited him the first day and went home to call his daughter to tell her. She said she already knew – it had been on TV in Europe. I thought how was that possible? I realised it must all have been planned."

It is an accusation both the French and the Bolivians deny. "We had been waiting to make our next move," said a French diplomat in La Paz, "until after the Supreme Court judgment." Césaire, in fact, was only convinced that Barbie was, indeed, arrested when the comptroller-general, one of the ambassador's numerous friends, telephoned to inform him. But if the event was a surprise, its potential was clear. The Embassy immediately notified Paris and decided to try to keep Barbie in prison until the Supreme Court judgment.

A great deal of fast thinking had been set in motion by Barbie's arrest. Back in France, an ad hoc "Barbie group" was put together under the guidance of Jean Louis Blanco, secretary-general of the presidency. His team consisted of three men with a close interest in the affair – Claude Cheysson, Foreign Minister, Robert Badinter, Justice Minister, and Charles Hernu, Minister of Defence, whose role it was to provide both transport and security for Barbie's final flight. Two other men provided help and advice – Régis Debray, by then adviser to the presidency, and Antoine Blanca, friend of Prime Minister Pierre Mauroy and roving ambassador to Latin America.

Feelers were put out to a nervous German government in Bonn, and it quickly became apparent that Germany would find the return of Barbie deeply embarrassing. There were several considerations: a trial would probably arouse unpleasant counter-demonstrations from pro-Nazi groups which, in the middle of an electoral campaign, the government was anxious to avoid. The sentence was likely to be lighter in a German court than in a French one, and this risked upsetting French public opinion. Finally, the government was anxious to avoid a repetition of the Maidanek trial in 1975 when former inmates of the concentration camp were treated as liars or mentally ill by defence lawyers acting for the former camp guards.

In La Paz, as the Minister of the Interior, Mario Roncal, waited for Germany to confirm its willingness to receive Barbie, an embarrassed German Embassy was checking on alternative possibilities. They drew a blank. The Peruvians, who formally wanted him, made it clear they were not actually interested. Brazil refused to receive him. As the Germans and the French agreed, the only country which did show interest was France.

For the French, the challenge was to keep their real intentions sufficiently secret to prevent a counter move by Barbie's friends, while at the same time galvanising the chaotic Bolivian administration into action.

"The Bolivian cabinet voted unanimously for his expulsion the day after his arrest," claimed Mario Rueda Pena, Bolivia's information minister. "The alternatives were to try him here for conspiracy and organising the para-military, which would be difficult actually to prove, or expelling him for infringement of immigration regulations."

The cabinet may have been unanimous, as Rueda Pena claimed, but an agonising nine days were to pass before the decision could be implemented.

The French too had realised that expulsion was the best way of getting their man. "We realised that if we asked for extradition, the same thing would happen," said a French diplomat.

Expulsion, however, was a delicate matter to manage. In the wake of the outcry over the violation of Bolivian sovereignty which had followed the Italian DC10 affair, there was no question of a foreign aircraft picking him up. It would have to be a Bolivian plane which carried Barbie out of Bolivia – but Barbie's contacts in the air force were well known. The French opted for Guyana as the nearest French territory. Siles, anxious to improve Bolivia's image in the world and establish a moral credibility, which might incidentally help to plead Bolivia's case for urgently needed economic aid, was persuaded to listen to the French plan, but had grave doubts as to whether it could be successfully executed.

As Barbie was held incommunicado and denied visits from either his lawyer or his doctor, the formidable Raymond Césaire began to lobby support. While the Bolivians prevaricated, Césaire, in a massive diplomatic effort, lobbied nearly two hundred Bolivians, quietly establishing who, in the Bolivian military, could be counted on to cooperate without organising a counter move. Some thought was given to the preparation of Bolivian public opinion for what was in train.

"We were in the secret ten days before the expulsion," said the Israeli ambassador to La Paz. "They asked if we could contribute material which might help convince the public. We supplied some films on the holocaust which were shown on television a few days before he was expelled."

De Castro meanwhile was trying to get his master released.

As the weekend approached, the atmosphere in the French Embassy was electric. Siles had come under heavy criticism from both left and right. Jaime Paz Zamorra, his vice-president, said publicly that Barbie should be tried in Bolivia for crimes committed there.

In the Ministry of the Interior, they knew that was hopeless. "When the military left the Ministry of the Interior," said one official, "they removed every document, every scrap of paper; they even took the furniture." The right wing argued that Barbie was a Bolivian citizen who deserved the protection of the government. Barbie's lawyer and his friends were beginning to claim publicly that Siles was preparing to sell a Bolivian citizen. It was becoming increasingly embarrassing for Siles to keep Barbie in prison and everyone knew that, once released, the prize would slip from their grasp.

Early that week, the French acquired a new and determined ally when Gustavo Sanchez, a member of Siles's party and a leftist, was appointed sub-secretary of the Ministry of the Interior. Sanchez has a reputation in La Paz as a devious man, but his objectives as far as Barbie were concerned were clear. "I wanted him expelled," he said. For the French, the arrival of Sanchez was a relief. The minister, Mario Roncal, who seemed no more enthusiastic over Barbie's expulsion than he had been over Pagliai's, had infuriated the French by vanishing for long periods of time during the intense and urgent negotiations which followed Barbie's arrest.

It was imperative for the French to keep Barbie in prison until the night of Friday, February 4, when the expulsion was planned. It was equally imperative for Barbie's friends to get him out. Once again, the ambassador's friendship with the comptroller-general was called into service.

"I could write a novel about that time," said de Castro. "He was incommunicado from the second day, but I got in to see him. It's like that here. The place was full of press, trying to take pictures. I took him magazines and food."

Belatedly, on Thursday, February 3, de Castro and Barbie decided to settle the debt at the official exchange rate.

It came to 1,450,000 pesos. And there were no hundred peso notes available, only fifties. It was a suitcase full. They made me sit there and count it out, then they made me count it again. Finally it was paid, but then they said it wasn't enough, they wanted the interest.

Their whole attitude had changed. The normal procedure is that you pay the debt and if they want the interest, they make a new order and have to arrest you again.

De Castro's anxieties were sharpened by a telephone call that evening, the first definite leak of the government's intentions. One of de Castro's ubiquitous friends rang him from the television station.

"They have nominated a TV crew to travel with Klaus tomorrow," he told de Castro. "They're going to expel your friend."

"Never," de Castro protested.

"I'm telling you the truth, believe me."

Shaken, de Castro went to see Barbie early the next morning. He found him playing *chaca* – a local game, similar to checkers.

"I told him about it, but he didn't seem very worried," said de Castro. "So I said I would go and sort out the interest."

De Castro went to the comptroller's office to try to find out how much the interest payment was. Neither the comptroller nor his deputy was there.

"They weren't there, because I had them practically under arrest in the Ministry of the Interior," said Sanchez. "I knew that if Barbie's friends managed to pay the interest, we had no more excuse to hold him."

De Castro waited all afternoon. "They turned up after four o'clock – I finally found out how much it was at 4.25 – I knew the banks would be closing, but I ran there anyway. The bank was closed. I was desperate. I even rang a friend, a money changer, and asked if he could get the bank to open. He said I was crazy."

The interest was in fact paid later that day by Gustavo Sanchez. Barbie was handed over from San Pedro gaol into his custody in the Ministry of the Interior. Sanchez, determined to find some evidence with which to prosecute some of Barbie's collaborators, arranged a bizarre confrontation. He hoped to extract some confession of his crimes in Bolivia before Barbie left for ever.

Adolfo Ustárez had been arrested that Friday morning and Mario Mingola some days earlier.

"I arranged a little party for Barbie and his friends," said Sanchez, "and a film crew, just to see what they would say."

After a nervous greeting between Ustárez and Barbie, the three men sat in silence. Sanchez was working to a deadline – a Bolivian Hercules was due to fly into La Paz, collect Barbie and fly him out to Cayenne. He was also working under siege. Since the day of Barbie's arrest press interest in the case had grown dramatically. As the final hours approached, El Alto airport was thronged with journalists, trying to anticipate how the Bolivians would expel him.

"The scene was incredible," said a diplomat. "A Lufthansa flight was leaving that night and several journalists had bought tickets, thinking he would be on it. They had to check in, and at the last moment they realised that he wasn't going. They were all trying to get their money back."

Another group was encamped outside the Ministry of the Interior. In the late afternoon a man was taken out with a coat over his head and put in a car headed for the airport. Most of the press set off in hot pursuit. A few minutes later Klaus Barbie was brought out, also with a coat over his head, and accompanied by Sanchez and Rueda Pena. "He still thought he was going to Germany. I kept on questioning him all the way to the airport. I wanted to frighten him," said Sanchez.

"What do you think of death?" he asked Barbie as the car climbed the twisting road to the airport.

"Death is cruel," said Barbie.

"It is just as cruel for those you sent to die in Lyon," Sanchez retorted.

Barbie was taken, not to El Alto, but to the military airport of La Paz, where he was rushed on to the plane. Waiting on board were a group of French secret service men and, at the last minute, a Bolivian television crew, headed by Ugo Roncal, the brother of the Minister of the Interior. The Hercules rolled down the runway and took off into the night.

Inside the aircraft it was nearly dark. There were no seats, and Barbie sat on the floor. He was still shaken from his confrontation with Sanchez, and reluctant to talk to the television journalist except on his own terms. In the long conversation which followed, he refused to talk about his wartime career, pursuing instead a futile rehearsal of his legal rights.

"The past is the past," he protested, "I want to talk about the way I was kidnapped. I want to say this on TV to all the people of Bolivia. It is a kidnapping. I haven't seen a single document. How can you expel a Bolivian citizen? My nationality dates from twenty-five years ago and it was signed by the president, Hernan Siles Zuazo."

"Nevertheless," persisted the interviewer, "there is some doubt about your nationality, because you changed your name to come to Bolivia."

"I didn't change my name," said Barbie, "I didn't change anything. I took another name, like lots of other people . . . because one has a right to defend oneself . . ."

Conscious that what he said would be watched avidly in Bolivia, Barbie gave his version of the past thirty years.

"I had sympathy for the people of Bolivia," he said, "not for any government. I was always neutral. I was interested in working, in making a little progress. I wanted to do the country some good. Whatever I could bring, I brought."

"Do you think your life has reached its last phase?" Barbie was asked.

"I understand so. Just as my wife's life reached its final stage."

"Are you afraid of death?"

"No. I've never feared death and I do not fear it now . . ."

It was not until the plane landed at Cayenne, in the small hours of the morning, that Barbie knew he was bound, not for Germany but for France. Waiting at the foot of the steps was a group of Guyanese officials.

"You are in French territory," said one, "and there is a warrant for your arrest."

An hour later a French DC-8 took off, taking Barbie on the last leg of his journey, a journey which ended, with a touch of official vengeance, when he swept through the gates of Montluc prison in Lyon, the scene of his past brutalities.

"The past is buried," Barbie had protested on his way to Guyana.

From that moment, the past was again present.

CHAPTER SIXTEEN

The Last Defence

There is a sense in which Klaus Barbie is already "as good as dead". His active life ended when he was driven into the old prison at Montluc, and for a man who had been restlessly, ingeniously, sometimes diabolically active for seventy years, that was the end of life itself. Perhaps he was ready for it. With anything like his old energy, he could have broken out of the net that finally closed round him in Bolivia in 1983. But, especially after the death of his wife and son, his nervous vitality seemed to drain away. Suddenly he was tired and old, almost resigned, and he let himself be taken without much effort to elude the hunters. Men of Barbie's temperament do not survive well in the boredom and passivity of prison life. It may be that he will die before the trial begins, sparing a great many people in France a great deal of anxiety. And it may also be that this would not matter. Serge Klarsfeld has observed that he does not particularly care what happens to Klaus Barbie now, whether he is found guilty or acquitted or what his sentence may be. The point for Klarsfeld is that justice has at last reached Barbie, and that the doors of a prison have closed upon him because of what he did forty years ago in France. Nothing else is important.

He passes his days in the solid old St Joseph prison at Lyon, just round the corner from the Hotel Terminus where he had his first torture chamber. Barbie is held on the first floor of the high-security wing, in a tract of nine cells whose other occupants were transferred when he arrived. To protect him against the very remote chance of an attempt at either rescue or assassination, he is moved to a different cell each night, taking with him the same bed. He eats the ordinary prison food, once complaining, in his early months, that he wanted croissants for breakfast. He reads books and listens to a radio, and is permitted to watch television on request. Occasionally the monotony is broken by a visit from his lawyer, Maître Jacques Vergès, or from his daughter Ute Messner, who travels up from her home in the Austrian Tyrol. From time to time, he is confronted by a potential witness invited to identify him; sometimes this takes place in St Joseph, but sometimes – these must be memorable days for Barbie – he is taken in a convoy of police wagons with screaming sirens for a short journey through the Lyon traffic to Montluc. To see Barbie in the Montluc fortress, the scene of so many of his crimes, may, the investigating judge Christian Riss hopes, stimulate the memories of elderly witnesses.

A year after his capture, there was still no sign when the Barbie trial would take place. French law states that a trial must begin at any time between three months and two years after the end of the investigative hearings. Given the leisurely pace of the investigation, and the congestion of cases already investigated and waiting to come to court, this could place the trial anywhere in 1985 or even 1986. But if and when Barbie is finally tried, it should be before the Cour d'Assises, the highest criminal court, in the enormous neo-classical Palais de Justice which dominates the Lyon waterfront along the quays of the river Saône. There will be three judges, one of whom will be the president of the court, and a jury of twelve who are required to produce at least a two-thirds majority vote for a conviction. Selecting jurors in the city where Barbie is so well remembered and so hated will not be simple; the defence will probably object that some or all of them are prejudiced, and many Lyonnais suspect that Maître Vergès may demand the transfer of the whole hearing to Paris or some other town on the grounds that it is impossible for his client to get a fair trial in Lyon.

In France, a grand "historical" trial of this kind seems to attract two extremes of personality. One is the great defence lawyer who turns the court into a political theatre and – sometimes at the expense of his client's interests – insists on arraigning the Republic or the government of the day for having brought the case at all. Vergès is plainly in this tradition, a descendant of Tixier-Vignancour, the defender of the right-wing rebels against de Gaulle, and of Maurice Garçon who defended René Hardy. The other is the austere, utterly dedicated and professional seeker after truth and justice. Christian Riss, the juge d'instruction who has led the investigation against Barbie, will not appear in the trial but belongs to that second category. Though he is young – too young to remember the German occupation – Riss became committed to uncovering the truth about those years when he took up the reopened case of Paul Touvier, head of the Lyon Milice, who was pardoned by President Pompidou in 1971 and has since disappeared. When the Barbie case came up, Riss refused an offer of promotion to a more senior post in order to take on the investigation. He works carefully and without haste, anxious to preserve the fiction that the Barbie case is no more important than the other dossiers on his desk and to avoid raising suggestions of a "show trial" by giving it precedence.

Vergès is an entirely different creature. He took over Barbie's defence in June 1983 from Alain de la Servette, chairman of the Lyon bar, and the Jesuit lawyer Robert Boyer, after the archbishop of Lyon had criticised the involvement of Father Boyer as a priest. Son of a French father and a Vietnamese mother, Jacques Vergès at fifty-nine is the most spectacular and mysterious figure of the French bar. He joined the Communist party just after the liberation, then left it during the Algerian war; his politics today are those of an independent revolutionary Marxism whose immediate aim is to challenge the "bourgeois state" and expose its hypocrisies. Vergès made his name as a defender of Algerian freedom fighters during the 1950s, and was for a time married to the Algerian heroine of the revolution, Djemila Bouhired, whose life he saved in court. Later he went through a pro-Chinese enthusiasm at the time of the Cultural Revolution, and edited in Paris a distinctly Maoist review called *Révolution*; it was Vergès, as editor, who sent the young student Régis Debray to Bolivia to find Ché Guevara and his guerrillas. (Debray is now an adviser to President Mitterand, while Vergès remains an unreconstructed survivor of the "spirit of 1968". Relations between them are distant these days.) In 1970, however, Jacques Vergès vanished for no less than eight years. He has never offered an explanation, and rumours suggest he was involved for part of that time in training Palestinian guerrillas in the Lebanon. His only remark upon his return was: "I have come back battle-hardened – note that word, it's the right one – and optimistic." After his reappearance, Vergès concentrated on defending the accused in terrorism trials, both of the right and the left, from Palestinians and associates of the Baader-Meinhof group to Klaus Barbie.

It is already many years since Vergès produced his theory of "defence by rupture" as opposed to "defence by connivance". A Vergès client must refuse to accept the legal procedures and rules imposed on him and challenge the entire "system" which has placed him on trial. In the Barbie case, Vergès intends in the first place not merely to demolish the charges against him but to break up the trial itself and the law under which it takes place as violations of the normal rules of justice. The second part of his "defence by rupture" will be to usurp the role of prosecutor for himself, and to turn the courtroom into the trial of the French bourgeois state by exposing its collaboration with Fascism in the past and accusing it of crimes against liberation fighters in Vietnam and Algeria which are even more atrocious than those laid to Barbie's account. That he as a left-winger is using a Nazi torturer as a weapon against his own enemies troubles Vergès not in the slightest.

In attacking the charges and the legal basis of the trial, Vergès has some powerful ammunition. Barbie is accused on eight charges of "crimes against humanity", an offence which did not exist in French law when the alleged crimes were committed. It dates back only to 1964, when the French National Assembly discovered that, as all crimes under French law fell under a twenty-year time bar or "prescription", the prosecution of Nazi war criminals would become impossible after 1965. The new category of "crimes against humanity" was therefore invented, on the model of the post-war Nuremburg indictment, which was not to be subject to prescription. This, of course, is "retroactive justice", a principle which all good jurists feel uneasy about.

For Barbie the new law means that he cannot be accused of individual crimes against members of the Resistance – including Jean Moulin – although he was twice sentenced to death *in absentia* by French courts, in 1952 and 1954, for torturing and murdering Résistants. Crimes against humanity, as the Lyon prosecutor defined them in 1983, "relate to massacres, murders and deportations inflicted upon civilian populations during the war and the occupation, such as genocide and the taking of hostages".

The charges brought by the prosecution are:

The arrest and murder of a district police officer and the massacre (at the École de Santé) of twenty-two hostages, including women and children, in 1944;

the arrest and torture of nineteen persons at Lyon in the summer of 1943;

"the liquidation of the Lyon Committee of the General Union of French Jews, at the end of which, following a raid on February 9 1943 on the offices of this organisation, eighty-six persons were deported";

the shooting of forty-two persons of whom forty were Jews at Lyon and nearby in 1943 and 1944;

a raid on the railway workshop at Oullins in August 1944 in the course of which two people were killed and several wounded;

"the deportation to Auschwitz and Ravensbruck concentration camps of some six hundred and fifty persons, of whom half were

Jews, by the last rail transport leaving Lyon on August 11 1944";

the shooting of seventy Jews at Bron on August 17 1944, and of other Jews and two priests on August 20 that year at St-Genis-Laval;

"the deportation of fifty-five Jews, of whom fifty-two were children, at Izieu in the Ain".

The definition of some of these charges as "crimes against humanity" may well collapse in court. François de Menthon, a leading French jurist, has provided a much more vivid summary of the problem than the Lyon prosecutor: "If a woman is arrested and tried by the authorities for acts of resistance, that is a legitimate procedure; if the authorities apply torture to her under interrogation, that is a war crime; if they deport her to an extermination camp or use her for medical experiments, that is a crime against humanity." Alain de la Servette, Barbie's first defence laywer, suggested that the fifth charge, the raid on the railway workshops, should be considered a war crime and struck off the indictment "if the investigation establishes that Barbie and his men acted that day in consequence of a denunciation informing them that a Resistance cell existed there".

Under French law, private individuals and groups can add their own accusations to those of the state, their lawyers acting alongside the state prosecutor. But at the Barbie trial, these "partis civiles", or private prosecutions, will for the most part try to add their own evidence to the state indictment without bringing additional charges. Some, like Itta Halaunbrenner and Simone Lagrange, are acting as individuals. But the great bulk of the "partis civiles", which may number over a hundred by the time the case comes to court, are associations of old Resistance members, of victims of Nazism or of French Jews, and here Vergès will certainly find another target. Most of these groups did not exist at the time that Barbie was operating in France. Vergès can therefore argue that they cannot possibly pose as injured parties, and should be thrown out of court.

Nailing down Barbie's guilt on the existing eight charges may be exceedingly difficult. A man or woman can find it hard enough to identify the officer who once tortured them, forty years after the crime. It is even harder for the survivor of a group of deportees, or for witnesses to a massacre, to pin down the man responsible for the action, especially given the casual and often chaotic way in which the Gestapo and the SS chain of command worked in Lyon.

There can be little doubt of Barbie's general involvement in most of these crimes. To prove that he was in direct command or issued the orders is another matter.

This is true even of the final and best-known charge, the tragedy of the Jewish children of Izieu. There are essentially two pieces of evidence against Barbie. The first is his identification by Julien Favet, now an old man, who on his own testimony saw Barbie only once for a few minutes while the children were being loaded into the trucks and was not told his name at the time. The second is the famous telex message to Paris, bearing Barbie's signature and reporting that the children's home had been emptied and that its inhabitants would be deported to the transit camp at Drancy, the last stop on the way to the gas chambers at Auschwitz. On the face of it, this telex dated April 6 1944 is damning proof that Barbie was in command of the operation. But closer inspection shows ambiguities which a clever lawyer like Vergès could exploit. The cable's full signature runs, in the abbreviated German bureaucratic jargon:

DER KDR DER SIPO UND DES SD LYON ROEM 4 B I.A. GEZ. BARBIE. SS-OSTUF.

Deciphered, this reads: "The commander of the Sicherheitspolizei and SD Lyon, Roman numeral IV B. Signed as representative (im Auftrage) Barbie, SS Obersturmführer." This probably means that Barbie commanded the operation as leader of section IV/B, under the general authority of the commander of the German security police at Lyon. It could, however, be argued that Barbie had put his name to the telex report on behalf of somebody quite different who was commanding IV/B but was not available to send the message at the time. Vergès may also try to show that Barbie, engaged on a hectic succession of operations up-country in those April days, was not in Lyon on April 6, but the possibility that he dictated the message to the Lyon office by telephone can hardly affect his guilt or innocence.

All that we know of Barbie's own attitude to the charges comes from an account of his first interrogation by Christian Riss, the investigating judge, which was leaked to the Lyon newspapers in March 1983. He claimed then that he was only the third man in the hierarchy of German security dealing with "enemies of the state", and that he had never tortured anyone. "Among my subordinates, there were SS men of Croat or Yugoslav origin wearing the cap with the death's-head badge. Some of them may have used torture." Barbie denied that he had taken any part in the clearing of the children's home at Izieu, and dismissed the witness Julien Favet as "a liar".

In the end, Barbie has few grounds either for hope or fear from the outcome of the trial. The death penalty is no longer applied in France. But in the unlikely event that he is acquitted, the Munich courts will immediately apply for his extradition to face trial in West Germany; they intend to try him not for "crimes against humanity" but – as Nazi "war crimes" are not time-barred in the Federal Republic – on the single charge of having murdered the Resistance leader Joseph Kemmler at St Claude in February 1944. Whatever remains of his life, Klaus Barbie seems certain to spend it in prison cells.

Not everyone would agree: Barbie's friends in La Paz still dream of ways to free him. Alvaro de Castro, his old bodyguard, claims that he has been involved in plans to kidnap Régis Debray as a hostage for Barbie's release and then, when Debray did not carry out an expected visit to Bolivia, to seize the French Ambassador instead. But there is little evidence to suggest that these plots advanced beyond mere café-table fantasy.

In France, there are those – like Christian Riss – who ask of the Barbie trial only that it should do justice, despite its disquieting foundation on "retroactive" law. But there are many more who demand that the trial should serve as a national lesson in history. The Klarsfelds have shown something of both motives. Serge Klarsfeld has suggested that it is enough for him that Barbie is now being punished, that the vengeance owed to the memory of the dead is being exacted. But he has also spoken of the importance of teaching France and the world, in a way they cannot forget, about the fate of the French Jews under the Nazis and the Vichy regime, and he intends to act as the lawyer for two of the "partis civiles", Itta Halaunbrenner and Simone Lagrange, at the trial. The Resistance historian Henri Noguères, in contrast, hopes for a quite different lesson about the past. "For me, the trial will have considerable importance if it allows the Jean Moulin affair to be cleared up, with the circumstances of the treason to which he fell victim."

This is an odd expectation, given that the indictment has nothing whatever to do with the fate of Jean Moulin and specifically excludes "war crimes" committed against members of the Resistance. But with Jacques Vergès as the defender, Noguères in fact has good grounds to be interested. It is Vergès, more than anyone else, who intends to transform the trial into a history lesson in which the Vichy regime will be presented as only one episode in a long tale of French imperialism and repression, and he fully intends to drag the Moulin affair into the courtroom. Vergès has already proclaimed, to the outrage and derision of most of France, that he can prove that Jean Moulin was sold to the Germans by other Resistance leaders, as part of a plot to remove him as a left-wing challenger to their own control of the movement, and that Moulin committed suicide in Montluc out of sheer despair over the treachery of his colleagues. The whole indictment, he will say, is a scandalous cover-up organised by the French bourgeoisie to conceal their own intimate relationship with Fascism. This would be "defence by rupture" indeed.

About the political reverberations of the Barbie trial, an enormous balloon of expectation has been puffed up in France. Some of the puffing has been done by Barbie himself, who at times in Bolivia would tell his cronies that the French would never dare to put him in court: his revelations about the cowardice of the Resistance and the treachery of prominent Frenchmen would tear the nation to ribbons. Most of the inflating, however, has been achieved by French journalists and politicians themselves. It is said that Barbie from the witness stand will recite compendious lists of collaborators now in high positions, or that he will expose the French Communist party for some secret deal with the Third Reich, or that he will explode for ever the heroic myth of the Resistance. Barbie's testimony, some speculate, will devastate French political life, perhaps rendering the leaders of the right open to prosecution for crimes against humanity, perhaps shattering the precarious left-wing coalition of Socialists and Communists which supports President François Mitterand. Maître Vergès is apparently seeking to delay the trial until 1986, for no other reason than that parliamentary elections are due that year.

But this is really a balloon full of flatulence. In the first place, Barbie's knowledge of wartime France was quite limited. An SS captain heading a counter-guerrilla squad in one provincial city was not likely to know the inner secrets of the German military or SS commanders in Paris; an officer as junior and as frantically busy as Obersturmführer Barbie had neither opportunity nor time to share the knowledge which men like Oberg and Knochen had accumulated. He would have had still less access to the complex politics of Vichy, or to the facts about the subtle balance of collaboration and disobedience which varied from one French city and region to another. Barbie probably knows some unpleasant facts about who denounced whom in Lyon and the surrounding region, but the political consequences will be trivial now. Moreover,

Barbie at seventy-two was already showing signs of forgetting names.

Secondly, almost all the French generation which encountered Barbie has left the political and professional scene. With a very few exceptions, his French contemporaries are dead or retired. It is just possible that Barbie's testimony could get one or two ancient police superintendents hauled out of their country villas to stand trial for helping to deport Jews, or shatter the reputation of a half-forgotten prefect. By French standards, this is not a high political score.

And yet there is something authentic about the interest which the case arouses in France, which is more than the chronic hankering for a political scandal. For a full generation after the liberation, France was ruled by those who emerged bearing the credentials of the Resistance, whether they were politicians of the Fourth Republic or servants of the Gaullist regime which followed it in 1958. The "true France", so the dominant version of history ran, had resisted; Vichy and the collaborators were presented officially as a handful of senile reactionaries supported by an eccentric minority of native Fascists. This historical consensus was broadly upheld not only by the centre and moderate right in politics but to a considerable extent by the Communist party as well. The idea that Vichy had been a genuine and quite widely-supported expression of the conservative tradition in France was repressed.

After the upheaval of May 1968 especially, this consensus began to disintegrate. Not only young neo-conservatives but a new generation of the left disillusioned both with the Communist party and the Socialists – neither of which had wholeheartedly opposed the disastrous colonial war in Algeria, with its accompaniment of torture and atrocity – demanded a new interpretation of history. They were assisted by the astonishing revival of the Jewish community in France, soon to become not only the largest but far the most militant and confident centre of the Diaspora in Europe, which insisted on bringing to light the role played by Vichy, the police, and to a considerable extent the French public in the deportation and murder of the French Jews.

Today, France's post-war efforts to deal with the consequences of Vichy seem at once half-hearted and one-sided. In southern and central France, the Maquis took the opportunity to kill off many local collaborators and political opponents. In Paris, some of the leading Vichy politicians and journalists were tried and shot; Pétain died in prison. But almost all the prosecutions dealt either with treachery to the French state or with crimes committed against the Resistance; the fate of the Jews counted for little. Barbie's two condemnations *in absentia* were on charges unconnected with the Jewish deportations. Darquier de Pellepoix, who had been Commissioner for Jewish Affairs until 1944, was condemned to death in his absence in 1947 for "espionage for a foreign power", rather than for the deportation of seventy-five thousand Jews. He died peacefully in Spain in 1980, and there was so little French interest in him that his passing was not reported for some two and a half years. René Bousquet, secretary-general of the police under Vichy, who had helped to organise the deportations and, on Laval's orders, had offered to deliver the stateless Jews in the zone libre to the Germans, became after the war a director of the Banque de l'Indochine and of the UTA airline. Jean Leguay, his subordinate in the "occupied zone", became a director of perfume firms, including Nina Ricci.

But this indifference is now being broken down. The Klarsfelds forced the West German authorities in 1980 to bring to trial and convict Kurt Lischka, Ernst Heinrichsohn and Herbert Hagen, all senior SS officers in France, for their part in the deportation of Jews. Through the pressure of "partis civiles", Christian Riss had reopened the dossier against the Lyon Milice leader Paul Touvier. Leguay is now to stand trial for crimes against humanity, and similar charges have now been brought against Maurice Papon. In terms of French politics, this is a much more sensational affair than the Barbie case. Papon, aged seventy-three, accused of assisting the arrest and deportation of Jews while he was secretary-general of the Bordeaux prefecture, went on to become prefect of police in Paris from 1958 to 1966 and ultimately budget minister in the cabinet of President Valéry Giscard d'Estaing from 1978 to 1981. If the Papon charges are proved, they would indeed be a shattering demonstration of the hypocrisy of post-war and even recent French governments, and of their inclination to cover up the most embarrassing realities of the Occupation. Serge Klarsfeld, once again, is representing "partis civiles" in the Papon case, and it is not surprising that Jacques Vergès has demanded that the Papon trial should be completed before Klaus Barbie comes to court.

How great a criminal was Barbie? We will probably never know. Much of the truth about what he did in France, Holland, Bolivia and Peru can be found in this book. Yet this may be only a part of what he has on his conscience, perhaps even a minor part. There is, for example, a suspicious blank in the last months of the war, in the spring of 1945, when Barbie joined the disintegrating German armies in the Ruhr. He has said, in one of his highly unreliable interviews with journalists, that he was in some unit charged with "special duties"; this was a period in which the SS was indiscriminately murdering deserters and slaughtering the inmates of prisons in cities like Düsseldorf or Essen in the last days before the American tanks arrived. Barbie may well have taken part in these executions.

Even more sinister was his claim, made in 1979 to the German journalist Gerd Heidemann, that he had been seconded to "anti-partisan" duties in Russia between July 1941 and early 1942. Although Heidemann was to go to gaol in West Germany in 1983 for his part in the forging of the so-called "Hitler Diaries", there is no reason to suppose that he doctored this tape-recording and – as we have mentioned in Chapter 2 (page 53) – there is negative evidence to suggest that Barbie was absent from Holland in that period. But if he had indeed been posted to such tasks in the Soviet Union, as an SD officer Barbie would have been attached to one of the four Einsatzgruppen.

The work of the Einsatzgruppen operating in Russia, the Ukraine and the Baltic republics behind the advancing German armies forms one of the most monstrous crimes in human history. Their written instructions from Heydrich, as chief of the SD, were to execute all Communist and Comintern officials, all opposition elements from partisans to agitators, and all "Jews in the service of party or state". To this was added the verbal instruction to exterminate the entire Jewish population in the conquered regions. This was the first stage in the "final solution".

By the end of November 1942 the Einsatzgruppen had accounted for well over a million Jews. Day after day, relays of SS and police troops lined up rows of naked men, women and children on the edge of wide trenches and shot them down, to fall on the corpses of the previous batch of victims. When a trench was full, it was covered in, often before all the sufferers were dead, and a new one was excavated. Heinrich Himmler once nerved himself to stand on the lip of such a trench and watch the process. After a few minutes his knees buckled and he made to turn away. It was SS General Karl Wolff, his adjutant and one of the men we interviewed for this book, who grasped the Reichsführer by the elbow and forced him to see the operation through. If Barbie really was in the Soviet Union, that is what he did.

Even on what is known for certain about his career, in Europe and South America, there is no defence for Barbie. And yet, although he cannot be defended or excused, there is one more thing to be said which only he or his lawyer can say. These chapters have shown, above all, that Klaus Barbie was a faithful servant, a useful henchman, a true handyman of our times. He is entitled to stand up in the French courtroom and to say to the world: "You all needed me, dictators and democrats, Germans, Americans and Bolivians. You all paid me for my services and were grateful for them in your time. Why, then, am I standing here alone?"

PRINCIPAL CHARACTERS IN SOUTH AMERICA

Major Roberto D'Aubuisson, extreme right wing Salvadoran politician.

Col. Luis Arce Gómez, drugs trafficker. Minister of the Interior of Bolivia July 1980–February 1981.

Luis Banchero Rossi, Peruvian fishmeal magnate. Murdered January 1st 1972.

Gen. Hugo Banzer, President of Bolivia 1971–1978.

Gen. René Barrientos, President of Bolivia November 1964–April 1969.

Alvaro de Castro, arms dealer, friend and bodyguard of Klaus Barbie.

Col. Juan Manuel Contreras, Head of Chilean secret police, DINA 1973–1977.

Orlando Letelier, Chilean ambassador to the USA, 1971, Minister of Defence August–September 1973. Assassinated in Washington, September 1976.

Gen. Luis García Meza Tejada, President of Bolivia July 1980–August 1981.

Gen. Alfredo Ovando Candia, President of Bolivia 1969–1970.

Gen. Augusto Pinochet, President of Chile since the military coup of 1973.

Mario Roncal, Minister of the Interior under Siles Zuazo.

Dr Santos Chichizola, Peruvian lawyer. Investigating judge on Banchero Rossi case.

Hernan Siles Zuazo, President of Bolivia 1956–1960, 1982–.

Roberto Suarez, major Bolivian cocaine producer and dealer.

Dr Adolfo Ustárez, Bolivian lawyer. Friend of Klaus Barbie. Comptroller of the Republic under García Meza regime.

GLOSSARY

AAA	Argentine Anticommunist Alliance; right-wing death squad
AIP	news agency financed by DINA (q.v.)
Allgemeine SS	general branch of SS
Amt	department in German bureaucracy; eg. Amt II/2 = department 2, section 2
APC	armoured personnel carrier
C-130	Hercules military aircraft of US manufacture
CBS	US television network
CEDADE	Spanish neo-Fascist organisation
CIA	US Central Intelligence Agency
CIC	US Counter Intelligence Corps
CNR	Conseil National de la Résistance
COB	Central Obrero Boliviano; Bolivian trade union confederation
COMIBOL	Bolivian state mining corporation
Condor	organisation for mutual aid between right-wing regimes in Latin America
CROWCASS	Central Registry of War Criminals and Security Suspects
DINA	Chilean state security service
DPs	displaced persons
ECIC	European Command Interrogation Center (US forces in Germany)
ELN	Peruvian left-wing guerrilla group
ERN	Bolivian left-wing guerrilla group
ETA	Basque separatist movement
EUCOM	US Military Command in Europe
G-2	senior intelligence officer attached to a major US military headquarters
Gestapo	German combined criminal and political police
HICOG	Office of the US High Commissioner in Germany
KPD	German Communist Party

Kripo	Kriminalpolizei, or criminal police, later integrated into Gestapo
MNAT	Mouvement National anti-Terroriste
MNR	Movimiento Nacional Revolucionario – populist Bolivian political party
MSI	Italian neo-Fascist party
Nazi; NSDAP	German National Socialist party
NCO	non-commissioned officer
NSB	Dutch Nazi movement
OAS	French Secret Army Organisation
ODESSA	Organisation der ehemaligen SS-Angehörigen; alleged Nazi post-war underground
OMGUS	Office of the Military Governor, US zone
OSI	Office of Special Investigations
OSS	Office of Strategic Services – US intelligence agency in World War Two
PIP	Peruvian Intelligence Police
PPF	Fascist party in wartime France
PX	US army rations department
RSHA	Reichssicherheitshauptamt
S-3	Operations officer in US Counter Intelligence Corps
SA	Sturmabteilung, stormtroopers
SD	Sicherheitsdienst, secret service of SS
SED	East German Communist party
SHAEF	Allied high command in the West at the end of World War Two
SID	Servizio Informazione Difesa, Italian secret service agency
Sipo; Sipo/SD	Sicherheitspolizei; security police
SOE	British Special Operations Executive
SS	Schutzstaffel
SSU	A forerunner of the OSS (q.v.)
STO	Service de Travail Obligatoire
UDBA	Tito's secret police
UGIF	Union Générale des Israelites de France
Ustasa/Ustase	Croatian terrorist organisation (Ustasa when used as adjective, Ustase as noun)
V-Mann	Vertrauensmann, informer and spy
VIP	persons accorded high priority
Waffen-SS	formerly the Politische Bereitschaften; expanded

	in wartime into regular divisions operating alongside the army
WDD	War Department Detachment, an early cover-name for the embryo CIA

BIBLIOGRAPHY

Barbie's early life and career in Germany

Books (selection)

Christoffel, Edgar, *Der Weg Durch die Nacht*, Trier, 1983.
Deschner, Günther, *Heydrich*, London, 1981.
Höhne, Heinz, *Order of the Death's Head*, London, 1969.
Krausnick, Helmut, and others, *Anatomy of the SS State*, London, 1968.
Schnabel, Reimund, *Macht ohne Moral*, Munich, 1957.
Springer, Max, *Loslösungsbestrebungen am Rhein, 1918–24*, Berlin, 1924.
Zenz, Emil, *Die Stadt Trier im 20. Jahrhundert*, Trier, 1981.

Archive sources

The Wiener Library, London; Berlin Document Center; Institut für Zeitgeschichte, Munich; Bundesarchiv, Koblenz; Stadtbibliothek, Trier; Karl-Marx-Haus, Trier; Stadtarchiv, Düsseldorf; Hauptstaatsarchiv, Düsseldorf; Stadtarchiv, Dortmund; Nordrhein-Westfälisches Staatsarchiv, Münster; newspaper archive of the Trierer Volksfreund, Trier; Stadtbibliothek, Koblenz.

Barbie in Holland

Kwiet, Konrad, *Reichskommissariat Niederlande*, Munich, 1968.
Knoop, Hans, *De Joodsche Raad*, Amsterdam, 1983.
Presser, J., *Ashes in the Wind*, London, 1968.
Stegman, H. and J. P. Vorsteveld, *Het Joodse werkdorp in de Wieringermeer*, Zutphen, 1983.

Barbie in France

Books (selection)

Amoretti, Henri, *Lyon Capitale*, Paris, 1964.
Amouroux, Henri, *L'Impitoyable Guerre Civile*, Paris, 1975.
Bourdet, Claude, *L'Aventure Incertaine*, Paris, 1975.
Bower, Tom, *Klaus Barbie, Butcher of Lyon*, London, 1984.
Calef, Henri, *Jean Moulin*, Paris, 1980.
Cobb, Richard, *French and Germans and Germans and French*, London, 1983.
Cole, Hubert, *Laval*, London, 1963.
Colly, Marcel, *Deux Semaines à Montluc*, Lyon, 1945.
De Bayac, Jacques, *Histoire de la Milice*, Paris, 1969.
De Bénouville, Guillain, *Le Sacrifice du Matin*, Paris, 1946.
De Gaulle, Charles, *Mémoires de Guerre*, Paris, 1973.
Delarue, Jacques, *Histoire de la Gestapo*, Paris, 1962.
Dreyfus, Paul, *Histoires Extraordinaires de la Résistance*, Paris, 1977.
Frenay, Henri, *La Nuit Finira*, Paris, 1973.
Fuchs, Gottlieb, *Le Renard*, Paris, 1973.
Harzer, Philippe, *Barbie et la Gestapo en France*, Paris, 1983.
Klarsfeld, Serge, *Vichy – Auschwitz*, Paris, 1983.
Marrus, Michel and Robert Paxton, *Vichy France and the Jews*, New York, 1981.
Mazel, Prof. Pierre, *La Mémoriale de l'Oppression*, Lyon, 1945.
Michel, Henri, *Jean Moulin L'Unificateur*, Paris, 1964.
Moulin, Laure, *Jean Moulin*, Paris, 1982.
Murphy, Brendan, *The Butcher of Lyon*, New York, 1983.
Noguères, Henri, with M. Degliame, *Histoire de la Résistance en France, 1940–1945*, Paris, 1976.
Pineau, Christian, *La Simple Vérité*, Paris, 1960.
Pryce-Jones, David, *Paris in the Third Reich*, London, 1981.
Rings, Werner, *Life with the Enemy*, London, 1982.
Ruby, Marcel, *La Résistance à Lyon* and *La Contre Résistance à Lyon*, Paris, 1981.
Ruby, Marcel, *Klaus Barbie de Montluc à Montluc*, Lyon, 1983.
Schoenbrun, David, *Soldiers of the Night*, New York, 1980.
Vistel, Alban, *La Nuit Sans Ombre*, Paris, 1970.

Archives and Sources

Archives of the Centre de Documentation Juive Contemporaine in Paris; Post-war depositions of: Francis André, Ernst Floreck, Ludwig Heinson, Lucien Guesdon, Lucien Doussot, Müller-Kulenkampf, Georges Delaye, Charles Perrin, Pierre Vincent, Eugene Delormé, Germaine Clément, Marie Prost, Gaston Muray, Lucie Aubrac, Antoine Chardon (Supt. of Judicial Police, Lyon).

Barbie's post-war career in Germany and escape

Books (selection)

Alexander, Stella, *Church and State in Yugoslavia*, Cambridge, 1979.
Bower, Tom, *Blind Eye to Murder*, London, 1983.
Höhne, Heinz and Hermann Zolling, *Network*, London, 1972.
Maclean, Fitzroy, *Disputed Barricades*, London, 1957.
Smith, Bradley, *The Shadow Warriors*, London, 1983.

Archive Sources

Zentralstelle der Landesjustizverwaltungen, Ludwigsburg; Zentralrat der Juden in Deutschland, Düsseldorf; Newspaper archives of *Augsburger Zeitung, Frankfurter Rundschau, Hessische Nachrichten*, Kassel; Staatsanwaltschaft, Munich.

The Neo-Fascists

Books (selection)

Evola, Julius, *Gli Uomini e le Rovine*, Italy, 1972.
Flamini, Gianni, *Il Partito del Golpe*, Italy, 1981.
Graziani, Clemente, *Processo a Ordine Nuovo Processo alle Idee*, Italy, 1973.
Paolucci, Ibio, *Il Processo Infame*, Italy, 1977.
Papuzzi, Alberto, *Il Provocatore*, Italy, 1976.
Pesenti, Roberto and Marco Sassano, *Fiasconaro e Alessandrini Accusano*, Italy, 1974.
Rognoni, Carlo (Ed.), *L'Italia della P2*, Italy, 1981.
Rosenbaum, Petra, *Il Nuovo Fascismo*, Italy, 1975.

BIBLIOGRAPHY

Archive sources

Franco Ferraresi's La Cultura della Destra Eversiva (Paper 83); Rosario Ninna's Per Una Storia del Terrorismo di Destra (Paper 83); Luciano Violante's Politica della Sicurezza, Relazioni Internazionali e Terrorismo (Paper 83); Lettera Aperta ai Militanti di Ordine Nuovo 73; Corte d'Assise di Roma Sentenza 14.7.78 (Golpe Borghese); Corte d'Assise di Firenze Sentenza (Omicidio Occorsio) 78; Tribunale di Roma Sentenza (Processo Contro Ordine Nuovo) 21.11.73.

Barbie and Neo-Fascists in Latin America

Books (selection)

Aspiazu, Rene Bascope, *La Veta Blanca*, La Paz, 1982.
Branch, Taylor, and Eugene Propper, *Labyrinth*, New York, 1982.
Christie, Stuart, *Stefano delle Chiaie, Portrait of a Black Terrorist*, London, 1984.
Dinges, John and Saul Landau, *Assassination on Embassy Row*, New York, 1980.
Domic, Marcos, *Ideologia y Mito*, Cochabamba, 1978.
Dunkerley, James, *Bolivia, Coup d'État*, London, 1980.
Kruger, Henrik, *The Great Heroin Coup*, London, 1980.
Laurent, Frederic, *L'Orchestre Noir*, Paris, 1978.
Narcotrafico y Politica, Ed. Iepala, Madrid, 1982.
Orellana, Amado Canelas, *Bolivia*, Coca Cocaina, Cochabamba, 1982.

Documents and Archives

US Justice Department Report on Klaus Barbie and his links with US Intelligence, and source documents, 1983; various US Army intelligence documents obtained under Freedom of Information Act on Barbie, Schwend, Draganovic, Merk, Rivez etc; CIA documents obtained under Freedom of Information Act; US Federal Records Center, Suitland, Maryland; National Archives, Washington.

INDEX

AAA 211, 278
Abwehr 36, 57–8
Acker *see* "Mouse"
Adam, Charles 63–4
Adenauer, Chancellor Konrad 25
Ägidienberg battle 26
Aginterpress agency 206, 212
AIP agency 278
Albrecht, Bertie 69–70, 77
Alexander, Alfredo 229
Algeria 205–6, 329
Alipasin Most camp (Yugoslavia) 188
Allende, Pres. Salvador 212, 262
Alsace-Lorraine 25, 55–6
Altamirano, Carlos 213
Altmann, Rabbi Adolf **23–4**, 37, 44, 45, 191
Altmann, Klaus *etc see* Barbie
Amsterdam 45–54
André, Francis 108, 110–11, 115, 116
Angeli, Alexandre 109
Anti-Defamation League 236
Aqui newspaper 283
Arce Gómez, Col. Luis 274–7, 281, 283, 284, 312
  coup 285
  drug industry 289–95
  resigns 297
Argentina 198, 217, 304
  delle Chiaie 278–82
  "dirty war" 18, 270, 278, 280
  KB 192, 194, 215
Assistenza Pontifica 189
Astier de la Vigerie, Emmanuel d' 68, 69
Atala, Sonia 293
Aubrac, Lucie 89, 102
Aubrac, Raymond 74, 87–9, 98–9, 102
Aubry, Henri ("Thomas") 78, 86–90, 94

Aubuisson, Maj. Roberto D' 279, 288
Augsburg, Dr Emil 147, 151, 162, 166–7
Augsburg (W. Germany) 162–70, 173–5, 183, 191–3
Auschwitz camp 16, 124, 251, 260
  Altmann 23
  Dutch Jews 45, 54
  French Jews 108, 109, 112, 114, 324–6
Austria 41, 138, 183–6, 190
Avanguardia Nazionale 205, 207, 208, 210
Ayers, Capt. William 226–7

Badinter, Robert 315
Banchero Rossi, Luis 252–5, 265
Banzer, Pres. Hugo 272, 274, 280, 294
  coup 247–8, 249
  KB 258–9, 261, 264, 310
Barbie, Anna (*née* Hees) (mother of KB) 25–8, 30, 40, 43, 137; cares for Ute 143; says goodbye to KB 193; visited by family 224
Barbie, Françoise (*née* Croisset) (wife of Klaus-Jörg) 232, 296
Barbie, Klaus (*alias* Altmann) ('KB') **16–19, 330–32**; childhood 24–9; high school 27–33, 34–5; Hitler Youth 30–32, 38; Deutsche Jungfolk 32–3; adjutant to Horrmann 33; recruited by SD 33, 38; Labour Service 33; police work prewar 38–43; army (*1938*) 41, (*1945*) 130–32, (*1942*) 53–4, 330–31; marriage 41–2, 44; Dortmund 43–4; Holland **44–54**; Russia 53–4, 330–31; France 58, **60–131**; children born 53, 98, 142–3; underground Germany

342

postwar **130–193**; recruited by
CIC **133**; imprisoned *by
Americans* 139, 141–2, 154–61, *by
British* 141–2; Marburg
University 139; emigration 190–
96, 215; "Altmann" pseudonym
adopted 23–4, 191; Spain 203;
Bolivia 212, **215–319**;
Argentina 215; wood business
220; Bolivian nationality **222**, 250,
258, 314, 317, 319; assists
Bolivian government 225, 248,
266–312; Transmaritima 225–
30; in Europe 227; arms-dealing
228–30, 237–8; with Schwend
237–57; Peru 242–57;
imprisoned *in Bolivia* 259–60,
264, 314–17; García Meza coup
275–87; expelled from Bolivia
15–16, 310–20; projected trial
322–32
Barbie (Altmann), Klaus-Jörg
(Klaus) (Jorge) (son of KB)
born 142–3, 263; baby 169–70;
emigrates 193–4, 215; visits
Germany 224; Transmaritima
227; student in Spain 227, 296;
marries 232; killed 295–6
Barbie, Kurt (brother of KB) 27, 32
Barbie, Nikolaus (father of KB) 25–
8, 32
Barbie (Altmann), Regine (*née*
Willms/Wilhelms) (wife of KB)
43, 97, 137, 162, 243; marriage
39–42; *and* Andrée 169–70;
emigration 193–4, 215; Bolivian
Indians 220; visits Germany
224; death of son 295–6; dies,
310, 311
Barbie (Altmann), Ute Regina (Ute
Maria) (*later* Messner)
(daughter of KB) 137, 143, 162,
311; born 53, 263; emigrates 193–
4, 215; visits Germany 224, 233,
239; capture of KB 314–15, 321
Barkhausen, Kurt 139, 142
Barrientos, Pres. René 224–7, 229,
230, 233
  Ché Guevara 231
Bartelmus, Erich 108, 115, 129
Barthelet, Superintendent 79–80

Basque separatists *see* ETA
Bastien, Lydie 85, 89–90
Bechtold, Herbert 165, 167, 168, 174,
176, 183
Becker, Fridolin 144
Belgium 44
Berlin, KB in 38–40
Bernhard, Prince (of Netherlands) 47
Bernhard Operation 235–6
Bibes, Louis 160–62, 175
Black Orchestra organisations 205*ff*
Blanca, Antoine 315
Blanco, Jean Louis 315
Blandon, Mario 124
Blood Putsch 37
Böhm (husband of Andrée) 55, 56, 57,
59
Bolívar, Simón 215
Bolivia 19, *map* 200–201, **215–319**
  Banzer govt 247–65, **266–84**
  Barrientos govt 224–33
  drug industry 271–5, 289–95
  García Meza govt 275, 285–97
  German community 216–21ff, 248
  Indians, S. American 215–16, 220
  Jews 216–18
  naval aspirations 225–30
  Ovando govt 228, 233–4
  Paz Estenssoro govt 221–5
  Siles Zuazo govt 266, 276, 284, 301,
  302–19
Bolivian Democratic Front 222
Bolivian Sugar Corpn 259
Bologna station bomb 17, 299–300
Bonnet, Nicole 256, 261
Borghese, Prince Valerio (Il
Commandante) 204, 208, 212
Bormann, Martin 137, 241
Bornewasser, Bishop (of Trier) 31
Bosnia 187
Bossé, Roger 122–3
Boudet, Maurice 74
Bouhired, Djemila 323
Bouness, Frau (cousin of KB) 224
Bourdet, Claude 68, 69
Bousquet, René 107, 330
Boyer, Fr Robert 323
Bramel, Gene 178
Brazil 315
Brigada Central de Informacion 210
Bron airfield 126–7, 325

Broszat, Martin 124
Browning, Maj. Earl 153, 154, 162,
    165–6, 178
Brun, Albert 256, 257, 261
Buchenwald camp 51, 118
Buckmaster, Col. Maurice 104
Budak, Mile 187
Burkhardt, Gertrud 159
Busch, Pres. German 217

Cahn, Ernst 50
Calderon, Otero 229
Camacho, Colonel 290
Canaris, Adml Wilhelm 58
Carbone, Emilio 277–8, 282, 300
Carrasco, Col. Jorge 212
Carrion, Constantino 261, 264, 313
Carter, Pres. Jimmy 297
Castro, Alvaro de 216, 220, 226, 264,
    311
  arms-dealing 228
  bodyguard to KB 261, 262–3, 298
  coup d'état 288–9, 293
  delle Chiaie/Pagliai 281, 301–3,
    308, 310
  KB's expulsion 312–18, 327
Cayenne (Guyana) 316, 318, 320
CBS 294
CEDADE 227
Central Intelligence Group 156
Césaire, Raymond 310, 315, 316
Chambon, Albert 255–6, 257, 258
Chambonnet, Albert ("Didier") 116,
    124, 125
Chavet, Pol 98
Cheysson, Claude 315
Chiaie see delle Chiaie
Chile 18, 198, 212–13, 269–70
  arms-deals 229–30, 238
  Rudel 228
Christoffel, Edgar 37
"Chrystal Night" 24, 41
Church/Vatican
  Nazi hostility to 29–31, 34–5, 37–8
  postwar Nazi aid 137–8
  refugee policy 185–6, 189
  Ustase involvement 187–9
  Vatican Concordat 31, 34
CIA 135, 156, 171, 191
  S. America 230–32, 269–71,
    299–308

CIC 18, 133ff, **140–41**, 236
  KB 141, **148–95**
  marriage rules 151
  Rat Line 183–95
Ciolini, Elio 299
Clay, Gen. Lucius D. 158–9, 175
Clissold, Stephen 188–9
CNR 69, 84
COB 221, 283, 285
Cochabamba 219–20, 263
Cohen, Prof. David 51, 52–3
"Cold War" 134–8, 140
Colliard-Masson (Maquisard)
    119–20
Colombani, Dominique 232
Colombia 272–4
Combined Travel Board 191
COMIBOL debt 312–14, 317–18
"Commandos de Acción" 210
Committee for the Defence of
    Democracy (Bolivia) 285
Compiègne camp 118
Concutelli, Luigi 210, 211, 213
Condor organisation 269–70
Confédération Nationale de la
    Résistance 179
Conseil National de la Résistance
    (CNR) 69, 84
Contemporary Jewish Documentation
    Centre 251
Contreras, Col. Manuel 213, 278
Cordier, Daniel 81
Corr, Edwin 298, 300–301, 303–4, 309
Cossio, Maj. Luis 291, 293
Croatia see Yugoslavia
Croisset, Françoise see Barbie
CROWCASS 136, 149
Cruzada del Mar 225–6
Cuba 239
Czechoslovakia 41

Dabringhaus, Erhard 160, 162–5, 167
Dachau camp 94, 117
Danet, Olivier 299
Daniels, Major 178
Dannecker, Theodore 107–8
Darnand, Émile-Joseph 62, 101, 111
Debray, Régis 258–9, 261, 323
  and KB 262, 315, 327
Debré, Michel 258–9
Degrelle, Léon 203–4, 208, 227

Delaye, Georges 124
Delestraint, Gen. Charles 69, 78–9,
    86, 94
Deletraz, Edmée 76, 77–8, 87
delle Chiaie, Leda 209
delle Chiaie, Stefano 17, 19, 198,
    204–14
    capture attempt 299–308
    S. America 211–13, 266, 270,
        278–308
    Spain 208–11, 213–14
Delorme, Eugène 118–19
Derner, John H. 147
Deutsche Jugendkraft 28
Deutsche Jungfolk 32
Devigny, André 75, 76, 102
DINA 212–13, 270, 278
Ditges, Karl 51
Dobson, Lt.-Col. Jack 193
Donar Mission 70
Dortmund 43–4
Draganovič, Dr Krunoslav 185–96,
    236
Drancy camp 108, 112, 114–15, 326
Dugoujon, Dr Frédéric 86–8, 90–91
Düsseldorf 40–43

ECIC see Oberursel
Eckmann, Lieutenant-Colonel 178
Ehinger, Major 58, 59
Eichmann, Adolf 16, 36, 38, 219, 258
    Dutch Jews 46
    "Erik" 218–19
    French Jews 107
    "Jewish Emigration" 52
Einsatzkommando/-gruppe (task
    force) 67, 331
Elio, Doctor 260–61
Ellersieck, Kurt 143
ELN 246
El Salvador see Salvador
ERN 267
Erskine, Col. David 156, 177–8,
    180–81
Espinal, Fr Luis 283
ETA 209–10, 212
Etkin, Capt. Max 156–7
EUCOM 180–81, 191, 193
European Command Interrogation
    Center see Oberursel
Europe-Bolivia Assn 288

Évosges reprisals 115

Fajardo, José 282, 289
Falange (Bolivia) 219, 248, 261, 266
Favet, Julien 113–14, 326, 327
Feldgendarmerie 71
Fernandez, Alfonso 226
Ferreira, Dantes 260–61
"Fiancés of Death" 273–4, 276, 277,
    289–95, 299
    García Meza coup 286
Fiebelkorn, Joachim 273–4, 276, 286,
    289–95
    Bologna 299
Fiebelkorn, Linda 273
Floreck, Ernst 74, 110
Flores, Mery 312
Forrestal, James 126
Forstner, Baroness von 139
France **58–131, 322–32**
    Algeria 205–6, 329
    Alsace-Lorraine 25, 55–6
    "armée secrète" 68, 69
    "Atilla Operation" 61, 64
    forced labour 100–101
    Free French 61, 68, 130
    French Voluntary Legion 62
    in Germany (post World War I) 25
        –6
    intelligence: wartime 70–72; postwar
        141, 156–63, 183
    invaded (1940) 56
    Italian zone 59, 103, 113
    KB: listed as war criminal 136;
        investigations 224, 232; extradition
        requests 258, 260, 264, 277; capture/
        trial aspects 310, 314–32
    legal procedures 322–8
    Merk listed as war criminal 156
    Milice 62, **101–2**, 115, 322; Bron
        127; Jews 108, 109, 111
    Resistance organisation 61, 67–9,
        83–4, 103–4
    Socialist (Mitterand) govt 296
    Vichy regime 56, **59**, **61–2**, 64, 327;
        "collaboration principle" 101–2,
        328–30
    zone libre 59, 61
    see also Lyon etc
Franco, Gen. Francisco 135, 198, 209,
    211, 213

François-Poncet, André 103
Freedom of Information Act (US) 7, 299
Free French *see* France
Freemasons 46, 47–9
Frenay, Henri **68–9**, 75, 77, 81, 83, 121
Fuchs, Gottlieb 60–61, 67, 92, 98
Fuerza Nueva party 204
Fünten, Ferdinand aus der 51, 52

García Meza, Pres. Luis 17, 274–5, 276–7, 283
  coup 287
  drug industry 289–95
  resignation/exile 279, 312
Garçon, Maître Maurice 96, 177, 322
Garvey, Lt.-Col. Dale 148–9, 154
Gasser, Erwin 248
Gaulle, Gen. Charles de 61, 100, 329
  and Moulin 68–9, 81, 83–4, 90, 91
Gay, Jack 193, 194
Gehlen, Gen. Reinhard 135
  intelligence organisation ("Rusty") 145, 166, 167, 171
Geissmann, Raymond 112–13, 251
Gentile, Claudio 299
Gerlier, Cardinal Pierre 109, 126, 129–30
Germany **23–44, 130–93**; Rhenish separatism 25–6; nazism, rise of 29–31, 37, 43; non-Nazi parties 29–30, 40; Vatican Concordat 31; prewar military ventures 41; S. American propaganda 217; postwar conditions 134*ff*, 164, 165, 167; West Germany and KB 223–4, 230, 233, 310–15, 327
Gestapo (Geheime Staatspolizei) 35, 42, **66–7**
  and Abwehr 58
  Donar Mission 70
Gex (France) 58, 60–61, 65
Giorgio, Maurizio 299–300
Giraud, Gen. Henri 130
Giscard d'Estaing, Pres. Valéry 330
Glas, Alfons 120–21
Godesberg (Germany) 25
Goebbels, Dr Josef 135
Goldberg, Michael 262

Great Britain
  and CIC 140–41, 143, 149–50, 155
  and KB 136, 140, 141–2, 146, 168
Greece 205, 211
Guatemala 198
Guérin-Serac, Yves 205–6, 207, 212
Guevara, Ché (Ernesto) 231–2, 261, 282
Gustmann, Wolfgang 139
Guyana (Cayenne) 316, 318, 320

Hagen, Herbert 330
Haig, Alexander 299
Hahn, Fritz 223
Hajdu, Camille 153–4, 156–60
Halaunbrenner, Itta 260, 325, 327
Hardick, Colonel 181
Hardy, René ("Didot") ("Carbon") **77–9, 84–90**, 122, 149, 161
  La Paz (*1972*) 262
  trials **96**, 160, 168, 173, 176–8
Harster, Wilhelm 47, 51
Hecht, Leo 183, 191, 193
Hees, Anna *see* Barbie
Heidemann, Gerd 53, 331
Heinrichsohn, Ernst 330
Henriot, Philippe 111
Hernu, Charles 315
Heydrich, Reinhard **35–6**, 38, 67, 74, 107
  Einsatzgruppen 331
  "Jewish Emigration" 51–2
HICOG 176, 179–81, 183
Hieber, Johann 239
Himmler, Heinrich 35, 36, 38, 40, 74
  Hardy capture 85
  Jews 51–2, 107, 331
  resistance leaders 95–6
  RSHA 66
Hindenburg, Pres. Paul von 29
Hirschfeld, Walter 147–8
Hitler, Adolf 26, 29, 30, 133, 203
Hitler Youth 30–32, 38, 134
Hobbins, Lt. John 190–91
Hoffmann, Emil 140, 141, 146, 153
Höhn, Prof. Reinhard 38
Holland/Netherlands 43–5, **45–54**
  "Anjerdag" 47
  Dutch Nazis (NSB) 47, 49–50
  "February Strike" 51
  Koko affair 50

Hollert, Heinz Fritz 66
Honduras 238
Horrmann, Karl 32, 33, 35
Höss, Rudolf 124
Höttl, Wilhelm 135, 166
Hoy newspaper 229
Huber, Eugen Albert 239
Huber, Otto 126–7

Ilgenfritz, Otto 138
"Incontrolados, Los" 210
Interamericana project 230
Israel 229, 316
Italy
    France: occupation zone 59, 103,
        113
    German surrender in 136
    Mussolini falls 103
    neo-fascism 198, **204–8**
    postwar Nazi aid 138
    Rat Line 185–6, 188–90, 191,
        193–4
    terrorist acts 206–8, 210–11, 213;
        Bologna bomb 17, 299–300
Izieu orphanage 113–15, 215, 260,
    325, **326**–7

Jaquin, André ("Milneuf") 110
Jasenovac camp (Yugoslavia) 187–8
Jewish Councils 51
Jews
    Bolivia 216–18*ff*
    "Chrystal Night" 24, 41
    Einsatzgruppen 331
    "Emigration Offices" 52
    France 107–15, 126–7, 324–5, 329
    Holland 45–6, 49–54
    Nuremberg Laws (*1934*) 37
    Peru 236
    refugees 60
    Trier prewar 23–4, 29, 37
    Wannsee Conference 54
    Zionist organisations 49
John, Herbert 241, 252–3, 257, 261,
    265
Joly, Cécile 119–20
"José" (drug racketeer) 272–3, 274,
    293, 294–5
Judenamt (Jewish section) of RSHA
    107

Kaddouche, Simone (*see also*
    Lagrange) 112
Kalb, Johan Peter (Josef) 48
Kaltenbrunner, Ernst 95, 96, 236
Kamber, Theophil 236
"Kameraden" (comrades) 237
Kapenauer, Ludwig 220
KB *see* Barbie, Klaus
Kemmler, Joseph 120–21, 310, 327
Kempin, Otto 48
Klarsfeld, Beate **250–52**, 257–8, 310,
    327, 330
    with Itta Halaunbrenner 260
    kidnap attempt 262
Klarsfeld, Serge **250–51**, 262, 321,
    327, **330**
Knab, Werner 66, 104, 115, 124, 126
    St-Genis-Laval 130
Knochen, Helmut 67, 328
Knolle, Colonel 50–51
Kolb, Eugene 168–9, 173–4
Kopplin, Ike 273, 289, 295
Kriminalpolizei/Kripo 67
Kuhlmann, Manfred 273, 289, 291–2
Kühn, Ellen 138, 142

Lages, Willy 51, 52–3
Lagrange, Simone (*see also*
    Kaddouche) 325, 327
La Paz 215, 216, 218, 220–21
    San Pedro prison 259–60, 264,
        314–17
Larea, Captain 300, 307
La Rue, Jacques de 66
La Servette, Alain de 323, 325
Latin America *see* South America
Latin American anti-Communist
    League 288
Lauhaus, Willy 50
Laval, Pierre 101, 108, 330
La Vista, Vincent 186
Lavoie, Dick 161
Lebrun, Pres. Albert 103
Lechin, Juan 283, 287
Le Clerc, Jean ("Napoleon") 273–4,
    294–5
Lecussan, Joseph 101
Ledezma, Gaston 263–4
Leguay, Jean 330
Leighton, Bernardo *and* Anita 213
LeMay, Gen. Curtis 168

Lemonnier, Adml Jean 126
Lesèvre, Georges *and* Jean-Pierre 117
Lesèvre, Lise 110, 111, 116–17
Letelier, Orlando 278
Lévy, Jean-Pierre **68**, 69, 75
Lischka, Kurt 330
Long, Dr Jean 111
Lopez Rega, José (El Brujo) 211–12
Ludolph, Manfred 251–2
Lutjens, Alfred 73
Lyon, Paul 184–6, 190
Lyon (France) 58, 61, **63–131**
  École de Santé Militaire 72, 112, 324
  KB trial 320–30
  occupation 63–7
  resistance organisation 67–9, 75, 77
  see also Montluc

McCloy, John 179–81
McFarren, Peter 297
Mader, Dr Julius 254
Magjerli, Mgr Junaj 194
Maidanek trial 315
Mandereau, Jean Louis 232
Maquis (field resistance) 101, 103–4, 105, 121–2, 329
Marburg University 139
Marx, Karl 25, 27
Mauroy, Pierre 315
Mauthausen camp 51, 53, 74, 75
Mehren (W. Germany) 26
Meiners, Heinrich 94
Meinike, Adolf 272
Memmingen (W. Germany) 147–62
Menthon, François de 325
Merk, Kurt ("Petersen") **57–60**, 74–5, 98; meets Andrée 57; meets KB 60; "Technica" 70–72; US agent 132–3, 144–6, **147–70**; wanted by France 156–62; dies 171–2
Merlen, Charles 71, 157–9
Merlino, Mario 207
Merzig (W. Germany) 25
Messner, Ute *see* Barbie
Milan (Italy) 206–7
Milano, Maj. (*later* Lt.-Col.) 166, 183–6, 190, 193
Mildenstein, Edler von 38
Milice *see* France

Mingola, Mario 281, 288, 318
Minnich, Franz 153
Miori Pereira, Maj. Hugo Raul 280
Mitterand, Pres. François 323
MNR 219, 221–2, 224–5, 248, 266
Monjaret, Joseph 75–6
Montluc prison 76, **98–100**, 112, 126–8, 322
  KB in 320–21
  liberated 130
  Moulin "suicide" 328
Moog, Robert ("Boby") 74–5, 76, 77–9, 84, 115
Moritz, August 67, 110–11
Morlot, Antoinette ("Mimiche") 97
Mortimore, Major 81
Mota, Jordi 227–8
Motsch, Father 220
Moulin, Jean ("Max") 75, **81–96**, 149, 160, 161
  appointed by de Gaulle 69
  and KB's trial 324, 327–8
  KB's view of 79–80, 227–8
Moulin, Laure 81, 95
"Mouse" (Acker) 140, 141–2
Mouvement National Anti-Terroriste (MNAT) 110
Movimiento Nacional Revolucionario (MNR) 219, 221–2, 224–5, 248, 266
MSI (Movimento Sociale Italiano) 205
Müller, Albert (Nazi official) 34
Müller, Rolf (Lyon SS) 66, 70
Müller (Munich prosecutor) 174
Multon, Jean ("Lunel") 75, 77–9, 84
Murillo, Mirna 267
Mussert, Anton 47, 49–50
Mussolini, Benito (il Duce) 103, 135, 198, 205

Nationalblatt see Trierer
National Bolshevism 40
Nazi party
  ODESSA 137–8
  organisations 35–7
  postwar 134–8, 143–4
  rise of 29–31
  see also SS *etc*
Nazi-Soviet Pact (1939) 41

Neagoy, George 191, 193, 194
Nebe, Artur 39
neo-fascism 17, **198**, **203–14**, 227
  "Fiancés of Death" 272–4, 276, 277
  Phoenix Commando 281–2
  strategy of tension 206–7, 209
Newsweek magazine 311
New York Times 297
Nicaragua 280
Niebüll (W. Germany) 33
Noguères, Henri 327
NSB 47, 49–50
Nuremberg Laws (1934) 37

OAS 205
Oberg, Gen. Karl 67, 107, 108, 328
Oberursel (ECIC: European
  Command Interrogation
  Center) 154–5, 157
Occorsio, Vittorio 210–11
ODESSA 137–8, 254
Office of Special Investigations (OSI)
  168
Ohlendorf, Otto 38
OMGUS 175, 176
Ondra, Hedwig 73–4
Ordine Nuovo 205, 210–11, 278
Organisation of American States 288
Organisation Armée Contre le
  Communisme International 206
OSI 168
OSS 152
Oullins (France) 324
Ovando Candia, Pres. Alfredo 212,
  226, 228, 233
Oyonnax (France) 104

Padua (Italy) 206
Pagliai, Pierluigi **278–82**, 297, **298**,
  299, 301
  capture 299–310, 311
  García Meza coup 285, 288–9
Palma, Colonel 259
Papon, Maurice 330
Paraguay 228, 238
Paris Match magazine 262
Paris-Presse: l'Intransigeant 172–3
Parti Populaire Français (PPF) 108,
  110–11
Pavelič, Ante 187, 188, 189
Payot, Max 128–9

Paz Estenssoro, Pres. Victor 221–2,
  224–5, 237, 267
Paz Zamorra, Jaime 316
"Pedro" (informant) 304, 308
Pellepoix, Darquier de 107, 330
Pereda, General 276
Perón, Pres. Juan Domingo 211
Peru 226
  KB **242–57**, 264–5, 315
  Schwend 228, 234, **236–65**
Pétain, Marshal Henri 56, **61–2**, 101,
  103, 109
  postwar 329
"Petersen Bureau" 145–50, **151–69**
Pfeiffer, Léon 125
Phoenix Commando 281–2
Pineau, Christian 93
Pinochet, Pres. Augusto 17, 212, 213,
  228
PIP 240, 241, 249, 254, 257
  Banchero Rossi case 252, 253
Piquet-Wicks, Maj. Eric 81
Pius XII, Pope 188
"Plan Vert" 77, 85, 91
Poland 41, 43
Pompidou, Pres. Georges 258, 322
Portugal 198, 205, 211
PPF 108, 110–11
Prado, Col. Gary 294
Progrès 251
Puerto Rico 309

Quadripartite Allied Intelligence
  Committee 158
Quiroga Santa Cruz, Marcelo 285–6

Rabl, Wolfgang 233, 251
Radio Fides 286
Raimers, Doctor 307
Ratliffe, Jim 154
"Rat Line" 183–6, 188, 190–95
Rauter, Hans 46–7, 50, 51, 54
Ravensbruck 117, 324–5
Reagan, Pres. Ronald 299
Red Brigade 205
Red Cross 185–6, 188, 194, 236
"Red Lilac" group 140–42
Rega, Lopez 278
Reichswehr (army 1921–35) 37
"René" (refugee-smuggler) 217,
  218–19

Révolution 323
Reyes, General 283
Reyes, Federico Nielsen (fascist) 226
Reyes, Simon (peasants' union) 286
Reynaudon, Jean 111
Rhineland 25–6, 41
Richard, Adrian 105–6
Richter, General 257
Riddleberger, James D. 179
Riggin, Major 168
Riss, Christian 322–3, 326, 327, 330
Rivera, Cespedes 222
Rivez, Andrée 9, 98, 151, 171–2
    collaboration 62, 70–72
    Germany postwar 132–3, 146, 162,
        165
    KB killings 107, 131, 148, 170–71
    meets Merk 55–60
    Regine Barbie 169–70
    wanted by France 156, 158–62
Rodes, Col. Peter 158
Röhm, Ernst 36–7, 217
Romac, Fr Roque (Fr Oswald Toth)
    192, 219–20
Romans-Petit, Henri 104
Rome 207–8, 210–11, 213
    see also "Rat Line"; Church
Roncal, Mario 308, 309, 315, 317
Roncal, Ugo 319
Röthke, Heinz 109
RSHA **42–3**, 66–7
Rudel, Hans Ulrich 228, 230, 238
Rueda Pena, Mario 316, 319
Rundschau von Illimani 218

SA (Sturmabteilung) 29–30, **36–7**
Saar region 25
Sachsenhausen camp 49
St Claude (France) 117–21, 310, 327
St-Genis-Laval killing 128–30, 325
Salazar, António de Oliviera 198, 211
Salvador (El Salvador) 17, 198, 238,
    270
    Chiaie 279, 280, 288
Sanchez, Gustavo 317, 318, 319
San Girolamo, Confraternity of 185,
    186, 189, 194, 195
Santa Cruz (Bolivia) 271
Santos Chichizola, José Antonio 237,
    241, 257

Banchero Rossi 252, 253–5, 265
Sauckel (Gauleiter) 101
Schade, Freiherr von 40–41
Schlageter, Albert Leo 25–6, 79–80
Schloss Hartheim (Germany) 51
Schneider-Merck, Volkmar Johannes
    242–7, 248–50, 253–5, 256–7,
    265
Schoenbrun, David, 84
Schoetker (Montluc prisoner) 99
Scholl, Hans *and* Sophie 174
Schow, Col. Robert 70–71, 158
Schumaker, Maria Isabel 297
Schwend, Friedrich/Fritz/Federico
    Paul 228, 233, **234–49**, 269;
    emigrates 136; meets KB 237;
    military secrets 237, 255; meets
    Schneider-Merck 243; Banchero
    Rossi appeals for KB 258–9,
    261; tried 265; dies 265
SD **35–6**, **42–3**
    KB recruited 33, 38
    postwar 134*ff*
    "Selection Board" operation 143–4,
        146, 147, 148–9, 154–6
Serbia/Serbs 187–8
Serre, Col. Richard 70–71, 158–9
Serreulles, Claude 87, 100
Service d'Ordre Légionnaire 101
Servizio Informazione Difesa (SID)
    207–8, 300
Sessarego, Eugenia 252, 265
Seta, Jean Baptiste 129
Seyss-Inquart, Arthur 46–7
SHAEF 136, 149
Shute, Benjamin 180
Sibert, Gen. Edwin 158
Sicherheitsdienst *see* SD
Sicherheitspolizei *see* Sipo
SID 207–8, 300
Siles Zuazo, Pres. Hernan 222, 266,
    276, 283, 295
    inaugurated 301–4, 309
    KB release 310–11, 316–17, 319
Silver, Arnold 155
Silverstein, Fr Aaron 244
Sipo 39, 42
Skorzeny, Col. Otto 135, 137, 206, 238
    visited by KB 203, 227
Sobibor camp 45, 54, 109
SOE 104

South America 137–8, **197–8**, *map*
  200–201, 255
  arms-dealing 228, 237*ff*
  Bolivian coup 288
  German propaganda 217
  inter-government liaison 269–70
  postwar immigration 184–6,
    189–90
  see also Bolivia *etc*
Spain 135, 198, 213, 227
  arms deals 238
  delle Chiaie 208–11, 213–14
  Nazi exiles 203–4
Special Refugee Commission 188, 189
Spiller, Captain 163, 165, 167, 168
SS **35–7**, 124, 134*ff*
  and Abwehr 58
  KB recruited 33, 38
  Marriage Decree 41–2
  Operation Bernhard 235–6
  slogan 205
SSU 152
Stellfeld, Hans 273, 292
Stenngritt, Harry 86
Stepinac, Archbishop 188
Stern magazine 50, 241
STO 100–101
Streicher, Julius 36
Stroessner, Pres. Alfredo 228
Stürmer, Der 36
Suarez, Roberto 271–4, 276, 289
Sucre (Bolivia) 216, 260
Switzerland 60

Taylor, Line 146, 151, 171
Taylor, Robert/Bob 133, 144–6,
  148–54, 157, 171
Taylor, Gen. Robert 180
"Technica" betrayal 70–72, 158–60
Terrazas, Dr Freddy 304–5, 306–7
"Tetsch net" 166
"Thédy" (secretary) 97
Theresienstadt camp 23
Thévenon, Maurice 104
Tito, Marshal Josip 192, 195
Tixier-Vignancourt, Maître 322
Tongeren, Charlotte van 47–9
Tongeren, Gen. Hermannus von 47–9
Tongeren, Jacoba van 48, 49
"Tora Tora" operation 208
Torrelio, Pres. Celso 297

Toth, Fr Oswald *see* Romac
Touvier, Paul 322, 330
Townley, Michael 212–13, 278
Transmaritima Boliviana company
  226–30, 238, 239, 244, 260
  COMIBOL debt 312–14, 317, 318
Trier (W. Germany) **23–6**, 27–30, 31,
  32, 37
  see also Barbie, Anna *and* Regine
Trierer Nationalblatt 24, 35, 37
  offices 32

UDBA 195
Udler (W. Germany) 26
UGIF 108, 112, 251, 324
Ultima Hora 259
Unrauth, Capt. Walter 182–3, 190
Urcullo, Jaime 313, 314
USA
  anti-terrorism (*1982*) 298–311
  enters war 61
  García Meza 284, 286, 289, 294, 297
  Italian coup 208
  postwar intelligence 133*ff*, 236
  S. America: subversion 230–32
  see also CIC; CIA
USSR 41, 61, 134, 139, 145
  KB and 53–4, 330–31
  see also "Cold War"
Ustárez, Dr Adolfo 261, 277, 286–7,
  292, 293
  arrested 318
Ustasa/e (*see* glossary) 186–9, 190, 195

Vallin (Maquisard) 119–20
Valpreda, Pietro 207
Vargas, Inspector 257
Vasquez, Noel 285–6
Vatican *see* Church
Velarde, Mario 314
Valasco, Gaston 225–8, 229
Vercors, République du 122
Vergès, Maître Jacques 321, 322, 323
  –30
Vichy regime *see* France
Vidal, Joseph 168, 173, 175, 177–9,
  180–81
Vildoso, President 298
Vilka, Juan 252, 265
Vincent, Jean *and* Marguerite 119
Vincent, Pierre 118

Vrij Nederland 49

Waffen-SS 137, 155
Wannsee Conference 54
Wannsee Institute 147
War Crimes Commission 136
War Dept Detachment (WDD) 156
Wehrmacht (armed forces) 63, 66, 117
Weissman, Marvin 284
Werwolf movement 135
"White Rose" group 174
Whiteway, Lt. John 159, 161, 168, 176, 177
Who's Who in the CIA 254
Wieringermeer (Holland) 52–3
Wiesenthal, Simon 250, 256
Willms, Regine *see* Barbie
Wilson, Major 178, 180
Winter, Alexander 139

Wolf, Heinz 222
Wolff, Gen. Karl 135–6, 203, 331
World War I 25
World War II: preliminaries 41; declared 42; N African campaign 61, 104; USSR enters 61; USA enters 61; Mussolini falls 103; D-Day 121–2; Allies land in S. France 126; V-E Day 133

Yugoslavia 152, 195, 326
   Croatians 185, 220, 236, 252–3: *Ustase* 186–9, 190, 195
Yungas region 220, 250, 269

Zarp, Christian 153
Zemun camp (Yugoslavia) 187
Zlatin, Miron *and* Sabrina 113–14